Studien zur Geschichte des Völkerrechts

Begründet von Michael Stolleis

Band 40

Christophe Wampach

Armed Reprisals from Medieval Times to 1945

Nomos

Funding for open access publication from the Max Planck Digital Library.

The Deutsche Nationalbibliothek lists this publication in the Deutsche Nationalbibliografie; detailed bibliographic data are available on the Internet at http://dnb.d-nb.de

a.t.: Bonn, Rheinische Friedrich-Wilhelms-Univ., Diss., 2020

ISBN 978-3-8487-7718-1 (Print)
978-3-7489-2111-0 (ePDF)

British Library Cataloguing-in-Publication Data
A catalogue record for this book is available from the British Library.

ISBN 978-3-8487-7718-1 (Print)
978-3-7489-2111-0 (ePDF)

Library of Congress Cataloging-in-Publication Data
Wampach, Christophe
Armed Reprisals from Medieval Times to 1945
Christophe Wampach
336 pp.
Includes bibliographic references.

ISBN 978-3-8487-7718-1 (Print)
978-3-7489-2111-0 (ePDF)

1st Edition 2020

Published by
Nomos Verlagsgesellschaft mbH & Co. KG
Waldseestraße 3-5 | 76530 Baden-Baden
www.nomos.de

Production of the printed version:
Nomos Verlagsgesellschaft mbH & Co. KG
Waldseestraße 3-5 | 76530 Baden-Baden

ISBN (Print): 978-3-8487-7718-1
ISBN (ePDF): 978-3-7489-2111-0

DOI: https://doi.org/10.5771/9783748921110

Onlineversion
Nomos eLibrary

To my grandfathers René and Emil

Acknowledgements

The present work is the result of a Ph.D. dissertation at the Rheinische Friedrich-Wilhelms-Universität Bonn defended in Summer Semester 2020. This book would not exist without the help and support of many persons.

I would like to first thank my supervisor, Prof. Dr. Mathias Schmoeckel from the University of Bonn, who encouraged me to embark on the doctoral journey, drew my attention to the topic of reprisals and showed great enthusiasm for my research. He also gave me an excellent environment at the Institut für Deutsche und Rheinische Rechtsgeschichte to broaden my knowledge on legal history and more particularly on the history of international law by making me one of his assistants.

My second acknowledgement goes to Prof. Dr. Dirk Heirbaut from the Universiteit Gent, who kindly agreed to become the second assessor. I am really thankful for his interest in my work, his pertinent remarks, and for exhorting me to pursue the path of academic investigation.

Thanks as well to Prof. Dr. Martin Schermaier from the University of Bonn, who organised and presided the defence under the particular circumstances of the COVID-19 pandemic that shook the world.

I am also very much obliged to the Gerda Henkel Stiftung which granted me a two-year scholarship that made the writing of my thesis financially possible.

I also want to thank my colleagues, fellow Ph.D. candidates and friends at the Institut für Deutsche und Rheinische Rechtsgeschichte for their unfailing support, our long talks about methodological issues and all the good time we spent together: PD Dr. Matthias Maetschke, Dr. Pierre Friedrich, Dr. Vincent Nossek, Dr. Gero Fuchs, Dr. Malte Becker, Dr. Alexander Kustermann, Prof. Dr. Joaquín Sedano Rueda and Frau Silvia Schmidt.

I am greatly indebted to the Milla Altabás family in Lima who welcomed me into their home and provided me with a place to serenely work, while helping me to sometimes take my mind off the naval battles, the stormy sessions in the British parliament and the fluctuating attitude of lawyers which all teemed in my head.

I would like also to express my deep gratitude to my good friends Hugo W. Smart, for helping with my punctual linguistic enquiries, and Connor A. Carey, for having endorsed the burdensome task of proofreading my work.

My eternal gratitude goes to my family who has always believed in me and provided me with emotional support in times of doubt and motivation drop. Thank you, Papa, Maman, Florent, Corinne, and my grandparents.

Finally, thank you, María Belén, for all your love giving me strength to keep going. You make me feel lucky everyday to have met you.

Brussels, July 2020

Table of Contents

Abbreviations

A.D.	*anno Domini*
AJIL	American Journal of International Law
a.m.	*ante meridiem*
Annuaire IDI	Annuaire de l'Institut de droit international
ArchVölkR	Archiv des Völkerrechts
Art.	Article(s)
BFSP	British and Foreign State Papers
BYIL	The British Yearbook of International Law
Cap.	*capitulo*
CaseWResJIntL	Case Western Reserve Journal of International Law
CathLaw	Catholic Lawyer
ch.	chapter(s)
Chinese JIL	Chinese Journal of International Law
CLJ	Cambridge Law Journal
Clunet	Journal du Droit International Privé et de la Jurisprudence Comparée
Cod. Just.	*Codex Justinianus*
col.	column(s)
CUP	Cambridge University Press
DAEM	Deutsches Archiv für Erforschung des Mittelalters
DJZ	Deutsche Juristen-Zeitung
ed(s).	editor(s)
edn.	edition
e.g.	*exempli gratia*
EHQ	European History Quarterly
EJIL	European Journal of International Law
esp.	especially
et al.	*et alii*
f./ff.	and following
fn.	footnote(s)
F. O.	Foreign Office
fol.	folio(s)

ForeignAff	Foreign Affairs
Fundamina	Fundamina: A Journal of Legal History
GeoLJ	Georgetown Law Journal
GPO	Government Printing Office
HUP	Harvard University Press
i.a.	*inter alia*
Ibid.	*ibidem*
ICJ	International Court of Justice
IIL	Institute of International Law
IntAff	International Affairs
IntlConciliation	International Conciliation
JHistIntIL	Journal of History of International Law = Revue d'histoire du droit international
J.O.R.F.	Journal officiel de la République française
JSSL	Journal of the Statistical Society of London
JTransnatLawPol	Journal of Transnational Law and Policy
JUFIL	Journal on the Use of Force and International Law
Just. *Nov.*	Justinian, *Novellae*
Lib.	*liber*
LJIL	Leiden Journal of International Law
LMR	Law Magazine and Review: A Quarterly Review of Jurisprudence, 5th series
LNOJ	League of Nations Official Journal
LNTS	League of Nations Treaty Series
LQR	Law Quarterly Review
MilRev	Military Law Review
MLLWR	Military Law and the Law of War Review
MP	Member(s) of Parliament (United Kingdom)
NAR	The North American Review
NordJIntLaw	Nordisk Tidsskrift for International Ret
no(s).	margin number(s)
Nr.	number
N.S.	New Style = Gregorian calendar
NYIL	Netherlands Yearbook of International Law
O.S.	Old Style = Julian calendar
OUP	Oxford University Press
Para(s).	paragraph(s)

PCA	Permanent Court of Arbitration at The Hague
PCIJ	Permanent Court of International Justice
PhilipLJ	Philippine Law Journal
p.m.	*post meridiem*
P. R. O.	Public Record Office
PUF	Presses universitaires de France
PUP	Princeton University Press
PYIL	Philippine Yearbook of International Law
Qu.	*quæstio*
r	recto
RdC	Recueil des Cours de l'Académie de Droit International de La Haye
RDFE	Revue de droit français et étranger
RDI	Revue de droit international, de sciences diplomatiques, politiques et sociales
RDILC	Revue de Droit International et de Législation Comparée
RevJurCat	Revista jurídica de Catalunya
RGBl.	Deutsches Reichsgesetzblatt
RGDIP	Revue Générale de Droit International Public
RHEF	Revue d'histoire de l'Église de France
RIAA	Report of International Arbitral Awards
RID comp.	Revue internationale de droit comparé
RivDirInt	Rivista di Diritto Internazionale
RLT	Roman Legal Tradition
Saint Louis LR	Saint Louis Law Review
s.d.	*sine dato*
Sec.	section(s)
ser.	series/*série*
s.l.	*sine loco*
s.n.	*sine nomine*
Suppl.	supplement(s)
TGS	Transactions of the Grotius Society
Tit.	*titulus*
tr.	translation
UChiLRev	University of Chicago Law Review
UN	United Nations

UPaLRe	University of Pennsylvania Law Review and American Law Register
U.S.	United States
v	verso
VillLRev	Villanova Law Review
viz.	*videlicet*
vol(s).	volume(s)
WWI	World War One
WWII	World War Two
YaleLJ	Yale Law Journal
YaleRev	The Yale Review
ZAkDR	Zeitschrift der Akademie für Deutsches Recht
ZaöRV	Zeitschrift für ausländisches öffentliches Recht und Völkerrecht
ZPE	Zeitschrift für Papyrologie und Epigraphik
ZRG GA	Zeitschrift der Savigny-Stiftung für Rechtsgeschichte – Germanistische Abteilung
ZVölkR	Zeitschrift für Völkerrecht

Introduction

I. Outline of a Burning Issue

1. Contextualisation of a Remark by Karl Strupp

> "Si l'on voulait dresser, au domaine du droit des gens, une liste des matières théoriquement et pratiquement brûlantes, on ne pourrait en trouver aucune qui le serait plus que le droit des *représailles*."[1]

The passage above opens an article written by German legal scholar Karl Strupp for a *liber amicorum* in honour of Belgian jurist Ernest Mahaim. The topic of reprisals was not unknown to the latter. The previous year, Mahaim presided the Institute of International Law's 1934 session in Paris, which saw the adoption of a regulation governing reprisals in peacetime. In this article, Strupp stressed that the question of reprisals, and more precisely of 'armed' reprisals, had been an acute problem since the creation of the League of Nations and the subsequent adoption of the Kellogg-Briand Pact. He nevertheless acknowledged that the issue was not new and was already of practical interest prior to 1919. However, the situation had grown worse, in his opinion, with the renunciation of aggressive war during the interwar years. As a result, the employment of armed reprisals offered a dangerous alternative to circumvent that prohibition. The question of the distinction between armed reprisals and war had thus become of critical importance.[2]

In order to understand the issue which Strupp referred to, it is necessary first to define 'reprisals' and explain their raison d'être.

---

1 Karl Strupp, 'Problèmes actuels du droit des représailles', in *Mélanges offerts à Ernest Mahaim par ses collègues, ses amis, ses élèves*, Liège, 5 Novembre 1935, 2nd vol. (Paris: Librairie du Recueil Sirey, 1935), 341–56, at 341 (emphasis in original).

2 Ibid., 341–2. Cf. Stephen C. Neff, *War and the Law of Nations: A General History* (Cambridge: CUP, 2005), 285–286 and 297. On Strupp, see Sandra Link, *Ein Realist mit Idealen – Der Völkerrechtler Karl Strupp (1886–1940)* (Studien zur Geschichte des Völkerrechts, 5; Baden-Baden: Nomos, 2003).

Etymologically, the word 'reprisals' goes back to Medieval Latin *reprehendere*, 'to retake', and evolved through the Italian *ripreso* (<*riprendere*) and the French *reprise* (<*reprendre*).[3] It originally meant the action of taking one's property back or its equivalent in nature or value.[4] Reprisals then pursued redress. Nevertheless, they came over time to be used for other goals such as law enforcement, deterrence, even punishment.[5] Hence, the pressure applied against the wrongdoer diversified and was not only limited to the mere retaking of property.[6]

---

3 Peter Haggenmacher, 'L'ancêtre de la protection diplomatique. les représailles de l'ancien droit (XIIe-XVIIIe siècles)', *Relations internationales* 143/3 (2010), 7–12, at 9. See also Émile Littré, *Dictionnaire de la langue française*, 4th vol. (Paris/Londres: Libraire Hachette et Cie, 1874), 1647.

4 Cf. Grover Clark, 'The English Practice with Regard to Reprisals by Private Persons', *AJIL* 27 (1933), 694–723, at 702.

5 Cf. Federica Paddeu, *Justification and Excuse in International Law: Concept and Theory of General Defences* (Cambridge Studies in International and Comparative Law; Cambridge: CUP, 2018), 248–9.

In the *Naulilaa* case, a panel of Swiss arbitrators where called to answer the questions whether the responsibility of Germany was engaged for damage caused during WWI to neutral Portugal in its southwestern African colony of Angola, and whether reprisals might justify Germany's actions. On that occasion, the award in 1928 spelt out reprisals as "aim[ing] to impose on the offending State reparation for the offense or the return to legality in avoidance of new offenses." (*Responsabilité de l'Allemagne à raison des dommages causés dans les colonies portugaises du sud de l'Afrique (Sentence sur le principe de la responsabilité*), Decision of 31 July 1928, RIAA 2 (1949), 1011–33, at 1026; extract translated in Andrew D. Mitchell, 'Does One Illegality Merit Another? The Law of Belligerent Reprisals in International Law', *MilLRev* 170 (2001), 155–77, at 156). Cf. Alfon Knetsch, 'Repressalien', in Paul Posener (ed.), *Rechtslexikon. Handwörterbuch der Rechts- und Staatswissenschaften*, mit Unterstützung durch zahlreiche Mitarbeiter, 2nd vol. (Berlin: Erich Weber Verlag, 1909), 379; Article 1 of the IIL's resolution governing reprisals in time of peace: Institut de Droit International (ed.), *Session de Paris, Octobre 1934* (Annuaire IDI, vol. 38; Bruxelles: Goemaere, 1934), 708.

Contemporary scholars have particularly emphasised the punitive character of the modern use of reprisals. See, e.g., Derek Bowett, 'Reprisals Involving Recourse to Armed Force', *AJIL* 66 (1972), 1–36, at 3; Robert W. Tucker, 'Reprisals and Self-Defence. The Customary Law', *AJIL* 66 (1972), 586–96, at 589. Cf. Neff, *War and the Law of Nations* (above, n. 2), 124. But when this punitive character prevails, the measure can hardly be regarded as peacetime reprisals. For instance, Ibid., 229, mentions instances of reprisals against savage tribes in the nineteenth century that, in truth, looked like punitive expeditions or small-scale wars.

6 Cf. Thomas Joseph Lawrence, *The principles of international law* (4th edn., Boston: D. C. Heath & Co., 1910), 337; Evelyn Speyer Colbert, *Retaliation in international law* (New York: King's Crown Press, 1948), 60–1.

According to Hans Kelsen, reprisals are "acts which, although normally illegal, are exceptionally permitted as reaction of one state against a violation of its right by another state."[7] So, reprisals imply the departure from the ordinary rules of international law in response to wrongful acts. They differ in such respect from other measures of coercion semantically or conceptually related. Retorsion, for example, is the unfriendly response by a State to another country's act or conduct. The difference with reprisals is, therefore, that the acts of retorsion are politically or morally discourteous, but do not constitute a breach of international law.[8] Another measure distinguishable from reprisals is self-defence, which means an immediate reaction to prevent or thwart an imminent or ongoing aggression. As to reprisals, there is, on the contrary, no requirement of temporal immediacy because the wrong is already done.[9] Finally, reprisals should not be confused with sanctions. Indeed, the former are a self-help method while sanctions are understood today as collective enforcement measures decided by an international organisation.[10]

---

7 Hans Kelsen, *Principles of international law* (New York: Rinehart & company, 1952), 23.

8 The suspension of diplomatic relations is, e.g., an act of retorsion. See Thomas Giegerich, 'Retorsion', in Rüdiger Wolfrum (ed.), *The Max Planck Encyclopedia of Public International Law*, published under the auspices of the Max Planck Institute for comparative public law and international law, 11 vols. (Oxford: OUP, 2012–2013; <http://www.mpepil.com>, accessed 15 December 2017); United Nations, *Materials on the Responsibility of States for Internationally Wrongful Acts* (United Nations Legislative Series, 25; New York: United Nations, 2012), 304–5.

9 Cf. Jean-Claude Venezia, 'La notion de représailles en droit international public', *RGDIP* 64 (1960), 465–98, at 474–477; Frits Kalshoven, *Belligerent Reprisals*, Preface by Jean Pictet (Scientific collection of the Henry Dunant Institute, 1; Leyden: Sijthoff, 1971), 26–7; Oscar Schachter, 'In Defense of International Rules on the Use of Force', *UChiLRev* 53 (1986), 113–46, at 132; Fiona Mckinnon, 'Reprisals as a Method of Enforcing International Law', *LJIL* 4 (1991), 221–48, at 231–232; The Chairman Pemmaraju Sreenivasa Rao, 2424th Meeting, 21 July 1995: United Nations, *Yearbook of the International Law Commission 1995: Summary records of the meetings of the forty-seventh session 2 May-21 July 1995*, 1st vol. (New York/Geneva: United Nations, 1997), 297 Para. 12.

10 Matthias Ruffert, 'Reprisals', in Rüdiger Wolfrum (ed.), *The Max Planck Encyclopedia of Public International Law*, published under the auspices of the Max Planck Institute for comparative public law and international law, 8th vol. (Oxford: OUP, 2012–2013; <http://www.mpepil.com>, accessed 13 December 2017), 927–30, here at no. 9. See also Hans Kelsen, *Collective security under international law* (2nd reprint [originally published: International law studies, 49; Washington: United States GPO, 1957], Clark, New Jersey: The Lawbook Exchange, 2011),

In contemporary legal terminology, as well as colloquially, reprisals mean the retaliatory action during a war in response to the opponent's violation of the *ius in bello*.[11] Those 'belligerent' reprisals often correspond to the idea of 'retaliation', namely returning a tit for a tat as retribution: the *lex talionis*.[12] However, the present study is all about peacetime reprisals, known today as 'countermeasures' but referred herein to as 'reprisals' in accordance with their pre-WWII meaning.[13]

A distinction exists between acts of reprisals involving the use of force and non-forcible ones. An example of the latter kind is the non-fulfilment of treaty obligations.[14] The compatibility of non-forcible reprisals with a state of peace has never raised serious doubts. On the contrary, it was far

---

104; United Nations, *Materials on the Responsibility of States for Internationally Wrongful Acts* (above, n. 8), 305.

11 On belligerent reprisals, see i.a. Louis Le Fur, *Des Représailles en temps de guerre: Représailles et Réparations* (Comité pour la Défense du Droit International; Paris: Recueil Sirey, 1919); Ellery C. Stowell, 'Military Reprisals and the Sanctions of the Laws of War', *AJIL* 36 (1942), 643–50; Kalshoven, *Belligerent Reprisals* (above, n. 9); Shane Darcy, 'The Evolution of the Law of Belligerent Reprisals', *MilLRev* 175 (2003), 184–251; Johannes Hebenstreit, *Repressalien im humanitären Völkerrecht* (Völkerrecht und Außenpolitik, 64; Baden-Baden: Nomos, 2004).

12 Cf. Joseph-Mathias Gérard de Rayneval, *Institutions du droit de la nature et des gens*, 1st vol. (new edn., Paris: Rey et Gravier, 1832), 318; Andrés Bello, *Principios de derecho internacional* (2nd edn., Caracas: J. M. de Rojas, 1847), 127; Haggenmacher, 'L'ancêtre de la protection diplomatique. les représailles de l'ancien droit (XIIe-XVIIIe siècles)' (above, n. 3), 9. Peacetime reprisals were sometimes classified under 'retaliation' as umbrella term (see, e.g., Colbert, *Retaliation in international law* (above, n. 6), 2–3 fn. 1) or were accounted for in a reductive manner as the application of the talion (see, e.g., Theodor Schmalz, *Das europäische Völker-Recht: in acht Büchern* (Berlin: Duncker und Humblot, 1817), 213–6). This categorisation may be the source of confusion and does not correctly render the character of reprisals used in time of peace. Therefore, the concept of retaliation is reserved here for belligerent reprisals only.

13 The shift from 'reprisals' to 'countermeasures' followed the arbitration award in *Case concerning the Air Service Agreement of 27 March 1946 between the United States of America and France*, Decision of 9 December 1978, RIAA 18 (2006), 471–93. See also United Nations, *Materials on the Responsibility of States for Internationally Wrongful Acts* (above, n. 8), 304; Federica Paddeu, 'Countermeasures', in Rüdiger Wolfrum (ed.), *The Max Planck Encyclopedia of Public International Law*, published under the auspices of the Max Planck Institute for comparative public law and international law, 11 vols. (Oxford: OUP, 2012–2013; <http://www.mpepil.com>, accessed 13 December 2017), no. 2.

14 In the past, the expulsion or the dismissal of nationals of the wrongdoing country was often regarded as a measure of reprisals. See, thereupon, Carl Albert von Kamptz, *Beiträge zum Staats- und Völkerrecht*, 1st vol. (Berlin: Nicolai, 1815), 204–

less certain when reprisals involved the employment of armed force.[15] Nonetheless, 'armed' (or 'forcible') reprisals have usually been classified amongst the non-amicable mode of self-help 'falling short of war', i.e. enforcement methods not amounting to war.[16]

The existence of reprisals in international law flows from the anarchic state of international relations. From the absence of an international organisation or a supreme authority results the decentralisation of law enforcement. Thus, the doctrine of self-help teaches that every sovereign State is permitted to take the law into its own hands.[17]

In the light of these explanations, Strupp's previous remarks arouse interest and raise a number of questions. In fact, one may wonder why armed reprisals were allowed during the interwar period while the League of Nations can be described as "an organized international community".[18]

---

6. More generally about non-forcible reprisals, see esp. Andrea de Guttry, *Le rappresaglie non comportanti la coercizione militare nel diritto internazionale* (Pubblicazioni della facoltà di giurisprudenza della università di Pisa, 90; Milano: Dott. A. Giuffrè, 1985); Omer Yousif Elagab, *The legality of non-forcible counter-measures in international law* (Oxford monographs in international law; Oxford: OUP, 1988).

15 See *infra*, Introduction I.2.

16 In German legal literature, armed reprisals are sometimes called *militärische Repressalien*. See, e.g., Josef L. Kunz, *Kriegsrecht und Neutralitätsrecht* (Wien: Julius Springer, 1935), 7ff.; Georg Kappus, *Der völkerrechtliche Kriegsbegriff in seiner Abgrenzung gegenüber den militärischen Repressalien* (Abhandlungen aus dem Staats- und Verwaltungsrecht mit Einschluss des Kolonialrechts und des Völkerrechts, 52; Breslau: M. & H. Marcus, 1936); Harald Heyns, *Die Anwendung von militärischen Repressalien unter Völkerbundmitgliedstaaten*, Inaugural-Dissertation zur Erlangung der Doktorwürde der Hohen Rechts- und Staatswissenschaftlichen Fakultät der Christian-Albrechts-Universität zu Kiel (Baruth/Mark-Berlin: J. Särchen, 1938). However, the attributive adjective 'military' may be misleading. The expression *nichtkriegerische Repressalien* —used, e.g., by Georg Jellinek, 'China und das Völkerrecht', *DJZ* 5 (1900), 401–4, at 402; Paul Schoen, 'Zur Lehre von den völkerrechtlichen nichtkriegerischen Mitteln der Selbsthilfe', *ZVölkR* 20 (1936), 14–64— is more suitable to highlight the separation between armed reprisals and belligerent reprisals (*Kriegsrepressalien*).

17 Cf. Yves de la Brière, 'Évolution de la doctrine et de la pratique en matière de représailles', *RdC* 22/II (1928), 237–94, at 278; Albert E. Hindmarsh, 'Self-Help in Time of Peace', *AJIL* 26 (1932), 315–26, at 320; Georges Scelle, 'Règles générales du droit de la paix', *RdC* 46 (1933), 327–703, at 671–673; Ruffert, 'Reprisals' (above, n. 10), no. 2.

18 See International Court of Justice, *South West Africa Cases (Ethiopia v. South Africa; Liberia v. South Africa), Preliminary Objections*, Judgement of 21 December 1962, I.C.J. Reports (1962), 319–48, at 329.

A cursory look in legal doctrine of the time shows, though, that there were conflicting views on that issue. On the one hand, some lawyers supported the opinion that the resort to armed reprisals was incompatible with the new obligations imposed by the Covenant of the League of Nations.[19] Strupp himself considered that the progress achieved in the organisation of the international community of States and in the prevention and settlement of disputes forbade the recourse to armed reprisals, if not normatively at least morally.[20] On the other hand, two doctoral theses on reprisals from the early 1930s both concluded that in the actual state of international law reprisals were still needed and therefore should not be abolished.[21] Indeed, although the collective security system of the League prevented the occurrence of conflicts between States and encouraged their settlement, it was not flawless. The League of Nations was an organised international community, yet decentralised.[22] So, in the absence of an effective method to guarantee law compliance and law enforcement in the form

19 E.g. "S'emparer de force du territoire de son adversaire comme garantie du payement d'une dette dont on proclame soi-même, sans nul contrôle, l'existence et le montant, c'est la forme la plus caractéristique de l'anarchie juridique qui, tolérable en l'absence de toute organisation sociale, ne saurait être tolérée dans la Société des Nations." (Nikolaos Sokrates Politis, 'Les représailles entre Etats membres de la Société des Nations', *RGDIP* 31 (1924), 5–16, at 14). See also Louis Le Fur, 'Le développement historique du droit international. De l'anarchie internationale à une communauté internationale organisée', *RdC* 41/III (1932), 505–601, at 533–535.

20 Strupp, 'Problèmes actuels du droit des représailles' (above, n. 1), 341–51. See also Brière, 'Évolution de la doctrine et de la pratique en matière de représailles' (above, n. 17), 248–250 and 278–288.

21 Alfred Müller, *Wandlungen im Repressalienrecht*, Inaugural-Dissertation zur Erlangung der Doktorwürde der Hohen Rechts- und Staatswissenschaftlichen Fakultät der Georg-August-Universität zu Göttingen (Göttingen: [A. Stenger], 1933), 107; André Haumant, *Les représailles*, Thèse pour le doctorat en droit présentée et soutenue le 12 Mars 1934, à 14 heures (Paris: Marcel Giard, 1934), 218–9. Cf. Erich Schumann, *Die Repressalie*, Inaugural=Dissertation zur Erlangung der Doktorwürde der Rechts= und Wirtschaftswissenschaftlichen Fakultät der Universität Rostock (Rostock: Carl Hinstorff, 1927), 38–40. Shortly after WWII, Colbert, *Retaliation in international law* (above, n. 6), 199–206, reached a similar conclusion. She urged then to regulate the employment of peacetime reprisals rather than abandon that mode of redress.

22 Josef L. Kunz, 'Sanctions in International Law', *AJIL* 54 (1960), 324–47, at 327.

of sanctions, the resort to reprisals did not completely lose its significance.[23]

However, this explanation remains largely unsatisfactory because, during the era of the League of Nations, many States had consented to waive their sovereign right to resort to war. Although the efforts in that regard did not ultimately succeed to ban war for good from the international relations, many prominent nations strove to outlaw its resort. On the contrary, nothing alike was ever decided regarding the employment of armed reprisals. One would thus look in vain for a similar prohibition or at least regulation adopted by States at the time. This difference in treatment between the two activities is all the more intriguing that the question of the distinction between war and armed reprisals was a thorny issue during the interwar period.

2. Blurry Line between Armed Reprisals and War

For want of restriction, the resort to armed reprisals presented a dangerous solution for bypassing the prohibition of war. In this way, real wars could be waged in the guise of alleged reprisals.[24] This situation ensued from the classification of reprisals under the law of peace. It means that reprisals were deemed consistent with a state of peace, even when they involved the use of armed force.[25]

---

23 Elisabeth Zoller, *Peacetime unilateral remedies: An analysis of countermeasures* (Dobbs Ferry, N.Y.: Transnational Publishers, 1984), 38. Cf. André Pépy, 'Après les ratifications du Plan Young. Révision et Sanctions', *RDI* 5 (1930), 441–77, at 476; Hindmarsh, 'Self-Help in Time of Peace' (above, n. 17), 324–6.

24 Scelle, 'Règles générales du droit de la paix' (above, n. 17), 677; Kunz, *Kriegsrecht und Neutralitätsrecht* (above, n. 16), 8 fn. 37, and 11; Wilhelm Georg Grewe, *Epochen der Völkerrechtsgeschichte* (Baden-Baden: Nomos, 1984), 735; Neff, *War and the Law of Nations* (above, n. 2), 296–7.

25 Nonetheless, numerous textbooks on international law covered the topic of reprisals in the second part or volume devoted to war. The idea was to stress the distinction between the so-called 'pacific' means of coercion and war. So, e.g., John Westlake explained that "[t]he consideration of measures [short of war] will naturally precede the detailed consideration of war, as being more akin to the subject of the preceding volume [on Peace], but first of all war must be defined or those measures could not be distinguished from it." (John Westlake, *International Law*, 2nd vol. (2nd edn., Cambridge: CUP, 1913), 1). Cf. Lassa Oppenheim, *International Law: A Treatise*, 2nd vol. (London: Longmans, Green, and Co., 1905), V. In other words, an excluding definition applied to the concept of war. Since

As a result, the employment of armed reprisals possessed obvious advantages over the resort to war. British legal scholar Thomas Erskine Holland mentioned that reprisals "are strictly limited in scope; they cease, when their object has been attained, without the formalities of a treaty of peace; and, no condition of "belligerency" existing between the Powers immediately concerned, third Powers are not called upon to undertake the onerous obligations of "neutrality.""[26] From a constitutional law viewpoint, the resort to reprisals could also be decided by the Executive alone, without the prior permission of the Parliament, which only was required to declare war.[27] The limited scope of armed reprisals also made them more beneficial to the target country than a war, which could take on dramatic proportions and bring about many calamities.[28] Besides, reprisals would cease immediately after the fulfilment of the demands for which the reprisal-taking State undertook the operation. In other words, the target country would

---

reprisals and the other measures short of war remained within the confines of peace, a forcible action not labelled as such could only mean war; and vice versa.

26 Letter of 18 December 1902: Thomas Erskine Holland, *Letters to "The Times" upon War and Neutrality (1881–1920): With some commentary* (3rd edn., London: Longmans, Green, and Co., 1921), 14. About the legal implications of war, see Alan N. Salpeter and Jonathan C. Waller, 'Armed Reprisals during Intermediacy – A New Framework for Analysis in International Law', *VillLRev* 17 (1971), 270–312, at 271 fn. 5.

27 "La collaboration des deux pouvoirs sera effective dans les véritables guerres, mais les gouvernements, de nos jours, prennent souvent l'initiative des hostilités, sans vouloir engager la guerre proprement dite; par exemple, sous forme de représailles violentes, de blocus pacifiques, d'expéditions, même occupations du territoire étranger." (Marius Maurel, *De la Déclaration de Guerre: Étude d'Histoire Diplomatique, de Droit Constitutionnel et de Droit Public International*, Préface de A. Mérignhac (Paris: Librairie générale de droit & de jurisprudence, 1907), 203f.). See also Frantz Despagnet, *Cours de droit international public* (4th edn., Paris: Libraire de la société du Recueil Sirey, 1910), 782.

28 The reprisal-taking States were well aware of that aspect, as it is apparent from a British Memorandum of 1902 drafted in the context of the blockade of Venezuela: "The various [coercive] measures mentioned are, no doubt, all of them, in essence acts of war; if Venezuela chose so to treat them, she would be justified in taking that course. It is, however, plainly in her interests not to regard them in this light, and they form a convenient *mitior usus* which is suitable to the case of a recalcitrant petty State in controversy with Great Powers of overwhelming strength, who, while desiring to obtain proper redress, are unwilling to dismember or destroy a puny antagonist." (British Memorandum of 29 November 1902 on pacific blockade reproduced by Lothar Kotzsch, 'Die Blockade gegen Venezuela vom Jahre 1902 als Präzedenzfall für das moderne Kriegsrecht', *ArchVölkR* 5 (1955–1956), 410–25, at 423).

not be compelled to meet other demands.[29] The prevailing pacific sentiment also accounts for the use of reprisals as a substitute for war.[30] In fact, reprisals were not only milder than war, but morally more acceptable too. Finally, the reprisal-taking States were not to abide by the rules of the *ius in bello*. That is why Fritz Grob argued in his major work *The Relativity of War and Peace* (1949) that military operations were named armed reprisals as sheer legal casuistry in order to avoid calling them war and hence falling under the scope of some rules of the law of war.[31]

The resort to reprisals had thus undeniable advantages and different legal implications than war. However, the distinction between reprisals and war was no easy matter. French jurist Yves de la Brière characterised reprisals as an unnamed war of small scale that did not break the state of peace.[32] He thus meant that armed reprisals looked like war but had distinct legal effects. Such description reveals the singular place of armed reprisals within international law for lying half-way between peace and war.[33] In fact, not only lay people could not distinguish armed reprisals

29 Colbert, *Retaliation in international law* (above, n. 6), 98–9.

30 Elagab, *The legality of non-forcible counter-measures in international law* (above, n. 14), 14.

31 Fritz Grob, *The Relativity of War and Peace: A Study in Law, History, and Politics*, Foreword by Roscoe Pound (New Haven: Yale University Press, 1949), 237–47.

32 Brière, 'Évolution de la doctrine et de la pratique en matière de représailles' (above, n. 17), 272.

33 In the Eighth Philippic, Section 4, Cicero stated "*Inter bellum et pacem medium nihil*", that is, between peace and war no intermediacy [exists]. This maxim has governed international law since at least Hugo Grotius who adopted it as an invariable principle. See Hugo Grotius, *Le droit de la guerre et de la paix*, Traduction de Jean Barbeyrac, 2 vols. (Bibliothèque de Philosophie politique et juridique: Textes et Documents; Caen [Amsterdam]: Centre de Philosophie politique et juridique de l'Université de Caen [chez Pierre de Coup], 1984 [1724]), Book III Ch. XXI § I.3, here at 2nd vol., 971. See also Lord Macnaghten in *Janson v. Driefontein Consolidated Mines* (1902): "[...] the law recognises a state of peace and a state of war, but that it knows nothing of an intermediate state which is neither the one thing nor the other—neither peace nor war." (Frederick Pollock and A. P. Stone, *The Law Reports or The Incorporated Council of Law Reporting. House of Lords, Judicial Committee of the Privy Council, and Peerage Cases: 1902.* (London: William Clowes and sons, 1902), 497). Armed reprisals could thus not escape from the dichotomy: they had to be either warlike or pacific. As a result, they fell within the law of peace. Kunz, *Kriegsrecht und Neutralitätsrecht* (above, n. 16), 8. Cornelius van Bynkershoek stated too that "[...], *Repressaliis locum non esse, nisi in Pace,* [...]." (Cornelius van Bynkershoek, *Quaestionum juris publici libri duo*, 2 vols. (The Classics of International Law, 14; [1st edn. of 1737], Oxford: Claren-

from war, but jurists too.[34] For example, Great Britain, Germany and Italy began to blockade the coasts of Venezuela in December 1902. The action

---

don Press, 1930), Book I Cap. 24, here 1st vol., 173 (tr. 2nd vol., 134)). So, legal doctrine ruled out the existence of a so-called 'state of reprisals'. See, e.g., Friedrich Heinrich Geffcken, 'La France en Chine et le droit international', *RDILC* 17 (1885), 145–51, at 145; Ernest Nys, *Le droit international: Les principes, les théories, les faits*, 3rd vol. (Bruxelles/Paris: Alfred Castaigne; Albert Fontemoing, 1906), 89.

Notwithstanding, few authors supported the opinion that an intermediate state, a *status mixtus*, under which armed reprisals would come, existed in international law. Shortly before the Second World War, Carl Schmitt believed to have identified, both *de facto* and *de jure*, the existence of a state of intermediacy. See Carl Schmitt, '„Inter pacem et bellum nihil medium"', *ZAkDR* (1939), 594–5. A few years later, Georg Schwarzenberger held the view based on his assessment of State practice that the alternative of peace and war was actually a construction *de lege ferenda*. In fact, the absence of an objective criterion to separate both concepts, owing to the legality of the limited use of force in peacetime, gave him the certainty that "The doctrine of the alternative character of peace and war, [...], minimizes or ignores the reality of State practice which has created rules pertaining neither to those of peace or war, but constituting a *status mixtus*." (Georg Schwarzenberger, 'Jus Pacis Ac Belli? Prolegomena to a Sociology of International Law', *AJIL* 37 (1943), 460–79, quotation at 474). Armed reprisals appertained thus to this state of intermediacy for they were "neither *pax bellicosa* nor *bellum pacificum*". See Georg Schwarzenberger, *Power Politics: A Study of World Society*, published under the auspices of the London Institute of World Affairs (The Library of World Affairs, 18; 3rd edn., London: Stevens & sons, 1964), 190–1. Cf. Georg Schwarzenberger, '[Book Review: *Retaliation in International Law*, by Evelyn Speyer Colbert]', *IntAff* 25 (1949), 336–7.

In 1954, Philip C. Jessup, having chiefly in mind the context of the Cold War, also urged to drop the old division in order to acknowledge a third intermediate status characterised by: (1) the permanent hostility between the parties; (2) the impossibility to settle the issues all at once owing to their fundamental and deep-rooted nature; (3) the avoidance of war to settle the disputes. He could glimpse some consequences, even benefits, of such intermediacy. See Philip C. Jessup, 'Should International Law Recognize an Intermediate Status between Peace and War?', *AJIL* 48 (1954), 98–103. The second characteristic surely prevents the classification of armed reprisals under such a third state. Nevertheless, the U.S. legal scholar observed regarding the measures short of war that "It does not seem to have been particularly helpful to have discussed some such situations as non-amicable modes of redress short of war, perhaps because of the uncertainty about the legal definition of war itself. The difficulty seems to arise from the legal necessity of fitting every situation into one of the two traditional categories of peace or war." (Ibid., 100).

Two decades later, Alan N. Salpeter and Jonathan C. Waller worked on the assumption that armed reprisals fell within a status of intermediacy. They argued for the adoption of a new standard to evaluate the use of this means because they considered both customary law and the United Nations rule inadequate. See

was undertaken at first by way of reprisals, but under the pressure of third States, the blockading Powers were forced to acknowledge the existence of a state of war. However, no declaration of war followed. Thomas E. Holland struggled to label the true nature of the state of things which superseded the acts of reprisals. In the absence of an accurate legal classification, he called it a state of "war *sub modo*" while warning against the obliteration of the dividing line between peace and war.[35]

In that case, the reprisal-taking States recognised the existence of war. Nevertheless, such admission was infrequent and for lack of a declaration of war by either party to the conflict or armed resistance by the assailed country, the war would not break out. In fact, the use of objective criteria usually proved unavailing to delineate the limit between the two activities. Some lawyers advocated, therefore, the identification of armed reprisals with war.[36] However, it was the subjective test that was commonly applied. So, if none of the States directly involved in the dispute had manifested a hostile intention, the absence of *animus belligerendi* defined the action as reprisals.[37] This test was a valid criterion which, nevertheless, could too easily lead to abuse, i.e. the oppression of the weak by the strong followed by the denial of the existence of war.

In comparison to war, armed reprisals appear as quite permissive while there was no inherent difference between the two activities. It is, therefore, beyond understanding why a separation between war and armed reprisals was held onto. The resort to armed reprisals allowed the maintenance of a fiction, namely that forcible measures like bombardment or military occupation could also be compatible with peace. Until today, the distinction has not been completely dropped.

Salpeter and Waller, 'Armed Reprisals during Intermediacy – A New Framework for Analysis in International Law' (above, n. 26).

34 Cf. Neff, *War and the Law of Nations* (above, n. 2), 226f.

35 Thomas Erskine Holland, 'War *Sub Modo*', *The Law Quarterly Review* 19 (1903), 133–5, at 135.

36 See, e.g., Paul Pradier-Fodéré, *Traité de droit international public européen et américain, suivant les progrès de la science et de la pratique contemporaines*, 9 vols. (Paris: A. Durand et Pedone-Lauriel, 1885–1906), 6th vol., 488; Théophile Funck-Brentano and Albert Sorel, *Précis du droit ges gens* (2nd edn., Paris: E. Plon, Nourrit et Cie, 1887), 229; Nys, *Le droit international* (above, n. 33), 89. Cf. Peter Wagner, *Zur Lehre von den Streiterledigungsmitteln des Völkerrechts. Eine historisch-kritische und thetische Untersuchung* (Darmstadt: Chr. Haun, 1900), 67.

37 See, e.g., Westlake, *International Law* (above, n. 25), 2.

3. Pre-1919 Practice

In view of the above remarks, the distinction between armed reprisals and war patently fell short of clarity. Nevertheless, this cannot be reduced to an issue specific to the League of Nations era. Strupp asserted that the creation of the League of Nations was the triggering factor which made reprisals grow quantitatively and qualitatively.[38] However, even by his own testimony, the issue about armed reprisals predated 1919. Thomas E. Holland's comments are symptomatic of a problem that had deeper roots.

The nineteenth century may be regarded as a landmark in the history of reprisals. Charles De Visscher —Belgian lawyer, who during his career held prominent positions including member of the PCA, judge of the PCIJ and later of the ICJ— called it "l'époque classique des représailles". He explained that the characteristics of nineteenth-century reprisals were their separation from war and their highly politicised nature. Indeed, the acts of reprisals in that century were intrinsically hostile. Notwithstanding, they seldom amounted to war because the target country was generally not in position to hit back. In fact, the asymmetric relations of power allowed the stronger reprisal-taking State to claim the absence of war with the weaker target country, regardless of the high degree of violence. Besides, the recourse to reprisals pursued chiefly opportunistic ends.[39]

The many instances of armed reprisals that occurred throughout the nineteenth century seem to confirm this pattern invariably. The reprisal-taking State was always a mighty Western Power, mainly France or Great Britain that were the leading States of that century.[40] On the other side, armed reprisals applied only to the smaller and weaker Powers. They were either peripheral European States —namely Greece, the Two Sicilies, Portugal and the Ottoman Empire— or Asian or American nations. These target countries were usually regarded as half-civilised, viz. "neither wholly re-

38 Strupp, 'Problèmes actuels du droit des représailles' (above, n. 1), 341.

39 Charles De Visscher, *Théories et réalités en droit international public* (Paris: A. Pedone, 1953), 348.

40 For example, in his authoritative study of pacific blockade, the German legal scholar and diplomat Horst P. Falcke identified six cases of pacific blockade by way of reprisals. All were established by either France or Great Britain, three cases each. See Horst P. Falcke, *Le blocus pacifique*, trans. Ant. Contat (Leipzig: Rossberg, 1919), 234–7.

spectable nor wholly responsible members of the family of nations".[41] Their recognition as full members of the family of civilised nations was a slow process throughout the nineteenth century.[42] Hence, when armed reprisals were contemplated or decided, the diplomatic correspondence often abounded with contemptuous remarks about the internal political, financial and economic situation of the target country: corruption, despotic government, political unrest, protectionism, etc.[43]

Based on this asymmetric power relation, the great Powers resorted to armed reprisals to enforce their demands, with a very low probability that the target country would treat them as acts of war. Furthermore, some lawyers approved this practice because it did not cause the outbreak of war and presented a lesser evil than war. Therefore, they rejected the objection that this mode of redress was inequitable on the grounds that the employment of such measure between Powers of equal strength would inevitably lead to war.[44] So, the separation between armed reprisals and war rested on mere factual and political asymmetry.

The second characteristic is that nineteenth-century reprisals took on a highly politicised aspect. The demands that the reprisal-taking country pressed against the target country sought redress for the violation of rights.

---

41 Colbert, *Retaliation in international law* (above, n. 6), 62–3. On the concept of 'civilisation', see Liliana Obregón, 'The Civilized and the Uncivilized', in Bardo Fassbender and Anne Peters (eds.), *The Oxford Handbook of the History of International Law* (Oxford: OUP, 2012), 917–39.
On the other hand, savage or barbarian nations were considered outside the sphere of international law. Washburn emphasised this when he told about the so-called pacific blockade that Great Britain instituted against the Kingdom of Dahomey (actual Benin) in 1876, thus diminishing the importance of the case. See Albert H. Washburn, 'The Legality of the Pacific Blockade', *Colum. L. Rev.* 21 (1921), 55–69/227–241/442–459, at 240.

42 Héctor Gros Espiell, 'La doctrine du Droit international en Amérique Latine avant la première conférence panaméricaine (Washington, 1889)', *JHistIntlL* 3 (2001), 1–17, at 4.

43 See, e.g., Mr Sanford to Mr Cass, 10 August 1857: Henry S. Sanford, *The Aves Island Case: with the Correspondence Relating Thereto and Discussion of Law and Facts, Being the Official Documents published by Order of the Senate of the United States* (Washington: [s.n.], 1861), 238–9.

44 Cf. Lucien de Sainte-Croix, *Étude sur l'exception de dol en droit romain/La déclaration de guerre et ses effets immédiats; Étude d'histoire et de législation comparée*, Thèse pour le doctorat; L'acte public sur les matières ci-après sera soutenu le Mercredi 20 Janvier 1892, à 2 heures et demie (Paris: Arthur Rousseau, 1892), 225; Letter of 18 December 1902: Holland, *Letters to "The Times" upon War and Neutrality (1881–1920)* (above, n. 26), 14.

However, political considerations were generally at stake, hiding in the background. Reprisals as a lawful mode of self-help could serve as a legalistic camouflage.[45] Depending on the angle from which it is viewed, a case of armed reprisals could thus be called an instance of armed intervention.[46] The concept of 'gunboat diplomacy', i.e. "the threat or use of naval

---

45 "Denn während die äusseren Anlässe sich oft als rein äusserliche Faktoren darstellen, sind die Motive in den meisten Fällen hochpolitischer Art, sei es, dass sie auf das Prestige des Staates zurückgreifen oder etwa Ausdehnungsgelüsten entspringen." (Ernst Hiller, 'Die Friedensblockade und ihre Stellung in Völkerrecht', Inaugural-Dissertation verfasst und der Hohen Rechts- und Staatswissenschaftlichen Fakultät der Bayer. Julius-Maximilians-Universität Würzburg zur Erlangung der staatswissenschaftlichen Doktorwürde (Würzburg, Hohe Rechts- und Staatswissenschafltiche Fakultät der Bayer. Julius-Maximilians-Universität Würzburg, 1923), 88). See also Ian Brownlie, *International Law and the Use of Force by States* (Oxford: Clarendon Press, 1963), 220.

46 Intervention is the interference by a State in the internal or external affairs of another State (William Edward Hall, *A treatise on international law* (4th edn., Oxford: Clarendon Press, 1895), 297). About intervention, see i.a. Adolph von Flöckher, *De l'intervention en droit international* (Paris: A. Pedone, 1896); Percy Henry Winfield, 'The History of Intervention in International Law', *BYIL* 3 (1922–23), 130–49; Percy Henry Winfield, 'The Grounds of Intervention in International Law', *BYIL* 5 (1924), 149–62; Charles G. Fenwick, 'Intervention. Individual and Collective', *AJIL* 39 (1945), 645–63; Miloš Vec, 'Intervention/Nichtintervention. Verrechtlichung der Politik und Politisierung des Völkerrechts im 19. Jahrhunderts', in Ulrich Lappenküper and Reiner Marcowitz (eds.), *Macht und Recht. Völkerrecht in den internationalen Beziehungen* (Otto-von-Bismarck-Stiftung Wissenschaftliche Reihe, 13; Paderborn: Ferdinand Schöningh, 2010), 135–60. Acts of reprisals also take the character "of a limited interference in the sphere of interests of another state" (Kelsen, *Principles of international law* (above, n. 7), 25). However, while reprisals are a response to the violation of rights, intervention seeks to defend interests not guaranteed by international law. As a result, there is a risk that reprisals serve as a flimsy pretext to pursue concealed illegitimate interests. Cf. Flöckher, *De l'intervention en droit international* (above, n. 46), 5–6; Kelsen, *Principles of international law* (above, n. 7), 25; Louis Delbez, *La notion de guerre: Essai d'analyse dogmatique* (Paris: A. Pedone, 1953), 94.
For example, the French intervention of 1861 in Mexico was "partly in nature of reprisals" (Robert Phillimore, *Commentaries Upon International Law*, 3rd vol. (2nd edn., London: Butterworths, 1873), 43). Indeed, Great Britain, France and Spain decided to jointly take coercive measures on account of the Mexican Government's failure to provide redress for damages sustained by their nationals, such as unpaid bonds. The protection of their nationals in the future was also one of their chief concerns. See the Convention of London signed between them on 31 October 1861: Friedrich Wilhelm August Murhard, Karl Murhard, J. Pinhas et al., *Nouveau recueil général de traités, conventions et autres transactions remarquables, servant à la connaissance des relations étrangères des puissances et États dans leurs rap-*

force to secure diplomatic concessions",[47] reflects this idea of intervention when the claimant State blockaded some ports or portions of the coast of the respondent State with gunboats, as a means of pressure. That expression, however, is not a legal concept. In fact, a blockade bereft of belligerency is known in international law as 'pacific blockade' and describes either an act of reprisals or an intervention.[48] Reprisals were actually acts ambivalent in nature.

---

ports mutuels. Continuation du grand Recueil de feu M. de Martens, 20 vols. (Goettingue: Librairie de Dieterich, 1843–1875), 17th vol., Part 2, 143. They agreed in that convention that the coercive measures could neither lead to the acquisition of territory or of special advantages nor interfere in the Mexican internal affairs (Art. 2). However, Spain and Great Britain withdrew their participation when it became obvious that France endeavoured to place on the Mexican imperial throne a European monarch (Francis Wharton, *A digest of the international law of the United States, taken from documents issued by Presidents and Secretaries of State, and from decisions of federal courts and opinions of Attorneys-General*, 3rd vol. (Washington: GPO, 1886), 97–99).

47 David Nicholson, 'Gunboat Diplomacy', in James C. Bradford (ed.), *International Encyclopedia of Military History*, Preface by Professor Jeremy Black (London/New York: Routledge, 2006), 574–5, at 574. Cf. Lea Heimbeck, *Die Abwicklung von Staatsbankrotten im Völkerrecht: Verrechtlichung und Rechtsvermeidung zwischen 1824 und 1907* (Studien zur Geschichte des Völkerrechts, 28; Baden-Baden: Nomos, 2013), 167 fn. 1. See, i.a., Anthony Preston and John Major, *Send a gunboat! A study of the gunboat and its role in British policy, 1854–1904* (London: Longmans, Green and Co., 1967); Miriam Hood, *Gunboat Diplomacy, 1895–1905: Great Power Pressure in Venezuela* (2nd edn., London: George Allen & Unwin, 1983); James Cable, *Gunboat diplomacy: Political applications of limited naval force.* (Studies in International Security, 16; 3rd edn., Basingstoke: Palgrave Macmillan, 1994); Andrew Graham-Yooll, *Imperial Skirmishes: War and Gunboat Diplomacy in Latin America* (Brooklyn, N.Y./Northampton, Mass.: Interlink Books, 2002). 'Gunboat diplomacy' refers to the resort to military measures by European States and the United States for political purposes. This is not a legal concept.
The concept of 'coercive diplomacy' is more general. See, thereupon, Alexander L. George, *Forceful Persuasion: Coercive Diplomacy as an Alternative to War*, Foreword by Ambassador Samuel W. Lewis (Washington, D.C.: United States Institute of Peace Press, 1991).

48 Cf. Oppenheim, *International Law* (above, n. 25), 43; Falcke, *Le blocus pacifique* (above, n. 40), 234; Ludwig Weber, 'Blockade, pacific', in Rudolf Bernhardt (ed.), *Encyclopedia of Public International Law. Use of Force, War and Neutrality, Peace Treaties (A–M)*, 3rd vol., Max Planck Institute for Comparative Public Law and International Law (Amsterdam/New York/Oxford: North-Holland Publishing Company, 1982), 51–3, here at 51.

Also, the resort to armed reprisals against another country required a great deal of caution and tact. For instance, the pacific blockade by way of reprisals that Great Britain instituted against Greece in 1850 seriously endangered the stability and peace of Europe. France and Russia, in their capacity as co-guarantors of the Greek independence, harshly protested against the British course of action.[49] According to De Visscher, the growing rivalry between the great Powers in all regions of the globe was precisely the strongest political incentive for the limitation, even prohibition, of armed reprisals.[50]

Finally, a last aspect of the pre-1919 practice is the absence of clear-cut regulation governing armed reprisals. Thomas J. Lawrence underlined the "great need of international legislation on the subject of reprisals."[51] As a matter of fact, apart from the 1887 Declaration on Blockade in the Absence of a State of War —i.e. pacific blockade— by the IIL and the Drago-Porter Convention of 1907, peacetime reprisals never were regulated by multilateral treaties.[52] Although the underlying principle of reprisals was sound, the question of their limitation raised a problem.[53] However, it does not mean that the resort to armed reprisals was not subject to any conditions. There were some tacitly recognised limits on armed reprisals in State practice and legal doctrine. For example, private innocent persons and their property ought to be spared.[54] The State that suffered a prior infringement of rights ought also to make a formal demand for redress be-

49 About this incident, see Derek Taylor, *Don Pacifico: The Acceptable Face of Gunboat Diplomacy* (London/Portland, Oregon: Vallentine Mitchell, 2008).

50 De Visscher, *Théories et réalités en droit international public* (above, n. 39), 349–50. Cf. Haumant, *Les représailles* (above, n. 21), 156.

51 Lawrence, *The principles of international law* (above, n. 6), 344. See also Jan de Louter, *Le droit international public positif*, 2nd vol. (Bibliothèque internationale du Droit des Gens; Oxford: OUP, 1920), 205.

52 Paddeu, *Justification and Excuse in International Law* (above, n. 5), 237. See also Louter, *Le droit international public positif* (above, n. 51), 201.

53 Robert Redslob, *Histoire des grands principes du droit des gens: Depuis l'Antiquité jusqu'à la veille de la Grande Guerre* (Paris: Rousseau et Cie, 1923), 466.

54 See esp. Charles Sumner's interesting speech in the U.S. Senate on 18 July 1868: Charles Sumner, *The works of Charles Sumner*, 15 vols. (Boston: Lee and Shepard, 1875–1883), 12th vol., 481–501. Cf. Pasquale Fiore, *Nouveau droit international public suivant les besoins de la civilisation moderne*, traduit de l'Italien et annotée par Charles Antoine, 2nd vol. (2nd edn., Paris: A. Durand et Pedone-Lauriel, 1885–1886), 666; Edwin Montefiore Borchard, 'Reprisals on Private Property', *AJIL* 30 (1936), 108–13; Ignaz Seidl-Hohenveldern, 'Reprisals and the taking of private property', in Redactie van het Nederlands Tijdschrift voor Internationaal Recht (ed.), *De Conflictu Legum. Bundel opstellen aangeboden aan Roeland Duco*

fore resorting to reprisals.[55] Despite those conditions, armed reprisals were actually known for being excessive and abusive.[56] This situation contrasts with the ancient practice of reprisals in force before the nineteenth century.[57]

II. Leading Question

The overall picture of armed reprisals that emerges from this tour d'horizon is one where a lack of clarity over the subject prevailed. Armed reprisals were shrouded in ambiguity. They appear to fall within that part of international law where there are more grey zones than absolute certainties.[58] As a consequence, armed reprisals gave rise to numerous abuses of all kinds from the early nineteenth century until 1945.

Kollewijn & Johannes Offerhaus ter gelegenheid van hun zeventigste verjaardag (Leiden: A. W. Sijthoff, 1962), 470–9.

55 See, e.g., August von Bulmerincq, 'Die Staatsstreitigkeiten und ihre Entscheidung ohne Krieg.', in Franz von Holtzendorff (ed.), *Handbuch des Völkerrechts. Auf Grundlage Europäischer Staatspraxis*, 4th vol. (Hamburg: A.-G. (vormals J. F. Richter), 1889), 3–127, at 87–90; Oppenheim, *International Law* (above, n. 25), 34–41.

56 Despagnet, *Cours de droit international public* (above, n. 27), 782–3; Louter, *Le droit international public positif* (above, n. 51), 202; Simon Maccoby, 'Reprisals as a Measure of Redress Short of War', *CLJ* 2 (1924–1926), 60–73, at 69. Some authors insisted on a requirement of proportionality between the damage suffered and the damage inflicted. See, e.g., Robert Piédelièvre, *Précis de droit international public ou droit des gens*, 2nd vol. (Paris: F. Pichon, 1895), 87–88; Oppenheim, *International Law* (above, n. 25), 39–40; Louter, *Le droit international public positif* (above, n. 51), 201. However, since armed reprisals were not used to secure compensation but rather to exert pressure on the target country with a view to reaching a satisfactory agreement, "a standard for proportionality would not be easy to establish[, should international regulation of reprisals be attempted.]" (Colbert, *Retaliation in international law* (above, n. 6), 77).

57 Cf. Ibid., 60–1. Neff, *War and the Law of Nations* (above, n. 2), 217: "There can be few ironies greater than the fact that, in this area of practice which descends so directly from the just-war outlook of the Middle Ages, with its stress on justice and the rule of law, the hard face of power politics should be so ubiquitously present."

58 Cf. Jellinek, 'China und das Völkerrecht' (above, n. 16), 402; Julius Stone, *Legal controls of International Conflict: A Treatise on the Dynamics of Disputes- and War-Law* (London: Stevens & sons, 1954), 285.

In 1935, when Strupp referred to armed reprisals as a burning issue, he believed that there was a dangerous loophole in international law. The use of armed reprisals presented, in many regards, a menacing alternative to war since it allowed evasion of the restrictions on the *ius ad bellum* as well as the limitations on the conduct of war. War could then be waged under the guise of reprisals. Also, before the creation of the League of Nations, nineteenth-century armed reprisals were no less controversial. They were resorted to abusively by great Powers against weak States because of the existing asymmetric relations of power between them. In the light of the absence of armed resistance, the reprisal-taking country could deny the existence of war.

Thus, during about a century and a half, the topic of armed reprisals was a burning issue, which, however, failed to be suitably addressed and resolved. The measure was considered as being permissive under international law, yet paradoxically no clear-cut regulation limited the right to reprisals involving the use of force; only vague and general principles governed it. This state of legal uncertainty was obviously the strongest recommendation of armed reprisals for powerful States. It reveals the inherent weakness (or strength) of this mode of redress.

The existence of a gap is particularly odd in the interwar era. In fact, the waging of war was subject to restrictions, whereas armed reprisals, despite the semblance to war, remained unconcerned by these efforts of limitation and regulation. Besides, the recourse to armed reprisals in that period seemed unwarranted given the system of collective security of the League of Nations (and notwithstanding the flaws of that system). It was only in 1945 that this loophole was closed when the UN-Charter enshrined the prohibition of the use of force in time of peace.[59]

The whole situation, thus, makes one wonder *why the law of armed reprisals remained in a legal limbo of international law from the outset of the nineteenth century up to 1945*.

This is a question about the longevity of a nebulous situation in international law. Emphasis is laid on the practice and theory of reprisals in order to identify the factors which may account for this legal limbo. Therefore, delicate issues such as the definition of the concept of war lie outside of the scope of the present investigation.[60] Likewise, the evolution of the law of

59 Brownlie, *International Law and the Use of Force by States* (above, n. 45), 223.

60 Cf. Schwarzenberger, '[Book Review: *Retaliation in International Law*, by Evelyn Speyer Colbert]' (above, n. 33), 336.

war and the law of neutrality are not covered by this question. The aim is to provide a global and coherent image of the history of armed reprisals.

III. State of Research

The fact that armed reprisals remained in a state of legal vagueness is a question of international legal history. Thus, the first step is to consult the general works on this topic.[61] Yet, an observation stands out: the narrative of the history of reprisals lacks cohesion and is descriptive rather than analytical. The general evolution of this measure is usually fragmented into three or four epochs which are remotely related. In each of them, reprisals are said to be characterised by certain distinguishing traits and by the general trend that emerged from the practice. However, the underlying reasons for the transformations of reprisals are often overlooked.[62] For example, the exclusive use of reprisals by great Powers against weak or small countries in the nineteenth century is said to contrast with the practice in

61 The history of reprisals also has a practical interest for various institutions of international law since it provides the key to understanding them. As a matter of fact, the topic of reprisals is one of the most curious chapters of the history of the development of international relations (Ernest Nys, *Le droit de la guerre et les précurseurs de Grotius* (Bruxelles/Leipzig: C. Muquardt, Merzbach et Falk, 1882), 38; Ernest Nys, *Les origines du droit international* (Bruxelles: Alfred Castaigne, 1894), 63). For example, the concept of denial of justice in international law, the international responsibility of States and the diplomatic protection of nationals abroad have a historical connection with reprisals. See, i.a., Charles De Visscher, 'Le déni de justice en droit international', *RdC* 52/II (1935), 369–442, at 370–374; Alwyn Vernon Freeman, *The International Responsibility of States for Denial of Justice* (New York: Kraus, 1938 [Reprod. 1970]), 53–67; Hans W. Spiegel, 'Origin and Development of Denial of Justice', *AJIL* 32 (1938), 63–81; Jan Paulsson, *Denial of Justice in International Law* (Hersch Lauterpacht memorial lectures, 17; Cambridge: CUP, 2005), 10–37; Haggenmacher, 'L'ancêtre de la protection diplomatique. les représailles de l'ancien droit (XIIe-XVIIIe siècles)' (above, n. 3).

62 Cf. Karl Josef Partsch, 'Repressalie', in Karl Strupp and Hans-Jürgen Schlochauer (eds.), *Wörterbuch des Völkerrechts*, begründet von Professor Dr. Karl Strupp, 3 vols. (2nd edn., Berlin: Walter De Gruyter & Co., 1960–1962), 3rd vol., 103–6, at 103; Grewe, *Epochen der Völkerrechtsgeschichte* (above, n. 24), 145–147, 237–240, 428–433, 616–622 and 733–735; Karl-Heinz Ziegler, *Völkerrechtsgeschichte: Ein Studienbuch* (Kurzlehrbücher für das Juristische Studium; 2nd edn., München: C. H. Beck, 2007), 109–110, 128, 154, 185 and 205; Ruffert, 'Reprisals' (above, n. 10), nos. 3–5.

the eighteenth century.[63] Stephen C. Neff refers to the nineteenth-century practice as a new species of reprisals that blended components of special and general reprisals previously used.[64] Still, there is no explanation why only great Powers had recourse to armed reprisals against weak and small States.

Monographs exclusively dedicated to the whole history of reprisals can be counted on the fingers of one hand.[65] In 1933, before the outbreak of WWII, German lawyer Alfred Müller wrote a doctoral thesis on the history of this measure. His historical investigation sought to answer the question of the legitimacy of reprisals in his time. He highlighted the increasing tendency to restrict the employment of this measure, mainly through treaties. Nevertheless, he concluded that, as long as the international community remained in an anarchical state, reprisals should not be deprived of relevance.[66] Evelyn Speyer Colbert's *Retaliation in international law* (1948) — unquestionably, the reference work on reprisals from a historical viewpoint— reaches a similar conclusion, but as the result of a different argument. Colbert engaged in an analysis based on primary sources of State practice from the early days of the institution of reprisals until the signature of the UN-Charter. It led her to assert that, unlike the medieval private reprisals which were governed by a uniform body of rules, modern public reprisals in time of peace, viz. reprisals as employed from the outset of the nineteenth century until 1945, were essentially lawless. Thence,

63 See, e.g., Geoffrey Butler and Simon Maccoby, *The Development of International Law* (Contributions to international law and diplomacy; London: Longmans, Green and Co., 1928), 181.

64 Neff, *War and the Law of Nations* (above, n. 2), 225–6.

65 There are, nevertheless, a great number of studies focusing on one specific aspect, one variety or an epoch of reprisals. It is particularly true regarding the old institution of 'private' or 'special' reprisals that developed in the Middle Ages and disappeared in the eighteenth century. A private individual that suffered an unredressed wrong could be granted a royal licence, in the form of a so-called letter of reprisals, for a limited goal, namely the seizure of property belonging to the countrymen of the original wrongdoer up to the value of the loss. See esp. René de Mas Latrie, *Du droit de marque ou droit de représailles au Moyen-Age: suivi de pièces justificatives* (2nd edn., Paris: Baur, 1875); Alberto Del Vecchio and Eugenio Casanova, *Le rappresaglie dei comuni medievali e specialmente in Firenze: Saggio storico* (Bologna: Nicola Zanichelli (Cesare e Giacomo Zanichelli), 1894); Friedrich Rudolf Hohl, 'Bartolus a Saxoferrato: Tractatus Represaliarum. Seine Bedeutung für die Entwicklungsgeschichte des Repressalienrechts' (Bonn, Rheinische Friedrich-Wilhelms-Universität Bonn, 1954).

66 Müller, *Wandlungen im Repressalienrecht* (above, n. 21). Cf. Haumant, *Les représailles* (above, n. 21).

strong Powers resorted to this method to pursue national policies. But notwithstanding the abuses to which such a lack of regulation might lead, she believed that, as a means of law enforcement, reprisals had lost none of their practical use for the international legal system.[67]

These works make it possible to collect valuable information on armed reprisals in their historical manifestation. Yet, they cannot account for the failure to solve the burning issue around the measure. Colbert's insightful study and Müller's work explain the maintenance of armed reprisals as the inevitable and necessary consequence of an anarchic state in the international relations, as the result of the deficiency of international law to prevent their use. Nevertheless, they do not suggest that this phenomenon might have other causes.

Another line of explanation could flow from the angle of the relation between armed reprisals and war. This aspect has often been studied in order to establish the precise meaning of the latter activity.[68] Two books are worth mentioning: Lothar Kotzsch's *The concept of war in contemporary history and international law* (1956) and Stephen C. Neff's *War and the Law of Nations* (2005).

Kotzsch looked into the evolution of reprisals secondarily, i.e. intending to define the concept of war as accurately as possible. He pointed out that the subjective test of *animus* prevailed in the nineteenth century for want of a factual criterion that could aptly separate armed reprisals and war. As a consequence, no state of war arose in the absence of an *animus belligerendi* on either side. However, because of their superiority of force, the great Powers could deny being at war and compel the target countries of inferior rank to yield and accept armed reprisals as not being tantamount to war. For the interwar years, Kotzsch observed that the question of the distinction between war and armed reprisals was full of inconsistencies. In the early days of the League of Nations, it was the objective test which enabled to determine the existence of war. Nevertheless, a shift occurred, and the subjective test superseded the objective one without depriving it entirely of all relevance on a subsidiary basis. Furthermore, since the blockade of Venezuela in 1902–1903, third States could bring about a state of war through the application of the law of neutrality, when the coercive mea-

67 Colbert, *Retaliation in international law* (above, n. 6). In the second part of her work, Colbert looked at the case of belligerent reprisals and the use of reprisals against or by neutral States in wartime.

68 See, e.g., Kappus, *Der völkerrechtliche Kriegsbegriff in seiner Abgrenzung gegenüber den militärischen Repressalien* (above, n. 16).

sures interfered with their rights. This had the effect of producing a change from material towards formal war.[69]

Despite being enlightening in regard to the distinction between armed reprisals and war, Kotzsch's explanations about the evolution of reprisals are quite concise.

Neff, on the other hand, offers a much more comprehensive panorama of the history of reprisals. He endeavours to show that the ambiguous relation of reprisals with war had existed from the Middle Ages until 1945. Neff specifically pinpoints that reprisals had been resorted to mainly as a form of law enforcement that rested on the medieval just-war tradition. He, thus, regards nineteenth-century reprisals as pursuing redress by armed means, unlike war which aimed at the subjection of the target State to the assailant Power's will. Indeed, reprisals differed from war owing to several factors: i.a., a limited scope, proportionality, the non-termination of treaties and the absence of impact on third States. However, he recognises that the line between the two activities was not always clear-cut and that armed reprisals were sometimes employed as a substitute for war, particularly by the great Powers. The absence of contest by the target State —since it took two to make a war— as well as the absence of *animus belligerendi* prevented armed reprisals from being classified as war. Neff points out that many lawyers protested against the abuses to which armed reprisals led; still, no general project to restrict this means succeeded to gather support. Unfortunately, Neff fails to provide an explanation.[70]

The attention of scholars has too often been drawn to the tight relationship between armed reprisals and war. The separate regime governing the two activities explains why States turned to armed reprisals as a more permissive measure than war, particularly when there was an asymmetry of power. But it does not answer the question of the absence of clarification on the law of armed reprisals.

Olivier Barsalou suggests in an article from 2010 that during the interwar years, international lawyers created a set of norms aiming at governing the use of armed reprisals. Thereby, they legalised the employment of this method, which led international law to incorporate the idea of violence as a source of authority, whereas the end of the whole international legal system is the eradication of violence. As an illustration of this tension, he

69 Lothar Kotzsch, *The concept of war in contemporary history and international law* (Études d'histoire économique, politique et sociale, 18; Genève: E. Droz, 1956), esp. 127–141 and 146–171.

70 Neff, *War and the Law of Nations* (above, n. 2).

used the Italian bombardment and occupation of the Greek island of Corfu in 1923 by way of reprisals. The legitimisation of violence, in fact, provided a legal justification to commit abuses in situations of asymmetric imbalance and to wage war in disguise.[71] However, Barsalou's article is too reductive as the author does not rely on an extensive study of contemporary legal doctrine. Indeed, the regulation adopted by the IIL in 1934 contradicts his argument. The Institute agreed upon the drastic restriction of the recourse to armed reprisals in the same way as the *ius ad bellum*, thence depriving the measure of practical relevance and condemning the use of force in peacetime just like war.

Finally, the master's thesis of Ross Williamson (2013) aims to explain the rise and fall of the practice of pacific blockade through the lens of identity performances. The author argues that the measure emerged as the result of multiple identities in tension. Indeed, when three European Powers (Great Britain, France and Russia) blockaded and then destroyed the Ottoman fleet in the bay of Navarino in 1827, they acted as Christian nations in support of the Hellenic Republic against the Muslim oppressor. Nevertheless, as members of the Concert of Europe, they refrained from calling their action an act of war. Williamson thus links the legitimisation of pacific blockade to the identity of great Powers. In fact, great Powers resorted to pacific blockade as a demonstration of force against States considered so inferior that it was not worth the expense of hostilities. In this way, they could assert power in the form of informal imperialism over the latter countries. Lastly, he contends that the normative changes that followed WWI prompted the disappearance without abrogation of pacific blockade. The great Powers could no longer perform their identity through this measure. Williamson therefore concludes that the fortunes of a norm depend mostly upon the normative environment and that international law precisely played an ambivalent role by allowing hierarchies and at the same

71 Olivier Barsalou, 'The History of Reprisals Up to 1945. Some Lessons Learned and Unlearned for Contemporary International Law', *MLLWR* 49 (2010), 335–71. Cf. Minerva Jean A. Falcon, 'Reprisals', *PYIL* 10 (1984), 26–37, at 30–31: "Turning now to the norms governing the more controversial use of armed force during peacetime, it might be mentioned that the evolution of norms to govern such types of reprisals did not follow the seemingly easier path followed by that of norms governing belligerent reprisals. Doctrine was laid down willy-nilly as certain questions began to be asked. One of the first of such questions raised was whether the resort to armed force during peacetime could constitute a legitimate reprisal. This question was raised in the *Corfu Affair* of 1923."

time challenging them.[72] Yet, Williamson's study can be criticised for placing too much emphasis on realpolitik and for leaving out the legal aspects of the topic of pacific blockade altogether. Besides, he fails to identify that pacific blockade fell within the broader pattern of coercion in time of peace. Hence, there were still cases of armed reprisals in the interwar period although pacific blockade vanished after 1919.

So, notwithstanding the interest that armed reprisals and more generally the use of force in peacetime arises in legal literature, the state of research is unsatisfactory. No direct explanation can account well enough for the persistence of the burning issue of armed reprisals in international law and the state of neglect that characterised the customary right of armed reprisals.

By analogy, however, Lea Heimbeck's study on the concepts of 'legal avoidance' (*Rechtsvermeidung*) and 'normatization' (*Verrechtlichung*) may enlighten as to this situation. She, indeed, identifies that two different strategies met the handling of State bankruptcy in international law throughout the nineteenth century. On the one hand, 'normatization' pursued the implementation of norms in order to fill the legal lacuna in some fields of human interaction. On the other hand, actors (mainly powerful nations) could also deliberately omit to introduce law, and let non-legal considerations (i.e. financial, economic, and political ones) decide on the course of action to be adopted on a case-by-case basis. The question of State bankruptcy in nineteenth-century international law was such a topic where the absence of norms enabled powerful creditor States to resort to some forms of coercion and pursue the control of the small debtor countries through informal imperialism.[73] But where Heimbeck suggests that the employment of armed reprisals was the consequence of legal avoidance in the field of State bankruptcy, it should be noted that the 'law' of reprisals itself was not much clearer. It is in fact not incongruous to argue

---

72 Ross Williamson, 'A Friendly Demonstration of Force. Pacific Blockade, International Law and State Identity, 1827 to 1921', Thesis submitted to the Faculty of Graduate and Postgraduate Affairs in partial fulfillment of the requirements for the degree of Master of Arts in Legal Studies (Ottawa, Ontario: Carleton University, 2013; <http://www.curve.carleton.ca>, accessed 27 December 2017).

73 Heimbeck, *Die Abwicklung von Staatsbankrotten im Völkerrecht* (above, n. 47); Lea Heimbeck, 'Legal Avoidance as Peace Instrument. Domination and Pacification through Asymmetric Loan Transactions', in Thomas Hippler and Miloš Vec (eds.), *Paradoxes of Peace in Nineteenth Century Europe* (Oxford: OUP, 2015), 111–27.

that the ill-defined legal situation of armed reprisals was *per se* subject to a voluntary omission of law-making.[74]

Therefore, a comprehensive and interpretative history of armed reprisals is still to be written. A study on such a topic may yield fascinating discoveries and shed light on a blind spot in the history of international law.[75]

IV. Research Hypotheses

In the light of all the remarks and reflections outlined above, some hypotheses can be formulated:

1. By the end of the eighteenth century, the absence of a clear legal regime governing reprisals was the result of their transformation into a measure of the law of nations applied only between States and the ensuing obsolescence of the well-elaborated medieval law of reprisals.
2. During the period 1831–1863, armed reprisals remained in a legal grey zone as this measure was shaped into an informal privilege of the great Powers.
3. The lack of clarity regarding the resort to armed reprisals between 1848–1912 was the consequence of the faint-heartedness of most legal scholars to deal too critically with a measure which they regarded as a lesser evil than war, this being why they did not seriously challenge the State practice.

---

74 An interwar German lawyer strongly hinted that the League of Nations intentionally avoided solving the question of the compatibility of armed reprisals with the Covenant: "Daß eine solche bedeutsame Frage nach mehr denn 12 jährigem Bestand des Bundes nicht positiv rechtlich eindeutig geregelt wurde, kennzeichnet die Übergangsnatur des gegenwärtigen Rechtszustandes in besonderem Maße. *Der Völkerbund ist hier einer verantwortungsschweren Aufgabe bisher offensichtlich mit Absicht aus dem Weg gegangen*, wodurch die Zweifel über die entwicklungsmäße Reife der Staaten, ja über die Möglichkeit überhaupt, die Selbsthilfe im zwischenstaatlichen Leben in all ihren gewaltsamen Formen auszuschalten, stark unterstrichen wurden." (Egon Gottschalk, 'Die völkerrechtlichen Hauptprobleme des Mandschureikonflikts', *ZVölkR* 17 (1933), 188–259 & 289–341, here at 209–210 (emphasis added)). He, indeed, suggested that the lack of objective criteria for the distinction between war and armed reprisals was the result of a politically intended twilight (*"eines politisch gewollten Halbdunkels"*) that allowed the United States and the European Powers to deny the existence of a state of war and the ensuing consequences (Ibid., 203–5).

75 Cf. Denyse Chast, '[Book Review: *As Represalias. Estudo de historia do direito português sécs. XV e XVI*, by Ruy de Albuquerque]', *RID comp.* 28 (1976), 621–2, at 621.

4. Despite the creation of the League of Nations that entailed a turnaround in legal doctrine, the great Powers strove in the interwar to keep armed reprisals in a state of unclarity by opposing resistance to any attempts to restrict their privilege.

V. Sources

As a work of legal history, close scrutiny of both contemporaneous primary and secondary sources is essential, especially for a topic like the present one. Indeed, the narrative about the general use of force told since the end of WWI by international legal scholarship has often emphasised the existence of a legal vacuum in the nineteenth century.[76]

The present study focuses on both State practice and legal theory.

State practice relies almost exclusively on precedents. Many cases which were called acts of reprisals by statesmen or which have been labelled as such in international law manuals are examined here.[77] Great importance is given to materials that provide evidence for the practice of the two leading reprisal-taking States, namely France and Great Britain.

Amongst the sources upon which the analysis of the cases is based is the diplomatic correspondence, such as the one printed in the *British and Foreign State Papers* (BFSP). In fact, the diplomatic transactions give an insight into the great Powers' diplomacy and discourse and allow the sounding out of the motivations and the attitude of the actors to a dispute where a resort to armed reprisals occurred or was contemplated. Diplomatic reports on the political and economic situation of the target countries also help to comprehend the causes of the issue and the whole course of action. In addition, certain aspects of international law were frequently discussed in diplomatic dispatches.

This State practice, however, was often questioned. In this respect, the national parliamentary debates are interesting, too. Indeed, the recourse to reprisals was, unlike war, not subject to approval by the Legislative branch.

---

76 See thereupon Agatha Verdebout, 'The Contemporary Discourse on the Use of Force in the Nineteenth Century. A Diachronic and Critical Analysis', *JUFIL* 1 (2014), 223–46.

77 The resort to armed reprisals was a relatively sporadic phenomenon, contrary to what one may think. Cf. Michael Tomz, *Reputation and International Cooperation: Sovereign Debt across Three Centuries* (Princeton, New Jersey/Oxford: PUP, 2007), who demonstrates that military force was employed to collect sovereign debts throughout the nineteenth century in a significantly small amount of cases.

Still, when a case of reprisals led to an international crisis, the national parliament felt compelled to examine the Government's foreign policy. This is precisely what happened following the British reprisals against Greece in the so-called *Don Pacifico* case in 1850. It was unusual at the time in Great Britain to discuss questions of foreign policy in either House.[78] So, those debates which contained a great deal of foreign policy statements and comments about international law actually reveal the tension caused by State practice. In the same vein are the conference proceedings like those of the Second Hague Peace Conference of 1907 and, for the interwar period, the minutes of the sittings of the League of Nations's political organ, viz. the Council.[79]

Finally, legal theory plays a non-negligible role. The writings of lawyers are enlightening as to the perception of the State practice with respect to the resort to armed reprisals. Following the development of international law as a science,[80] legal doctrine began in the wake of the *Don Pacifico* affair to look into the situation of reprisals, principally in the form of pacific blockade. The opinion of legal scholars on this topic can be found in monographs, general books on international law and in articles published in the most renowned journals of the time. There are also many post-graduate theses on reprisals and pacific blockade, mainly from French and German universities, which attests to the great interest for reprisals during four decades (from 1890 to 1940).[81] The works of the Institute of International Law is to be scrutinised too, because they contain the views of the

78 Taylor, *Don Pacifico* (above, n. 49), 220.

79 The *League of Nations Official Journal* (LNOJ) published the official documents of that intergovernmental organisation. For instance, the whole discussion about the Corfu crisis of 1923 in the Council is reproduced in this periodical.

80 See Martti Koskenniemi, *The Gentle Civilizer of Nations: The Rise and Fall of International Law, 1870–1960* (Cambridge, New York: CUP, 2002).

81 See, i.a., Charles Barès, *Le blocus pacifique* (Toulouse: G. Berthoumieu, 1898); Louis Ducrocq, *Représailles en temps de paix: Blocus pacifique suivi d'une étude sur les affaires de Chine (1900–1901)*, Thèse pour le doctorat de la Faculté de droit de Paris, soutenue le 20 Mars 1901, à 1 heure (Paris: A. Pedone, 1901); Jean Teyssaire, *Le blocus pacifique*, Thèse de Faculté de droit de l'université de Paris pour le doctorat présentée et soutenue le Mardi 8 Novembre 1910, à une heure et demie (Beauvais: Imprimerie centrale administrative, 1910); Robert Roth, *Die Repressalie: Eine völkerrechtliche Studie*, Inaugural=Dissertation der juristischen Fakultät der Friedrich=Alexanders=Universität zu Erlangen (Nürnberg: Benedikt Hitz, 1918); Pao Jin Ho, 'Reprisals in international law', Master of Arts in Political Science (Urbana, Ill.: University of Illinois, 1922); Hiller, 'Die Friedensblockade und ihre Stellung in Völkerrecht' (above, n. 45); Jakob Baenziger, *Die Repressalien im Völkerrecht*, Dissertation zur Erlangung der Würde eines Doktors beider Rechte

most distinguished legal experts who dealt with the issue of armed reprisals.

VI. Structure

Four chapters make up the investigation and divide it chronologically. This periodisation aims to highlight the crucial stages in the evolution of armed reprisals up to the point where the issue had reached a dead end at the time of the League of Nations and could only be ended through a drastic step: their prohibition, pursuant to Art. 2(4) of the UN-Charter.

The first chapter deals with the development of reprisals prior to the nineteenth century. It seeks to show the process of deregulation up to the end of the eighteenth century that undermined the rules governing reprisals and to explain the malleability of the law of reprisals in the following century. It, thus, begins with the emergence of reprisals and the first norms that were adopted in the High Middle Ages to restrict the new practice. Great emphasis is laid on Bartolus de Saxoferrato's tractate which thoroughly theorised reprisals. This theorisation allowed a high degree of standardisation for the rules governing reprisals. The chapter then addresses the decline of this theory following the emergence of the modern State. That part pinpoints to what extent the State practice departed from the well-accepted regulation of reprisals and widened the gap with legal theory.

The second chapter covers the period 1831–1863. The present Writer believes that these dates delimit at best the crucial epoch of formation of armed reprisals as a State practice employed exclusively by great Powers against smaller States. The year 1831 provides the first example of armed reprisals of this kind: the French operation against Portugal. The British reprisals against Brazil in 1863 close the period of development as no sig-

---

vorgelegt der hohen juristischen Fakultät der Universität Freiburg in der Schweiz (Zug: J. Kündigs Erben, 1925); Schumann, *Die Repressalie* (above, n. 21); Pao Jin Ho, 'Pacific blockade with special reference to its use as a measure of reprisal', Doctor of Philosophy in Political Science (Urbana, Ill.: University of Illinois, 1925); Müller, *Wandlungen im Repressalienrecht* (above, n. 21); Haumant, *Les représailles* (above, n. 21); Robert von Förster, *Schiedssprechung und Repressalie*, Inaugural-Dissertation zur Erlangung der juristischen Doktorwürde der Rechts- und Staatswissenschaftlichen Fakultät der Universität zu Göttingen (Würzburg: Konrad Triltsch, 1936); Heyns, *Die Anwendung von militärischen Repressalien unter Völkerbundmitgliedstaaten* (above, n. 16).

nificant case of armed reprisals were recorded thereafter in textbooks during more than twenty years until 1884. Besides, the subsequent instances of armed reprisals in the late nineteenth century and in the first half of the twentieth century followed closely the same pattern and were justified on the basis of precedents that mostly came from the period 1831–1863. Indeed, the most emblematic cases of this measure are from that period. During these three decades, the practice of reprisals also saw innovations like the use of blockades short of war by way of reprisals, later known as pacific blockades. Finally, another salient feature of the epoch considered in this chapter is the absence of doctrinal interest. For those reasons, the State practice is of particular relevance to understand the reshaping of reprisals by the great Powers.

The next chapter is devoted to the general dispute over armed reprisals that arose in legal doctrine. It, thus, focuses on the opinion of lawyers. Indeed, throughout the third quarter of the nineteenth century, there was a lively debate in doctrine about the legality of pacific blockade. This legal discussion originated from the late 1840s when precursors raised awareness on the dangerous development of armed reprisals. Yet, it is only from the 1860s onwards that the place of pacific blockade in international law was seriously challenged. In 1887, however, the IIL confirmed pacific blockade to be a legitimate institution of international law. The position of legal scholars is thoroughly examined here to understand the real issues of the debate and to highlight the considerations that prevailed. In this context, the observations and criticisms of fierce opponents of armed reprisals are of great interest. The last part of the chapter considers the controversy about the blockade of Venezuela in 1902–1903. This incident had not only an impact on State practice with the adoption of the Drago-Porter Convention of 1907 but also divided legal scholars.

The last chapter deals with the epoch of the League of Nations. The importance that the topic of armed reprisals gained in this period is examined in details, both in legal doctrine and in State practice. Two cases (namely the French occupation of the Ruhr in 1923 and the Italian bombardment and occupation of the island of Corfu in the same year) are studied to bring out the attitude of the great Powers following the resort to acts of armed reprisals. Of great interest is the reaction of the other States and the statements they made on those occasions. In addition, the opinions of lawyers are analysed because they began to criticise more than ever the resort to armed reprisals. One of the detractors of this measure was the Greek lawyer Nicolas Politis who was entrusted with the task of drafting a regulation governing reprisals in peacetime for the IIL's session of Paris in

1934. The works and debates of the Institute will be the subject of close scrutiny, too.

By following this structure, it is hoped to provide a consistent story of armed reprisals which clarifies the grey areas about the persistence of this measure in spite of the changes in international law.

Chapter One. From Regulation to Deregulation up to the End of the Eighteenth Century

I. Introduction

Reprisals are an ancient measure that had evolved in time. This chapter focuses on the development of reprisals up to the end of the eighteenth century in order to get a clear image of the legal situation of this means on the eve of the next century. It is argued here that in the early years of the nineteenth century, reprisals were barely regulated as a consequence of uncontrolled State practice and the lack of suitable adaptation of the medieval law of reprisals. It is, indeed, in the Middle Ages that reprisals developed and became the subject of a highly sophisticated set of rules. On the contrary, the State practice of reprisals in the seventeenth and eighteenth centuries did not seem to have been governed by a clear regulation.

II. Elaboration of the Medieval Law of Reprisals

1. Emergence and Development of Reprisals in the Early and High Middle Ages

Reprisals were a medieval legal innovation that reached, in the last centuries of the Middle Ages, a high degree of sophistication, clarity and uniformity.[82] From the preliminary steps to their complete enforcement, they were governed by a well-elaborated legal framework.[83] Broadly speaking, the Sovereign granted his subject the right to seize property belonging to countrymen of the wrongdoer or even arrest them when justice could not be obtained in the latter's country for the wrong committed (e.g., unpaid

82 Cf. Colbert, *Retaliation in international law* (above, n. 6), 3.

83 See esp. Mas Latrie, *Du droit de marque ou droit de représailles au Moyen-Age* (above, n. 65).

debt or robbery).[84] Three elements emerge: self-help, collective responsibility and denial of justice.[85] It was thus a measure used to seek compensation when the victim and the wrongdoer were not subjects of the same suzerain.

Some authors have supported the view that reprisals already existed in Ancient Greece as an elaborate legal institution regulated by municipal law and treaties which differed from piracy and brigandage. Indeed, there was a self-help measure in that time which rested on the theory of community responsibility, in this extent comparable to medieval reprisals. A whole community could be held responsible for the wrong committed by one of its members against an alien when it failed to give the latter justice. As a consequence, property or persons of that community could be seized by the victim's own community.[86]

---

84 Cf. Ibid., 4; Giulio Vismara, 'Repressalien(recht)', in Norbert Angermann, Robert-Henri Bautier, Robert Auty et al. (eds.), *Lexikon des Mittelalters*, 10 vols. (München/Zürich/Stuttgart/Weimar: Artemis & Winkler/LexMA-Verlag/J. B. Metzler, 1980–1999), 7th vol., col. 746; G. Fahl, 'Repressalie', in Wolfgang Stammler, Adalbert Erler, Ekkehard Kaufmann et al. (eds.), *Handwörterbuch zur deutschen Rechtsgeschichte*, 4th vol. (Berlin: Erich Schmidt, 1990), col. 911–913, here at 911–912; W. Ogris, 'Repressalienarrest', in Wolfgang Stammler, Adalbert Erler, Ekkehard Kaufmann et al. (eds.), *Handwörterbuch zur deutschen Rechtsgeschichte*, 4th vol. (Berlin: Erich Schmidt, 1990), col. 913–916; Neff, *War and the Law of Nations* (above, n. 2), 77.

85 Hohl, 'Bartolus a Saxoferrato: Tractatus Represaliarum. Seine Bedeutung für die Entwicklungsgeschichte des Repressalienrechts' (above, n. 65), 1st vol., 36.

86 See about the measure of 'reprisals' practised in Ancient Greece, i.a., Charles-Albert Lécrivain, 'Le droit de se faire justice soi-même et les représailles dans les relations internationales de la Grèce', *Mémoires de l'Académie de sciences, inscriptions et belles-lettres de Toulouse* 9 (9th ser.) (1897), 277–90; Rodolphe Dareste, *Nouvelles études d'histoire du droit* (Paris: Librairie de la société du recueil général des lois et des arrêts, 1902), 38–54; Coleman Phillipson, *The international law and custom of Ancient Greece and Rome*, 2nd vol. (London: Macmillan and Co., 1911), 349–66; Jean Rougé, *La marine dans l'Antiquité* (L'historien, 23; Paris: PUF, 1975), 161; Benedetto Bravo, 'Sulân. Représailles et justice privée contre des étrangers dans les cités grecques (*Étude du vocabulaire et des institutions*)', *Annali della Scuola Normale Superiore di Pisa. Classe di Lettere e Filosofia* 10 (3rd ser.)/3 (1980), 675–987; Andrew Lintott, '*Sula*–Reprisal by Seizure in Greek Inter-Community Relations', *The Classical Quarterly* 54 (2004), 340–53. Nevertheless, the distinction between piracy and this ancient form of reprisals is not necessarily easy to make as the former activity was also considered respectable at times. See A. H. Jackson, 'An Oracle for Raiders?', *ZPE* 108 (1995), 95–9.

But in the days of the Roman Empire, there was no such thing as reprisals.[87] According to medieval Italian lawyers Bartolus de Saxoferrato and Giovanni da Legnano,[88] who were the first to thoroughly deal with the topic of reprisals, the measure actually stemmed from the decay of the Roman Empire and the ensuing disappearance of a superior authority (previously, the Roman Emperor) who could dispense justice.[89] Nevertheless, statements of law by Emperors in the fifth and sixth centuries still reminded that Roman law did not admit vicarious liability, i.e. holding a third party responsible for someone else's debt or wrong.[90] The new Western European kingdoms also reaffirmed several times the principle of individual responsibility for one's own debt.[91] The reassertion of this principle, however, suggests that the rule was not often abided by.

---

87 Mas Latrie, *Du droit de marque ou droit de représailles au Moyen-Age* (above, n. 65), 6.

88 For a biography and a bibliography of Bartolus, see Friedrich Carl von Savigny, *Geschichte des Römischen Rechts im Mittelalter*, 6th vol. (2nd edn., Heidelberg: J. C. B. Mohr, 1850), 137–84; Peter Weimar, 'Bartolus de Saxoferrato (1313/14–1357)', in Michael Stolleis (ed.), *Juristen. Ein biographisches Lexikon; Von der Antike bis zum 20. Jahrhundert* (München: C. H. Beck, 1995), 67–8; Axel Krauß, 'Bartolus de Saxoferrato (1313/14–1357)', in Gerd Kleinheyer and Jan Schröder (eds.), *Deutsche und Europäische Juristen aus neun Jahrhunderten. Eine biographische Einführung in die Geschichte der Rechtswissenschaft* (6th edn., Tübingen: Mohr Siebeck, 2017), 45–9. On Giovanni da Legnano, see Thomas Erskine Holland's 'Introduction' in Giovanni da Legnano, *Tractatus de Bello, de Represaliis et de Duello*, edited by Thomas Erskine Holland (The Classics of International Law, 8; Oxford: OUP, 1917).

89 Bartolus de Saxoferrato, *Omnium Iuris Interpretum Antesignani Consilia, Quaestiones et Tractatus: Nunc recens Quadragintaquatuoraliis Consiliis, tum Criminalibus, tum Ciuilibus, & vno Tractatu de Procuratoribus locupletata; Atque etiam, praeter alias Additiones ad hanc diem editas, Aureis Adnotationibus. Initia Consiliorum, Quæstionum,& Tractatuum ad literarum seriem subsequentia indicabunt*, 10th vol. (Venetiis: apud Iuntas, 1590), Proemium, here at fol. 119v; Legnano, *Tractatus de Bello, de Represaliis et de Duello* (above, n. 88), Cap. CXXIII, here at 155 (tr. at 307–308).

90 See *Cod. Just.*, XII, 60.4; *Cod. Just.*, XI, 57; Just. *Nov.*, LII, 1, quoted in Phillipson, *The international law and custom of Ancient Greece and Rome* (above, n. 86), 365–6.

91 An example is Clause 247 of the seventh-century Lombard law called *Edictum Rothari*, transcribed in Friedrich Bluhme, 'Edictus Langobardorum', in Georg Heinrich Pertz (ed.), *Monumenta Germaniae Historica. Inde ab anno Christi quingentesimo usque ad annum millesimum et quingentesimum*, Auspiciis Societatis aperiendis fontibus rerum germanicarum medii aevi (Hannover: Hahn, 1868), 1–225, at 60. In a letter written by Cassiodorus (*Variae*, IV, 10), the Ostrogothic ruler of Italy Theoderic the Great stressed this principle, too. He condemned the practice of '*pignoratio*' as a "monstrous perversion of all the rule of law" (Cas-

So, reprisals developed unchecked and probably gave rise to numerous abuses before norms were finally adopted to control their use.[92] Indeed, this means constituted an obstacle to trade and a serious threat to peace, although it allowed obtaining redress. Attempts were thus made to regulate reprisals and limit their adverse effects.[93] Through treaties and domestic law, a whole set of procedures and requirements were agreed upon with the aim of attaching guarantees to the use of reprisals and limiting their recourse. From the tenth centuries onwards, first in Northern Italy and then everywhere in Europe, the number of treaties containing a stipulation about reprisals multiplied.[94] This phenomenon followed the resumption of trade in the Mediterranean region around 950.[95] By the thirteenth century, a provision restricting reprisals was inserted into almost every treaty of friendship of the time.[96]

---

siodorus, *The letters of Cassiodorus: being a condensed translation of the Variae epistolae of Magnus Aurelius Cassiodorus Senator*, With an Introduction by Thomas Hodgkin (London: Henry Frowde, 1886), 240–1).

92 Cf. Colbert, *Retaliation in international law* (above, n. 6), 12.

93 Del Vecchio and Casanova, *Le rappresaglie dei comuni medievali e specialmente in Firenze* (above, n. 65), 60–1.

94 For treaties including a reference to reprisals, see Ibid., 69–71; Hans Planitz, 'Studien zur Geschichte des deutschen Arrestprozesses. Der Fremdenarrest', *ZRG GA* 40 (1919), 87–198, at 171–175; Hohl, 'Bartolus a Saxoferrato: Tractatus Represaliarum. Seine Bedeutung für die Entwicklungsgeschichte des Repressalienrechts' (above, n. 65), 1st vol., 38 fn. 1.

95 Marie-Claire Chavarot, 'La pratique des lettres de marque d'après les arrêts du parlement (XIIIe-début XVe siècle)', *Bibliothèque de l'école des chartes* 149 (1991), 51–89, at 54.

96 Spiegel, 'Origin and Development of Denial of Justice' (above, n. 61), 69. It is also by that time that the vulgar term 'reprisals' (*represalias*) began to prevail in legal documents over some legal expressions in Latin that were used earlier as synonyms, like '*pignoratio*' which refers to a pledge in Roman property law, or '*clarigo*', i.e. a demand for redress. Cf. Butler and Maccoby, *The Development of International Law* (above, n. 63), 173. In fact, in order to avoid misunderstanding, the Second Council of Lyon of 1274 spoke of "[…] *pignorationes, quas vulgaris elocutio repressalias nominat,* […]."(Sexti Decretal. Lib. V. Tit. VIII. Cap. Un., reproduced in Emil Ludwig Richter and Emil Friedberg, *Corpus Iuris Canonici: Editio Lipsiensis Secunda*, 2nd vol. (Graz: Akademische Druck- u. Verlagsanstalt, 1959), col. 1089). In the eighteenth century, Bynkershoek maintained that there was actually no suitable Latin equivalent to 'reprisals' since the measure did not exist under Roman law. See Bynkershoek, *Quaestionum juris publici libri duo* (above, n. 33), Book I Cap. 24, here 1st vol., 171 (tr. 2nd vol., 133).
In medieval England, reprisals were called 'withernam' when they were exercised between towns within the same realm, i.e. town-to-town reprisals. See thereupon D. A. Gardiner, 'The History of Belligerent Rights on the High Seas in the Four-

In most cases, a denial of justice was declared the condition *sine qua non* for reprisals.[97] As early as the ninth century, bilateral treaties like the agreement entered between the Lombard prince Sicard of Benevento and the Neapolitans in 836 made the recourse to self-help subject to such a requirement.[98] It meant that the victim had to exhaust first the local remedies in the wrongdoer's country before turning to his Sovereign for letters of reprisal. Later treaties often laid down the criteria to identify the existence of a denial of justice.[99] For example, the commitment made by James I of Aragon to the viscount and archbishop of Narbonne provided that a denial of justice would exist if the authorities of Narbonne failed to give a satisfactory answer within twenty-one days after receiving the official demand for redress sent by the Aragonese Crown on behalf of its subjects who did not obtain compensation. In such a case, reprisals could be granted.[100]

---

teenth Century', *LQR* 48 (1932), 521–46, at 538; Clark, 'The English Practice with Regard to Reprisals by Private Persons' (above, n. 4), 704–5; Colbert, *Retaliation in international law* (above, n. 6), 14; J. Duncan M. Derrett, 'Withernam. A Legal Practice Joke of Sir Thomas More', *CathLaw* 7 (1961), 211–222 & 242; J. Duncan M. Derrett, 'Withernam. A Postscript', *CathLaw* 9 (1963), 124–37. This kind of reprisals was forbidden in 1275 under Edward I. See the First Statutes of Westminster, Clause 23, reproduced in Great Britain, *The Statutes of the Realm*, Printed by command of his majesty King George the Third. In pursuance of an address of the House of Commons of Great Britain. From Original Records and Authentic Manuscripts. 1st vol. (London: Dawsons of Pall Mall, 1810 [Reprinted 1963]), part "The Statutes", 33. Yet, instances of withernam were still documented in the seventeenth century. See, e.g., Katherine Maud Elisabeth Murray, *The Constitutional History of the Cinque Ports* (Publications of the University of Manchester: 235. Historical series, 68; Manchester: Manchester University Press, 1935), 176. That is why the Statutes of Westminster I can be regarded as a "noble experiment" lacking acceptation (Erwin F. Meyer, 'Anent the statute of Westminster I and liability', *Saint Louis LR* 17 (1931), 22–6).

97 Spiegel, 'Origin and Development of Denial of Justice' (above, n. 61), 66. Indeed, reprisals and denial of justice were closely linked to such an extent that denial of justice remained for a long time the main condition to resort to reprisals until the concept of international delinquency, i.e. illegality, replaced it. See Ibid., 63–4.

98 See Clause 8 transcribed in Bluhme, 'Edictus Langobardorum' (above, n. 91), 219. About the so-called *Pactum Sicardi* and its background, see Barbara M. Kreutz, *Before the Normans: Southern Italy in the Ninth and Tenth Centuries* (Philadelphia: University of Pennsylvania Press, 1996), 20–3.

99 Colbert, *Retaliation in international law* (above, n. 6), 28.

100 Mas Latrie, *Du droit de marque ou droit de représailles au Moyen-Age* (above, n. 65), 26f. and 58–59.

Sometimes the stipulation aimed to prevent reprisals by holding the sole wrongdoer or debtor responsible. A treaty concluded in 1216 between Florence and Bologna had precisely this content.[101] More pragmatically, Hanseatic cities concluded bilateral treaties that made judgements against the debtor or wrongdoer enforceable within the jurisdiction of both cities.[102] Another method to restrict the resort to reprisals was the creation by the contracting parties of a compensation fund financed through special duties levied on the goods of their merchants, such as in a treaty of 1218 between Florence and Perugia.[103]

Thirteenth-century treaties of peace and truces between France and England occasionally set up a conciliation commission, composed of magistrates called 'the keepers of the peace', that endeavoured to bring the complaints between subjects of both nations to an amicable agreement. This approach sought to prevent the resurgence of violence in the form of either new hostilities or reprisals. However, in case of failure and after a certain period of time had elapsed, the imposed restraint of violence ceased.[104]

In addition to treaty law, domestic law addressed the issue of reprisals, too. Sovereigns sometimes attempted to abolish reprisals within their realm. For instance, the Holy Roman Emperor Frederick II forbade in a

---

101 Ibid., 49.

102 Karl Theodor Pütter, *Beiträge zur Völkerrechts-Geschichte und Wissenschaft* (Leipzig: Adolph Wienbrack, 1843), 151.

103 Colbert, *Retaliation in international law* (above, n. 6), 13. However, a tax levy on merchandise of trade to recompense the aggrieved individuals was not necessarily the best alternative to reprisals. Merchants often protested against such method. But the case of Jacques Cœur, 'argentier' of Charles VII of France, also shows that this process was used for personal enrichment. Indeed, Cœur, himself a victim of piracy and in this capacity entitled to compensation by way of reprisals, was accused in 1453 of extorting and acquiring large sums of money as commissioner and farmer of such a tax. See Kathryn Reyerson, 'Commercial law and merchant disputes. Jacques Coeur and the law of Marque', *Medieval Encounters* 9 (2003), 244–55.

104 Henry Wheaton, *Histoire des progrès du droit des gens en Europe et en Amérique depuis la paix de Westphalie jusqu'à nos jours: Avec une introduction sur les progrès du droit des gens en Europe avant la paix de Westphalie*, 1st vol. (4th edn., Leipzig: F. A. Brockhaus, 1865), 80; Mas Latrie, *Du droit de marque ou droit de représailles au Moyen-Age* (above, n. 65), 49; Nys, *Le droit de la guerre et les précurseurs de Grotius* (above, n. 61), 36–37 and 43. See, e.g., the truces of June 1228 and July 1255: Jean Dumont, *Corps universel diplomatique du droit des gens*, 8 vols. (Amsterdam: P. Brunel, R. et G. Wetstein, les Janssons à Waesberge, L'Honoré et Chatelain, 1726–1731), 1st vol., Part I, 166 and 398.

constitution of September 1231 from taking reprisals or waging private war on one's own initiative. In order to maintain peace in his dominion, each claim had, therefore, to be brought before a competent judicial body.[105]

By the thirteenth century, local regulations largely began to impose the procurement of a licence authorising the taking of reprisals.[106] It was equivalent in many respects to the *auctoritas* necessary for a just war.[107] The victim's Sovereign alone —namely the King, in France and England; the Podestà, in Florence; the Doge, in Venice and Genoa; etc.— or his delegates could allow reprisals.[108] The idea naturally was to examine the justice of the demands and prevent the escalation of private violence, which could

---

105 Deutsches Institut für Erforschung des Mittelalters and Wolfgang Stürner, *Monumenta Germaniae Historica: Inde ab anno Christi Quingentesimo usque ad annum millesimum et quingentesimum* (Legum sectio IV. Constitutiones et acta publica imperatorum et regum, 2 Suppl.; Hannover: Hahn, 1996), 158–9. Another decree of the same month provided the penalty for the transgressors: those who undertook a private war had to be deprived of all their goods; in case of reprisals, it would be the half. See Ibid., 159–60.

106 Hohl, 'Bartolus a Saxoferrato: Tractatus Represaliarum. Seine Bedeutung für die Entwicklungsgeschichte des Repressalienrechts' (above, n. 65), 1st vol, 110. The letter of reprisal granted by John I of England to John of Rye in 1216 is one of the earliest examples. See Verein für Hansische Geschichte and Konstantin Höhlbaum, *Hansisches Urkundenbuch*, 1st vol. (Halle: Buchhandlung des Waisenhauses, 1876), 48.

107 Neff, *War and the Law of Nations* (above, n. 2), 78.

108 Mas Latrie, *Du droit de marque ou droit de représailles au Moyen-Age* (above, n. 65), 18. Since 1353, the King of England had the exclusive right to allow reprisals. See Edward III's Ordinance of the Staples, Clause 17, reproduced in Great Britain, *The Statutes of the Realm* (above, n. 96), part "The Statutes", 339. In France prior to the fifteenth century, some authorities more or less independent like the viscount of Béarn could authorise reprisals. It was also true for some cities like Marseille. See Joseph Eiglier, *Étude historique sur le droit de marque ou de représailles à Marseille aux XIIIème, XIVème & XVème siècles* (Marseille: Aschero et Sacomant, 1888). In 1443, under Charles VII, the power to grant reprisals was limited to the King and the parlements "parce que pluseurs marques ont esté par cy-devant adjugées pour peu de chose, & que matiere de marque doit estre discutée par grant deliberacion & bon conseil" (Eusèbe Jacob de Laurière, Denis-François Secousse, Louis-Guillaume de Villevaut et al., *Ordonnances des Roys de France de la Troisième Race*, 21 vols. (Paris: Imprimerie Royale, 1723–1849), 13th vol., 368). It finally became a regalian privilege in 1485. See, i.a., Jean Bodin, *Les six livres de la République* (Paris: Chez Iacques du Puys, Librairie Iuré, 1576), Book I, ch. 10, here at 216; René Choppin, *Trois livres du domaine de la couronne de France: Composez en latin [...]. Et traduits en langage vulgaire sur la derniere impression de l'an 1605. Avec une table alphabetique fort ample des*

lead to general warfare.[109] Without such a licence, the acts of violence against aliens amounted to piracy.[110] This licence made clear that the ruler delegated to the victim a small portion of his sovereign powers to accomplish a law enforcement purpose.[111]

The licence is called either 'letter of reprisal' (when reprisals were executed within the territory of the Sovereign allowing them) or 'letter of marque' (when the seizure was carried out beyond the boundary *—marca* — of his jurisdiction).[112] These letters teach a great deal about the procedure governing the practice of reprisals. They usually set out the reasons justifying their granting (initial wrong and denial of justice) and specified the conditions under which reprisals were allowed and carried out (target group, amount to be seized and control of the authorities).[113]

---

matieres, & choses plus remarquables y contenuës. (Paris: Chez Estienne Richer, 1634), 377; *Guidon de la mer*, ch. X, Art. 1, reproduced in Jean-Marie Pardessus, *Collection de lois maritimes antérieures au XVIII.ᵉ siècle*, 2nd vol. (Paris: Imprimerie Royale, 1831), 410–411.

109 Butler and Maccoby, *The Development of International Law* (above, n. 63), 174–5. The unpunished murder of a Norman sailor in a brawl with English sailors in the port of Bayonne (back then part of the English realm) in 1292 led to a series of retaliating acts on both sides after the King of France flippantly told the Norman seamen to take the matter into their own hands. The Normans then captured an English ship and hung part of the crew on the spot. The English retaliated against French ships without the authorisation of their King. War eventually broke out between both nations. See Robert Plumer Ward, *An Enquiry Into the Foundation and History of the Law of Nations in Europe, from the Time of the Greeks and Romans, to the Age of Grotius*, 1st vol. (London: J. Butterworth, 1795), 295–6; Charles Mac Farlane, *The Cabinet History of England: Being an Abridgment, by the Author, of the Chapters Entitled "Civil and Military History" in "The Pictorial History of England," with a Continuation to the Present Time*, 3th vol. (London: Charles Knight and Co., 1845), 45–7. Such an incident might have prompted Sovereigns to generalise the requirement of a licence to resort to reprisals.

110 Butler and Maccoby, *The Development of International Law* (above, n. 63), 175; Clark, 'The English Practice with Regard to Reprisals by Private Persons' (above, n. 4), 702.

111 Neff, *War and the Law of Nations* (above, n. 2), 80.

112 Jan H. W. Verzijl, *International law in historical perspective*, 12 vols. (Nova et vetera iuris gentium / Publications of the Institute for International Law of the University of Utrecht; Series A. Modern International Law, vols. 4, 6–14, 16, 19; Leiden: A. W. Sijthoff, 1968–1998), Part IX-C, 153. But see Mas Latrie, *Du droit de marque ou droit de représailles au Moyen-Age* (above, n. 65), 12.

113 For a more detailed account of these requirements, see Clark, 'The English Practice with Regard to Reprisals by Private Persons' (above, n. 4). See also Colbert, *Retaliation in international law* (above, n. 6), 32–3; Hohl, 'Bartolus a Saxoferrato:

Beyond that and in order to prevent adverse effects on trade caused by reprisals, domestic law also provided for immunities from reprisals in favour of foreign merchants.[114] These exemptions were granted to some particular merchants, to all those belonging to a certain nation or generally to any merchant going to this fair or that market.[115] When the 'parlement' of Paris condemned in 1272 the Countess of Flanders, who had ordered the seizure of a Welsh merchant's wool on account of the unredressed grievances of her subjects in England, it was not because the parlement did not recognise her the right to grant reprisals, although she was at the time a vassal of the King of France, but because she violated the immunity that she had granted to all merchants travelling to and returning from a fair in Lille.[116]

Tractatus Represaliarum. Seine Bedeutung für die Entwicklungsgeschichte des Repressalienrechts' (above, n. 65), 1st vol., 115 fn. 1. As illustration, Clark referred to a letter of reprisal dated from 1295 that was granted by Edward I of England to a Gascon subject who suffered losses at the hands of Portuguese people. Translated by Reginald Godfrey Marsden, *Documents relating to law and custom of the sea*, 2 vols. (Publications of the Navy Records Society, 49–50; London: Navy Records Society, 1915–1916), 1st vol., 38–41, from the Latin original.

114 Paul-Louis Huvelin, *Essai historique sur le droit des marchés & des foires* (Paris: Arthur Rousseau, 1897), 442–3.

115 Mas Latrie, *Du droit de marque ou droit de représailles au Moyen-Age* (above, n. 65), 45. For examples from the first half of the fourteenth century, see Colbert, *Retaliation in international law* (above, n. 6), 40–1. See also, e.g., the privileges granted by the Kings of France in favour of the Jews in 1360 (Art. 5) and the Lombards of Paris in 1382 (Art. 17). Laurière et al., *Ordonnances des Roys de France de la Troisième Race* (above, n. 108), 3rd vol., 475; 6th vol., 656, respectively. This was done in consideration of their commercial significance as bankers and pawnbrokers. Mas Latrie, *Du droit de marque ou droit de représailles au Moyen-Age* (above, n. 65), 20. In England, the Magna Carta of 1215 ensured foreign merchants the right to enter, reside in and leave the kingdom without suffering exactions, except in wartime (Magna Carta, Clause 41, reproduced in Great Britain, *The Statutes of the Realm* (above, n. 96), part "Charters of Liberties", 11). Wheaton, *Histoire des progrès du droit des gens en Europe et en Amérique depuis la paix de Westphalie jusqu'à nos jours* (above, n. 104), 81, implied that this immunity protected against reprisals, too.

116 Arthur Auguste Beugnot, *Les Olim ou registres des arrêts rendus par la cour du roi sous les règnes de Saint Louis, de Philippe le Hardi, de Philippe le Bel, de Louis le Hutin et de Philippe le Long* (Collection de documents inédits sur l'histoire de France publiés par ordre du roi et par les soins du ministre de l'instruction publique. Première série: Histoire politique; Paris: Imprimerie Royale, 1839), 914–916, § LXXXI. See, thereupon, Mas Latrie, *Du droit de marque ou droit de représailles au Moyen-Age* (above, n. 65), 20; Chavarot, 'La pratique des lettres de marque d'après les arrêts du parlement (XIIIe–début XVe siècle)' (above, n. 95),

Exemptions were also granted to some other categories of persons such as students.[117] Another important immunity was declared in favour of ecclesiastical men and their property. Indeed, after pointing out that reprisals were "forbidden by civil regulation as iniquitous and contrary to laws and natural equity" ("*tanquam graves legibus et aequitati naturali contrariae civili sint constitutione prohibitae*"), the Second Council of Lyon in 1274 placed an interdict on their use against ecclesiastical persons or their goods on pain of excommunication.[118] Finally, certain commodities could also be declared free of reprisals.[119]

56–7. It was frequent to grant merchants such protection against reprisals during fairs and on their journey to and from there. See, e.g., G. Des Marez, 'La lettre de foire au XIIIe siècle. Contribution à l'étude sur les origines des papiers de crédit.', *RDILC* 31 (1899), 533–44, at 541f. Such an immunity even became customary (Saxoferrato, *Omnium Iuris Interpretum Antesignani Consilia, Quaestiones et Tractatus* (above, n. 89), Qu. 7, Ad octauum, 23, here at fol. 123v). See, however, Henry Joosen, *Représailles exercées contre des marchands malinois aux foires de Champagne (1300–1305)*, extrait de la Chronique Mensuelle « Mechlinia » (Malines: H. Dierickx-Beke Fils, 1934).

117 At the Diet of Roncaglia in November 1158, Frederick I Barbarossa gave the *Privilegium Scholasticum*. It did not only grant students at Bologna protection during their stay and their journey to and from the university, but also immunity from reprisals. See Deutsches Institut für Erforschung des Mittelalters and Ludwig Weiland, *Monumenta Germaniae Historica: Inde ab anno Christi Quingentesimo usque ad annum millesimum et quingentesimum* (Legum sectio IV. Constitutiones et acta publica imperatorum et regum, 1; Hannover: Hahn, 1893), 249. However, according to this text, the privilege applied only in case of '*delictum*'. Heinz Koeppler, 'Frederick Barbarossa and the Schools of Bologna. Some Remarks on the 'Authentica Habita'', *The English Historical Review* 54 (1939), 577–607, at 597–600., on the other hand, argued that the authentic privilege dealt with '*debitum*' since it was a much common source of complaint. Cf. Winfried Stelzer, 'Zum Scholarenprivileg Friedrich Barbarossas (Authentica „Habita")', *DAEM* 34 (1978), 123–65. See also Honoré Bonet, *L'arbre des batailles*, publié par Ernest Nys (Bruxelles/Leipzig: C. Muquardt, Merzbach et Falk, 1883), Part 4, Ch. LXXXVI, here at 192–194.

118 Sexti Decretal. Lib. V. Tit. VIII. Cap. Un., reproduced in Richter and Friedberg, *Corpus Iuris Canonici* (above, n. 96), col. 1089. This rule was the 28th canon adopted by the Second Council of Lyon. It was repeated, often literally, by successive provincial Councils. See Charles Du Fresne Du Cange, *Glossarium mediæ et infimæ latinitatis*, Conditum a Carolo Du Fresne, domino Du Cange, auctum a monachis ordinis S. Benedicti cum supplementis integris D. P. Carpenterii, Adelungii, aliorums suisque digessit G. A. L. Henschel sequuntur glossarium gallicum, tabulæ, indices auctorum et rerum, dissertationes: Editio nova aucta pluribus verbis aliorum scriptorum a Léopold Favre, Toustain, Le Pelletier, Dantine et al., 7th vol. (new edn., Niort: L. Favre, 1886), 134, on 'Repræsaliæ';

As can be seen, reprisals had become by the thirteenth century a well-established legal institution.[120] The practice spread all over Europe. In many respects, the development of a law of reprisals can be regarded as a progress in medieval legal thinking rather than a relic of barbaric times since it resulted from a plural and multicultural experience.[121]

2. Theory: Bartolus de Saxoferrato's Tractatus Represaliarum

(a) Significance for the Law of Reprisals

Although there were many restrictions and procedural rules governing reprisals, the practice was far from homogenous. It lacked standardisation. In this context, Bartolus de Saxoferrato, a renowned Italian law professor at Perugia who wrote on a wide variety of legal subjects, completed in 1354, three years before his demise, a treatise dedicated to the theory of reprisals: the *Tractatus Represaliarum*.[122] His interest in this topic might

---

Louis Boisset, 'Les conciles provinciaux français et la réception des décrets du IIe concile de Lyon (1274)', *RHEF* 69 (1983), 29–59, at 49.

119 Mas Latrie, *Du droit de marque ou droit de représailles au Moyen-Age* (above, n. 65), 21–2; Colbert, *Retaliation in international law* (above, n. 6), 41. For instance, the charter granted by the King Peter III of Aragon to the city of Barcelona in 1283 provided that victuals brought to that city by land or sea could not be seized by way of reprisals. See Antonio de Capmany y de Montpalau, *Memorias históricas sobre la marina, comercio y artes de la antigua ciudad de Barcelona*, publicadas por disposicion y a expensas de la Real Junta y Consulado de Comercio de la misma ciudad, Real Junta y Consuldado de Comercio de Barcelona, 2nd vol. (Madrid: en la imprenta de don Antonio de Sancha, 1779), 42f., Cap. XIII.

120 Hindmarsh, 'Self-Help in Time of Peace' (above, n. 17), 316; Hohl, 'Bartolus a Saxoferrato: Tractatus Represaliarum. Seine Bedeutung für die Entwicklungsgeschichte des Repressalienrechts' (above, n. 65), 1st vol., 38.

121 Andrés Díaz Borrás, 'Marca, arte de la mercadería y protorganización de la estructura recaudatoria en la Valencia del trescientos', *Anuario de Estudios Medievales* 41 (2011), 3–29, at 7.

122 Saxoferrato, *Omnium Iuris Interpretum Antesignani Consilia, Quaestiones et Tractatus* (above, n. 89), fol. 119v–124v. See esp. Proemium, here at fol. 119v. A French translation of Bartolus's *Tractatus Represaliarum* has recently been completed by Dominique Gaurier of the University of Nantes and is available in PDF since June 2019 on the website https://globalhistoryofinternationallaw.files.wordpress.com/. The document is titled '*Tractatus Bartoli Represaliarum* – une traduction' and includes an introduction by the translator.

have been aroused by the frequency of reprisals in his days and the urgent need to regulate and limit their use.[123]

Bartolus's *Tractatus Represaliarum* is the first academic work to examine the matter of reprisals thoroughly and explain the practice of his time in a coherent manner.[124] Lawyers have largely acknowledged the importance of this study for the institution of reprisals.[125] In fact, the *Tractatus* was quickly positively received by his contemporaries. For instance, Albericus de Rosate (†1360) praised Bartolus's work in these terms: "*De istis repræsaliis fecit pulcherrimum tractatum Bart. de Saxoferrato, qui mihi postea superuenit, & ponam in fine operis ad eius laudem.*"[126] Bartholus's fame as a jurisconsult and the intrinsic quality of the theory of reprisals, which he developed by leaning on municipal statutes and the practice of his time, can mainly account for the positive reception of his treatise.[127] So, in the middle of the eighteenth century, Ludovico Antonio Muratori could still write "*Bartolus, Jurisperitorum suo tempore princeps, in istud argumentum invasit, ediditque Tractatum de Represaliis, quem veluti loco Legis habuere post illum nati.*"[128]

123 Cf. Ibid., Proemium, here at fol. 119v; Jasonne Grabher O'Brien, 'In Defense of the Mystical Body. Giovanni da Legnano's Theory of Reprisals', *RLT* 1 (2002), 25–55, at 26.

124 But see Nys, *Le droit de la guerre et les précurseurs de Grotius* (above, n. 61), 44.

125 See, i.a., Del Vecchio and Casanova, *Le rappresaglie dei comuni medievali e specialmente in Firenze* (above, n. 65), XXII–XXIV; M. H. Keen, *The Laws of War in the Late Middle Ages* (Studies in political history; London/Toronto: Routledge & Kegan Paul/University of Toronto Press, 1965), 219; Ziegler, *Völkerrechtsgeschichte* (above, n. 62), 109. Grewe, *Epochen der Völkerrechtsgeschichte* (above, n. 24), 145, called Bartolus's *Tractatus Represaliarum* a "höchst scharfsinnigen und eingehenden Darstellung des Repressalienrechtes".

126 Commentarium de Statutis Lib. I Qu. LIII, in Albericus de Rosate, Bartolus de Saxoferrato, Giorgio Natta et al., *Tractatus de statutis, diversorum autorum et JC. in Europa præstantiisimorum,* (Francofurti: ex officina Wolffgangi Richteri, curante Iohanne Theobaldo Schönvvettero & Conrado Meulio ciuibus, 1606), 32.

127 Del Vecchio and Casanova, *Le rappresaglie dei comuni medievali e specialmente in Firenze* (above, n. 65), XXIII–XXIV; Hohl, 'Bartolus a Saxoferrato: Tractatus Represaliarum. Seine Bedeutung für die Entwicklungsgeschichte des Repressalienrechts' (above, n. 65), 1st vol., 132.

128 Disseratio LV De Represaliis: Ludovico Antonio Muratori, *Antiquitates italicæ medii ævi, sive dissertationes: De Moribus, Ritibus, Religione, Regimine, Magistratibus, Legibus, Studiis Literarum, Artibus, Lingua, Militia, Nummis, Principibus, Libertate, Servitute, Fœderibus, aliisque faciem & mores Italici Populi referentibus post declinationem Rom.*, 4th vol. (Mediolani: ex Typographia Societatis Palatinæ in Regia Curia, 1741), col. 758.

For centuries, the *Tractatus* remained authoritative.[129] Generations of jurists were influenced, directly or indirectly, by the theory of reprisals laid down by Bartolus.[130] Indeed, Giovanni da Legnano,[131] Martinus Garatus

129 Haggenmacher, 'L'ancêtre de la protection diplomatique. les représailles de l'ancien droit (XIIe-XVIIIe siècles)' (above, n. 3), 11.

130 See Hohl, 'Bartolus a Saxoferrato: Tractatus Represaliarum. Seine Bedeutung für die Entwicklungsgeschichte des Repressalienrechts' (above, n. 65), 1st vol., 132–138.

131 Legnano, *Tractatus de Bello, de Represaliis et de Duello* (above, n. 88), Cap. CXXII–CLXVII, at 155–174 (tr. at 307–331).

Laudensis,[132] Johannes Jacobus Canis,[133] Honoré Bonet,[134] etc. [135] —just to name a few— dealt with reprisals in similar terms as Bartolus. [136]

132 Martinus Garatus Laudensis, 'De Represaliis', in Franciscus Zilettus (ed.), *Tractatus illustrium in utraque tum pontificii, tum cæsarei iuris facultate Iurisconsultorum, De Fisco, & eius Priuilegiis. Ex multis in hoc volumen congesti, additis plurimis, etiam nunquam editis, hac nota designatis; & multò, quàm antea, emendatiores redditi; Summariis singulorum Tractatuum locupletißimis illustrati. Indices accessere ita lucupletes, ut omnes materiæ, quæ sparsim leguntur, facillimè distinctæ Lectoribus appareant*, 12th vol. (Venetiis: [s.n.], 1584), fol. 279r- fol. 281r.

133 Johannes Jacobus Canis, 'De Represaliis', in Franciscus Zilettus (ed.), *Tractatus illustrium in utraque tum pontificii, tum cæsarei iuris facultate Iurisconsultorum, De Fisco, & eius Priuilegiis. Ex multis in hoc volumen congesti, additis plurimis, etiam nunquam editis, hac nota designatis; & multò, quàm antea, emendatiores redditi; Summariis singulorum Tractatuum locupletißimis illustrati. Indices accessere ita lucupletes, ut omnes materiæ, quæ sparsim leguntur, facillimè distinctæ Lectoribus appareant*, 12th vol. (Venetiis: [s.n.], 1584), fol. 275r–fol 279r.

134 Bonet, *L'arbre des batailles* (above, n. 117), Part 4, Ch. LXXIX–XC, here at 180–196.

135 In the seventeenth and eighteenth centuries, an impressive amount of doctoral theses on reprisals —where Bartolus's influence can be identified— were defended at Dutch, German and Swiss universities. See a list in Dietrich Heinrich Ludwig von Ompteda, *Litteratur des gesammten sowohl natürlichen als positiven Völkerrechts*, 2nd vol. (Regensburg: bey Johann Leopold Montags sel. Erben, 1785), 609–13; Carl Albert von Kamptz, *Neue Literatur des Völkerrechts seit dem Jahre 1784; als Ergänzung und Fortsetzung des Werks des Gesandten von Ompteda* (Berlin: Duncker und Humblot, 1817), 316–7; Hohl, 'Bartolus a Saxoferrato: Tractatus Represaliarum. Seine Bedeutung für die Entwicklungsgeschichte des Repressalienrechts' (above, n. 65), 1st vol., 136 fn. 5. The enthusiasm for this topic can be explained by the fragmentation of the Holy Roman Empire into numerous independent principalities and the ensuing question whether reprisals between German Princes were allowed (Ibid., 1st vol., 136–137). See, e.g., Adam Friedrich Glafey, *Vernünfft- Und Völcker-Recht*: *Worinnen die Lehren dieser Wissenschafft auf demonstrative Gründe gesetzet/ und nach selbigen die unter souverainen Völckern/ wie auch denen Gelehrten biß daher vorgefallene Strittigkeiten erörtert werden, Nebst einer Historie des vernünfftigen Rechts/ worinnen nicht nur die Lehren eines jeden Scribenten in Jure Naturæ angezeigt und examinirt werden, sondern auch eine vollständige Bibliotheca Juris Naturæ & Gentium zu befinden ist, welche die biß anhero in dieser disciplin heraus gekommene Bücher, Dissertationes, Deductiones und andere pieçes volantes nach ihren Materien in Alphabetischer Ordnung darlegt*, Samt einen vollständigen Real-Register (Franckfurt/Leipzig: Christoph Riegel, 1723), Book VI, Ch. 1, § 21, here at 7–8, for a negative answer to this question. Cf. Georg Friedrich von Martens, *Précis du droit des gens moderne de l'Europe fondé sur les traités et l'usage*: *Pour servir d'introduction à un cours politique et diplomatique* (2nd edn., Gottingue: Librairie de Dieterich, 1801), 378.

The importance of Bartolus's treatise is indisputable and therefore makes it essential to examine now the major aspects of his theory of reprisals, leaving the questions of detail aside.

(b) Justification of Reprisals

Bartolus addressed first the problematic question of the justification of the use of reprisals. It was no easy task as this remedy involved despoiling innocent persons. This posed a dilemma. On the one hand, the victim deserved justice. On the other, there was the principle that one should not be held vicariously liable for another's debt.[137]

Firstly, Bartolus wondered whether reprisals were morally (*in foro conscientiae*) permitted. He pointed out in this respect that natural law (*ratio naturali*) condemned reprisals. Yet, Saint Augustine of Hippo and Saint Thomas of Aquinas's theory of just war helped to legitimise their use. The question of the legitimacy of reprisals *in foro conscientiae* could actually be solved if the three cumulative conditions which made war 'just' were met, viz. *authoritas superioris* (the superior's permission), *causa iusta* (a just cause) and *intentio recta* (a rightful intention). Bartolus mainly laid great emphasis on the last requirement. Indeed, reprisals could be morally illicit in the absence of a rightful intention, notwithstanding the superior's consent and the justice of the cause.[138] However, his successors did not really insist on the condition of the *intentio recta*, probably because subjective criteria are hard to prove.[139]

Finally, reprisals could also be justified from a legal viewpoint (*in foro civili*). Bartolus drew here again an analogy with the legality of war under *ius divinum* (divine law) and *ius gentium* (law of nations).[140] Indeed, war

136 Hohl, 'Bartolus a Saxoferrato: Tractatus Represaliarum. Seine Bedeutung für die Entwicklungsgeschichte des Repressalienrechts' (above, n. 65), 1st vol., 132–135. Also Keen, *The Laws of War in the Late Middle Ages* (above, n. 125), 219.

137 Hohl, 'Bartolus a Saxoferrato: Tractatus Represaliarum. Seine Bedeutung für die Entwicklungsgeschichte des Repressalienrechts' (above, n. 65), 1st vol., 61.

138 Saxoferrato, *Omnium Iuris Interpretum Antesignani Consilia, Quaestiones et Tractatus* (above, n. 89), Qu. 1, Ad primum, 3, here at fol. 119v–120r. On the just-war doctrine, see Neff, *War and the Law of Nations* (above, n. 2), 49–54.

139 Markus Schrödl, *Das Kriegsrecht des Gelehrten Rechts im 15. Jahrhundert: Die Lehren der Kanonistik und der Legistik über De bello, de represaliis et de duello* (Rechtsgeschichtliche Studien, 14; Hamburg: Dr. Kovač, 2006), 211.

140 Saxoferrato, *Omnium Iuris Interpretum Antesignani Consilia, Quaestiones et Tractatus* (above, n. 89), Qu. 1, Ad secundum, 5, here at fol. 120r.

could be regarded as a salutary remedy originating from God and used to restore peace and tranquillity.[141] As to the Roman *ius gentium*, war was lawful when an authority having no superior agreed on its resort.[142] But a just cause, like the defence of one's own body or of the 'mystical' body, was also needed.[143] A mystical body referred to a community composed of various members who together formed one sole body.[144] This concept especially calls to mind the allegory on the frontispiece of Thomas Hobbes's *Leviathan*. As a result, the whole body could repel an attack on one part, e.g. one of its citizens.[145] For Bartolus, reprisals were thus fully tantamount to war: "*nam concedere represalias est indicere bellum*".[146]

So, in order to be lawful, reprisals had to fulfil the two main conditions of the just-war theory: the superior's consent and the just cause.

141 Joachim von Elbe, 'The Evolution of the Concept of the Just War in International Law', *AJIL* 33 (1939), 665–88, at 672.

142 Ibid., 672–3.

143 Saxoferrato, *Omnium Iuris Interpretum Antesignani Consilia, Quaestiones et Tractatus* (above, n. 89), Qu. 1, Ad secundum, 5–6, here at fol. 120r.

144 The expression 'mystical' body (*corpus mysticus*) is borrowed from Legnano, *Tractatus de Bello, de Represaliis et de Duello* (above, n. 88), Cap. CXXIII, at 155 (tr. at 308). For his part, Bartolus spoke of "*corpus [...] de uno corpore mixto*." (Saxoferrato, *Omnium Iuris Interpretum Antesignani Consilia, Quaestiones et Tractatus* (above, n. 89), Qu. 1, Ad secundum, 5, here at fol. 120r).

145 Ibid., Qu. 1, Ad secundum, 6, here at fol. 120r. According to Giovanni da Legnano, reprisals were considered a particular war waged in defence of one part of the mystical body. It differed from self-defence which pursued the defence of an individual's own body. See Legnano, *Tractatus de Bello, de Represaliis et de Duello* (above, n. 88), Cap. LXXIX, at 130 (tr. at 277). See further O'Brien, 'In Defense of the Mystical Body. Giovanni da Legnano's Theory of Reprisals' (above, n. 123), 31. Reprisals were thus the response of the mystical body. Seen from this angle, reprisals had little to do with the right to feud, contrary to what claimed Pütter, *Beiträge zur Völkerrechts-Geschichte und Wissenschaft* (above, n. 102), 149.

146 Saxoferrato, *Omnium Iuris Interpretum Antesignani Consilia, Quaestiones et Tractatus* (above, n. 89), Qu. 3, Ad secundum, 3, here at fol. 121r. See also Bonet, *L'arbre des batailles* (above, n. 117), Part 4, Ch. LXXXII, here at 183.

(c) Conditions

i) Superior's Consent

Reprisals, in the same conditions as just war, could only be allowed by an authority which had no superior. Indeed, the theory of just war taught that "*bellum iustum non potest indicere, nisi ille qui superiorem non habet*".[147] The same maxim applied to reprisals, too. Since the emergence of reprisals was the consequence of the disappearance of a superior authority able to provide justice, it thus logically implied that only an overlord could permit them.

However, given the political situation in the Italian peninsula in Bartolus's time, it was not necessarily easy to say who the overlord was.[148] Thence, it was not unusual to distinguish between ruler *de jure* and ruler *de facto*. The Pope and the Holy Roman Emperor were often recognised as being superior *de jure* in many dominions. Yet, their authority was not firmly established *de facto* everywhere. Such was the case of the Emperor who resided in Germany. Although he was the *de jure* overlord, he did not wield the *de facto* power in some parts of his Empire like the Italian territories.[149] As a result, the Italian cities (*civitas*) where the Emperor's *de facto* authority failed were entitled to grant reprisals.[150]

147 Saxoferrato, *Omnium Iuris Interpretum Antesignani Consilia, Quaestiones et Tractatus* (above, n. 89), Qu. 3, Ad secundum, 3, here at fol. 121r.

148 See thereupon Cecil Nathan Sidney Woolf, *Bartolus de Sassoferrato: His position in the history of medieval political thought* (Cambridge: CUP, 1913), esp. 203–207.

149 Saxoferrato, *Omnium Iuris Interpretum Antesignani Consilia, Quaestiones et Tractatus* (above, n. 89), Qu. 2, Ad quintum, here at fol. 121r.

150 Ibid., Qu. 3, Ad secundum, 4, here at fol. 121r. According to Bartolus, this power to grant reprisals was delegated through statutes by the citizens to the podestà or lord.

ii) Just Cause

In addition, reprisals required a just cause (*causa iusta*).[151] It means first that the initial injustice should be quite grave because reprisals were an odious measure and a subsidiary remedy.[152] Bartolus did not specify the nature of this injustice, but it could be in all likelihood either a wrong or a debt. This reading can be inferred from the passage where he said that reprisals were legal when the target nation neglected to give justice and to enforce payment of the debt ("*qui iustitiam facere, & debitum reddere neglegit*").[153]

Following an injustice, the victim had then to bring his claim before the local judge of the wrongdoer.[154] If he obtained justice, the question of reprisals would not even arise. On the contrary, if he suffered a denial of justice, the recourse to reprisals would have a just cause.

A denial of justice could be of two kinds: either the absence of judgement or an iniquitous decision.[155] There was a denial of justice in the former case when the judges at all levels of the judicial hierarchy, including the ruler, remained elusive and avoided rendering justice.[156] Bartolus did not answer after which delay the victim could deem justice to be denied. He merely stated that reprisals could be granted when this denial was duly recognised in the victim's country.[157] In the latter case, the exhaustion of the local remedies was also the rule: the victim had to appeal to the superi-

151 About the Roman-law origin of the just cause for reprisals, see Jacob Giltaij, 'Roman law and the *causa legitima* for reprisal in Bartolus', *Fundamina* 20 (2014), 349–56.

152 Saxoferrato, *Omnium Iuris Interpretum Antesignani Consilia, Quaestiones et Tractatus* (above, n. 89), Qu. 2, Ad quartum, here at fol. 121r.

153 Ibid., Qu. 1, Ad secundum, 4, here at fol. 120r. Cf. Colbert, *Retaliation in international law* (above, n. 6), 18.

154 Saxoferrato, *Omnium Iuris Interpretum Antesignani Consilia, Quaestiones et Tractatus* (above, n. 89), Qu. 2, Ad primum, here at fol. 120v. Nevertheless, there were exceptions to this rule. See Qu. 2, Ad secundum, here at fol. 120v.

155 There were in practice other forms of denial of justice that could be imagined. For instance, when no legal action was available to the plaintiff in the wrongdoer's country (e.g., to Christians before Ottoman judges), the result was an obvious denial of justice. See Mas Latrie, *Du droit de marque ou droit de représailles au Moyen-Age* (above, n. 65), 25. Justice could also be deemed denied when the wrongdoer's overlord was unable or intentionally obstructed the enforcement of the judgement (Colbert, *Retaliation in international law* (above, n. 6), 20–1).

156 Saxoferrato, *Omnium Iuris Interpretum Antesignani Consilia, Quaestiones et Tractatus* (above, n. 89), Qu. 2, Ad tertium, 9, here at fol. 120v.

157 Ibid., Qu. 2, Ad primum, here at fol. 120v.

or instances. However, if the unjust judgement was confirmed on appeal or there was no existing appellate instance, justice could rightly be considered denied.[158]

The next step consisted then of confirming the existence of the denial of justice. To this end, the records of the first judge could be requested. If he refused to produce them, he would commit an injustice. Witnesses could also be called in order to prove the denial.[159] In general, the ruler of the victim sent an official demand for redress. The categorical refusal or the persistent silence by the authorities of the wrongdoer's nation would confirm the denial of justice.[160]

Only then would the cause be just. The consequence was, therefore, that every individual subject of the delinquent country could be held responsible, not because of the initial wrong but precisely because of the denial of justice.[161] The parallel between reprisals and just war is also evident here. Indeed, reprisals could target innocent persons, just like in war innocents could be captured.[162] This flowed from the concept of 'mystical body' after which all the individual members had to bear the burden of the community. The use of reprisals thus aimed to incite the nation found at fault to guarantee the legal protection of aliens within its jurisdiction.[163]

158 Ibid., Qu. 2, Ad tertium, here at fol. 120v–121r. See also Qu. 6, Ad primum, here at fol. 122v; Qu. 2, Ad quintum, here at fol. 121r.

159 Ibid., Qu. 4, Ad quintum, here at fol. 121v.

160 Hohl, 'Bartolus a Saxoferrato: Tractatus Represaliarum. Seine Bedeutung für die Entwicklungsgeschichte des Repressalienrechts' (above, n. 65), 1st vol., 113.

161 Saxoferrato, *Omnium Iuris Interpretum Antesignani Consilia, Quaestiones et Tractatus* (above, n. 89), Qu. 10, Ad primum, here at fol. 124r.

162 Ibid., Qu. 6, Ad quartum, 6, here at fol. 122v.

163 Hohl, 'Bartolus a Saxoferrato: Tractatus Represaliarum. Seine Bedeutung für die Entwicklungsgeschichte des Repressalienrechts' (above, n. 65), 1st vol., 96.

(d) Execution

If granted,[164] reprisals had a compensatory character since they were limited to the value of the loss sustained plus costs.[165] In other words, a criterion of proportionality applied.

During this phase, the superior authority was in charge of supervising the lawful execution of reprisals. Bartolus pointed out that the letter holder was, in principle, not entitled to carry out reprisals by seizing persons and goods himself, except in some derogatory cases.[166] Even so, the authorities controlled almost the whole procedure. For example, the letter holder could, in some cases, arrest a countryman of the wrongdoer. But then the captive had to be brought before a judge unless the letter holder was expressly authorised to detain the alien in his own jail.[167] Regarding the seizure of property, the presence of a judge was not necessary.[168] However, a judge had to oversee the sale and appraisal of those goods.[169] The reason

164 The ruler had no obligation to grant reprisals. In fact, common good could actually take precedence over private interests. See Ibid., 1st vol., 114–115. Nevertheless, according to Bartolus, there was a tacit (social) contract between the citizen and the *civitas*. In echange for bearing the burdens of the nation, the citizen deserved defence and protection from the *civitas*. See Saxoferrato, *Omnium Iuris Interpretum Antesignani Consilia, Quaestiones et Tractatus* (above, n. 89), Qu. 5, Ad primum, 2, here at fol. 122r.

165 Hohl, 'Bartolus a Saxoferrato: Tractatus Represaliarum. Seine Bedeutung für die Entwicklungsgeschichte des Repressalienrechts' (above, n. 65), 1st vol., 123.

166 Saxoferrato, *Omnium Iuris Interpretum Antesignani Consilia, Quaestiones et Tractatus* (above, n. 89), Qu. 9, Ad primum, here at fol. 124r.

167 Ibid., Qu. 9, Ad secundum, 2, here at fol. 124r.

168 Ibid., Qu. 9, Ad secundum, 3, here at fol. 124r.

169 Ibid., Qu. 9, Ad tertium, here at fol. 124r. Such supervision was, of course, not for free. As Bartolus stressed, procedural costs had to be withheld from the sale: "*Dico etiam quod in comparatione eius, quod quis recipit, debet fieri detractio expensarum factarum*" (Ibid). Hohl signaled that these costs varied between 10 and 30 % (Hohl, 'Bartolus a Saxoferrato: Tractatus Represaliarum. Seine Bedeutung für die Entwicklungsgeschichte des Repressalienrechts' (above, n. 65), 1st vol., 127). British Admiralty judges expressed an opinion in 1652 regarding letters of reprisal. They signaled that normally 10 % were reserved for the State. See Marsden, *Documents relating to law and custom of the sea* (above, n. 113), 2nd vol., 14. See also Art. 2 of French letters patent, dated 6 August 1582, reproduced in Sylvain Lebeau, *Nouveau code des prises*: *ou recueil des édits, déclarations, lettres patentes, arrêts, ordonnances, réglemens et décisions sur la Course et l'administration des Prises, depuis 1400 jusqu'au mois de mai 1789 (v. st.); suivi de toutes les lois, arrêtés, messages, et autres actes qui ont paru depuis cette dernière époque jusqu'à présent*, 1st vol. (Paris: Imprimerie de la République, an VII), 21.

for so many precautions against abuses was, of course, the risk of counter-reprisals.[170]

3. Risks of Abuse

The medieval law and theory of reprisals convey the general image of a minutely regulated institution which sought to prevent, at any cost, the commission of abuses by private individuals. Indeed, the three above conditions of (a) the Sovereign's consent, (b) the just cause and (c) the proportionality aimed to impede the taking of reprisals in an impulsive, unilateral and excessive way. This also explains why the role played by the authorities was so central in controlling the enforcement of reprisals.

In fact, when the execution fell upon the letter holder, excesses could be committed under the guise of reprisals. For example, Louis XII of France complained in late 1509 that, for the last twenty years, expired letters of reprisal had been used by French individuals against Spanish citizens and vice versa, much to the detriment of trade between both countries.[171] Such cases were, nevertheless, the exception rather than the general rule.[172]

However, the regulation of reprisals seemed to contain a serious loophole because the importance of political considerations in the decision-making to resort to reprisals had not been taken enough into account. This flaw left the door open to abuse; this time not by the victim but by the superior authority. For instance, the political character of reprisals was quite apparent when a prominent citizen of an Italian city who was elected podestà of another, was either barred from taking office or dismissed while in office. The hindrance or dismissal was felt as a national insult in the home city and could give rise to reprisals motivated politically.[173]

---

170 See Saxoferrato, *Omnium Iuris Interpretum Antesignani Consilia, Quaestiones et Tractatus* (above, n. 89), Qu. 10, Ad tertium, here at fol. 124v.

171 René de Maulde La Clavière, *La diplomatie au temps de Machiavel*, 1st vol. (Paris: Ernest Leroux, 1892), 232–233.

172 Colbert, *Retaliation in international law* (above, n. 6), 47.

173 See Hohl, 'Bartolus a Saxoferrato: Tractatus Represaliarum. Seine Bedeutung für die Entwicklungsgeschichte des Repressalienrechts' (above, n. 65), 1st vol., 100–101.

As a matter of fact, the Sovereign of the victim enjoyed a broad discretionary power. It could either grant or refuse to grant letters of reprisal, suspend their enforcement and even revoke them.[174] He was actually under no obligation to authorise reprisals.[175] Policy generally dictated such decisions, depending on whether rivalry or friendly relationship with the nation at fault was on the agenda.[176] Reprisals could likewise be granted lightly to private individuals without the condition of a denial of justice being fulfilled.[177] This requirement was more easily omitted when the ruler himself or a high lord suffered an injustice. In such a case, the claims were not brought before the local judge of the wrongdoer but directly to the overlord. When in 1445 a royal galley loaded of grain was captured by pirates from Genoa, the King of France sought redress from the Genoese authorities but failed. Thus, he ordered the sequestration of the property of Genoese people found in Languedoc.[178] This confusion of identity between the grantee of reprisals and the grantor presented the apparent danger that an all-out war was likelier to break out.

So, the more reprisals involved policy, the more they lost their original compensatory function.[179] They, indeed, were guided by questions of prestige and commercial supremacy rather than by the pursuit of redress for

174 Ibid., 1st vol., 113–115. See also Mas Latrie, *Du droit de marque ou droit de représailles au Moyen-Age* (above, n. 65), 51; Colbert, *Retaliation in international law* (above, n. 6), 33–4.

175 However, according to eighteenth-century French jurist René-Josué Valin, the Sovereign who refused to issue a letter of reprisal on the pretext that war might ensue, would tarnish his reputation and violate his duty of justice. See René-Josué Valin, *Nouveau commentaire sur l'Ordonnance de la marine du mois d'août 1681: Où se trouve la Conférence des anciennes Ordonnances, des Us & Coutumes de la Mer, tant du Royaume que des Pays étrangers, & des nouveaux Réglemens concernans la Navigation & le Commerce maritime. Avec des Explications prises de l'esprit du Texte, de l'Usage, des Décisions des Tribunaux & des meilleurs Auteurs qui ont écrit sur la Jurisprudence nautique. Et des Notes historiques & critiques, tirées de la plupart des divers Recueils de Manuscrits conservés dans les dépôts publics*, dédié à S. A. S. Mgr le Duc de Penthièvre, Amiral de France., 2nd vol. (La Rochelle: chez Jérôme Legier, 1766), 419.

176 Mas Latrie ingenuously believed, though that the granting of reprisals was seldom biased or illegal. See Mas Latrie, *Du droit de marque ou droit de représailles au Moyen-Age* (above, n. 65), 15f.

177 Cf. Colbert, *Retaliation in international law* (above, n. 6), 47f.

178 Maulde La Clavière, *La diplomatie au temps de Machiavel* (above, n. 171), 229. See also at 237.

179 Cf. Colbert, *Retaliation in international law* (above, n. 6), 47; Hohl, 'Bartolus a Saxoferrato: Tractatus Represaliarum. Seine Bedeutung für die Entwicklungsgeschichte des Repressalienrechts' (above, n. 65), 1st vol., 104–105.

injustice.[180] Against this background, the importance of the rules governing reprisals that aimed to maintain them within tolerable limits cannot be minimised.[181]

However, the medieval law of reprisals was about to lose a large amount of relevance following the emergence of the modern State around the sixteenth century. Indeed, reprisals became a public matter as the process of centralisation of power led to the politicisation of all spheres of international relation and consequently to a decline in standards.

III. Politicisation of Reprisals (XVIth–XVIIIth c.)

1. Transition from Private to Public Reprisals

(a) Diplomatic Interposition of the Sovereign

With the development of the modern State system, reprisals underwent slow transformations. They, indeed, progressively stopped involving a relation between private individuals to become solely a State-to-State matter.[182] This process especially had an impact on the conditions governing reprisals. The result was that the medieval law of reprisals became ill-adapted to the new circumstances, which led to a decline in standards. This was particularly true in respect of the *causa iusta*.

Bartolus laid great emphasis on the element of just cause. A denial of justice was the fundamental requirement to allow reprisals. On the contrary, the initial wrong had little importance. It was nothing more than the triggering event. For Bartolus, it did not matter whether the wrong arose from a debt or an injury, so long as it was of certain gravity. The next step was the most important: the victim had to bring his claim before the local judge of the wrongdoer. However, sixteenth-century Italian lawyer Alberico Gentili observed that, if a public person committed the wrong, judicial

---

180 Ibid., 1st vol., 105.

181 Cf. Colbert, *Retaliation in international law* (above, n. 6), 49–50; Hohl, 'Bartolus a Saxoferrato: Tractatus Represaliarum. Seine Bedeutung für die Entwicklungsgeschichte des Repressalienrechts' (above, n. 65), 1st vol., 107–108.

182 Haumant, *Les représailles* (above, n. 21), 51f.

remedies were unavailable to the victim.[183] The distinction depending on whether the wrongdoer turned out to be a private individual or a public authority heralded the development of reprisals into a political coercive measure and the replacement of denial of justice by the notion of international delinquency.[184]

Even so, denial of justice as a requisite for reprisals did not immediately lose relevance. In fact, lawyers kept stressing the importance of this condition. The two main classes of denial of justice were the delay of justice and the manifestly unjust judgement.[185] In the former class, justice was generally regarded as abusively neglected after "a fit time".[186] But there was no clear criterion unless expressly provided by treaty. As for the second class, judgements were *prima facie* just because a presumption of impartiality should prevail in case of doubt.[187] Nevertheless, Bynkershoek pointed out that both the plaintiff and his Sovereign too readily regarded an unfavourable decision as being unjust.[188]

In theory, the victim could turn to his Sovereign and call him for assistance only after a denial of justice had occurred. The monarch would then interpose on behalf of his aggrieved subject by seeking to obtain redress from the wrongdoing community through the action of the national am-

---

183 "*quam circa represalias: ubi distinguitur, quod aut iniuria facta a priuato est, et petenda iustitia sit a magistratu loci unde iniuria est; aut a publico facta est, et tum dentur represaliae nec petita iustitia prius.*" (Alberico Gentili, *De Iure Belli Libri Tres* (Oxford: Clarendon Press, 1877), Lib. II Cap. I, here at 127).

184 Spiegel, 'Origin and Development of Denial of Justice' (above, n. 61), 73–4. See also Hohl, 'Bartolus a Saxoferrato: Tractatus Represaliarum. Seine Bedeutung für die Entwicklungsgeschichte des Repressalienrechts' (above, n. 65), 1st vol., 139.

185 "Justice is held to be denied, not only if judgment can not be obtained against a guilty person, or a debtor, within a reasonable time, but also if in a clear case a judgment is given which is obviously contrary to law, since the authority of the judge has not the same validity against foreigners as against subjects." (Richard Zouche, *Iuris et Iudicii Fecialis, Sive, Iuris Inter Gentes, et Quaestionum de Eodem Explicatio: Qua Quae ad Pacem & Bellum inter diversos Principes, aut Populos spectant, ex praecipuis Historico-jure-peritis, exhibentur*, 2 vols. (The Classics of International Law, 1; Washington: Carnegie Institution, 1911), 2nd vol., 33). See also Grotius, *Le droit de la guerre et de la paix* (above, n. 33), Book III Ch. II § V.1, here at 2nd vol., 747.

186 Charles Molloy, *De Jure Maritimo et Navali: Or, A Treatise of Affairs Maritime and of Commerce. In Three Books.* (7th edn., London: Printed for John Walthoe junior, and J. Wotton, 1722), 27.

187 Ibid., 32.

188 Bynkershoek, *Quaestionum juris publici libri duo* (above, n. 33), Book I Cap. 24, here 1st vol., 176 (tr. 2nd vol., 136).

bassador at the foreign Court.[189] The Sovereign's interposition was a precursor of diplomatic protection that had been customarily in use since the fourteenth century at least and figured as a requirement in treaties since the sixteenth century.[190] It precisely aimed to confirm the existence of a denial of justice.[191]

However, against the background of the emergence of modern States, it was no longer a denial of justice that constituted a *causa iusta* for reprisals, but the neglect of the foreign Sovereign to compel the author of the injustice to make reparation.[192] Indeed, Articles 1 and 2 under Title X on the letters of reprisal in Louis XIV's *Grande ordonnance de la marine d'août 1681* did not say a word about a prior denial of justice sustained by the victim, but stipulated that the ambassadors of France were charged with pressing the claims.[193] According to maritime law expert René-Josué Valin who commented the Ordinance, the issuance of letters of reprisal could only

189 Robert Kolb, 'The Protection of the Individual in Times of War and Peace', in Bardo Fassbender and Anne Peters (eds.), *The Oxford Handbook of the History of International Law* (Oxford: OUP, 2012), 317–37, at 333.

190 Colbert, *Retaliation in international law* (above, n. 6), 24–5.

191 Gabriel Bonnot de Mably, *Le droit public de l'Europe, fondé sur les traités: Précédé des principes de négociations, pour servir d'Introduction*, avec des Remarques Historiques, Politiques & Critiques par Mr. Rousset, 2nd vol. (2nd edn., Amsterdam/Leipzig: Arkstée & Merkus, 1773), 444.

192 For example, Francisco de Vitoria wrote in his *De Jure Belli* at § 41: "[...], although [...] Sovereign might initially be blameless, yet it is a breach of duty, as St. Augustine says, for them to neglect to vindicate the right against the wrongdoing of their subjects, [...]. There is, accordingly, no inherent injustice in the letters of marque and reprisals which princes often issue in such cases, because it is on account of the neglect and breach of duty of the other prince that the prince of the injured party grants him this right to recoup himself even from innocent folk." (Translation by James Brown Scott, *The Spanish Origin of International Law: Francisco de Vitoria and His Law of Nations* (Oxford: Clarendon Press, 1934), LXIV). Cf. Balthazar Ayala, *De Jure et Officiis Bellicis et Disciplina Militari Libri III*, 2 vols. (The Classics of International Law, 2; Washington, D.C.: The Carnegie Institution of Washington, 1912), 2nd vol., 31–33; Grotius, *Le droit de la guerre et de la paix* (above, n. 33), Book III Ch. II §§ I.3 – 4 and II.1 – 4, here at 2nd vol., 743–744; Francis Hutcheson, *A Short Introduction to Moral Philosophy: in Three Books; Containing the Elements of Ethicks and the Law of Nature*, translated from the Latin (2nd edn., Glasgow: Robert & Andrew Foulis, 1753), 320–1; Louis de Jaucourt, 'Représailles', in Denis Diderot and Jean Le Rond d'Alembert (eds.), *Encyclopédie ou Dictionnaire raisonné des sciences, des arts et des métiers.*, 14th vol. (Neufchastel: chez Samuel Faulche & Compagnie, [1751–1765]), 142–3.

193 See Valin, *Nouveau commentaire sur l'Ordonnance de la marine du mois d'août 1681* (above, n. 175), 416–420.

follow from the ambassadors' unsuccessful attempt at the foreign court to obtain satisfaction.[194] In the so-called Jay Treaty of 1795 between Great Britain and the United States, it also was no longer about a citizen being denied justice personally.[195]

In this context, the interposition of his Sovereign was indispensable for the victim. But by doing so, the claims left the private sphere to be fully endorsed by the State.[196] Thus, German scholar Christian Wolff regarded the question of reprisals as an issue between two States. He, indeed, explained that the refusal by the wrongdoing nation to repair an injury done to the other nation or its citizens justified the lawful taking of reprisals.[197]

The result of this evolution was the exclusion of the subjects from the procedure. Before turning to his ruler, the aggrieved individual was no longer formally bound to first exhaust all local remedies in the wrongdoer's country. Thence, the disappearance of this condition made likelier a resort to reprisals guided by political considerations, given that the merits of the claim did not have to be examined by a judicial body, but by the central authority of the State. Such a situation left the door open for power struggle as the State demanding redress on behalf of its citizen expected the delinquent State to yield unconditionally. Nonetheless, Valin ingenuously believed that a powerful nation like France never traded on its superiority to press claims, although he acknowledged that this dominant position certainly made a rupture of peace less likely.[198]

---

194 Ibid., 2nd vol., 419.

195 "Article 22. It is expressly stipulated that neither of the said Contracting Parties will order or Authorize any Acts of Reprisal against the other on Complaints of Injuries or Damages until the said party shall first have presented to the other a Statement thereof, verified by competent proof and Evidence, and demanded Justice and Satisfaction, and the same shall either have been refused or unreasonably delayed." (David Hunter Miller, *Treaties and other international acts of the United States of America*, 2nd vol. (Washington, D. C.: GPO, 1931–1948), 261).

196 Maulde La Clavière, *La diplomatie au temps de Machiavel* (above, n. 171), 251.

197 "there is no place for reprisals, except when another people does an injury to us or to our citizens, and, *when asked*, is unwilling to repair it within a proper time, that is, without delay." (Christian Wolff, *Jus Gentium Methodo Scientifica Pertractatum*, 2nd vol. (The Classics of International Law, 13; Oxford: Clarendon Press, 1934), § 589 (emphasis added)).

198 Valin, *Nouveau commentaire sur l'Ordonnance de la marine du mois d'août 1681* (above, n. 175), 419.

There is, however, one remarkable case in the history of the law of nations where the complaining State was compelled to recognise the condition of denial of justice: the *Silesian Loan* case.[199] This episode is in many respects illustrative of power struggle and the transition from denial of justice to the Sovereign's interposition as a condition for permitting reprisals.

In 1751, at the time of the War of the Austrian Succession, Frederick II of Prussia withheld the last instalment he owed English lenders, pursuant to Article 7 of the Treaty of Breslau of 11 June 1742 by which Prussia committed to paying a loan contracted by Emperor Charles VI in exchange for the cession of the Duchy of Silesia. This act was justified as lawful reprisals in response to judgements of the English Admiralty courts which declared Prussian vessels and cargoes —albeit Prussia remained neutral during the war— good prizes for transporting contraband of war. A commission of jurisconsults set up by the Prussian monarch, indeed, considered that the English Admiralty courts did not offer sufficient guarantees of impartiality. So, since the appeal to the High Court of Admiralty would remain unavailing for the aggrieved Prussian nationals, the issue could only be treated from Sovereign to Sovereign.[200] The commission, therefore, concluded that Frederick II was rightfully entitled to confiscate by way of reprisals the debt he owed since all diplomatic remonstrances to obtain redress had been frustrated.

However, in Great Britain, the Law Officers of the Crown drafted an answer that asserted, amongst other things, that reprisals could only be allowed when justice was "absolutely denied, *in Re minime dubiâ*, by all the

199 The following account of the facts is based on Karl von Martens, *Causes célèbres du droit des gens*, 5 vols. (2nd edn., Leipzig: F. A. Brockhaus, 1858–1861), 2nd vol., 97–168; and Ernest Mason Satow, *The Silesian loan and Frederick the Great* (Oxford: Clarendon Press, 1915). See also Henry Wheaton, *History of the Law of Nations in Europe and America; From the Earliest Times to the Treaty of Washington, 1842* (New York: Gould, Banks & Co., 1845), 206–17.

200 Thereupon, the commission's report stated the following: "§ 47. Quand deux puissances se trouvent avoir entr'elles quelques différends, on ne peut d'aucun des deux côtés en appeler aux lois du pays, parce que l'une des deux parties ne les reconnait point; l'affaire se traite alors par voie de négociation, et de cour à cour, et le différend ne se decide du consentement des deux parties, que selon le droit des gens, ou par des principes qui s'y trouvent fondés." (reproduced in Martens, *Causes célèbres du droit des gens* (above, n. 199), 2nd vol., 125).

Tribunals, and afterwards by the Prince."[201] For Emer de Vattel, the whole answer was "un excellent morceau de Droit des Gens"[202], and, for Montesquieu, "une réponse sans réplique"[203]. As a result, the Prussian commission corrected its statement and explained that the action was actually not an act of reprisals, but rather an offsetting transaction. This argument probably aimed to avoid addressing the question of denial of justice as a condition for reprisals, which would put Frederick II in an uncomfortable position from a legal perspective.[204] But the issue was not settled until a declaration was added to the Treaty of Westminster of 16 January 1756. On the one hand, Frederick II agreed to pay the last instalment; on the other, George II of Great Britain promised the payment of twenty thousand pounds sterling to extinguish the claims of Prussian subjects.

In this case, the principle that justice ought to be absolutely denied for allowing reprisals was strongly reaffirmed. Still, it remained in theory. The facts are here more eloquent: Sovereigns proceeded to reprisals whenever they deemed the exhaustion of local remedies from the aggrieved subjects useless. Indeed, from the moment when reprisals stopped being treated as an issue between private individuals to become a State-to-State matter, the question of denial of justice lost all its relevance. Another interesting element here is also that Frederick II did not admit the illegality of the reprisals. Instead, he withheld the payment until the final settlement in

201 Satow, *The Silesian loan and Frederick the Great* (above, n. 199), 82. A couple of years later, the Archdeacon of Essex Thomas Rutherforth echoed this statement of law that local remedies ought to be exhausted for the lawful resort to reprisals. See Thomas Rutherforth, *Institutes of Natural Law: Being the Substance of a Course of Lectures on Grotius De Jure Belli Et Pacis read in S. Johns College, Cambridge*, 2nd vol. (Cambridge: J. Bentham, 1756), 598–600.

202 Emer de Vattel, *Le Droit des Gens. Ou Principes de la Loi naturelle, Appliqués à la conduite & aux affaires des Nations & des Souverains*, 1st vol. (Londres: [s.n.], 1758), 318 fn. (a).

203 Letter Nr. 72 to Father Guasco, 5 March 1753: Charles Louis de Montesquieu, *Œuvres complètes de Montesquieu: avec des notes de Dupin, Crevier, Voltaire, Mably, Servan, La Harpe, etc., etc.* (Paris: chez Firmin Didot frères, fils et Cie, 1857), 668. The report of the Law Officers has actually been acclaimed as a "legal masterpiece". See, e.g., Van Vechten Veeder, *Legal Masterpieces: Specimens of Argumentation and Exposition by Eminent Lawyers*, 1st vol. (St. Paul, Minn.: Keefe-Davidson Company, 1903), 20–32.

204 In all likelihood, there was also a desire to avoid open hostility between both countries as the reference to 'reprisals' might lead to that. In fact, the relationship between Frederick II and his uncle George II was already strained due to personal dislike and conflicting territorial claims in the Holy Roman Empire. See Satow, *The Silesian loan and Frederick the Great* (above, n. 199), 132–5.

1756. It shows that Sovereigns did not feel compelled to observe the rules to the letter. In fact, they acted as judge in the case of their aggrieved subjects.[205] This evolution definitely represented a step back from the medieval law of reprisals as political considerations were likelier to influence the decision on their resort.

(b) Progressive Exclusion of Private Individuals from the Execution

With the consolidation of the central power from the sixteenth century onwards, reprisals became less necessitated as inland security increased.[206] Besides, aliens had easier access to justice and enjoyed better protection from their homeland through diplomatic protection.[207] Nevertheless, when the Sovereign failed to obtain redress for the wrong suffered by his subjects, he could then allow the resort to reprisals.

---

205 Johann Jacob Moser, *Versuch des neuesten Europäischen Völker=Rechts in Friedens= und Kriegs=Zeiten: vornehmlich aus denen Staatshandlungen derer Europäischen Mächten, auch anderen Begebenheiten, so sich seit dem Tode Kayser Carls VI. im Jahr 1740. zugetragen haben*, 8th vol. (Frankfurt am Mayn: Varrentrapp Sohn und Wenner, 1779), 502.

206 Hohl, 'Bartolus a Saxoferrato: Tractatus Represaliarum. Seine Bedeutung für die Entwicklungsgeschichte des Repressalienrechts' (above, n. 65), 1st vol., 141.

207 De Visscher, *Théories et réalités en droit international public* (above, n. 39), 348; Antônio Augusto Cançado Trindade, 'Denial of justice and its relationship to exhaustion of local remedies in international law', *PhilipLJ* 53 (1978), 404–20, at 404f.; Paulsson, *Denial of Justice in International Law* (above, n. 61), 14. Cf. Colbert, *Retaliation in international law* (above, n. 6), 58; F. Parkinson, 'Reprisals in international maritime law. A historical paradigm', *Marine Policy* 12 (1988), 276–85, at 282. About the link between diplomatic protection and reprisals, see Alwyn Vernon Freeman, 'Recent Aspects of the Calvo Doctrine and the Challenge to International Law', *AJIL* 40 (1946), 121–47, at 139; Haggenmacher, 'L'ancêtre de la protection diplomatique. les représailles de l'ancien droit (XIIe-XVIIIe siècles)' (above, n. 3). Also, the Prussian commission of jurists in the Silesian Loan case stressed that "Le roi [...] ne peut, sans manquer à ses devoirs de souverain et à sa gloire, refuser de protéger ses sujets" (Martens, *Causes célèbres du droit des gens* (above, n. 199), 2nd vol., 128).

In the Middle Ages, the authorities closely supervised the execution of reprisals. In fact, according to Bartolus, reprisals should be made within the ruler's territory.[208] However, this was detrimental to trade because reprisals were usually made in ports.[209] Sovereigns thus prohibited reprisals in such places, like Ferdinand II of Aragon in an ordinance dated 18 March 1511.[210] During the negotiations with France in 1599, British diplomat Sir Henry Neville advocated the addition of a provision by which reprisals would be allowed only at sea. He explained that this was to the benefit of English merchants since there were more English goods in France than the reverse. He also put forward another argument: the English superiority at sea. Therefore, it would be harder for the French to make reprisals. Still, Neville pointed out that the French diplomats sup-

---

208 Bartolus considered that reprisals must be carried out within the ruler's jurisdiction who granted them unless there was an express derogation. The reason he brought forward was that the exercise of reprisals on the territory of the delinquent State would hardly fail to be seen as a *casus belli* or as a cause of major disturbance.See Saxoferrato, *Omnium Iuris Interpretum Antesignani Consilia, Quaestiones et Tractatus* (above, n. 89), Qu. 8, Ad tertium, here at fol. 123v. However, Giovanni da Legnano disagreed with this view. He argued that reprisals could be made abroad just like an act of self-defence. Moreover, he stressed that the wrongdoing country could be quite remote and that no property belonging to members of that nation could be found within the territory of the ruler who granted reprisals. See Legnano, *Tractatus de Bello, de Represaliis et de Duello* (above, n. 88), Cap. CXXXI, at 161 (tr. at 315). Indeed, reprisals were possible mostly when a "reciprocity of intercourse" existed (Koeppler, 'Frederick Barbarossa and the Schools of Bologna. Some Remarks on the 'Authentica Habita'' (above, n. 117), 595). But as reprisals became over time a method of coercion rather than compensation, the question of "reciprocity of intercourse" lost relevance since the idea behind reprisals was to compel the wrongdoing nation to give redress, and not to secure compensation oneself. That is why Great Britain chose to blockade the coasts of Venezuela in 1902 because the Venezuelan mercantile marine was not large enough to exert enough pressure by seizing and sequestrating merchant vessels. See British Memorandum of 29 November 1902, reproduced in Kotzsch, 'Die Blockade gegen Venezuela vom Jahre 1902 als Präzedenzfall für das moderne Kriegsrecht' (above, n. 28), 423.

209 Colbert, *Retaliation in international law* (above, n. 6), 44–5. See a letter of ca. 1484, reproduced in Henry Elliot Malden, *The Cely papers: Selections from the correspondence and memoranda of the Cely family, merchants of the Staple; A.D. 1475–1488* (London: Longmans, Green, and Co., 1900), 146, in which the Lord Lieutenant of Calais refused to execute reprisals against several Flemish merchants as that might adversely affect trade in the said port.

210 Maulde La Clavière, *La diplomatie au temps de Machiavel* (above, n. 171), 233.

ported this proposition on account of the adverse effect of reprisals on trade when taken on land or in ports.[211]

As a result, reprisals moved from land to the high seas at a time when maritime trade was growing.[212] So, at the turn of the seventeenth century, treaties and national law confined the enforcement of reprisals to the high seas.[213] This shift probably made the resort to reprisals easier to decide because the country that allowed them was less likely to see its trade directly impacted.

Now, since the State navy was still modest in size at the beginning of the Early Modern Times, the enforcement of the letters of reprisal was generally entrusted to private individuals: either the letter holder himself, when he had the means to do so, or a third party to whom the letter was sold.[214] This is what the *Guidon de la mer*, an anonymous sixteenth-century French compilation of practices relating to maritime trade, told in Article 3 of

---

211 Sir Henry Neville to Mr Secretary Cecyll, 18 July 1599: Edmund Sawyer, *Memorials of Affairs of State in the Reigns of Q. Elizabeth and K. James I.: Collected (chiefly) from the Original Papers Of the Right Honourable Sir Ralph Winwood, Kt. Sometime one of the Principal Secretaries of State. Comprehending likewise the Negotiations of Sir Henry Neville, Sir Charles Cornwallis, Sir Dudley Carleton, Sir Thomas Edmondes, Mr. Trumbull, Mr. Cottington and other, At the Courts of France and Spain, and in Holland, Venice, &c. Wherein the Principal Transactions of those Times Are faithfully related, and the Policies and Intrigues of those Courts at large discover'd. The whole digested in an exact Series of Time. To which are added Two Tables: One of the Letters, the other of the Principal Matters*, 1st vol. (London: Printed by W. B. for T. Ward, 1725), 73–4.

212 Hohl, 'Bartolus a Saxoferrato: Tractatus Represaliarum. Seine Bedeutung für die Entwicklungsgeschichte des Repressalienrechts' (above, n. 65), 1st vol., 141–142.

213 Clark, 'The English Practice with Regard to Reprisals by Private Persons' (above, n. 4), 720. See, e.g., the Anglo-French treaty of 29 March 1632, Art. 2: Dumont, *Corps universel diplomatique du droit des gens* (above, n. 104), 6th vol., Part I, 33; the Anglo-French treaty of 3 November 1655, Art. 3: Ibid., 6th vol., Parts II & III, 121. In a letter to the Lords of the Admiralty, Charles I of England authorised in 1637 the High Court of Admiralty to grant any English subject, who "have been or shalbe robbed, pillaged, or dampnified at sea or in port, by the said French King, or any of his subjects", letters of reprisal. The only constraint was that the seizure of ships and property had to take place exclusively "upon the seas, but not in any port or harbour, unlesse yt be the shipps or goods of the party that did the wronge" (Marsden, *Documents relating to law and custom of the sea* (above, n. 113), 1st vol., 501. See also Ibid., 2nd vol., 3–4 and 27).

214 Cf. Mas Latrie, *Du droit de marque ou droit de représailles au Moyen-Age* (above, n. 65), 36–7; Hohl, 'Bartolus a Saxoferrato: Tractatus Represaliarum. Seine Bedeutung für die Entwicklungsgeschichte des Repressalienrechts' (above, n. 65), 1st vol., 141–142; Neff, *War and the Law of Nations* (above, n. 2), 81.

Chapter X about the letters of marque or reprisal.[215] In addition to the private origin of the claim, it explains why international law historiography usually calls them 'private reprisals' in order to make a distinction with acts of reprisals carried out by the State.[216]

However, the public force was sometimes mobilised to exercise reprisals on the high seas on behalf of private individuals. For example, Edward Popham, general of the English fleet, was directed in 1650 to execute letters of reprisal against the French on behalf of their holder since "many of the English soe spoyled are not able to undergoe the charge of setting forth ships of their owne to make seizures by such letters of marque; and for that by the law used amongst nations any state may in such case cause justice to be executed by their owne immediate officers and ministers immediately where they finde it requisite".[217] As a matter of fact, private individuals were required by the English Council of State in 1652 to equip a ship "which shall not be of the burden of 200 tons at least, and carry in her twenty guns at least" in order to execute letters of reprisal.[218]

---

215 "Le plus frequent usage se pratique pour les marchands depredez sur mer, trafiquans en estrange pays, lesquels, en vertu d'icelle, trouvent par mer aucuns navires des sujets de celuy qui a toleré la premiere prise, l'abordant, s'ils sont les plus forts, mettent en effet leurs represailles." (Pardessus, *Collection de lois maritimes antérieures au XVIII.e siècle* (above, n. 108), 411).

216 Colbert, *Retaliation in international law* (above, n. 6), 9. See, e.g., De Visscher, 'Le déni de justice en droit international' (above, n. 61), 371, quoting Littré, *Dictionnaire de la langue française* (above, n. 3), 1647; Grewe, *Epochen der Völkerrechtsgeschichte* (above, n. 24), 237–8; Elagab, *The legality of non-forcible counter-measures in international law* (above, n. 14), 6; Neff, *War and the Law of Nations* (above, n. 2), 108.

217 Marsden, *Documents relating to law and custom of the sea* (above, n. 113), 2nd vol., 8. Another example is the seizure of French ships by two English warships at Cromwell's behest. Villemain tells the story of a Quaker merchant who turned to the Lord Protector after his vessel was confiscated in France. Cromwell sent the Quaker with a letter summoning Mazarin to give back the vessel and cargo within three days. After the failure of his mission, the Quaker returned to see Cromwell who then ordered reprisals on the former's behalf. The merchant was repaid on the sale of the prizes. As for the residue, the Lord Protector put it into the hands of the French ambassador. See Abel-François Villemain, *Histoire de Cromwell: D'après les mémoires du temps et les recueils parlementaires.* (Bruxelles: Meline, Cans et comp., 1851), 331.

218 Samuel Rawson Gardiner, *Letters and papers relating to the First Dutch War, 1652–1654* (Publications of the Navy Records Society, 13; [London]: Navy Records Society, 1899), 359.

Over time, as reprisals became more and more tightly linked with the affairs of State, Sovereigns stopped issuing letters of reprisal to private individuals. In France, since the Ordinance of 1681 until the end of the eighteenth century, merely four licences were granted.[219] In Great Britain, the issuance of the last letters of reprisal appears to be in 1738 to merchants aggrieved by Spain, in accordance with the Anglo-Spanish treaties of 1667

219 Joseph-Nicolas Guyot, 'Représailles (lettres de)', in Philippe-Antoine Merlin (ed.), *Répertoire universel et raisonné de jurisprudence. Réduit aux objets dont la connaissance peut encore être utile, et augmentée 1° des changemens apportés aux lois anciennes par les lois nouvelles, tant avant que depuis l'année 1814; 2° de dissertations, de plaidoyers et de réquisitoires sur les unes et les autres*, 15th vol. (5th edn., Paris: Garnery, 1828), 48–9, at 49. See further the correspondence regarding the execution of the letter of reprisal of 1702 granted to the Abbé de Polignac against the Danzigers (Lebeau, *Nouveau code des prises* (above, n. 169), 306–7); the text of the 1778 letter of reprisal issued in favour of two merchants of Bordeaux against the British (Wilhelm Georg Grewe, *Fontes historiae iuris gentium*, In Zusammenarbeit mit dem Institut für Internationales Recht an der Freien Universität Berlin, 2nd vol. (Berlin: Walter de Gruyter, 1988), 507–509); and the text of the decree adopted by the French National Convention by which Joseph Caudier was granted a letter of reprisal against the citizens of Genoa (Guyot, 'Représailles (lettres de)' (above, n. 219), 49).
However, regarding the licence given in 1778, Georg Friedrich von Martens, *Essai concernant les Armateurs, les Prises et sur tout les Reprises. D'après les loix, les traités, et les usages des Puissances maritimes de l'Europe* (Gottingue: Jean Chretien Dieterich, 1795), 30 fn. (e), considered it null on account of the war between France and Great Britain that had already begun since 17 June 1778. See the letter to the Admiral of France, 5 April 1779 (Athanase Jean Léger Jourdan, François André Isambert, Decrusy et al., *Recueil général des anciennes lois françaises: Depuis l'an 420 jusqu'à la Révoution de 1789*, 29 vols. (Paris: Belin-Leprieur, 1821–1833), 26th vol., 65; and also Balthazard-Marie Émérigon and Pierre-Sébastien Boulay-Paty, *Traité des assurances et des contrats à la grosse d'Émérigon, conféré et mis en rapport avec le nouveau code de commerce et la jurisprudence; suivi d'un vocabulaire des termes de marine et des noms de chaque partie d'un navire*, 1st vol. (2nd edn., Rennes: Molliex, 1827), 75–76). Moreover, both sides ordered general reprisals. See Louis XVI of France's issuance of general reprisals, 10 July 1778 (Jourdan et al., *Recueil général des anciennes lois françaises* (above, n. 219), 25th vol., 354; the British Order in Council allowing general reprisals against the French, 29 July, mentioned in the preamble of an Act reproduced in Danby Pickering, *The Statutes at Large: From Magna Charta To the End of the Eleventh Parliament of Great Britain, Anno 1761.*, 32nd vol (Cambridge: Charles Bathurst, 1778), 178). In those circumstances, the letter of reprisal actually amounted to a privateering commission.

and 1670.[220] But apart from these exceptions, it was the State alone that conducted reprisals in defence of its nationals.[221] Thus, reprisals ceased to imply a private issue as a result of the complete exclusion of the individual victims, from the procedure and the execution. Reprisals then became a means of coercion in the hands of States.

After the eighteenth century, no letter of reprisals was ever granted. There were, however, attempts by private individuals to obtain such a licence, but their efforts remained in vain.[222] Some international lawyers also argued that obsolescence does not mean abrogation, thence suggesting

220 See Newcastle's note to the Spanish ambassador at London on this subject (Marsden, *Documents relating to law and custom of the sea* (above, n. 113), 2nd vol., 283–285). See also Grewe, *Epochen der Völkerrechtsgeschichte* (above, n. 24), 430.

221 "Il est même rare aujourd'hui qu'un état accorde de telles lettres de represailles, en tems de paix, tandis que d'un côté les traités même bornent les cas où l'on pourrait user de ce moyen, et de l'autre, s'ils existent, c'est plutôt l'état qui use de represailles en faveur de ses sujets." (Martens, *Précis du droit des gens moderne de l'Europe fondé sur les traités et l'usage* (above, n. 135), 382). See also Domenico Alberto Azuni, *Droit maritime de l'Europe*, 2nd vol. (Paris: L'Auteur/Ant. Aug. Renouard, 1805), 440; Friedrich Saalfeld, *Handbuch des positiven Völkerrechts* (Tübingen: C. F. Osiander, 1833), 186. Cf. Mr Sanford's report on special reprisals addressed to Mr Cass, 16 August 1857: Sanford, *The Aves Island Case* (above, n. 43), 261.

222 An example is the legal proceedings initiated by the French citizen Rougemont against the French State before the Conseil d'État. He was shipowner of a privateer that captured several enemy ships in 1810 and 1811. But as they were brought to the port of neutral Algiers, the dey, who alleged the violation of his rules of neutrality, confiscated them and gave them back to their respective owners. However, these prizes were later confirmed as good by the French prize courts. Rougemont then turned to the Ministry of Foreign Affairs in order to receive compensation from the French State or, on a subsidiary basis, to be granted a letter of reprisal which he could enforce himself against the Regency of Algiers. This latter demand was motivated on the argument that the Ordinance of Marine of 1681 was still in force. Nevertheless, both appeals he introduced before the Conseil d'État were dismissed in 1823 and 1826. See Louis-Antoine Macarel, *Recueil des arrêts du Conseil, ou Ordonnances royales rendues en Conseil d'État, sur toutes les matières du contentieux de l'administration*: *Année 1823*, 5th vol. (Paris: Bureau d'administration du recueil, 1823), 674–8; and Louis-Antoine Macarel, *Recueil des arrêts du Conseil, ou Ordonnances royales rendues en Conseil d'État, sur toutes les matières du contentieux de l'administration*: *Année 1826*, 8th vol. (Paris: Bureau d'administration du recueil, 1826), 225–7.
In another instance, the so-called *Aves Island* case (1854–1861), Boston merchants who collected guano on an uninhabited island were evicted *manu militari* by Venezuelan soldiers. The victims then pressed the U.S. Government for many years to seek redress. At a point, they urged the Executive to grant them a

that letters of reprisal could still be granted to private individuals.[223] Nevertheless, those who maintained this opinion were a minority. Most legal scholars considered that private reprisals (a practice they viewed as inherited from barbaric times) had entirely fallen into disuse.[224]

---

letter of reprisal against Venezuela. Despite their insistence, no such licence was issued. See Sanford, *The Aves Island Case* (above, n. 43), for the correspondence. The fact is that the United States never authorised an individual to resort to special reprisals (John Bassett Moore, *A digest of international law: As embodied in diplomatic discussions, treaties and other international agreements, international awards, the decisions of municipal courts, and the writings of jurists, and especially in documents, published and unpublished, issued by Presidents and Secretaries of State of the United States, the opinions of the Attorney-General, and the decisions of courts, federal and state*, 7th vol. (Washington: GPO, 1906), 122).

223 See, e.g., Alphonse de Pistoye and Charles Duverdy, *Traité des prises maritimes: dans lequel on a refondu le traité de Valin en l'appropriant à la législation nouvelle*, Ouvrage contenant un grand nombre de décisions inédites de l'ancien Conseil des prises, et les actes émanés en 1854 des gouvernements belligérants et neutres, 1st vol. (Paris: Auguste Durand, 1855), 91; Phillimore, *Commentaries Upon International Law* (above, n. 46), 30. In support of their argument, they referred to legal provisions in national code that reminded the time when letters of reprisal were still in use. For example, Article 350 of the French *Code de commerce* of 1807 took up literally the wording of the provision in the Ordinance of Marine concerning the insurer's liability in case of loss caused, i.a., by reprisals. See thereupon Robert-Joseph Pothier and Jean-Julien Estrangin, *Traité du contrat d'assurance de Pothier: avec un discours préliminaire, des notes et un supplément* (Marseille: Sube et Laporte, 1810), 70 fn. (a) and 97. But see Ferdinand de Cussy, *Phases et causes célèbres du droit maritime des nations*, 2 vols. (Leipzig: F. A. Brockhaus, 1856), 1st vol., 125–126.

224 See, e.g., Théodore Ortolan, *Règles internationales et diplomatie de la mer*, 1st vol. (4th edn., Paris: Henri Plon, 1864), 359; Travers Twiss, *The law of nations considered as independent political communities: On the rights and duties of nations in time of war* (2nd edn., Oxford: Clarendon Press; London: Longmans, Green, and Co, 1875), 25; Carlos Calvo, *Le droit international théorique et pratique: précédé d'un exposé historique des progrès de la science du droit des gens*, 3rd vol. (4th edn., Paris: Guillaumin et Cie, 1888), 519–520 (§ 1811). Cf. Cussy, *Phases et causes célèbres du droit maritime des nations* (above, n. 223), 1st vol., 125–126.

2. Public Character of Reprisals

(a) General Aspects

The involvement of the State in the claims of its citizens —e.g., itself by exercising reprisals— sometimes made it hard to differentiate between 'public' and 'private' reprisals. In fact, the State would more and more treat an injury sustained by a subject as a direct injury to its dignity.[225] This was especially true when the subject represented the State. So, when the secretary of the Dutch ambassador to England was imprisoned in 1665, the province of Holland put the English ambassador's secretary in jail by way of reprisals.[226] Repeated attacks on subjects could also be regarded as a wrong committed against the whole State. In such cases, private claims were no longer treated individually but wholesale. Finally, States could resort to reprisals when it suffered a wrong or a loss personally.[227]

---

225 Butler and Maccoby, *The Development of International Law* (above, n. 63), 178.

226 Bynkershoek, *Quaestionum juris publici libri duo* (above, n. 33), Book I Cap. 24, here 1st vol., 177f. (tr. 2nd vol., 137). See further Cornelius van Bynkershoek, *Traité du Juge Competent des Ambassadeurs, Tant pour le Civil, que pour le Criminel* (La Haye: Thomas Johnson, 1723), 263–4. This form of reprisals, by which a person rather than property was arrested until the wrongdoing community gave satisfaction, was referred to by the Greek learned term 'androlepsia' (Grotius, *Le droit de la guerre et de la paix* (above, n. 33), Book III Ch. II § III.1, here at 2nd vol., 745. See also Neff, *War and the Law of Nations* (above, n. 2), 123). Examples of androlepsia were not uncommon in the seventeenth and eighteenth centuries. For instance, Johann Jacob Moser told that the King of Prussia arrested two Russian officers in his service as reprisals —actually in retalation— for the imprisonment of the baron of Stackelberg by the Empress of Russia in 1740 (Moser, *Versuch des neuesten Europäischen Völker=Rechts in Friedens= und Kriegs=Zeiten* (above, n. 205), 504–5). The peculiarity of this case is that Stackelberg was a Russian subject who served as an officer in the Prussian army. It is precisely on this latter basis that androlepsia followed, not on a bond of 'nationality'. For other examples of androlepsia, see Alphonse Rivier, *Principes du droit des gens*, 2nd vol. (Paris: Arthur Rousseau, 1896), 196.

227 See "[...], le Souverain demande justice, ou use de répresailles, non seulement pour ses propres affaires, mais encore pour celles de ses Sujets, qu'il doit protéger, & dont la Cause est celle de la Nation." (Vattel, *Le Droit des Gens. Ou Principes de la Loi naturelle, Appliqués à la conduite & aux affaires des Nations & des Souverains* (above, n. 202), 534).

From the sixteenth century until the early years of the nineteenth century, the most genuine public cause of complaint justifying a resort to reprisals was perhaps the infringement of neutrality law.[228] The neutral Sovereign initially granted letters of reprisal to his aggrieved subjects, e.g. when the prize courts of a warring nation condemned their ship and cargo.[229] However, the violation of neutral rights affected the neutral State directly too and gave it the unquestionable right to make reprisals on its own account against the wrongdoing warring party.[230] Such a course of action was not without danger, as the latter could treat it as an act of war.[231] Therefore, neutrals sometimes allied together to apply joint pressure by

---

228 About neutral reprisals, see Colbert, *Retaliation in international law* (above, n. 6), 107–23; Verzijl, *International law in historical perspective* (above, n. 112), Part IX-B, 36–38; Stephen C. Neff, *The rights and duties of neutrals: A general history* (Melland Schill studies in international law; Yonker, N.Y./Manchester: Juris Publishing/Manchester University Press, 2000), 71–3.

229 See the example cited by Zouche, *Iuris et Iudicii Fecialis, Sive, Iuris Inter Gentes, et Quaestionum de Eodem Explicatio* (above, n. 185), 1st vol., 131–132 (tr. 2nd vol., 125–126).

230 Cf. Martin Hübner, *De la Saisie des Batimens Neutres, ou Du Droit qu'ont les Nations Belligérantes d'arrêter les Navires des Peuples Amis*, 1st vol. (La Haye: [s.n.], 1759), 45–49; Joseph-Mathias Gérard de Rayneval, *De la liberté des mers*, 1st vol. (Paris: Treuttel et Wurtz/Arthus Bertrand/Delaunay, 1811), 250. For nineteenth-century opinions, see, i.a., Cesareo Fernandez, *Nociones de derecho internacional maritimo* (Habana: Imprenta del tiempo, 1863), 37; Laurent-Basile Hautefeuille, *Des droits et des devoirs des nations neutres en temps de guerre maritime*, 3rd vol. (3rd edn., Paris: Guillaumin et Cie, 1868), 346; Richard Kleen, *Lois et usages de la neutralité: D'après le droit international conventionnel et coutumier des États civilisés*, 1st vol. (Paris: A. Chevalier-Marescq, 1898), 130. Article 10 of the Fifth Hague Convention of 1907 respecting the Rights and Duties of Neutral Powers and Persons in Case of War on Land also seems to confirm this right: "The fact of a neutral Power resisting, even by force, attempts to violate its neutrality cannot be regarded as a hostile act."

231 Colbert, *Retaliation in international law* (above, n. 6), 115. That is why Thomas Jefferson warned against the recourse to reprisals in May 1793 in the so-called *The Little Sarah* affair. Indeed, when a French privateer ship purchased in Philadelphia captured a British vessel, the neutral United States were held responsible by Great Britain. Jefferson said on that occasion: "the making of reprisal on a nation is a very serious thing. [...] when reprisal follows it is considered as an act of war, & never yet failed to produce it in the case of a nation able to make war." (Paul Leicester Ford, *The Works of Thomas Jefferson*, 12 vols. (New York/London: G. P. Putnam's sons, 1904–1905), 7th vol., 335). However, a neutral nation could not eternally tolerate the violation of its neutrality. Therefore, the Harvard Draft on the Rights and Duties of Neutral States in Naval and Aerial War of 1939 expressly provided at Article 14 that "A neutral

way of reprisals on the delinquent belligerent.[232] This method allowed them to assert their rights and demand the recognition of some principles of neutrality law while not getting involved in the ongoing war.[233] Conversely, a belligerent also had a right to exercise reprisals against a neutral country that failed to maintain perfect impartiality.[234]

State shall not be deemed to have violated Article 4 of this Convention [i.e. the duty of impartiality laid upon neutrals] by resorting to acts of reprisal or retaliation against a belligerent because of illegal acts of the latter." (Harvard Research in International Law (ed.), *Drafts of conventions prepared for the codification of international law: I. Judicial Assistance, II. Rights and Duties of Neutral States in Naval and Aerial War, III. Rights and Duties of States in Case of Aggression*, Under the Auspices of the Faculty of the Harvard Law School, *AJIL* 33 (1939), Suppl., 329).

232 The bilateral treaties of alliance between neutral nations commonly contained a provision concerning the resort to joint reprisals until satisfaction would be obtained by all. See, e.g., the Articles of the Dano-Swedish Treaty of Stockholm of 17 March 1693 (Dumont, *Corps universel diplomatique du droit des gens* (above, n. 104), 7th vol., Part II, 325–327); Art. 7–8 of the Conventions of 9 July 1780 between Russia and Denmark, and 1 August 1780 between Russia and Sweden (Francis Taylor Piggott and George William Thomson Omond, *Documentary history of the armed neutralities, 1780 and 1800: together with selected documents relating to the war of American independence 1776–1783 and the Dutch war 1780–1784* ("Law of the Sea" Series, 1; London: University of London Press, 1919), 235–236, 242); Art. 12 of the Convention of 27 March 1794 between Denmark and Sweden-Norway (James Brown Scott, *The armed neutralities of 1780 and 1800: A collection of official documents preceded by the views of representative publicists* (Carnegie Endowment for International Peace: Division of International Law; New York: OUP, 1918), 443).

233 About those neutral alliances or leagues, see, i.a., Johann Eustach von Görtz, *Mémoire, ou précis historique sur la neutralité armée et son origine, Suivi de pièces justificatives* (Basle: J. Decker, 1801); Martens, *Causes célèbres du droit des gens* (above, n. 199), 3rd vol., 254–309; 4th vol., 219–302; Carl Bergbohm, *Die bewaffnete Neutralität, 1780–1783: Eine Entwicklungsphase des Völkerrechts im Seekriege* (Berlin: Puttkammer & Mühlbrecht, 1884); Carl Jacob Kulsrud, *Maritime Neutrality to 1780: A History of the Main Principles Governing Neutrality and Belligerency to 1780* (Boston: Little, Brown, and Company, 1936); Thorvald Boye, 'Quelques aspects du développement des règles de la neutralité', *RdC* 64/II (1938), 157–231, at 166–190.

234 Grotius, *Le droit de la guerre et de la paix* (above, n. 33), Book III Ch. I § V.5 – 8, here at 2nd vol., 717–719. Grotius did not explicitly refer to reprisals, but it flows from his explanation that the belligerent could obviously resort to this means as a form of compensation and coercion. See also Edward James Castle, *The law of commerce in time of war: with particular reference to the respective rights and duties of belligerents and neutrals* (London: William Maxwell & son, 1870), 54; Ludwig Gessner, *Le droit des neutres sur mer* (Bibliothèque diplomatique;

The fact that reprisals became 'public' had an impact on the law governing them. In the Middle Ages, rules were laid down by the Princes in order to limit reprisals and keep them within the bounds of what was acceptable. Yet, since the State no longer played the role of an authority of control but instead got directly involved in the procedure and execution of reprisals as main actor, those rules ceased to be treated as binding. As already seen, a denial of justice was no more required; the failure to obtain redress through diplomatic ways became the condition for reprisals. In fact, political considerations were pervasive.[235]

In this context, the plaintiff State felt the refusal to provide redress as a personal insult. It might explain why public reprisals did not observe a requirement of proportionality between the wrong and the amount of force employed and were principally used as a form of coercion applied on the wrongdoing nation, similar to some kind of punishment.[236] The so-called 'general' reprisals, a particular class of public reprisals, precisely followed this logic.

General reprisals consisted of the authorisation given by a Sovereign to all his subjects and the public fleet to capture property and persons from the rival country.[237] The proof of a personal loss was not necessary to make use of this right to fall upon property and persons of the enemy country.

2nd edn., Berlin: Charles Heymann, 1876), 125–7; Robert W. Tucker, *The Law of War and Neutrality at Sea* (U.S. Naval War College International Law Studies, 50; Washington: GPO, 1957), 261–2; Verzijl, *International law in historical perspective* (above, n. 112), Part IX-B, 38. The principle that a belligerent could make reprisals against the neutral party that committed a violation of neutrality was inserted into the Harvard Draft, at Article 24: "A belligerent may not resort to acts of reprisal or retaliation against a neutral State except for illegal acts of the latter, and a State is not to be charged with failure to perform its duties as a neutral State because it has not succeeded in inducing a belligerent to respect its rights as a neutral State." (Harvard Research in International Law (ed.), *Drafts of conventions prepared for the codification of international law* (above, n. 231), 419).

235 Cf. De Visscher, *Théories et réalités en droit international public* (above, n. 39), 348.

236 Cf. Colbert, *Retaliation in international law* (above, n. 6), 54–5; Hohl, 'Bartolus a Saxoferrato: Tractatus Represaliarum. Seine Bedeutung für die Entwicklungsgeschichte des Repressalienrechts' (above, n. 65), 1st vol., 142–143.

237 Cf. Grewe, *Epochen der Völkerrechtsgeschichte* (above, n. 24), 238; Neff, *War and the Law of Nations* (above, n. 2), 108. Orders of general reprisals were usually written in these terms: "his said Highnes, [...], doeth further alsoe by these presents grant, [...] universall reprisals against all and all manner of shipps and goods whatsoever belonging to the said the King of Spaine, and all and every his subjects whatsoever, both of Spaine and Flanders, and all other his dominions

The British Admiralty judges defended this opinion in 1652: general reprisals "may be issued, without proof of losses to individuals, against the Dutch, for redress of public losses, and to curb their insolences."[238]

This measure was much resorted to throughout the seventeenth and eighteenth centuries.[239] Although the reprisal-ordering country and the target country were still officially at peace due to the absence of a declaration of war, in many respects an order of general reprisals looked like a privateering commission in time of peace.[240] That is why general reprisals were often regarded as initiating the war, albeit it did not necessarily entail

---

and territories whatsoever; and doth hereby give full licence and authority that the said shipps and goods, and all shipps and goods whatsoever, belonging to the said king or his subjects, and every of them, may bee surprised and seized, either at sea or in ports or in land, and wheresoever they may be found, surprized, or seized, by the fleet and shipps of this Commonwealth or any other shipps or vessels to bee specially authorized and commissionated by the advice of his Councell, […]." (English Order in Council of 1655: Marsden, *Documents relating to law and custom of the sea* (above, n. 113), 2nd vol., 23–24).

238 Ibid., 2nd vol., 14. See also Neff, *War and the Law of Nations* (above, n. 2), 108.

239 See, e.g., general reprisals ordered in 1655 by England against Spain (Marsden, *Documents relating to law and custom of the sea* (above, n. 113), 2nd vol., 23–24); in 1664 by England against the Netherlands (Ibid., 2nd vol., 48–50), starting the Second Anglo-Dutch War; in 1689 by England against France (Ibid., 2nd vol., 123–124); in 1739 by Great Britain against Spain (Ibid., 2nd vol., 286), initiating the hostilities which culminated in the so-called War of Jenkin's Ear; in 1779 by Great Britain against Spain (James Dodsley, *The Annual Register: Or a View of the History, Politics and Literature, for the Year 1779*, 22nd vol. (London: Printed for J. Dodsley, 1780), 361–2). The last example —in fact, an isolated event since general reprisals were no longer in use by the nineteenth century— was the British Order in Council of 29 March 1854 marking Great Britain's entry into the Crimean War. See Francis Taylor Piggott, *The Declaration of Paris, 1856: A Study -documented-* ("Law of the Sea" Series of Historical and Legal Works, 4; London: University of London Press, 1919), 243–4.

240 Reprisals and privateering shared a common origin. See, i.a., W. L. Rodgers, 'Future International Laws of War', *AJIL* 33 (1939), 441–51, at 443; Verzijl, *International law in historical perspective* (above, n. 112), Part IX-C, 153; David J. Starkey, *British privateering enterprise in the eighteenth century* (Exeter Maritime Studies, 4; Exeter: University of Exeter Press, 1990), 20–1; Ziegler, *Völkerrechtsgeschichte* (above, n. 62), 128. Since the Middle Ages, Sovereigns had granted individuals privateering commissions —often called indistinctly 'letter of marque', 'letter of reprisal' or 'letter of marque or reprisal'— in order to augment the naval force in wartime. Cf. Charles La Mache, *La guerre de course dans le passé, dans le présent et dans l'avenir* (Paris: A. Pedone, 1901), 17; Marsden, *Documents relating to law and custom of the sea* (above, n. 113), 1st vol., XXVI–XXVII; Neff, *War and the Law of Nations* (above, n. 2), 109. Furthermore, general reprisals were similar to privateering because the seizure was not limited to a

all the legal consequences attached to war.[241] In any case, the use of a belligerent measure under the guise of reprisals highlights the political nature of general reprisals.[242]

---

certain amount for compensation and because a share of the spoils went to the captor —one half of the prize, according to the opinion of the British Admiralty judges in 1652. See Marsden, *Documents relating to law and custom of the sea* (above, n. 113), 2nd vol., 14; Verzijl, *International law in historical perspective* (above, n. 112), Part IX-C, 156; Neff, *War and the Law of Nations* (above, n. 2), 108–9.
This led to some confusion between reprisals as a means for obtaining redress and privateering activities. See, e.g., William Oke Manning, *Commentaries of the law of nations* (London: S. Sweet, 1839), 111–6; [Anonymous], 'The law relating to letters of marque and reprisals.', *The Legal Observer, or Journal of Jurisprudence* 19 (1839–1840), 481–2; B. F., 'The International Law of Embargo and Reprisal', *The Law Magazine; Or Quarterly Review of Jurisprudence* 24 (1840), 73–9. That is why it has been asserted that the Declaration of Paris respecting maritime law of 16 April 1856 abolished not only privateering but also special or general reprisals. See, e.g., Mr Sanford's report on special reprisals addressed to Mr Cass, 16 August 1857: Sanford, *The Aves Island Case* (above, n. 43), 262; Frederick Edwin Smith and Norman Wise Sibley, *International law as interpreted during the Russo-Japanese War* (2nd edn., London: T. Fisher Unwin, William Clowes and sons, 1907), 354f.; Percy Bordwell, *The Law of War Between Belligerents: A History and Commentary* (Chicago: Callaghan & Co., 1908), 18; Fahl, 'Repressalie' (above, n. 84), col. 912; Mckinnon, 'Reprisals as a Method of Enforcing International Law' (above, n. 9), 223. Cf. Pierre Bravard-Veyrières, *Des prises maritimes d'après l'ancient et le nouveau droit tel qu'il résulte du traité de Paris et de la déclaration du 16 avril 1856*, avec des notes par P. Royer-Collard (Paris: Cotillon, 1861), 21.

241 For statesmen, there was overall no difference between general reprisals and open war. See the opinion of Johan de Witt who was Grand Pensionary of Holland in the seventeenth century, quoted by Twiss, *The law of nations considered as independent political communities* (above, n. 224), 31; Albert Gallatin to Edward Everett, 5 January 1835: Henry Adams, *The Writings of Albert Gallatin*, 2nd vol. (Philadelphia: J.B. Lippincott, 1879), 477. See also Georg Friedrich von Martens, *Précis du droit des gens moderne de l'Europe, fondé sur les traités et l'usage*, Auquel on a joint la liste des principaux traités conclus depuis 1748 jusqu'à présent avec l'indication des ouvrages où ils se trouvent, 2nd vol. (Gottingue: chez Jean Chret. Dieterich, 1789), 328f. In the judgement of *The Maria Magdalena*, pronounced on 11 January 1779, the Judge of the High Court of Admiralty, Sir James Marriott, also argued that an order of general reprisals was tantamount to a declaration of war (Edward Stanley Roscoe, *Reports of prize cases determined in the High Court of Admiralty, before the Lords Commissioners of Appeals in prize causes, and before the Judicial Committee of the Privy Council, from 1745 to 1859*, 1st vol. (London: Stevens and sons, 1905), 23). Cf. with the opinion of seventeenth-century English jurist Sir Matthew Hale who became Chief Justice of the King's Bench (Matthew Hale, *Historia Placitorum Coronæ: The History of the Pleas*

(b) Blurring of the Line between War and Peace

By ceasing to aim at compensation, reprisals became a form of coercion used by the State. In the process, they could no longer be differentiated from other measures, especially war. Indeed, reprisals were rarely proportionate to the offence, and their employment was often arbitrary.

However, reprisals had always shared a close affinity with war. The whole law of reprisals laid down in the Middle Ages was largely modelled on the just-war theory.[243] For medieval jurists, reprisals were thus equivalent to war.[244] Yet back then, the concept of war covered a broader spectrum of measures: from war in the true sense to 'particular' forms such as reprisals, self-defence and duel.[245] But as a military revolution began in the sixteenth century, war became "far more disruptive than it had been be-

---

of the Crown, 1st vol. (new edn., London: T. Payne, H. L. Gardner, W. Otridge, E. and R. Brooke and J. Rider, J. Butterworth, W. Clarke and Son, R. Phenet, J. Cuthell, J. Walker, J. Bagster, and R. Bickerstaff, 1800), 161–2). However, in other judgements, Sir Marriott attributed to general reprisals legal effects different from those of a declaration of war. See *The Pere Adam*, judgement of 13 November 1778 (George Hay and James Marriott, *Decisions in the High Court of Admiralty: During The Time of Sir George Hay, and of Sir James Marriott, Late Judges of That Court. Michaelmas Term, 1776, to Hilary Term, 1779.*, 1st vol. (London: R. Bickerstaff, 1801), 141); *The Renard*, judgement of 9 December 1778 (Roscoe, *Reports of prize cases determined in the High Court of Admiralty, before the Lords Commissioners of Appeals in prize causes, and before the Judicial Committee of the Privy Council, from 1745 to 1859* (above, n. 241), 19). Another legal effect, according to U.S. President Thomas Jefferson, was that hostilities could be ended by merely repealing the order of general reprisals, whereas the termination of war required the signature of a peace treaty (Thomas Jefferson to Lieutenant Governor Levi Lincoln, 13 November 1808: Ford, *The Works of Thomas Jefferson* (above, n. 231), 11th vol., 74).

242 Colbert, *Retaliation in international law* (above, n. 6), 57.

243 Grewe, *Epochen der Völkerrechtsgeschichte* (above, n. 24), 145–6; Neff, *War and the Law of Nations* (above, n. 2), 80; Ziegler, *Völkerrechtsgeschichte* (above, n. 62), 110. This remained true beyond the Middle Ages. For example, Diego de Covarrubias still dealt in the sixteenth century with reprisals in the same just-war fashion (Diego de Covarrubias y Leyva, *Opera omnia: in duos tomos divisa* (Genève: Gabriel de Tournes & filiorum, 1724), 636).

244 See, e.g., Legnano, *Tractatus de Bello, de Represaliis et de Duello* (above, n. 88), Cap. II, at 79 (tr. at 217); Bonet, *L'arbre des batailles* (above, n. 117), Part 4, Ch. LXXXII, here at 183.

245 Haggenmacher, 'L'ancêtre de la protection diplomatique. les représailles de l'ancien droit (XIIe-XVIIIe siècles)' (above, n. 3), 11.

fore."[246] As a consequence, the maintenance of peaceful relations was no longer possible during a conflict and, hence, war and peace separated into two different states of affairs.[247] In this context, reprisals could not be assimilated to war anymore since their use did not completely disrupt the state of peace. In fact, unlike 'perfect' war (*bellum plenum*) which implied an armed conflict between two nations as a whole (*"ex bellis plenis quæ populi populis inferunt"*, according to Hugo Grotius), reprisals amounted to an 'imperfect' form of war, i.e. the enforcement of a right through the limited resort to force.[248]

Nevertheless, the opinion that reprisals were compatible with peace — although it was acknowledged that they might prelude war[249]— related mainly to 'private' reprisals as a means to obtain compensation, which fol-

246 Randall Lesaffer, 'The classical law of nations (1500–1800)', in Alexander Orakhelashvili (ed.), *Research Handbook on the Theory and History of International Law* (Cheltenham/Northampton, Mass.: Edward Elgar, 2011), 408–40, at 427.

247 Ibid., 428.

248 Hugo Grotius, *De Jure Belli ac Pacis Libri Tres*, 2 vols. (The Classics of International Law, 3; Oxford: Clarendon Press, 1923–1925), 1st vol., 444. See also Jean-Jacques Burlamaqui, *Principes du droit politiques*, 2nd vol. (Bibliothèque de Philosophie politique et juridique: Textes et Documents; Caen [Amsterdam]: Centre de Philosophie politique et juridique de l'Université de Caen [chez Zacharie Chatelain], 1987 [1752]), 56–57; Jaucourt, 'Représailles' (above, n. 192), 142; Wolff, *Jus Gentium Methodo Scientifica Pertractatum* (above, n. 197), § 603. But cf. with the opinion of the Supreme Court of the State of New York about imperfect war in the judgement *The People v McLeod* (July 1841) related to the famous *Caroline* affair (John Lansing Wendell, *Reports of Cases Argued and Determined in the Supreme Court of Judicature and in the Court for the Trial of Impeachments and the Correction of Errors of the State of New-York*, 25th vol. (2nd edn., New-York: Published by the reporter, 1850), 576–7). About imperfect war, see further Neff, *War and the Law of Nations* (above, n. 2), 119–120 and 122–126; Kathryn L. Einspanier, 'Burlamaqui, the Constitution and the Imperfect War on Terror', *GeoLJ* 96 (2007–2008), 985–1026, at 988–990.

249 See, e.g., Francisco de Vitoria's *De Jure Belli*, § 41, translated by Scott, *The Spanish Origin of International Law* (above, n. 192), LXIV; Samuel von Pufendorf, *Le droit de la nature et des gens*, Traduction de Jean Barbeyrac, 2nd vol. (Bibliothèque de Philosophie politique et juridique: Textes et Documents; Caen [Bâle]: Centre de Philosophie politique et juridique de l'Université de Caen [chez E. & J. R. Thourneisen], 1987 [1732]), 466. But cf. Pothier and Estrangin, *Traité du contrat d'assurance de Pothier* (above, n. 223), 97.
Since reprisals could lead to an all-out war between the reprisal-taking country and the target country, nineteenth-century criminal laws frequently provided harsh punishment for those citizens who, by their acts or behaviour, gave rise to reprisals (Roy Emerson Curtis, 'The Law of Hostile Military Expeditions as Applied by the United States', *AJIL* 8 (1914), 224–55, at 240). See, e.g., § 136 of the

lowed a well-elaborated set of rules.[250] The situation was different for public reprisals.

For being ordered by the Sovereign after the failure of diplomatic negotiations and for being conducted by the State's armed forces or the whole nation, the resemblance of reprisals to war was troubling.[251] At a time when war used to begin in the vast majority of cases without a formal declaration,[252] the resort to reprisals was thus not insignificant. It actually could aim at the intimidation of the target country in the hope that the latter would submit to the demands. Reprisals could be used likewise to secure a dominant position over the opponent in anticipation of overt hostil-

Allgemeines Landrecht für die Preussischen Staaten of 1794 (Prussia, *Allgemeines Landrecht für die Preussischen Staaten*, 4th vol. (2nd edn., Berlin: Pauli, 1794), 1193f.); Art. 84 and 85 of Napoleon's Penal Code of 1810 (reproduced in Pistoye and Duverdy, *Traité des prises maritimes* (above, n. 223), 91); Art. 123 of the Peruvian Penal Code (mentioned in Paul Pradier-Fodéré, 'Note sur la question du Luxor', in Institut de Droit International (ed.), *Session d'Oxford – Septembre 1880* (Annuaire IDI, vol. 5; Bruxelles: C. Muquardt, Merzbach et Falk, 1882), 183–200, at 189); the Norwegian law of 16 May 1904 (referred to in Maurel, *De la Déclaration de Guerre* (above, n. 27), 173 fn. 1).

250 See, e.g., Molloy, *De Jure Maritimo et Navali* (above, n. 186), 31; Glafey, *Vernünfft- Und Völcker-Recht* (above, n. 135), Book VI, Ch. 1, § 14, here at 4; Valin, *Nouveau commentaire sur l'Ordonnance de la marine du mois d'août 1681* (above, n. 175), 417; Bynkershoek, *Quaestionum juris publici libri duo* (above, n. 33), Book I Cap. 24, here 1st vol., 173 (tr. 2nd vol., 134). See further Clark, 'The English Practice with Regard to Reprisals by Private Persons' (above, n. 4), 711.

251 At a time when the use of public reprisals was still not fully established, it is not surprising that their enforcement was regarded as amounting to war. A French ambassador stressed this feature before the British Parliament in 1652: "Ce droit [viz. the right of reprisals] a été introduit et réservé par les traités de paix, pour réparer les pertes de ceux à qui la justice est déniée, en leur permettant de se venger sur le bien des particuliers, mais il est encore inouï qu'aucune nation l'ait étendu sur le bien d'un Prince, ni qu'on ait employé les forces publiques pour le mettre à exécution. Il n'y aurait point autrement de différence entre une déclaration de guerre et des lettres de marques." (France, Ministère des Affaires étrangères, *Recueil des instructions données aux ambassadeurs et ministres de France depuis les traités de Westphalie jusqu'à la Révolution française*, 24th vol. (Paris: E. De Boccard, 1929), 159). The French ambassador here complained that reprisals were executed by the public force and targeted ships belonging to the King of France. Therefore, he did not see any difference between war and reprisals.

252 See John Frederick Maurice, *Hostilities Without Declaration of War: An Historical Abstract of the Cases in which Hostilities have occurred between civilized Powers prior to Declaration or Warning. From 1700 to 1870* (London: Her Majesty's Stationery Office, 1883), 4.

ities: by weakening the adversary materially, by gaining time to forge alliances or by letting the target country bear the responsibility of declaring war.[253]

Such employment of reprisals created situations where two contesting States were engaged in hostilities on a large scale but were not at war *de jure*. The so-called sixteenth-century 'Wars of Reprisals' are good examples where two countries, viz. France and England (1547–1549) and England and Spain (1563–1573), committed depredations in ports or on the high seas against each other under the pretext that subjects were denied justice for their loss.[254] Those episodes of violence, in fact, introduced an ambiguous state of affairs. By the middle of the eighteenth century, the use of reprisals thus pertained to an intermediate state between peace and war.[255]

---

253 Cf. Colbert, *Retaliation in international law* (above, n. 6), 55; Grewe, *Epochen der Völkerrechtsgeschichte* (above, n. 24), 431.

254 Cf. Thomas Alfred Walker, *A history of the law of nations*, 1st vol. (Cambridge: CUP, 1899), 187–8; Colbert, *Retaliation in international law* (above, n. 6), 48; Hohl, 'Bartolus a Saxoferrato: Tractatus Represaliarum. Seine Bedeutung für die Entwicklungsgeschichte des Repressalienrechts' (above, n. 65), 1st vol., 143; Grewe, *Epochen der Völkerrechtsgeschichte* (above, n. 24), 238. See further the secret instructions which were given: Germain Lefèvre-Pontalis, *Correspondance politique de Odet de Selve, ambassadeur de France en Angleterre (1546–1549)*, publiée sous les auspices de la Commission des Archives Diplomatiques (Inventaire analytique des archives du Ministère des affaires étrangères; Paris: Félix Alcan, 1888), 450; Michael Oppenheim, *A history of the administration of the royal navy and of merchant shipping in relation to the navy: From MDIX to MDCLX with an introduction treating of the preceding period*, 1st vol. (London and New York: John Lane The Bodley Head, 1896), 104f.

255 Maurice, *Hostilities Without Declaration of War* (above, n. 252), 5; Julian Stafford Corbett, *England in the Seven Years' War: A Study in Combined Strategy*, 1st vol. (London: Longmans, Green, and Co., 1907), 24.
Sir William Scott's judgement in *The Boedes Lust* (1804) illustrates perfectly the ambiguity of the use of coercion such as reprisals. In this case, Great Britain placed an embargo upon all Dutch ships in English harbours following the declaration of war against France on 16 May 1803. The idea behind this measure was to compel the Batavian Republic to remain neutral and not side with France. Nevertheless, war eventually broke out between the said Republic and Great Britain. A legal issue was raised before the High Court of Admiralty whether prior to the beginning of war the ships had been merely sequestrated or confiscated as good prizes. Sir William Scott pronounced the confiscation for the following grounds: "[The seizure] was at first equivocal; and if the matter in dispute had terminated in reconciliation, the seizure would have been converted into a mere civil embargo, so terminated. That would have been the retroactive effect of that course of circumstances. On the contrary, if the transactions end in hostility, the retroactive effect is directly the other way. It impresses the

(c) Vattel's Pertinent Remark

It is clear that the resort to reprisals was far from being justified in each case. Indeed, the decision to make use of this measure was sometimes guided by considerations of a purely political and strategic nature. For example, jealousy over the French expansion in North America drove Great Britain to capture all kinds of French ships between 1754 and 1756 despite the absence of an order of general reprisals or a declaration of war. It was ultimately in 1756 that the Seven Years' War officially began.[256] By not declaring war and resorting to so-called reprisals, Great Britain manifestly aimed to put the onus of the declaration of war on France, prevent a Spanish attack and receive the support of Dutch troops pursuant to a defensive alliance agreement.[257]

---

direct hostile character upon the original seizure. It is declared to be no embargo; it is no longer an equivocal act, subject to two interpretations; there is a declaration of the *animus*, by which it was done, that it was *done hostili animo*, and is to be considered as an hostile measure *ab initio*. The property taken is liable to be used as the property of persons, trespassers *ab initio*, and guilty of injuries, which they have refused to redeem by any amicable alteration of their measures. This is the necessary course, if no particular compact intervenes for the restitution of such property taken before a formal declaration of hostilities." (Christopher Robinson, *Reports of Cases Argued and Determined in the High Court of Admiralty: Commencing with the Judgments of the Right Hon. Sir William Scott. Michaelmas Term, 1798*, 6 vols. (Boston: Little, Brown and Company, 1853), 5th vol., 246 (emphasis in original)). Cf. Sir William Scott's judgement of 19 July 1799 in *The Herstelder* case (Ibid., 1st vol., 116–119). In other words, the use of embargo was tantamount to a conditional declaration of war. Reprisals in that epoch and already in the eighteenth century followed the same logic. They constituted a double-edged sword. On *The Boedes Lust* case, see Horst Sasse, 'Boedes Lust-Fall', in Karl Strupp and Hans-Jürgen Schlochauer (eds.), *Wörterbuch des Völkerrechts*, begründet von Professor Dr. Karl Strupp, 3 vols. (2nd edn., Berlin: Walter De Gruyter & Co., 1960–1962), 1st vol., 219.

256 See Alfred Thayer Mahan, *The influence of sea power upon history, 1660–1783* (12th edn., Boston: Little, Brown and Company, 1890), 283–5; John Westlake, 'Reprisals and War', *The Law Quarterly Review* 25 (1909), 127–37, at 129–130; Grewe, *Epochen der Völkerrechtsgeschichte* (above, n. 24), 430f.

257 Colbert, *Retaliation in international law* (above, n. 6), 56. Yet, France was not ready to bear that responsibility. The King of France, therefore, required the restitution of the French vessels and made some amicable offers, but stressed that Great Britain's refusal would be tantamount to an open declaration of war (François-Joachim de Pierre de Bernis, *Memoirs and letters of Cardinal de Bernis in two volumes*, with an introduction by C.-A. Sainte-Beuve. Translated by Katharine Prescott Wormeley. Illustrated with portraits from the original, 1st vol. (New York: P. F. Collier & Son, [1901]), 222).

Those occurrences inspired the famous Swiss international lawyer Emer de Vattel[258] a reflection on the use of reprisals in his days:

> "Il est des cas cependant, où les Répresailles seroient condamnables, lors même qu'une Déclaration de Guerre ne le seroit pas; & ce sont précisément ceux dans lesquels les Nations peuvent avec justice prendre les armes. Lorsqu'il s'agit dans le différend, non d'une voie de fait, d'un tort reçu, mais d'un droit contesté; après que l'on a inutilement tenté les voies de conciliation, ou les moyens pacifiques d'obtenir justice, c'est la Déclaration de Guerre qui doit suivre, & non de prétendues Répresailles, lesquelles, en pareil cas, ne seroient que de vrais actes d'hostilité, sans Déclaration de Guerre, & se trouveroient contraires à la foi publique, aussi bien qu'aux devoirs mutuels des Nations."[259]

Vattel made a shrewd observation in this quote. Indeed, he stressed here the hypocrisy of the employment of reprisals. He argued that in the situations where a declaration of war was a legitimate option (e.g., when a right was challenged), the use of reprisals should be precluded because it would be a cowardly way to begin the hostilities. That is why he called them '*pretended* reprisals' since they fooled nobody about their true nature and their real implications. These pretended reprisals were actual acts of war.[260]

---

258 On Vattel, see Emmanuelle Jouannet, 'Emer de Vattel (1714–1767)', in Bardo Fassbender and Anne Peters (eds.), *The Oxford Handbook of the History of International Law* (Oxford: OUP, 2012), 1118–21.

259 Vattel, *Le Droit des Gens. Ou Principes de la Loi naturelle, Appliqués à la conduite & aux affaires des Nations & des Souverains* (above, n. 202), 540–541. Joseph Chitty's English translation of this passage reads: "There are cases, however, in which reprisals would be justly condemnable, even when a declaration of war would not be so: and these are precisely those cases in which nations may with justice take up arms. When the question which constitutes the ground of a dispute, relates, not to an act of violence, or an injury received, but to a contested right,—after an ineffectual endeavour to obtain justice by a conciliatory and pacific measures, it is a declaration of war that ought to follow, and not pretended reprisals, which, in such a case, would only be real acts of hostility without a declaration of war, and would be contrary to public faith as well as to the mutual duties of nations." (Emer de Vattel, *The Law of Nations; Or Principles of the Law of Nature, applied to the Conduct and Affairs of Nations and Sovereigns*, edited by Joseph Chitty (6th edn., Philadelphia: T. & J. W. Johnson, 1844), 289).

260 During the peace negotiations of the Seven Years' War, Louis XV's Chief Minister Étienne-François de Choiseul demanded the restitution of the French ships captured before the declaration of war in 1756. His observations about the British reprisals curiously echoed Vattel's remark. Indeed, he argued that if

This remark concludes the part on reprisals in his *Law of Nations*. It thus makes the reader wonder to what extent reprisals were still valid as a compensatory measure in the second half of the eighteenth century. In fact, the impression which comes out of Vattel's comment is that the use of reprisals no longer obeyed clear rules; in other words, that States employed reprisals in a discretionary and arbitrary manner to apply pressure on the target country without bearing the responsibility for declaring war.

However, it does not mean that Vattel disapproved reprisals altogether. He regarded them as a milder measure; war being the *ultima ratio*.[261] But the case had to lend itself to their use. He actually explained that reprisals aimed at compensation. So, the claims giving rise to them had to be capable of a pecuniary statement. It did not matter whether those claims resulted from a debt or an injury suffered by either the State itself or its subjects, as long as they were well-ascertained, undeniable and assessable in money terms.[262] For Vattel, it was thus clear that the resort to reprisals was not allowed for political claims.[263]

Only when a claim could be valued in money terms was the recourse to reprisals commendable and preferable to war as a means of settlement of dispute.[264] Still, Vattel knew that their use did not mean that the issue would be terminated without a hitch. He, indeed, noted that war was like-

---

Great Britain had motives for complaint against France on account of hostilities in the American colonies, the adequate response was not to engage into dubious reprisals but rather to declare war. On this basis, the refusal to return the captures was considered by Choiseul unlawful (The French Memorial, 15 July 1761: Étienne-François de Choiseul, *An Historical Memorial of the Negotiation of France and England, From the 26th of March, 1761, to the 20th of September of the same Year*, With the Vouchers. Translated from the *French Original*, published at *Paris* by Authority (London: Printed for D. Wilson, and T. Becket and P. A. Dehondt in the Strand, 1761), 51–3).
However, Moser, *Versuch des neuesten Europäischen Völker=Rechts in Friedens= und Kriegs=Zeiten* (above, n. 205), 501–2, considered that nobody could judge the justice of reprisals because of the independence of the Sovereigns between each other. In fact, he argued that reprisals were preferable when the Sovereign wanted to avoid waging an all-out war.

261 Vattel, *Le Droit des Gens. Ou Principes de la Loi naturelle, Appliqués à la conduite & aux affaires des Nations & des Souverains* (above, n. 202), 539.

262 Ibid., 1st vol., 531 and 534.

263 Westlake, 'Reprisals and War' (above, n. 256), 129–30. But cf. Spiegel, 'Origin and Development of Denial of Justice' (above, n. 61), 76–7.

264 Vattel, *Le Droit des Gens. Ou Principes de la Loi naturelle, Appliqués à la conduite & aux affaires des Nations & des Souverains* (above, n. 202), 540. See further on peaceful settlement of international disputes in Vattel's, Lucius Caflisch, 'Vattel

lier to happen when reprisals targeted a Power of strength equal to the reprisal-taking State.[265]

IV. Interim Conclusion

The legal situation of reprisals was far from being clear-cut at the end of the eighteenth century. Indeed, the transformation of reprisals from a measure of private international law into one of public international law greatly affected the law governing them. Reprisals, which were initially used to protect private interests, soon became resorted to by States as an instrument of public policy. And yet, the rules were not adapted to fit the political reality of sovereign States.

Throughout the Middle Ages, the concern prevailed that reprisals, if they could not be abolished entirely, had at least to be strictly regulated. The idea behind the elaboration of rules governing reprisals was the conciliation of two interests: on the one hand, the public interest consisted in the protection of commerce and the preservation of peace; on the other, the defence of private interests when no compensation could be obtained by judicial means, hence the reason why reprisals were a necessary evil. The result was the adoption of restrictions at both local and international levels in the form of procedural norms which regulated in detail all the aspects of the practice. This process of 'normatization' was then consolidated and standardised through the work of influential jurists like Bartolus de Saxoferrato, who modelled the law of reprisals on the law of just war.

However, the centralisation of power, as a consequence of the creation of modern States which began in the sixteenth century, led to the politicisation of reprisals and thence to the dismantling of this legal framework. Indeed, States became the only actors in the whole procedure of reprisals, excluding the individuals at all stages and turning the question of reprisals into an affair of State. Sovereigns often departed from the strict observance of the rules of the law of reprisals in order to achieve their own political

---

and the peaceful settlement of international disputes', in Vincent Chetail and Peter Haggenmacher (eds.), *Vattel's International Law in a XXIst Century Perspective* (Graduate Institute of International and Development Studies, 9; Leiden/Boston: Martinus Nijhoff Publishers, 2011), 257–66; Hersch Lauterpacht, *The Function of Law in the International Community* (1st edn. of 1933, Oxford: OUP, 2011), 7–9.

265 Vattel, *Le Droit des Gens. Ou Principes de la Loi naturelle, Appliqués à la conduite & aux affaires des Nations & des Souverains* (above, n. 202), 540.

goals. In this context, the political considerations concretely superseded the legal rules governing reprisals. In State practice, these rules had then been reduced to abstract principles, i.e. mere guidelines for the use of reprisals.

Therefore, when the nineteenth century began, it can be said that the employment of reprisals was no longer subject to a clear-cut regulation but was instead governed by vague standards and influenced by national policy.

Chapter Two. Shaping of a Prerogative, 1831–1863

I. Introduction

The State practice of reprisals prior to the nineteenth century had mainly led to the obliteration of the significance of the ancient law of reprisals. The weight of national policy in the decision to resort to reprisals gained ascendency over the strict observance of some rules. Therefore, there was, in a way, a gap between State practice and doctrine as lawyers sometimes still emphasised the importance of some requirements like a denial of justice. Moreover, the difference between war and reprisals was almost non-existent. It was in this context that Vattel warned against the practice that prevailed in his days, around the middle of the eighteenth century. Although he regarded reprisals as a milder means than war and thus maintained that they had to be preferred over the latter measure whenever possible, he did not fail to observe that the employment of reprisals against a Power of equal strength was almost impossible without creating a state of war. However, between 1831 and 1863, reprisals were actually about to become a measure claimed to be consistent with peace and employed only by great Powers against small and weak States against which the enterprise of war was not worthwhile.

The present chapter argues that, during those three decades when the frequency of occurrences of acts of coercion classified as reprisals was high, the State practice of the great Powers shaped armed reprisals into a privilege in international law. Indeed, by playing on the asymmetric power relation existing to their advantage, the great Powers claimed the non-interruption of peace while at the same time using a vast amount of force as a form of coercion, even the kind of violence typically confined to wartime. Reprisals were an alternative to war, but reserved only to the strongest countries acting against weaker States. If the conditions of power relations were different —viz, when the target country was of equal or superior strength as the reprisal-taking State—, the employment of reprisals involving armed force would inexorably be treated as an act of war and then lead to open warfare. The resort to armed reprisals was consequently reserved to a limited group of countries, i.e. those that always had the upper hand when an issue occurred with a weaker State: the great Powers.

II. Asymmetric Power Relation

1. Portrait of Target Countries

(a) Preliminary Observation: 'Reprisal Clause' in Bilateral Treaties

Until the end of the eighteenth century, bilateral treaties of peace and commerce between European States systematically included a standard clause that governed the lawful use of reprisals between them.[266] Nonetheless, by the turn of the next century, this practice was discontinued, at least between Western Powers.[267]

In the course of the nineteenth century, Western Powers and the newly founded Latin American countries concluded amongst themselves many bilateral treaties of amity and peace which were modelled on the U.S.–French treaty of peace, friendship and commerce of 30 September 1800.[268]

266 Cf. Stephen C. Neff, *Justice among Nations: A History of International Law* (Cambridge, Mass.: HUP, 2014), 202.

267 Indeed, the standard clause is nowhere to be found in Georg Friedrich von Martens, *Nouveau recueil de traités d'Alliance, de Paix, de Trêve, de Neutralité, de Commerce, de Limites, d'Echange etc. et de plusieurs autres actes servant à la connoissance des relations étrangères des Puissances et Etats de l'Europe tant dans leur rapport mutuel que dans celui envers les Puissances et Etats dans d'autres parties du globe depuis 1808 jusqu'à présent*, 16 vols. (Göttingen: Dans la librairie de Dieterich, 1817–1842). However, there were still occasional references to reprisals in some treaties between Western Powers, such as Art. 11 of a project of convention in 1825 between Spain and the United States (Great Britain, F. O., *BFSP 1830–1831* (18th vol.; London: James Ridgway, 1833), 6f.). But this kind of mention became more seldom as the nineteenth century moved on. Quite peculiar in this respect are the custom union treaties between German principalities which stipulated the adoption of measures of reprisals or retorsion (mostly in the form of an increase of custom duties), either by the union as a whole or by each Member State separately, against non-Member States. See, e.g., Art. 9 and 18 of the Treaty of Kassel, 24 September 1828: Martens, *Nouveau recueil de traités d'Alliance, de Paix, de Trêve, de Neutralité, de Commerce, de Limites, d'Echange etc. et de plusieurs autres actes servant à la connoissance des relations étrangères des Puissances et Etats de l'Europe tant dans leur rapport mutuel que dans celui envers les Puissances et Etats dans d'autres parties du globe depuis 1808 jusqu'à présent* (above, n. 267), VII/2, 697f. and 701; Separate Article 20 Para. 3 to Art. 39 of the Treaty of Berlin, 4 April 1853: Great Britain, F. O., *BFSP 1855–1856* (46th vol.; London: William Ridgway, 1865), 1176.

268 Alejandro Álvarez, *Le droit international américain: Son fondement – sa nature, d'après l'Histoire diplomatique des Etats du Nouveau Monde et leur Vie Politique et Économique* (Paris: A. Pedone, 1910), 89. See the said U.S.-French Convention in

However, while the latter convention did not contain any reference to reprisals, it is striking that a 'reprisal clause' ordinarily figured in those bilateral treaties with a Latin American State. The provision —a kind of standard clause due to the identical wording, with sometimes slight modifications— stipulated that, if any article of the said treaty should be infringed or violated, neither reprisals nor war could be resorted to, unless justice and satisfaction were refused or unduly delayed despite the fact that a formal complaint substantiated by proof had been presented.[269]

Miller, *Treaties and other international acts of the United States of America* (above, n. 195), 457ff.

269 The standard clause was generally the same as Art. 31 Sec. 3, of the U.S.–Colombia treaty of 3 October 1824. See Martens, *Nouveau recueil de traités d'Alliance, de Paix, de Trêve, de Neutralité, de Commerce, de Limites, d'Echange etc. et de plusieurs autres actes servant à la connoissance des relations étrangères des Puissances et Etats de l'Europe tant dans leur rapport mutuel que dans celui envers les Puissances et Etats dans d'autres parties du globe depuis 1808 jusqu'à présent* (above, n. 267), 6th vol., Part II, 1008. Without claiming to be exhaustive, cf. the conventions between U.S.A.–Confederation of Central America, 5 December 1825, Art. 33 Sec. 3 (Ibid., VI/2, 839); U.S.A.–Brazil, 12 December 1828, Art. 33 Sec. 3 (Ibid., 9th vol., 67); U.S.A.–Mexico, 5 April 1831, Art. 34 Sec. 3 (Great Britain, F. O., *BFSP 1831–1832* (19th vol.; London: James Ridgway, 1834), 231); U.S.A.–Chile, 16 May 1832, Art. 31 Sec. 3 (Great Britain, F. O., *BFSP 1833–1834* (22nd vol.; London: James Ridgway and sons, 1847), 1363); France–Bolivia, 9 December 1834, Art. 31 (Great Britain, F. O., *BFSP 1834–1835* (23rd vol.; London: James Ridgway and sons, 1852), 186f.); U.S.A.–Venezuela, 20 January 1836, Art. 34 Sec. 3 (Martens, *Nouveau recueil de traités d'Alliance, de Paix, de Trêve, de Neutralité, de Commerce, de Limites, d'Echange etc. et de plusieurs autres actes servant à la connoissance des relations étrangères des Puissances et Etats de l'Europe tant dans leur rapport mutuel que dans celui envers les Puissances et Etats dans d'autres parties du globe depuis 1808 jusqu'à présent* (above, n. 267), 13th vol., 570); U.S.A.–Peru-Bolivian Confederation, 13 November 1836, Art. 29 Sec. 3 (Ibid., 15th vol., 125f.); Hanse Towns–Venezuela, 27 May 1837, Art. 25 (Ibid., 14th vol., 248); U.S.A.–Ecuador, 13 June 1839, Art. 35 Sec. 3 (Great Britain, F. O., *BFSP 1840–1841* (29th vol.; London: James Ridgway and sons, 1857), 1305f.); Spain–Ecuador, 16 February 1840, Art. 19 Sec. 2 (Ibid., 1319); U.S.A.–Portugal, 26 August 1840, Art. 14 Sec. 3 (Ibid., 1311f.); France–Venezuela, 3 April 1843, Art. 30 (Alexandre Jehan Henry de Clercq and Jules de Clercq, *Recueil des traités de la France*, publié sous les auspices de S. Exc. M. Drouyn de Lhuys, Ministre des Affaires Étrangères, 23 vols. (Paris: Amyot, 1864–1917), 5th vol., 16f.); France–Ecuador, 6 June 1843, Art. 28 Sec. 2 (Ibid., 5th vol., 99); Spain–Chile, 25 April 1844, Art. 12 (Great Britain, F. O., *BFSP 1845–1846* (34th vol.; London: Harrison and sons, 1860), 1111); France–New Granada, 28 October 1844, Art. 27 Para. 2 (Great Britain, F. O., *BFSP 1846–1847* (35th vol.; London: Printed by Harrison and sons, 1860), 1026); Spain–Venezuela, 30 March 1845, Art. 19 Sec. 2 (Ibid., 305); Spain–Uruguay, 26 March

The Latin American countries might have wished to insert this 'reprisal

---

1846, Art. 19 Sec. 2 (Murhard et al., *Nouveau recueil général de traités, conventions et autres transactions remarquables, servant à la connaissance des relations étrangères des puissances et États dans leurs rapports mutuels.* (above, n. 46), 9th vol., 97); U.S.A.–New Granada, 12 December 1846, Art. 35 Sec. 5 (Great Britain, F. O., *BFSP 1847–1848* (36th vol.; London: Harrison and sons, 1861), 1005); Hanse Towns–Guatemala, 25 June 1847, Art. 27 (Great Britain, F. O., *BFSP 1850–1851* (40th vol.; London: James Ridgway and sons, 1863), 1366); Sardinia–New Granada, 18 August 1847, Art. 15 and 24 Para. 2 (Great Britain, F. O., *BFSP 1848–1849* (37th vol., London: Harrison and sons, 1862), 766 and 769); France–Guatemala, 8 March 1848, Art. 28 Sec. 2 (Ibid., 1374f.); U.S.A.–Guatemala, 3 March 1849, Art. 33 Sec. 3 (Great Britain, F. O., *BFSP 1849–1850. [2]* (39th vol.; London: Harrison and sons, 1863), 60); U.S.A.–Nicaragua, 3 September 1849, Art. 36 Sec. 4 (Great Britain, F. O., *BFSP 1850–1851* (above, n. 269), 1063); U.S.A.–San Salvador, 2 January 1850, Art. 35 Sec. 3 (Great Britain, F. O., *BFSP 1849–1850. [2]* (above, n. 269), 71); Spain–Costa Rica, 10 May 1850, Art. 16 Sec. 2 (Ibid., 1346); Spain–Nicaragua, 25 July 1850, Art. 16 Sec. 2 (Ibid., 1338); U.S.A.–Peru, 26 July 1851, Art. 40 Sec. 3 (Great Britain, F. O., *BFSP 1850–1851* (above, n. 269), 1108); France–Dominican Republic, 8 May 1852, Art. 31 Para. 2 (Great Britain, F. O., *BFSP 1851–1852* (41st vol.; London: William Ridgway, 1864), 917); Spain–Dominican Republic, 18 February 1855, Art. 45 Sec. 2 (Great Britain, F. O., *BFSP 1855–1856* (above, n. 267), 1296); France–Honduras, 22 February 1856, Art. 28 Sec. 2 (Great Britain, F. O., *BFSP 1856–1857* (47th vol.; London: William Ridgway, 1866), 816); France–New Granada, 15 May 1856, Art. 27 Para. 2 (Ibid., 781); France–Venezuela, 24 October 1856, Art. 15 (Clercq & Clercq, *Recueil des traités de la France* (above, n. 269), 7th vol., 185); France–Salvador, 2 January 1858, Art. 33 (Great Britain, F. O., *BFSP 1859–1860* (50th vol.; London: William Ridgway, 1867), 399); U.S.A.–Bolivia, 13 May 1858, Art. 36 Sec. 3 (Great Britain, F. O., *BFSP 1857–1858* (48th vol.; London: William Ridgway, 1866), 771); France–Nicaragua, 11 April 1859, Art. 35 Sec. 2 (Great Britain, F. O., *BFSP 1859–1860* (above, n. 269), 377); Hanse Towns–Venezuela, 31 March 1860, Art. 27 (Great Britain, F. O., *BFSP 1861–1862* (52nd vol.; London: William Ridgway, 1868), 518); France–Peru, 9 March 1861, Art. 49 Sec. 2 (Clercq & Clercq, *Recueil des traités de la France* (above, n. 269), 8th vol., 209). Later in the nineteenth century when it became a strong continental Power in Europe, Germany signed bilateral treaties with Latin American Governments containing a similar provision. See, e.g., Germany–Dominican Republic, 30 January 1885, Art. 30 (Great Britain, F. O., *BFSP 1884–1885* (76th vol.; London: William Ridgway, 1892), 136).

It should be pointed out that the Western Powers also signed unequal treaties with 'inferior' nations. These conventions often stated quite bluntly that the right to take reprisals was reserved to the Western Power if the other contracting party failed to give redress when demanded. See, e.g., Art. 7 Para. 2 of the Treaty of Andrinople between Russia and the Ottoman Empire, 14 September 1829 (Martens, *Nouveau recueil de traités d'Alliance, de Paix, de Trêve, de Neutralité, de Commerce, de Limites, d'Echange etc. et de plusieurs autres actes servant à la connoissance des relations étrangères des Puissances et Etats de l'Europe tant dans*

clause', as it was not uncommon at the time in conventions between them to add an arbitration clause. The underlying idea was to preclude the use of reprisals or the beginning of hostilities before the exhaustion of all remedies available.[270] Viewed in this light, the insertion of a 'reprisal clause' in bilateral treaties concluded with Western Powers responded perhaps to the Latin American desire to assert the importance of the rule of exhaustion of local remedies.[271] Maybe, Great Britain did not sign any treaty that contained such a provision limiting the use of reprisals to clear cases of denial of justice, precisely because it did not want to lay down an intangible principle that would have restricted its freedom of decision and action.[272]

On the other hand, the presence of this 'reprisal clause' might also strongly suggest that the contracting Western Powers pursued the legitimisation of potential future acts of reprisals against the Latin American countries.[273] As a matter of fact, the use of reprisals was likelier to happen

---

leur rapport mutuel que dans celui envers les Puissances et Etats dans d'autres parties du globe depuis 1808 jusqu'à présent (above, n. 267), 8th vol., 148); Art. 5 of the Treaty between France and Khasso chiefs (in actual Mali and Senegal), 30 September 1855 (Clercq & Clercq, *Recueil des traités de la France* (above, n. 269), 6th vol., 578).

270 For some examples, see William Ray Manning, *Arbitration Treaties among the American Nations: To the Close of the Year 1910* (Publications of the Carnegie Endowment for International Peace: Division of International Law (Washington); New York: OUP, 1924), 9, 35, 42, 49, etc. The so-called U.S.–Mexican treaty of Guadalupe Hidalgo of 2 February 1848, e.g., incorporated an arbitration clause which limited the resort to reprisals or hostility of any kind. See Art. 21: Great Britain, F. O., *BFSP 1848–1849* (above, n. 269), 577. However, arbitration in this agreement was by no means mandatory (James Brown Scott, 'Mexico and the United States and Arbitration', *AJIL* 10 (1916), 577–80, at 578). More generally about the interplay between reprisals and arbitration, see u.a. Müller, *Wandlungen im Repressalienrecht* (above, n. 21), 75–9; Förster, *Schiedssprechung und Repressalie* (above, n. 81).

271 The Latin American notion of State responsibility carries weight in favour of this interpretation. Cf. J.-M. Yepes, 'Les problèmes fondamentaux du droit des gens en Amérique', *RdC* 47/I (1934), 1–143, at 97–105; Chittharanjan Felix Amerasinghe, *Local Remedies in International Law* (Cambridge Studies in International and Comparative Law; 2nd edn., Cambridge: CUP, 2004), 32–3.

272 Cf. Álvarez, *Le droit international américain* (above, n. 268), 122–3; Yepes, 'Les problèmes fondamentaux du droit des gens en Amérique' (above, n. 271), 105.

273 Although the clause theoretically applied against the contracting Western Power too, the latter was in actual fact in a position of strength due to the existence of an asymmetry of power. More generally, Latin American countries were not

against such latter States than against a European Power (apart from some exceptions) for the reasons that should be now examined.

(b) Characteristics of Inferiority

The explanations regarding the importance of the said clause in bilateral treaties between the South American States and the Western Powers belong to the realm of conjecture. Yet, nineteenth-century armed reprisals were, in actual fact, invariably taken by a first-rank Power against an inferior State. Indeed, in all the main instances listed in textbooks, the reprisal-taking country was either France or Great Britain, or to a much lesser extent, the United States.[274] Since these Powers were the world hegemons of their time, all the countries inferior to them could, in principle, be targeted by reprisals. Nevertheless, the target countries generally shared common characteristics.

The location of the target countries does not indicate much since European, Latin American, and even sometimes Asian countries were subject to acts of armed reprisals in the nineteenth century. From a geographical per-

---

considered in the nineteenth century as fully responsible members of the family of nations (Gros Espiell, 'La doctrine du Droit international en Amérique Latine avant la première conférence panaméricaine (Washington, 1889)' (above, n. 42), 4). So, the international agreements, which the Governments of Western Powers negotiated with them supposedly under the principle of sovereign equality, were actually in many respects unequal. This situation allowed Western Powers to make extensive use of diplomatic protection, which sometimes amounted to the actual use of force with the aim of securing redress for injured subjects or collecting public debt. See Arnulf Becker Lorca, *Mestizo International Law: A Global Intellectual History 1842–1933* (Cambridge Studies in International and Comparative Law, 115; Cambridge: CUP, 2014), 88–93; and also Álvarez, *Le droit international américain* (above, n. 268), 91–101.

274 Cf. Colbert, *Retaliation in international law* (above, n. 6), 61f. Statesmen who attempted to justify the lawfulness of acts of reprisals never failed to stress that all the great European Powers and the United States made frequent use of such means. See, e.g., the Marquess of Lansdowne, House of Lords, 17 June 1850: Great Britain, Parliament, *Hansard's Parliamentary Debates: Third Series, commencing with the accession of William IV.* (111th vol.; London: Cornelius Buck, 1850), col. 1335–1336; Lord J. Russell, House of Commons, 20 June 1850: Great Britain, Parliament, *Hansard's Parliamentary Debates: Third Series, commencing with the accession of William IV.* (112th vol.; London: Cornelius Buck, 1850), col. 102f.

spective, they generally had a maritime border and may be considered to be 'peripheral'.

What is more relevant is that the reprisal-taking Powers held the target countries with contempt for "being neither wholly respectable nor wholly responsible members of the family of nations".[275] They generally had a bad opinion of the latter's political organisation. The Latin American countries, e.g., were frequently shaken by instability, crises and civil conflicts.[276] As a result, the successive domestic upheavals gave rise to claims engaging the responsibility of the local Governments. Still, as they quickly changed, the next Government in office rarely consented to assume responsibility for the acts of the overthrown predecessors.[277] Regarding the European target countries —namely Portugal, the Two Sicilies and Greece—, the problem was of a quite different nature. Although being constitutional States, they were said to be governed by monarchs exercising despotic and arbitrary powers.[278] As a consequence, the administration of justice in those countries could not be wholly trusted.[279]

---

275 Colbert, *Retaliation in international law* (above, n. 6), 62.

276 Cf. Álvarez, *Le droit international américain* (above, n. 268), 92.

277 Mr Sanford to Mr Cass, 10 August 1857: Sanford, *The Aves Island Case* (above, n. 43), 239.

278 Such was, e.g., the opinion of Palmerston. See Viscount Palmerston to Count Ludolf, 12 October 1838: Great Britain, F. O., *BFSP 1839–1840* (28th vol.; London: Printed by Harrison and sons, 1857), 1218; Viscount Palmerston to Sir Edmund Lyons, 7 August 1846: Great Britain, F. O., *BFSP 1849–1850. [2]* (above, n. 269), 431–2. It has also been reported that British diplomatic agents spoke of Ferdinand II of the Two Sicilies as a "petty monarch" (François Guizot, *An Embassy to the Court of St. James's in 1840* (London: Richard Bentley, 1862), 89) or called Dom Miguel of Portugal a "Monster and Usurper, Tyrant, and [other terms] in use by the newspaper writers, but surely most indecent in the mouth of a diplomatic Agent." (Brigadier-General Sir John Campbell to the Marquis of Londonderry, 1831: Great Britain, F. O., *BFSP 1830–1831* (above, n. 267), 323).

279 This is the position that Palmerston defended in the House of Commons in 1850. He argued that Don Pacifico did not go before the Greek tribunals because he would not have obtained compensation for the injury he suffered because "the tribunals are at the mercy of the advisers of the crown, the judges being liable to be removed, and being often actually removed upon grounds of private interest and personal feeling." In fact, the Greek Government made no attempt to either prosecute or identify the looters as powerful persons were involved. Besides, no witness would have thus testified in favour of Don Pacifico. So, "[i]f the man I prosecute is rich, he is sure to be acquitted; if he is poor, he has nothing out of which to afford me compensation if he is condemned." Viscount Palmerston, House of Commons, 25 June 1850: Great Britain, Parliament, *Hansard's Parliamentary Debates* (above, n. 274), col. 395–396.

Another reason of disdain was also the fact that those States were regularly unable to fulfil their pledges because of misappropriation of government revenue, mismanagement of public funds and a protectionist economic policy detrimental to general wealth.[280] More generally, a factor of inferiority was the situation of economic or financial dependency on the great Powers. The South American and Southern European countries were massively indebted to the Western Powers or private investors and companies under the latter's protection.[281] This economic dependence was precisely an argument of leverage in the negotiations that the great Powers used to compel the target countries to accede to their demands. For example, Viscount Palmerston, the British Secretary of State for Foreign Affairs, threatened the Two Sicilies that Great Britain would search for new sources of sulphur if the Southern Italian kingdom persisted in refusing to consent to the withdrawal of a monopoly on Sicilian sulphur.[282] Also, when Brazil suspended the diplomatic relations with Great Britain because of the latter's refusal to indemnify damage caused in the exercise of reprisals in 1862–1863, the British Prime Minister, Earl Russell, was of the opinion that Great Britain should not give in because British trade could go on without commercial intercourses with Brazil, unlike the latter.[283] Altogether, it was in the interest of the target countries to yield, lest they might lose an important commercial partner. It can thus be said that the reprisal-taking States enjoyed a degree of impunity regarding the use of armed reprisals on account of this commercial superiority.

---

280 See, e.g., the remarks of Viscount Palmerston, House of Commons, 6 July 1847: Great Britain, Parliament, *Hansard's Parliamentary Debates: Third Series, commencing with the accession of William IV.* (93rd vol.; London: G. Woodfall and son, 1847), col. 1300–1303.

281 The demands made by the reprisal-taking States prove the enormous debts owed by the target countries. See, e.g., the one owed by Gran Colombia to the merchant James Mackintosh (Paulsson, *Denial of Justice in International Law* (above, n. 61), 18–9); or by Venezuela to British and German companies in 1902 (see Memorandum communicated by Count Metternich, 13 November 1902: Great Britain, F. O., *BFSP 1901–1902* (95th vol.; London: His Majesty's Stationery Office, 1905), 1084).

282 Viscount Palmerston to Count Ludolf, 12 October 1838: Great Britain, F. O., *BFSP 1839–1840* (above, n. 278), 1222f.

283 Earl Russell to Countr Lavradio, 10 October 1864: Great Britain, F. O., *Papers respecting the Renewal of Diplomatic Relations with Brazil* (London: Harrison and sons, 1866), 12.

Finally, the military weakness of the target countries in comparison to the strong Powers was crucial to make the employment of armed reprisals expedient. For instance, Great Britain did not hesitate to send fourteen vessels for an operation of reprisals against Greece in the *Don Pacifico* affair in 1850, whereas the whole Greek navy only comprised about ten ships of war.[284] So, it is not without reason that Lord Stanley could regard Greece as being "defenceless".[285] At any rate, the target country was often fully aware of its weakness.[286]

2. Informal Imperialism through Reprisals

(a) Issues of Commercial Nature

The great Powers had an interest to exploit the inferiority of the other countries and keep them in a situation of dependence and deference: it allowed them to achieve their own ends. For this purpose, reprisals presented for the great Powers with an excellent instrument of informal imperialism when one of those small countries refused to give way to their will.[287] As a matter of fact, this measure was employed in cases when grounds of public policy were at stake. The *Sulphur Monopoly* incident is illustrative of the importance of reprisals to settle issues of commercial nature between a

---

284 Mr Wyse to Viscount Palmerston, 28 January 1850: Great Britain, F. O., *BFSP 1849–1850. [2]* (above, n. 269), 524–5; Falcke, *Le blocus pacifique* (above, n. 40), 14. Another example is the British reprisals against the Two Sicilies in 1840. Although that Kingdom made preparations to repel a British attack, it was manifestly not in position to stand up militarily to Great Britain and had ultimately to give in. Cf. Dennis W. Thomson, 'Prelude to the Sulphur War of 1840. The Neapolitan Perspective', *EHQ* 25 (1995), 163–80, at 175; Guizot, *An Embassy to the Court of St. James's in 1840* (above, n. 278), 85.

285 Lord Stanley, House of Lords, 17 June 1850: Great Britain, Parliament, *Hansard's Parliamentary Debates* (above, n. 274), col. 1332.

286 See, e.g., Mr Londos to Mr Wyse, 19 January 1850: Great Britain, F. O., *BFSP 1849–1850. [2]* (above, n. 269), 515.

287 So, reprisals were sometimes employed to provoke a change in the target country's policy. For instance, British reprisals against Brazil in 1862–1863 were believed to strive for the abolition of slavery. See Falcke, *Le blocus pacifique* (above, n. 40), 110 fn. 9. Cf. the debate in the House of Commons, 16 July 1863: Great Britain, Parliament, *Hansard's Parliamentary Debates: Third Series, Commencing with the accession of William IV.* (172nd vol.; London: Cornelius Buck, 1863), col. 879–928; Earl Russell to Mr Eliot, 6 June 1863: Great Britain, F. O., *BFSP 1863–1864* (54th vol.; London: William Ridgway, 1869), 843.

great Power —in the present case, Great Britain— and an inferior one — namely, the Kingdom of the Two Sicilies.

When in the summer of 1838 the Neapolitan Government granted a monopoly on Sicilian sulphur to a private company chiefly made up of Frenchmen, Great Britain protested and sought the revocation of the grant by invoking the bilateral treaty of 1816, which, in addition to the most favoured nation clause, stipulated that no privileges detrimental to British trade could be granted to subjects of other nations. The monopoly was thus construed as a breach of the said treaty.[288]

As a matter of fact, the use of reprisals was inadequate to pursue formal imperialism, unlike war. Nevertheless, he operations of reprisals, indeed, often hid expansionist ambitions or territorial claims. For example, it was believed that Great Britain had views on Panama when it exercised reprisals against New Granada in 1836 (see Ulysse Tencé, *Annuaire historique universel pour 1836: Avec un Appendice contenant les actes publics, traités, notes diplomatiques, papiers d'états et tableaux statistiques, financiers, administratifs et nécrologiques; – une Chronique offrant les événements les plus piquants, les causes les plus célèbres, etc; et des notes pour servir à l'histoire des sciences, des lettres et des arts*, Nouvelle série (Paris: Thoisnier-Desplaces, 1837), 649). British reprisals against Greece in 1850 in the *Don Pacifico* case took also place against the background of claims over two Greek islands, viz. Sapienza and Cervi (see the diplomatic correspondence about the dispute over these islands between Greece and the Ionian Islands under British protectorate: Great Britain, F. O., *BFSP 1849–1850. [2]* (above, n. 269), 932–73). Yet, the acts of reprisals against Greece did not officially seek a settlement of these territorial claims (see Viscount Palmerston to Mr Wyse, 25 February 1850: Ibid., 604). Art. IV of the convention of 18 July 1850 between Great Britain and Greece explicitly excluded these claims from the settlement (Great Britain, F. O., *BFSP 1849–1850. (1)* (38th vol.; London: Harrison and sons, 1862), 19). For an assessment of the real causes behind the *Don Pacifico* affair, see David Hannell, 'Lord Palmerston and the 'Don Pacifico Affair' of 1850. The Ionian Connection', *EHQ* 19 (1989), 495–507.

288 See the diplomatic correspondence on the issue: Great Britain, F. O., *BFSP 1839–1840* (above, n. 278), 1163ff.; Great Britain, F. O., *BFSP 1840–1841* (above, n. 269), 175ff.; and also the treaty between Great Britain and the Two Sicilies, 26 September 1816: Jonathan Elliot, *The American Diplomatic Code, Embracing A Collection of Treaties and Conventions between the United States and Foreign Powers: From 1778 to 1834. With an Abstract of Important Judicial Decisions on Points connected with Our Foreign Relations. Also, A Concise Diplomatic Manual, containing a Summary of the Law of Nations, from the Works of Wicquefort, Martens, Kent, Vattel, Ward, Story, &c. &c. and Other Diplomatic Writings on Questions of International Law.*, 2nd vol. (Washington: Printed by Jonathan Elliot, 1834), 198–200. However, according to the Law Officers of the Crown, the monopoly did not violate the provisions of the treaty of 1816. See the separate opinions of Sir Frederick Pollock and Joseph Phillimore, 12 and 26 March 1840 respectively: Great Britain, Parliament, *Documents and statements respecting the Sulphur Monopoly,*

Indeed, the monopoly had a proven disastrous effect on British trade. The customs revenues registered a significant drop from 35.000£ a year to almost nothing.[289] Import of sulphur decreased by 50 per cent compared with 1838 before the introduction of the monopoly and consequently, the price of sulphur increased by 100 per cent.[290] Now, Great Britain's industry heavily relied on sulphur to produce sulphuric acid and other sorts of acids employed in various industrial processes such as bleaching and dyeing, manufacturing gunpowder and for medical purposes.[291] Finally, the introduction of the monopoly prejudiced British mine owners and holders of Sicilian sulphur as well as the shipping industry.[292]

The issue of the monopoly was thus no insignificant cause of complaint. It evolved into an economic doctrinal dispute that opposed protectionism and free trade. On the one hand, since 1823, the Neapolitan Government had pursued a model of economic protectionism, which explains why it considered the monopoly as a way to limit the exports of Sicilian sulphur and increase control over this trade which was *de facto* in British hands.[293] On the other hand, Great Britain advocated a free trade system. Palmerston argued that free trade enabled the discovery of alternatives to Sicilian sulphur: new mines will open in other regions of the world, what would

constituting grounds for Parliamentary inquiry into the conduct of the Foreign Secretary. (London: John Reid and Co., 1841), 76–7.

289 Phillimore, *Commentaries Upon International Law* (above, n. 46), 36.

290 R., 'On the Sulphur Trade of Sicily, and the Commercial Relations between that Country and Great Britain', *JSSL* 2/6 (1840), 446–57, at 446.

291 Ibid., 446.

292 See Ibid., 453–5. For the French ambassador in London, François Guizot, Great Britain was entitled to complain because the cause was just. However, he was of the opinion that the argument of a violation of the treaty of commerce weakened its claim. Great Britain should instead have based the demands solely on the losses incurred by British nationals and on the Neapolitan false promises to abrogate the monopoly (Guizot, *An Embassy to the Court of St. James's in 1840* (above, n. 278), 88–9). Indeed, only a breach of the law could justify reprisals, but not a decision detrimental to some mere interests. See Christian Friedrich Wurm, 'Selbsthilfe (völkerrechtliche)', in Carl von Rotteck and Carl Welcker (eds.), *Das Staats-Lexikon. Encyklopädie der sämmtlichen Staatswissenschaften für alle Stände*, 12th vol. (2nd edn., Altona: Johann Friedrich Hammerich, 1845–1848), 111–32, at 126–127.

293 Marcello De Cecco, 'The Italian Economy Seen from Abroad', in Gianni Toniolo (ed.), *The Oxford Handbook of the Italian Economy Since Unification* (Oxford: OUP, 2013), 134–54, at 136. See Thomson, 'Prelude to the Sulphur War of 1840. The Neapolitan Perspective' (above, n. 284), on the tension between free trade and protectionism partisans within the Neapolitan government up to 1840.

lead Sicilian mines to lose value.[294] So, for him, the Neapolitan Government was mistaken to suppose that monopolies contributed to the public good; an ignorance he ascribed to the political system of the Two Sicilies, i.e. a despotic monarchy.[295] In conclusion, "Palmerston showed that the Neapolitan Crown was scientifically backward and incorrect, politically offensive, ungrateful, and would also be easily proved to be militarily weak compared with Britain."[296]

On 12 March 1840, Palmerston instructed the ambassador in Naples — his brother, William Temple— to formally demand the immediate abolition of the monopoly and to seek compensation for losses sustained by British subjects as a result of this monopoly. The Neapolitan Government had a week to comply with the demands, failing which reprisals in the form of seizure and detention of Neapolitan and Sicilian ships would be ordered.[297] However, the answer being unsatisfactory, reprisals began on 17 April 1840. A number of Neapolitan and Sicilian vessels were seized in the Mediterranean Sea and detained by way of embargo in the ports of Malta.[298] Nonetheless, the dispute was eventually settled through the mediation of France that wished to avert the oppression of the Two Sicilies by Great Britain.[299]

A monopoly was also in the interest of the Frenchmen behind the project. In fact, the increased demand for sulphur from France and Great Britain caused price inflation in 1832 and an overproduction of Sicilian sulphur. Consequently, the markets were overstocked and the price significantly slumped in 1835. In this process, Frenchmen who had speculated on the price of sulphur almost went bankrupt. Hence, they sought from the Neapolitan Government the granting of a monopoly. See R., 'On the Sulphur Trade of Sicily, and the Commercial Relations between that Country and Great Britain' (above, n. 290), 449–50.

294 Viscount Palmerston to Count Ludolf, 12 October 1838: Great Britain, F. O., *BFSP 1839–1840* (above, n. 278), 1222–3.

295 Viscount Palmerston to Count Ludolf, 12 October 1838: Ibid., 1218–21.

296 De Cecco, 'The Italian Economy Seen from Abroad' (above, n. 293), 138.

297 Viscount Palmerston to Mr Temple, 12 March 1840: Great Britain, F. O., *BFSP 1840–1841* (above, n. 269), 187. See also Viscount Palmerston to the Lords Commissioners of the Admiralty, 12 March 1840: Ibid., 187–8.

298 Phillimore, *Commentaries Upon International Law* (above, n. 46), 37; Twiss, *The law of nations considered as independent political communities* (above, n. 224), 35.

299 See the speech of Alphonse Jobez, *Assemblée nationale*, 2 September 1848: Félix Wouters, *Histoire parlementaire de l'Assemblée nationale, précédée du récit de la révolution de Paris*, sous la surveillance de M. Alexandre Gendebien et de M. Maynz, 4th vol. (Bruxelles: Aux bureaux de l'association des ouvriers typographes, 1848), 453; and the ordinance of the King of Two Sicilies abolishing the monopoly, 21 July 1840: Great Britain, F. O., *BFSP 1840–1841* (above, n. 269), 1225–6. Apart from the political aspects of the incident, the French

The *Sulphur Monopoly* incident is noteworthy because it shows that great Powers used reprisals to keep and strengthen control over the target country in commercial matters, without having to turn to the extremity of war. Indeed, Great Britain came out on top as the monopoly was abolished and the British mine owners and holders of sulphur were compensated. Incidentally, it offered Palmerston the opportunity to teach the Two Sicilies a lesson about Neapolitan military inferiority and misconception about political economy.

Nevertheless, in other cases of commercial nature, armed reprisals were resorted to with the aim of imposing a dominant position over the target country. It happened in 1838 when France blockaded Mexican ports or with the so-called First Opium War (1839–1842) between Great Britain and China. Both operations started at first as acts of reprisals allegedly in response to the mistreatment of French and British nationals, respectively. However, the primary purpose since the beginning seemed to have been the concession of commercial privileges.[300] In fact, in the ultimatum addressed to the Mexican Government, France demanded —apart from damages for the French victims— the treatment of the most favoured nation and some commercial guarantees.[301] Although reprisals ultimately evolved into war in both cases, the peace treaties concluded with the defeated nations, namely Mexico and China, finally yielded the commercial advantages that the victors coveted: the most favoured nation principle was introduced in the mutual relations of France and Mexico while Great Britain

---

Government was really concerned about the Sicilian sulphur trade and sought the abolition of the monopoly, too. As a matter of fact, France also consumed Sicilian sulphur, although half less than Great Britain. See R., 'On the Sulphur Trade of Sicily, and the Commercial Relations between that Country and Great Britain' (above, n. 290), 446–448; 450f. French merchants suffered important losses as a consequence of this monopoly. But while the British use of reprisals achieved their end, namely the abolition of the monopoly and the settlement of the private British claims through a mixed arbitral tribunal, the aggrieved French merchants' claims remained unsettled until 1844. See France, *Pétition des réclamans français contre le gouvernement napolitain adressée à MM. les membres de la Chambre des Députés* (Marseille: Imprimerie Ed. Buret et Co, 1845); Thomson, 'Prelude to the Sulphur War of 1840. The Neapolitan Perspective' (above, n. 284), 176.

300 About the so-called Pastry War between France and Mexico, see Jacques Penot, 'L'expansion commerciale française au Mexique et les causes du conflit franco-mexicain de 1838–1839', *Bulletin Hispanique* 75 (1973), 169–201.

301 See Clercq & Clercq, *Recueil des traités de la France* (above, n. 269), 4th vol., 403–416, esp. 412.

obtained the opening of Chinese ports to British trade as well as the transfer of Hong Kong.[302]

(b) Assertion of National Dignity: 'Civis Romanus Sum', 1850

Not only commercial considerations were used to keep an inferior country in line. The great Powers also extended their influence and domination by demanding respect to their national dignity. If the inferior country showed disrespect towards the agents of the State, nationals or things representing the national sovereignty such as ships, the great Power sometimes had to demand obedience. Reprisals presented then an interesting option to reach such a goal. The *Don Pacifico* case of 1850 links the idea of maintenance of national honour with the taking of reprisals.[303]

When in Easter 1847 the Greek Government banned the burning of Judas Iscariot's effigy out of respect for the visit of Baron Rothschild in Athens,[304] an angry Greek mob looted the house and assaulted the household of David Ricardo, a Jewish Gibraltar-born British national nicknamed Don Pacifico, while the police remained passive.[305] The British minister at Athens immediately made representations to the Greek Government, but the Greek Foreign Minister denied him the right to demand redress on behalf of Don Pacifico as long as the latter had not exhausted the domestic

---

302 See Art. 3 of the Peace Treaty between France and Mexico, 9 March 1839 (Great Britain, F. O., *BFSP 1840–1841* (above, n. 269), 223); the Treaty of Nanking between Great Britain and China, 29 August 1842 (Great Britain, F. O., *BFSP 1841–1842* (30th vol.; London: James Ridgway and sons, 1858), 389–92). See thereupon Stephen C. Neff, 'Peace and prosperity: commercial aspects of peacemaking', in Randall Lesaffer (ed.), *Peace Treaties and International Law in European History. From the Late Middle Ages to World War One* (Cambridge: CUP, 2004), 365–81, at 374; Neff, *War and the Law of Nations* (above, n. 2), 230.

303 However, Cussy, *Phases et causes célèbres du droit maritime des nations* (above, n. 223), 2nd vol., 490, believed that Great Britain exercised reprisals in this case as an attempt to curb the growth of the Greek merchant navy.

304 Sir Edmund Lyons to Viscount Palmerston, 20 May 1847: Great Britain, F. O., *BFSP 1849–1850. [2]* (above, n. 269), 332.

305 See the account of the facts as told by Mr Pacifico himself to Sir Edmund Lyons, 7 April 1847: Ibid., 333–4.

remedies.[306] Nevertheless, convinced of the justness of the cause, Palmerston instructed to keep pressing Greece for compensation.[307]

Negotiations remained in a stalemate for a long time until the new British minister at Athens, Thomas Wyse, presented the Greek Government with a 24-hour ultimatum in early 1850.[308] But Greece refused. For that reason, Vice-Admiral Sir William Parker, Commander-in-Chief in the Mediterranean, who had already been enjoined by Palmerston to adopt coercive measures if the demands were not complied with, began a blockade of the port of Piraeus which applied at first only against the Greek ships of war.[309] Yet, the obstinacy of the Greek Government compelled Great Britain to take more stringent measures. The blockade was thus extended to other Greek ports and also enforced against Greek merchant vessels, provided they exclusively transported Greek property.[310]

---

306 Mr Glarakis to Sir Edmund Lyons, 27 December 1847 (O.S.)/8 January 1848 (N.S.): Ibid., 347–9. For this reason, Lassa Oppenheim viewed the British reprisals in this case as unjustified (Oppenheim, *International Law* (above, n. 25), 36). On the other hand, Freeman Snow considered that Don Pacifico's claims would, in all likelihood, be dismissed due to anti-Semitism in Greece and the fact that the attacking mob was numerous and hence 'faceless' (Freeman Snow, *Cases and opinions on international law: with notes and a syllabus* (Boston: The Boston Book Company, 1893), 248). In a letter to Sir Edmund Lyons, dated 24 January 1848, Don Pacifico refuted Glarakis's allegations and explained in detail the motives why he did not elect to pursue a judicial remedy. See Great Britain, F. O., *BFSP 1849–1850. [2]* (above, n. 269), 352–67.

307 Viscount Palmerston to Sir Edmund Lyons, 24 March 1848: Ibid., 370–1. Besides reparation on behalf of Don Pacifico, Great Britain claimed redress in other cases: (1) the uncompensated expropriation of Mr Finlay's land which had been inclosed within the gardens of the royal palace in Athens, (2) the ill-treatment of Ionians by Greek authorities —the Ionian Islands were at the time under British protectorate—, (3) the injurious detention of an officer and crewmen of the H.M.S. Fantome in Patras. See respectively Ibid., 410–479, 254–331, 216–253; and Falcke, *Le blocus pacifique* (above, n. 40), 88 fn. 2. This last complaint touched directly Great Britain's national honour and contrarily to the other claims was not of private origin.

308 Mr Wyse to Mr Londos, 17 January 1850: Great Britain, F. O., *BFSP 1849–1850. [2]* (above, n. 269), 491.

309 See Viscount Palmerston to the Lords Commissioners of the Admiralty, 30 November 1849: Ibid., 483–4; Mr Wyse to Viscount Palmerston, 18 January 1850: Ibid., 495–6.

310 See Mr Wyse to Viscount Palmerston, 25 January and 18 February 1850: Ibid., 525–526 and 653. The underlying idea of this measure was to avoid hindering trade of third Powers. Nevertheless, some complaints were formulated. See, e.g., Baron Brunnow to Viscount Palmerston, 20 March (O.S.)/1 April (N.S.) 1850: Ibid., 750–3.

The operation aroused outcry and condemnation abroad. Great Britain's co-guarantors of Greek independence, viz. France and Russia,[311] vehemently protested. Palmerston thus felt constrained to accept the French good offices. In the meantime, the harshness of the coercive means ought not to be increased.[312] The blockade remained effective; yet, vessels were not to be captured.[313]

However, the French mission failed. Reprisals were, therefore, resumed. But shortly after, in April 1850, the Greek Government agreed to come to terms. All the demands were unconditionally accepted.[314] In return, the blockade was lifted, and the detained vessels were released.[315] In total, the operation of reprisals lasted a little bit more than three months.

Although the whole issue with Greece was ultimately settled, the affair still caused great commotion in Great Britain. Indeed, Palmerston's light handling of the matter was strongly disapproved.[316] France judged that its good offices were mocked and for this reason recalled its ambassador from London. It created a climate of tension which augured war between both

---

311 See Art. IV of the convention signed on 7 May 1832 between the three Powers, on one hand, and Bavaria, on the other: Martens, *Nouveau recueil de traités d'Alliance, de Paix, de Trêve, de Neutralité, de Commerce, de Limites, d'Echange etc. et de plusieurs autres actes servant à la connoissance des relations étrangères des Puissances et Etats de l'Europe tant dans leur rapport mutuel que dans celui envers les Puissances et Etats dans d'autres parties du globe depuis 1808 jusqu'à présent* (above, n. 267), 10th vol., 554.

312 Viscount Palmerston to Mr Wyse, 5 February 1850: Great Britain, F. O., *BFSP 1849–1850. [2]* (above, n. 269), 505–6.

313 Order of Vice-Admiral Sir W. Parker to Commander Foote, 24 February 1850: Ibid., 673.

314 See the convention signed on 18 July 1850 between Great Britain and Greece for the settlement of the claims: Great Britain, F. O., *BFSP 1849–1850. (1)* (above, n. 287), 16–9. Art. II stipulated though that the amount of compensation owed by the Greek Government for the destruction of documents connected with Don Pacifico's claims on the Portuguese Government had to be determined by a mixed commission. Such a mixed commission met in Lisbon in 1851 and valued the loss at only 150£. See Great Britain, F. O., *BFSP 1850–1851* (above, n. 269), 617–42.

315 Mr Wyse to Viscount Palmerston, 28 April 1850: Great Britain, F. O., *BFSP 1849–1850. [2]* (above, n. 269), 877–8.

316 However, Palmerston had referred the question of the legality of the operation to the consideration of the Advocate-General who validated it. See Viscount Palmerston to Mr Wyse, 6 March 1850: Ibid., 661.

countries.[317] In this context, the British Parliament saw with great preoccupation the interruption of diplomatic relations with France.[318] Therefore, a motion of censure on the British Government was moved in the House of Lords.[319] Lord Stanley, who presented the resolution, argued that the policy followed by Palmerston had endangered peace with the other continental Powers.[320]

During the ensuing debate, the question of national dignity was central. All the Peers concurred with the view that Great Britain was a great and mighty Power. The laudatory expressions they used bear testament to the strong national pride and belief in their country's ascendancy. So, the British maritime superiority was often stressed as well as Great Britain's status as a leading commercial nation.[321] Nevertheless, many Peers considered that the show of force against a comparatively weak State like Greece was beneath Great Britain's dignity.[322] The abusive use of Great Britain's

317 Mr de La Hitte to Mr Drouyn de Lhuys, 14 May 1850: Martens, *Causes célèbres du droit des gens* (above, n. 199), 5th vol., 518–519. See also Mr Wyse to Viscount Palmerston, 31 May 1850: Great Britain, F. O., *BFSP 1849–1850. [2]* (above, n. 269), 921. Already since the beginning of the acts of reprisals, the French seemed to have entertained hostile feelings towards Great Britain. See, e.g., Lord Bloomfield to Viscount Palmerston, 12 February 1850: Ibid., 611.

318 See the parliamentarian discussion of this matter: House of Lords, 17 May 1850 (Great Britain, Parliament, *Hansard's Parliamentary Debates* (above, n. 274), col. 159–166); House of Commons, 23 May 1850 (Ibid., col. 237–268).

319 For a contextualisation of the debate, a summary of the discussions as well as nuances and correction of some information given in speeches, see Taylor, *Don Pacifico* (above, n. 49), 218–33.

320 Lord Stanley's motion read: "To resolve, that while the House fully recognizes the right and duty of the Government to secure to Her Majesty's subjects residing in foreign States the full protection of the laws of those States, it regrets to find, by the correspondence recently laid upon the table by Her Majesty's command, that various claims against the Greek Government, doubtful in point of justice or exaggerated in amount, have been enforced by coercive measures directed against the commerce and people of Greece, and calculated to endanger the continuance of our friendly relations with other Powers." (Lord Stanley, House of Lords, 17 June 1850: Great Britain, Parliament, *Hansard's Parliamentary Debates* (above, n. 274), col. 1332).

321 For example, Lord Eddisbury held Great Britain as "a great commercial country [...], with interests spread over every quarter of the globe, with our merchants in every port, and our ships on every sea," and Lord Stanley insisted on "her immense maritime superiority," (House of Lords, 17 June 1850: Ibid., col. 1388 and 1323, respectively).

322 See, e.g., Lord Stanley, House of Lords, 17 June 1850: Ibid., col. 1295.

superior naval might for such petty and doubtful claims was, thus, considered a "prostitut[ion]" of the honour of the British flag.[323]

Still, not all the Peers shared this view. Many defended the concordance of the measures with national dignity. The Marquess of Lansdowne, the then Lord President of the Council, contended that the presence of a large force in the Greek waters was not only efficacious to enforce the demands but also imparted prestige to the Greek Government for submitting to Sir William Parker, who was backed by a considerable fleet rather than a small squadron.[324] Lord Eddisbury added that a large fleet served the double goal to demonstrate British determination and prevent resistance. Besides, a wrongdoing State could not hide behind its weakness to escape reparation for the violation of the law of nations and the commission of injustices.[325] However, these latter arguments did not convince as the adoption of Lord Stanley's resolution passed by a majority of 37 votes (For: 169; Against: 132).[326]

Following this vote, Lord John Russell, who was Prime Minister at the time, was asked in the House of Commons if the Government would resign. He answered that not only the Government had no intention of resigning but also that it would not follow the policy laid down in the Peers' motion, i.e. to refrain from interfering on behalf of aggrieved British subjects.[327] This reply prompted a second round of debates that lasted from Monday 24 June until Friday 28 June 1850.[328] The Members of Parliament were well aware of the paramount importance of the issue under discussion. They knew that they were about to lay down some principles of foreign policy for the British Government, while it was usually not the custom of the Parliament to address such issues.[329]

John Roebuck, MP for Sheffield, introduced then a motion in the House of Commons by which the foreign policy conducted by the British Government would receive the approval of that House for being oriented to-

323 Lord Stanley, House of Lords, 17 June 1850: Ibid., col. 1321.

324 The Marquess of Lansdowne, House of Lords, 17 June 1850: Ibid., col. 1346.

325 Lord Eddisbury, House of Lords, 17 June 1850: Ibid., col. 1395–1396.

326 House of Lords, 17 June 1850: Ibid., col. 1401.

327 Lord J. Russell, House of Commons, 20 June 1850: Great Britain, Parliament, *Hansard's Parliamentary Debates* (above, n. 274), col. 102 and 104–105.

328 On these debates, see Taylor, *Don Pacifico* (above, n. 49), 234–51.

329 See, e.g., Sir W. Molesworth, House of Commons, 27 June 1850: Great Britain, Parliament, *Hansard's Parliamentary Debates* (above, n. 274), col. 505.

wards the maintenance of the national honour and dignity.[330] So, instead of focusing on the acts of reprisals against Greece, Roebuck widened the debate to fifteen years of foreign policy led by Palmerston. The real *tour de force* of this resolution was, indeed, to shift the centre of gravity of the discussion from the limited operation against Greece to Palmerston's foreign policy as a whole.[331]

The intervention of the British Government, and more precisely Palmerston's, into the internal affairs of foreign countries was amply discussed. A large part of the House professed a doctrine of non-intervention. William Ewart Gladstone, for instance, supported the principles of independence and equality between nations.[332] Thence, he believed that the passing of Roebuck's motion would establish a two-speed rule: a foreign policy accommodating towards strong Powers, on the one hand, and a bullying attitude towards weak nations, on the other.[333] Such a feature of Palmerston's foreign policy was reprehended by the opposition.[334] He even earned the nickname 'lucifer match' for his quick temper against weak countries when they failed to comply with his demands.[335]

However, when Palmerston took the floor, he held a memorable speech, the so-called '*Civis Romanus Sum*' speech, where he set forth the doctrine that British citizens deserved as much respect as the citizens of Rome in ancient times:

330 Roebuck's motion read: "That the principles on which the Foreign Policy of Her Majesty's Government has been regulated, have been such as were calculated to maintain the honour and dignity of this country; and, in times of unexampled difficulty, to preserve peace between England and the various nations of the world." (House of Commons, 24 June 1850: Ibid., col. 255).

331 Dolphus Whitten, 'The Don Pacifico Affair', *The Historian* 48 (1986), 255–67, at 264.

332 William Ewart Gladstone, House of Commons, 27 June 1850: Great Britain, Parliament, *Hansard's Parliamentary Debates* (above, n. 274), col. 589.

333 "I conclude that this House will not be of opinion that there is to be one rule for the weak and another for the strong, and that, because Greece is a kingdom of small extent and resources, therefore we are to establish for resident Englishmen immunities as against her, which we should not claim from Russia, or from Austria, or from France, and which we never should concede, as against ourselves, to any Power upon earth." (William Ewart Gladstone, House of Commons, 27 June 1850: Ibid., col. 561).

334 See, e.g., Lord John Manners, House of Commons, 25 June 1850: Ibid., col. 342–355 passim, esp. 343–344 and 355.

335 "No sooner does he meet with an obstruction than a flame immediately bursts forth." (Sir F. Thesiger, House of Commons, 24 June 1850: Ibid., col. 260).

> "as the Roman, in days of old, held himself free from indignity, when he could say *Civis Romanus sum*; so also a British subject, in whatever land he may be, shall feel confident that the watchful eye and the strong arm of England, will protect him against injustice and wrong."[336]

This doctrine, which strikingly echoed the verses "Rule, Britannia, rule the wave/ Britons never will be slaves" of James Thompson's eighteenth-century poem, raised the protection of British nationals abroad as a pillar of the British Government's foreign policy. Through it all, Palmerston's speech means that the other countries of the globe, and particularly those of inferior rank, had to show obedience to Great Britain. Therefore, under such circumstances, the employment of reprisals appears as a display of strength and superiority, which aimed to assert the national honour and impose the respect expected from weak and small States.

Palmerston's eloquent speech bore fruit because the motion passed by a majority of 46 votes (For: 310; Against: 264).[337] Beyond the political implications of this vote for the Government's survival, Palmerston's legacy lived on. So, when Great Britain made reprisals against Brazil in 1863, the connection between the taking of reprisals and the maintenance of national dignity was reaffirmed. Earl Russell, the Secretary of State for Foreign Affairs at the time, stated in the House of Lords that the '*Civis Romanus Sum*' doctrine had achieved to make the name of England respected. Indeed, it had become a duty for the British Government to interfere and demand redress on behalf of aggrieved nationals: "we, when a wrong is done, must, without regard to the wrong-doing Power being strong or weak, demand redress; and by demanding redress, depend upon it, we shall insure the protection of our commerce in all parts of the world."[338] When the Power failing to provide redress was weak, reprisals were undoubtedly a weapon of choice.

336 Viscount Palmerston, House of Commons, 25 June 1850: Ibid., col. 444.

337 House of Commons, 28 June 1850: Ibid., col. 739.

338 Earl Russell, House of Lords, 19 June 1863: Great Britain, Parliament, *Hansard's Parliamentary Debates: Third Series. Commencing with the accession of William IV.* (171st vol.; London: Cornelius Buck, 1863), col. 1145.

III. Unrestricted Resort to Reprisals

1. A Question of Political Opportunism: Palmerston's Policy, 1847

The process of politicisation of reprisals which began in the sixteenth century caused the departure of the practice of States from the legal theory framework that had been developed in the Middle Ages to govern the use of this self-help measure. In the nineteenth century, this state of affairs favoured the ends of the great Powers since the resort to reprisals was hardly restricted. The only limitations which they agreed to abide by were mainly those dictated by circumspection and public policy. It was actually in their interest that the law governing reprisals remained rudimentary.

The first important step regarding reprisals was the decision to have recourse to them. It was primarily a matter of expediency, i.e. a political question, but certainly no legal one.[339] Palmerston made quite clear what was the British Government's policy in that respect, on the occasion of a discussion in the House of Commons about the preoccupying situation of the so-called Spanish bondholders in Summer 1847.

On 6 July 1847, Lord George Bentinck brought to the attention of the House of Commons a petition presented by British bondholders who asked for redress and assistance on account of the sizeable unpaid debt owed by the Spanish Government. He demonstrated that Spain was actually in a position to fulfil its financial obligations. Therefore, he supported the view that Great Britain should not fear to take forcible measures for the recovery of the bondholders' just debts since the law of nations allowed such way to proceed. The motion Lord Bentinck moved forward aimed thus to invite the British Government to adopt the necessary steps

---

339 This is what the U.S. Secretary of State, Daniel Webster, stressed in a letter he wrote in the context of the well-known *Caroline* affair (1837) which strained the relations between the United States and Great Britain for many years: "All that is intended to be said at present is, that since the attack on the *Caroline* is avowed as a national act which may justify reprisals, or even general war, if the Government of The United States, in the judgment which it shall form of the transaction and of its own duty, should see fit so to decide, yet that it raises a question entirely public and political—a question between independent nations, [...]." (Mr Webster to Mr Crittenden, 15 March 1841: Great Britain, F. O., *BFSP 1840–1841* (above, n. 269), 1140).

to secure redress from Spain. He pointed out, furthermore, that no real resistance should be expected due to the weakness of the Spanish navy.[340]

However, the then-Minister of Foreign Affairs Viscount Palmerston, present that day, urged the House to withdraw this motion "upon grounds of public policy". Although agreeing with the principles of the law of nations set out by Lord Bentinck, he differed as to their application. Indeed, the British Government generally interposed on behalf of British citizens, who had entered into commercial transactions with foreign subjects, when the law in the latter's country was not properly administered. If, however, the contracting party was a foreign Government —e.g., in the case of loans —, the British Government could not give the assurance to step in so readily, should the former fail to meet its obligations. That would, otherwise, amount to the adoption of a binding policy for the future. Palmerston elaborated on the case of Spain. In his opinion, any private investment in that country, although being in principle a solvent and trustworthy Government, was actually a venture due to the Spanish economic protectionism and the inadequate public expenditures. Under such circumstances, Great Britain could not just have recourse to force to blindly defend the interests of speculators. Nevertheless, he supported the idea of sending a warning to those foreign Governments that owed money to British nationals.[341] He thus concluded saying the following:

> "That we have the means of enforcing the rights of British subjects, I am not prepared to dispute. It is not because we are afraid of these States, or all of them put together, that we have refrained from taking the steps to which my noble Friend would urge us. England, I trust, will always have the means of obtaining justice for its subjects from any country upon the face of the earth. *But this is a question of expediency, and not a question of power*; therefore let no foreign country who has done wrong to British subjects deceive itself by a false impression either that the British nation or the British Parliament will for ever remain patient under the wrong; or that, if called upon to enforce the rights of the people of England, the Government of England will not have ample power and means at its command to obtain justice for them."[342]

---

340 Lord Bentinck, House of Commons, 6 July 1847: Great Britain, Parliament, *Hansard's Parliamentary Debates* (above, n. 280), col. 1285–1298.

341 Viscount Palmerston, House of Commons, 6 July 1847: Ibid., col. 1298–1305.

342 Viscount Palmerston, House of Commons, 6 July 1847: Ibid., col. 1305–1306 (emphasis added).

In other words, Palmerston asserted that weakness or phlegm were not the reasons of the British Government's inaction. Foreign Governments should not then test the patience of Great Britain because the day might come that the taking of forceful reprisals should be decided. It was all about expedience and public policy.

The result was that Palmerston's speech and determination convinced the assembly to withdraw the motion.[343] However, this withdrawal also means that the House of Commons agreed not to dispute the broad discretionary power of the Foreign Minister to decide in the circumstances of each case when he saw fit to have recourse to acts of reprisals against a delinquent country.

2. Eluding Legal Requirements

(a) Denial of Justice debated in the British Parliament, 1850

Not all disputes led to the making of reprisals. However, once a Government had decided to have recourse to this measure when the grounds of public policy were favourable, it expected not to be hindered by a series of legal requirements.

Before the nineteenth century, there was a gap between State practice and legal theory regarding the conditions governing the use of reprisals. While bilateral treaties often reminded that justice had to be denied or neglected in order to resort to reprisals, the practice of States actually shows that it was generally not expected from the victim to exhaust the local remedies or even to seek reparations before national courts in the wrongdoer's country. The failure of the Sovereign's diplomatic interposition instead gave the justification for having recourse to reprisals.

This situation did not evolve much in the first half of the nineteenth century, notwithstanding that the bilateral treaties concluded between Western Powers and Latin American countries stressed the importance of denial of justice as a condition *sine qua non* for reprisals. In fact, the Gov-

343 Peter Borthwick, MP for Evesham, even believed that "the speech of the noble Lord [Palmerston] would be more effectual than the sending of an army to enforce the rights of British subjects." House of Commons, 6 July 1847: Ibid., col. 1307.

ernment rarely waited until the victim exhausted all the local remedies.[344] But at a time when the independence of States was a cornerstone of international law and the division of powers a fundamental constitutional principle, such a way of acting was unacceptable. Yet, the argument which the reprisal-taking States usually put forward in order to elude the observance of the requirement, consisted of drawing up a value judgement on the lack of independence of the judiciary in the target country or on the iniquity of the local laws.

Indeed, in the *Don Pacifico* affair, the British Government supported the view that the Greek tribunals did not offer sufficient guarantees of impartiality and independence.[345] However, this opinion was disputed by the opposition in the British Parliament.

On the one side, the opposition maintained in both Houses of the Parliament that, *de lege lata*, the recourse to reprisals could only be justified by a denial of justice. In support of this view, Peers and MPs of the opposition referred to Vattel's *The Law of Nations* and Lord Mansfield's authoritative opinion in the *Silesian Loan* case.[346] That is why Palmerston's proceeding against Greece was strongly disapproved. For example, Viscount Canning argued that not reprimanding the course pursued by the British Government in this affair could establish a dangerous precedent in the practice of nations, a "new principle of international law". Redress would then be demanded only through extrajudicial channels, and the aggrieved country would be its own judge to fix the compensation.[347] Sir John Walsh, MP for Radnorshire, concurred with this view when he said that the British Gov-

---

344 Colbert, *Retaliation in international law* (above, n. 6), 69. Cf. Amerasinghe, *Local Remedies in International Law* (above, n. 271), 28–9.

345 As Phillimore rightly pointed out, "the real question of International Law at issue in this case was, whether the state of the Greek tribunals was such as to warrant the English Foreign Minister in insisting upon Mr Pacifico's demand being satisfied by the Greek Government, before that person had exhausted the legal remedies which, it must be *presumed*, are afforded by the ordinary legal tribunals of every civilized State." (Phillimore, *Commentaries Upon International Law* (above, n. 46), 38 (emphasis in original)).

346 See the Earl of Aberdeen and Viscount Canning, House of Lords, 17 June 1850: Great Britain, Parliament, *Hansard's Parliamentary Debates* (above, n. 274), col. 1353–1354 and 1379; Sir F. Thesiger and Mr Gladstone, House of Commons, 24 June 1850: Great Britain, Parliament, *Hansard's Parliamentary Debates* (above, n. 274), col. 266–267 and 556–557.

347 Viscount Canning, House of Lords, 17 June 1850: Great Britain, Parliament, *Hansard's Parliamentary Debates* (above, n. 274), col. 1378ff., esp. 1381 and 1385–1386.

ernment would be "not merely a court of appeal, but a sort of court of *premiere instance*, totally setting aside the laws and tribunals of all foreign States. No doctrine could be more dangerous, or more infallibly lead to collision with great States, or to aggressive movements on small ones."[348] Nevertheless, Lord Stanley, Leader of the Opposition in the House of Lords, acknowledged that in some exceptional cases, i.e. when "the full protection of the laws of those States" could not be guaranteed —because either the foreign Government was despotic or the laws were corruptly administered—, the British Government could act without requiring the injured British nationals to exhaust local remedies.[349]

The supporters of the Government used this concession to their advantage. They criticised Lord Stanley for implicitly admitting such an exception to the rule, yet without explicitly adding it in the resolution he presented to the House of Lords. For the Peers and MPs in favour of the British Government, it was clear that the Greek judiciary was corrupted and lacked independence. Under such circumstances, it would be inconsistent with Great Britain's honour and primacy as a great Power and a leading commercial nation to wait until the prior exhaustion of local remedies. Furthermore, they referred to the recent practice of all the major Powers (France, Great Britain and the United States) in order to evidence the fact that denial of justice was no prerequisite for reprisals.[350]

The debate has some merit because it enables the assessment of the evolution of the law of reprisals in practice and the departure from long-established theoretical standards. Albeit the argumentation of the opposition can mainly be regarded as a political ploy,[351] the vast majority of British parliamentarians agreed, whether expressly or tacitly, on the point that the exhaustion of local remedies was not required in every case before making

348 Sir J. Walsh, House of Commons, 27 June 1850: Great Britain, Parliament, *Hansard's Parliamentary Debates* (above, n. 274), col. 480 (emphasis added).

349 Lord Stanley, House of Lords, 17 June 1850: Great Britain, Parliament, *Hansard's Parliamentary Debates* (above, n. 274), col. 1296–1297.

350 See the Marquess of Lansdowne and Lord Beaumont, House of Lords, 17 June 1850: Ibid., col. 1333–1335 and 1368–1369; Mr Roebuck, House of Commons, 24 June 1850: Great Britain, Parliament, *Hansard's Parliamentary Debates* (above, n. 274), col. 238ff.; Mr C. Anstey and Viscount Palmerston, House of Commons, 25 June 1850: Ibid., col. 370–371 and 381–382; Lord J. Russell, House of Commons, 28 June 1850: Ibid., col. 711.

351 Falcke, *Le blocus pacifique* (above, n. 40), 258. See, on this subject, Geoffrey Hicks, 'Don Pacifico, Democracy, and Danger. The Protectionist Party Critique of British Foreign Policy, 1850–1852', *The International History Review* 26 (2004), 515–40.

use of reprisals. That means that this condition was actually *à la carte*, namely contingent upon the very own impression that the reprisal-taking Power had of the target country and its judicial system. Indeed, it was Palmerston's opinion that only the British Government could judge whether the tribunals of the offending State were free.[352] In the context of asymmetric power relation, it signified that great Powers could cynically allege that the standards of justice were not met in the latter country in order to directly press the demands through diplomatic channel and, then eventually, have recourse to reprisals.

So, it can be said that the requirement of denial of justice meant nothing more than the refusal by the Government of the wrongdoing country to accede to the demands of the offended State.[353]

(b) Preventive Recourse to Amicable Means of Settlement

i) The Principle laid down in the 23rd Paris Protocol of 1856

The exhaustion of local remedies was therefore not an imperative prerequisite for the diplomatic action of the State on behalf of aggrieved nationals. So, when the wrongdoing country failed to fulfil the demands of redress, there was no impediment to the employment of reprisals, except for some possible grounds of public policy. This implies that there was no legal obligation to prefer amicable means of settlement —like good offices, mediation or arbitration— over a resort to armed reprisals, unless provided by treaty. The offended State enjoyed a wide margin of appreciation with regard to the measure which it deemed best fitted to carry out.

Nonetheless, the European Powers, convened at the Paris Peace Congress to discuss the end of the Crimean War, signed on 30 March 1856 a multilateral treaty which provided in Article 8 that any dispute which might arise between Turkey and one or several contracting parties ought to be referred to the other Powers' mediation ("*action médiatrice*") previous

352 Viscount Palmerston, House of Commons, 25 June 1850: Great Britain, Parliament, *Hansard's Parliamentary Debates* (above, n. 274), col. 382.

353 Already at the time when U.S. President Jackson threatened France to take reprisals if the latter kept withholding payment of compensation, the distinguished U.S. statesman Albert Gallatin likened denial of justice to the refusal by a political body, such as the French Chambers in that case, to give in to the demands. See Albert Gallatin to Edward Everett, January 1835: Adams, *The Writings of Albert Gallatin* (above, n. 241), 478.

to any use of force.[354] At the Plenipotentiaries' session on 14 April 1856, this provision was declared of general application at the suggestion of the Earl of Clarendon, yet without binding effect. Thus, Protocol 23 recommended that the use of good offices ought to precede the recourse to force. It stipulated, furthermore, that the Governments not represented at the Congress were invited to associate with this statement.[355]

The following year, an incident involving the Two Sicilies and Great Britain arose and gave rise to the practical application of the Protocol.

ii) The Cagliari affair, 1857–1858

The *Cagliari* was a Sardinian mail steamer that sailed from Genoa to Tunis on 25 June 1857. During the journey, partisans of Guiseppe Mazzini took over the ship, attacked the Neapolitan island of Ponza, liberated about 300 political prisoners and took ammunition before landing at Sapri to continue their revolution in the Kingdom of the Two Sicilies. The response of the Neapolitan authorities consisted of seizing the steamer and imprisoning the crew amongst whom were two British engineers.[356] The Secretary of State for Foreign Affairs of Great Britain at the time was precisely the Earl of Clarendon, who thus instructed the acting consul at Naples to afford protection to them since they were probably ignorant of the insur-

---

354 Great Britain, F. O., *BFSP 1855–1856* (above, n. 267), 12.

355 Édouard Gourdon, *Histoire du Congrès de Paris*, avec une introduction par M. J. Cohen (Paris: Librairie nouvelle, 1857), 124–6. The Protocol only spoke of the good offices of a friendly Power, but not of arbitration. And yet, the assembled Powers did not commit to having recourse to this step if they believed that it would be contrary to their dignity. For the British historian and lawyer Frederic Seebohm, this declaration showed that arbitration was not viewed as an appropriate means to settle disputes between sovereign States. Therefore, he argued that international law needed first to be laid down before thinking of mandatory arbitration, so that arbitral decisions would offer greater predictability (Frederic Seebohm, *On International Reform* (London: Longmans, Green, and Co., 1871), 104–8). But see Christian Friedrich Wurm, 'Selbsthülfe der Staaten in Friedenszeiten.', *Deutsche Vierteljahrs-Schrift* 21/4 (1858), 71–94, at 87.

356 See Sir J. Hudson to the Earl of Clarendon, 2 July 1857: Great Britain, F. O., *BFSP 1857–1858* (above, n. 269), 326; Acting Consul Barbar to the Earl of Clarendon, 30 June 1857: Ibid., 327–8. See the whole diplomatic correspondence regarding this incident: Ibid., 326–557.

gents' plot.[357] In March and April 1858, both engineers were released on account of their health.[358]

With the favourable opinion of the Law Officers of the Crown,[359] the Earl of Malmesbury, who had succeeded the Earl of Clarendon at the head of the Foreign Office, demanded compensation from the Neapolitan Government.[360] Great Britain claimed 3.000£ as Naples had declined the offer to fix the amount of compensation itself.[361] The British Government warned that if the Two Sicilies persisted in refusing this reparation, Great Britain would be fully entitled to take measures of embargo or reprisals to enforce compliance with the demands. However, as proof of moderation, it was ready to refer the issue to a third State's mediation, pursuant to the 23rd Protocol of Paris to which the Neapolitan Government had subscribed.[362] In fact, apart from moderation, the British Government felt in some way morally bound to abide by the Protocol, given that this public act was of great importance in Europe and that a British minister pushed for the adoption of the principle laid down in it.[363] Regarding the identity of the mediator, the Earl of Malmesbury proposed Sweden or another second-rank Power like the Netherlands, Belgium or Portugal. He, nevertheless, expressly ruled out the choice of a great Power. Arbitration, likewise, was altogether out of the question.[364]

In the end, mediation proved unnecessary, for the Neapolitan Government consented to fulfil the demands entirely.[365] The fear of British reprisals could explain the payment of 3.000£ since the force of the Two

---

357 Mr Hammond to Acting Consul Barbar, 24 July and 14 August 1857: Ibid., 331.

358 Mr Lyons to the Earl of Malmesbury, 19 March and 10 April 1858: Ibid., 433 and 462.

359 The Law Officers of the Crown to the Earl of Malmesbury, 29 January and 12 April 1858: Ibid., 391–392; 463–464.

360 The Earl of Malmesbury to Mr Carafa, 15 April 1858: Ibid., 472.

361 The Earl of Malmesbury to Mr Carafa, 25 May 1858: Ibid., 538.

362 The Earl of Malmesbury to Mr Carafa, 25 May 1858: Ibid.

363 "Had not so public and important an act received the assent of Europe, Her Majesty's Government might, perhaps, have proceeded, on receiving the refusal of the Neapolitan Government to satisfy their just demands, to take such measures as would at once have secured the pecuniary payment required; but they do not, under the present circumstances, consider themselves justified in resorting to extremities until they have first appealed to the good offices of a friendly Power to assist them in settling their claim on the Neapolitan Government." (The Earl of Malmesbury to Mr Lyons, 25 May 1858: Ibid., 541).

364 Earl of Malmesbury to Mr Lyons, 25 May 1858: Ibid., 541–2.

365 Mr Carafa to the Earl of Malmesbury, 8 June 1858: Ibid., 552.

Sicilies did not match Great Britain's.[366] As for the release of the Sardinian crew and the restitution of the *Cagliari*, the Neapolitan Government certainly knew —without acknowledging it formally, though— that the capture of the steamer and the imprisonment of its company were hardly lawful in terms of international law. For these reasons, it probably gave up.

So, the system of conflict resolution enacted in the Protocol revealed successful in this case, and reprisals did not make beyond mere threats. Nevertheless, Great Britain's course of action here was justified by the general context of the affair that called for much caution. As a matter of fact, the reference to the Protocol aimed to avert a general European war owing to the fear that the Kingdom of Sardinia would resolve to wage war on the Two Sicilies for the insult.[367] That is why the termination of the dispute was received with relief at the British Parliament.[368]

iii) The Prince of Wales case: British Reprisals against Brazil, 1862–1863

However, in another instance where the political situation was not so dire, the British Government showed less readiness to abide by the principle of the Protocol.

When the British barque *Prince of Wales* was shipwrecked off the Brazilian coast in June 1861, the circumstances surrounding the discovery of the wreck led the British consul at Rio Grande do Sul to suspect that the locals murdered the surviving sailors and plundered the remaining cargo, while the Brazilian authorities either colluded with them or acted with gross negligence.[369] Therefore, the British Government was firmly convinced that Brazil's responsibility was engaged. Hence, the former demanded the latter's commitment to pay compensation. Although the losses were estimated at 6.525,19£, Great Britain was ready to accept arbitration at the request of the Brazilian Government, yet on the sole issue of the amount of com-

366 See Mr Carafa to the Earl of Malmesbury, 8 June 1858: Ibid.

367 Earl of Malmesbury, House of Lords, 29 April 1858: Great Britain, Parliament, *Hansard's Parliamentary Debates*: *Third Series. Commencing with the accession of William IV.* (149th vol.; London: Cornelius Buck, 1858), col. 1938f.

368 Entry for 12 June 1858: James Howard Harris, Earl of Malmesbury, *Memoirs of an ex-minister*: *An autobiography*, 2nd vol. (3rd edn., London: Longmans, Green, and Co., 1884), 123.

369 Consul Vereker to the Secretary to the Board of Trade, 25 June 1861: Great Britain, F. O., *BFSP 1863–1864* (above, n. 287), 579–83.

pensation to be paid.[370] If, however, Brazil refused the demands and made no proposal for arbitration, Brazilian ships or property should be seized by way of reprisals.[371]

The Brazilian Government turned down the demands, which compelled Great Britain to make use of force. Thus, Admiral Warren, in accordance with the British ambassador to Brazil William Christie, blockaded the port of Rio de Janeiro from 31 December 1862 until 6 January 1863, when the Brazilian Government finally agreed under protest to pay whatever sum. Three warships closed off the entrance of the bay while two steamers were dispatched to capture Brazilian vessels, resulting in five prizes valued at about 13.000£. Following the announcement of the settlement of the dispute, the detained vessels were at once released.[372]

After revaluation, the British Government fixed the compensation at 3.200£.[373] Brazil paid the sum but stressed that the payment was the result of coercion and not the admission of responsibility in the plunder of the *Prince of Wales*.[374] Besides, the Brazilian Government directly challenged the conduct of reprisals. Indeed, it regarded the blockade of Rio de Janeiro harbour and the capture and detention of vessels in Brazilian territorial waters as being acts of war and a wanton affront since captures on the high seas would perfectly have attained their goal and remained within the

---

370 Mr Christie to the Marquis of Abrantes, 5 December 1862: Ibid., 736–7. See Seymour FitzGerald's criticism of such settlement terms, House of Commons, 16 July 1863: Great Britain, Parliament, *Hansard's Parliamentary Debates* (above, n. 287), col. 884.

371 Earl Russell to Mr Christie, 8 November 1862: Great Britain, F. O., *BFSP 1863–1864* (above, n. 287), 718.
Another cause of complaint was the supposed ill-treatment of three British naval officers who were arrested and put in a cell for many hours. They were accused of aggression on a Brazilian policeman while they were reportedly drunk on leave. The British Government demanded satisfaction for the outrage in the form of the punishment of the culprits and an official apology. See Mr Christie to the Marquis of Abrantes, 5 December 1862: Ibid., 732–4.

372 See Mr Christie to Earl Russell, 8 January 1863: Ibid., 740–9; Rear-Admiral Warren to the Secretary to the Admiralty, 8 January 1863: Ibid., 802. Regarding the ill-treatment of the officers of H.M.S. *Forte*, the issue was referred to the arbitration of Leopold I, King of the Belgians. On 18 June 1863, he ruled that the application of Brazilian municipal laws to the British officers neither was intended nor amounted to an insult to the British Navy. See the award: Great Britain, F. O., *BFSP 1862–1863* (53rd vol.; London: William Ridgway, 1868), 150–1.

373 Earl Russell to Mr Moreira, 24 February 1863: Great Britain, F. O., *BFSP 1863–1864* (above, n. 287), 818.

374 Mr Moreira to Earl Russell, 26 February 1863: Ibid., 819–20.

bounds of a state of peace. Therefore, the Brazilian Government demanded satisfaction for the violation of its national territory as well as compensation for the damage caused to the prizes.[375] In other words, the point of contention was the manner in which the acts of reprisals had been executed, not their cause.[376]

Nevertheless, the British Secretary of State for Foreign Affairs, Earl Russell, rejected the Brazilian demands on the grounds that the question of the expediency or execution of reprisals was indivisible from the issue that led to their adoption. He, thus, contended that since Great Britain was entitled to exercise reprisals and did not attempt to humiliate or attack Brazil, the issue should remain closed.[377] But this answer was deemed unsatisfactory and, consequently, the Brazilian plenipotentiary minister at London announced the suspension of diplomatic relations between the two countries.[378]

The crisis triggered a lively debate in the British Parliament about the impropriety of reprisals in the present case. The opposition strongly criticised Earl Russell's behaviour in the affair. For example, the Earl of Malmesbury accused his successor at the head of the Foreign Office of neglecting the principle of the 23rd Protocol of 1856. According to him, the right course of action would have been to refer the issue to mediation or arbitration.[379] At the sitting of the House of Commons on 16 July 1863, Seymour FitzGerald, MP for Horsham, also argued that the Protocol could not be interpreted —unlike the assertion of the Under Secretary for Foreign Affairs, Austen Henry Layard— as ascribing to the target country the duty to propose arbitration. For FitzGerald, this interpretation was against the spirit of the Protocol. He instead defended the view that the State which intended to resort to forcible measures first had to propose arbitration. That is why he condemned the British Government for omitting to

375 Mr Moreira to Earl Russell, 5 May 1863: Ibid., 835–7.

376 This was made very clear in Mr Moreira's letter to Earl Russell, 25 May 1863: Ibid., 838–40. He wrote: "C'est cette série d'actes de guerre pratiqués dans un état de profonde paix, actes aussi offensifs que superflus; ce sont ces représailles prétendues "pacifiques," avec lesquelles on a fermé toute discussion entre les deux Gouvernements, qui établissent le droit du Gouvernement Impérial à la réparation demandée dans la note du 5 courant, droit que rien ne saurait infirmer, quelles que soient d'ailleurs les raisons qui aient pu amener le Gouvernement Britannique à avoir recours à l'expédient de la force." (Ibid., 839f.).

377 Earl Russell to Mr Moreira, 19 May 1863: Ibid., 838.

378 Mr Moreira to Earl Russell, 25 May 1863: Ibid., 841.

379 The Earl of Malmesbury, House of Lords, 19 June 1863: Great Britain, Parliament, *Hansard's Parliamentary Debates* (above, n. 338), col. 1135.

make such a formal offer of arbitration. This was clear evidence for him that rules only bound weak parties, whereas stronger Powers would not hesitate over departing from the stipulations if they judged it necessary or more convenient.[380]

Another charge against the British Government was the uncritical acceptance of ambassador Christie's conduct in this affair. FitzGerald drew to the attention of the House of Commons that the last instruction which Christie received contained the British Government's consent to submit the whole issue to arbitration if Brazil would request it. Instead, the British ambassador deliberately communicated a previous despatch that limited the scope of arbitration to the sole question of the amount of compensation.[381] For another MP, Mr Henley, "[t]he facts were just as much a matter for arbitration as the amount of damages." Otherwise, it would deprive the Protocol of its original meaning.[382]

Finally, the execution of reprisals was blamed, too. The Earl of Malmesbury argued that Great Britain abused its power. If reprisals had to be taken, the least offensive acts of reprisals like an embargo on the hundred Brazilian vessels present in British harbours ought to have been preferred.[383]

The British Government refuted these accusations and attempted to justify the course of action against Brazil. Earl Russell maintained that an offer of arbitration would have prompted the Brazilian Government to delay settlement further. Moreover, referring to Viscount Palmerston's doctrine and policy towards other nations against which claims existed, he contend-

380 Seymour FitzGerald, House of Commons, 16 July 1863: Great Britain, Parliament, *Hansard's Parliamentary Debates* (above, n. 287), col. 882–883. Cf. Paulsson, *Denial of Justice in International Law* (above, n. 61), 19: "It has often been observed in international relations, and elsewhere, that the weak seek the protection of the law, while the strong do not need to be punctilious about its observance."

381 Seymour FitzGerald, House of Commons, 16 July 1863: Great Britain, Parliament, *Hansard's Parliamentary Debates* (above, n. 287), col. 884–886. On the other hand, Charles Buxton, MP for Maidstone, regarded as an effective precedent for future disputes the offer of arbitration by Great Britain, a powerful nation, on the principle of the claim. (House of Commons, 6 March 1863: Great Britain, Parliament, *Hansard's Parliamentary Debates: Third Series. Commencing with the accession of William IV.* (169th vol.; London: Cornelius Buck, 1863), col. 1160–1161).

382 Mr Henley, House of Commons, 16 July 1863: Great Britain, Parliament, *Hansard's Parliamentary Debates* (above, n. 287), col. 923.

383 The Earl of Malmesbury, House of Lords, 19 June 1863: Great Britain, Parliament, *Hansard's Parliamentary Debates* (above, n. 338), col. 1135.

ed that Great Britain was entitled to seek redress to ensure the protection of its commerce in every part of the world. Weak nations, thus, could not hide behind their weakness to evade responsibility.[384] In the House of Commons, Layard also laid emphasis on the incentive effect that reprisals against Brazil had upon the South American countries against which Great Britain had many pending claims. He pointed out the improvement of Great Britain's relations with those countries and their readiness to provide redress. However, he noted that the recent protest of Brazil seemed to have reversed this trend.[385]

In the negotiations with Brazil under the good offices of the King of Portugal, Earl Russell stressed the legality of the proceeding. He maintained that neither the blockade of Rio de Janeiro nor the capture of Brazilian vessels in the territorial waters amounted to war because, on the one hand, this blockade did not impede the ingress and egress of vessels under a foreign flag and, on the other, legal experts made no difference between seizures on the high seas and in the territorial waters. He also added that Great Britain's reprisals were less questionable than the Brazilian military occupation of Uruguayan territories as reprisals. As for the indemnification for losses suffered as a result of reprisals, Earl Russell firmly rejected any compensation. He argued that it would, otherwise, be as if Great Britain confessed that the acts of reprisals were, in actual fact, unjust.[386] For the Secretary of State for Foreign Affairs, "we can never admit that the power given by the Law of Nations, which the Emperor of Brazil has exercised, Her Majesty, as the Sovereign of a great maritime Power, should not also possess."[387]

384 Earl Russell, House of Lords, 19 June 1863: Ibid., col. 1143–1145.

385 Mr Layard, House of Commons, 16 July 1863: Great Britain, Parliament, *Hansard's Parliamentary Debates* (above, n. 287), col. 898–899.

386 Earl Russell to Count Lavradio, 10 October 1864: Great Britain, F. O., *Papers respecting the Renewal of Diplomatic Relations with Brazil* (above, n. 283), 10–2. On this last point, the *Institut de Droit International* in 1887 laid down the rule that the vessels detained in the course of a pacific blockade had to be restored after its termination, "but without any compensation whatsoever." See James Brown Scott (ed.), *Resolutions of the Institute of International Law dealing with the Law of Nations: With an Historical Introduction and Explanatory Notes*, Collected and translated under the supervision of and edited by James Scott Brown (Carnegie Endowment for International Peace: Division of International Law; New York: OUP, 1916), 69f.

387 Earl Russell, House of Lords, 7 February 1865: Great Britain, Parliament, *Hansard's Parliamentary Debates: Third Series, Commencing with the accession of William IV.* (177th vol.; London: Cornelius Buck, 1865), col. 35. See also Earl

In the end, the diplomatic relations between Great Britain and Brazil were restored in 1865. The former obtained to pay no compensation, in return for giving the formal assurance that it did not intend to offend the latter's dignity.[388]

It should be remarked that both Great Britain and Brazil had acceded to the Protocol of Paris, the latter at the former's invitation. And yet, the Brazilian Government did not protest that Great Britain had not abided by the principle of the Protocol.[389] So, after six or seven years, the recommendation enshrined in the 23rd Protocol did not play a significant role any longer to prevent the recourse to armed reprisals. The question merely had relevance in the political debate that took place in the British Parliament.

Altogether, the resort to reprisals was barely subject to the observance of legal prerequisites. It actually depended mostly on political considerations.

IV. On the Questionable Edge of Peace

1. Disproportionate Use of Force

(a) Standard of Proportionality versus Efficacy

Nineteenth-century reprisals were generally disproportionate to the offence.[390] Indeed, because reprisals were public, States mainly pursued coercion and were little concerned about the amount of force exercised. Nevertheless, it does not mean that proportionality in the form of a general requirement ceased to apply.[391] The reprisal-taking countries were, in fact, often criticised for exercising acts of reprisals too harsh. They were, therefore, reminded of the standard of proportionality.

So, in the context of the *Don Pacifico* affair of 1850, Russia raised serious concerns about the overwhelming force used by Great Britain. Without challenging the just cause of complaint against Greece that entitled Great Britain to have recourse to reprisals, Philipp von Brunnow, the Russian ambassador at London, insisted that the acts of reprisals could not have

Russell to Count Lavradio, 7 February 1865: Great Britain, F. O., *Papers respecting the Renewal of Diplomatic Relations with Brazil* (above, n. 283), 16.

388 See Senhor Saraiva to Senhor Vasconcellos, 23 June 1865: Ibid., 19.

389 Cf. The Earl of Malmesbury, House of Lords, 19 June 1863: Great Britain, Parliament, *Hansard's Parliamentary Debates* (above, n. 338), col. 1135.

390 Colbert, *Retaliation in international law* (above, n. 6), 76.

391 Neff, *War and the Law of Nations* (above, n. 2), 226.

any hostile character. The coercive measures ("*mesures comminatoires*") thus had to remain within the limits of what was necessary to secure compensation equal to the amount claimed. That is why he argued that a blockade of the Greek coasts was utterly inconsistent with mere reprisals and a state of peace.[392] The Russian foreign minister, Count Karl Nesselrode, likewise believed that the coercive measures were disproportionate to the amount claimed and the object of the action.[393] Also in the British Parliament, Lord Stanley and the Earl of Aberdeen pointed out that the naval fleet sent to Greek waters was as big as Admiral Nelson's armada at the battle of the Nile.[394]

On another occasion, in 1864 at the time of the negotiations for resuming diplomatic relations between Great Britain and Brazil, the Portuguese ambassador to the former country referred to Vattel's remark on proportionality of reprisals. In fact, he considered that out of the five vessels seized by Great Britain one alone would have sufficed to secure the amount claimed.[395]

However, the reprisal-taking countries generally defended the opinion that the only way to beat the stubbornness of a target country was to show a strong arm.[396] For that purpose, the force employed had to be considerable. Only then could reprisals be coercive while making resignation honourable for the target country.[397] As a matter of fact, the use of reprisals in

---

392 Baron Brunnow to Viscount Palmerston, 22 January (O.S.)/8 February (N.S.) 1850: Great Britain, F. O., *BFSP 1849–1850. [2]* (above, n. 269), 499–504. See, thereupon, Cussy, *Phases et causes célèbres du droit maritime des nations* (above, n. 223), 2nd vol., 487.

393 Count Nesselrode to Baron Brunnow, 19 February 1850: Great Britain, F. O., *BFSP 1849–1850. [2]* (above, n. 269), 616.

394 Lord Stanley and the Earl of Aberdeen, House of Lords, 17 June 1850: Great Britain, Parliament, *Hansard's Parliamentary Debates* (above, n. 274), col. 1310 and 1350, respectively. See also Cussy, *Phases et causes célèbres du droit maritime des nations* (above, n. 223), 2nd vol., 491.

395 Count Lavradio to Earl Russell, 14 October 1864: Great Britain, F. O., *Papers respecting the Renewal of Diplomatic Relations with Brazil* (above, n. 283), 14.

396 E.g. "Certain it is, that with respect to most of the Hispano-American governments, the records of the department [i.e. the U.S. Department of State] will show that amicable remonstrance, diplomatic correspondence, and negotiation are totally unavailable to procure justice for outrages upon American citizens, *unless accompanied by use of means of coercion*." (Mr Sanford to Mr Cass, 10 August 1857: Sanford, *The Aves Island Case* (above, n. 43), 239 (emphasis added)).

397 See, e.g., Mr C. Anstey, House of Commons, 25 June 1850: Great Britain, Parliament, *Hansard's Parliamentary Debates* (above, n. 274), col. 371–372; Viscount Palmerston, House of Commons, 25 June 1850: Ibid., col. 397.

the nineteenth century responded to a preoccupation of coercion. Reprisals were not used as a source of compensation but rather pursued "the attainment of some satisfactory arrangement".[398] So, in the mind of the great Powers, reprisals had to be efficacious, whatever the amount of force used, before being proportionate.

As a result of this way of thinking, the acts of reprisals resorted to could be harsher than the mere seizure of property since the idea was to teach a lesson to the target country. For example, when Greytown (in today's Nicaragua) refused to comply with several demands of the United States — namely the payment of an indemnity for injuries to an American company and for outrages to American citizens, the apology for the indignity committed to the American Minister to Central America and the promise to prevent the recurrence of similar abuses—, the U.S.S. *Cyane* shelled and destroyed the town in 1854.[399] Although the U.S. Secretary of the Navy, James C. Dobbin, instructed Captain Hollins on 10 June 1854 to act with restraint, he actually believed that the people of Greytown "should be taught that the United States will not tolerate these outrages, and that they have the power and the determination to check them."[400] In the present case, the use of a considerable force aimed to deter the recurrence of unlawful acts.

So, throughout the nineteenth century, a standard of proportionality between the amount of force employed and the seriousness of the offence did not guide the exercise of reprisals, since this self-help measure pursued the main idea of compulsion. It would take until 1928 before a mixed arbitral tribunal strongly reaffirmed in the *Naulilaa* case that such a requirement is indispensable to make reprisals lawful.[401]

398 Colbert, *Retaliation in international law* (above, n. 6), 77.

399 Moore, *A digest of international law* (above, n. 222), 112–4. See also Cussy, *Phases et causes célèbres du droit maritime des nations* (above, n. 223), 2nd vol., 528–533.

400 Quoted in Moore, *A digest of international law* (above, n. 222), 113f.

401 "Même si l'on admettait que le droit des gens n'exige pas que la représaille se mesure approximativement à l'offense, on devrait certainement considérer, comme excessives et partant illicites, des représailles hors de toute proportion avec l'acte qui les a motivées." (*Responsabilité de l'Allemagne à raison des dommages causés dans les colonies portugaises du sud de l'Afrique (Sentence sur le principe de la responsabilité*), Decision of 31 July 1928, RIAA 2 (1949), 1011–33, at 1028).

(b) Widening of the Category of Reprisals

Following this logic of coercion, the acts of reprisals had to be as intimidating as possible. However, during the period 1831–1863, reprisals were often understood *sensu stricto* as the seizure of ships or property.[402] That is why they were usually accompanied by other means of duress for the sake of efficacy.[403] As a consequence, the concept of 'reprisals' progressively came to cover any kind of coercive measure taken with the aim of attaining a satisfactory agreement with the offending State.

Whereas reprisals in the form of the seizure on the highs seas or in ports (embargo) were regarded as consistent with a state of peace as long as the target country did not treat them as constituting acts of war,[404] the legality of the other measures of coercion in time of peace was in many respects doubtful.

The reprisal-taking countries often had recourse, i.a., to a naval blockade of specific ports or stretches of coastline of the target country as a means accompanying the capture of ships. However, before the nineteenth century, a blockade referred exclusively to a belligerent right sanctioned by the law of nations.[405] Therefore, the use of such blockades outside a state of

---

402 See, e.g., Viscount Palmerston, House of Commons, 4 March 1850: Great Britain, Parliament, *Hansard's Parliamentary Debates*: *Third Series, commencing with the accession of William IV.* (109th vol.; London: Cornelius Buck, 1850), col. 316; Viscount Palmerston to Baron Brunnow, 30 March 1850: Great Britain, F. O., *BFSP 1849–1850. [2]* (above, n. 269), 738; Earl Russell to Mr Christie, 8 November 1862: Great Britain, F. O., *BFSP 1863–1864* (above, n. 287), 718.

403 E.g. "[…] it was necessary at length to resort to measures of reprisal and coercion, to show a force far more than sufficient to enforce our demands." (Lord J. Russell, House of Commons, 28 June 1850: Great Britain, Parliament, *Hansard's Parliamentary Debates* (above, n. 274), col. 711). As Westlake pointed out, pacific blockade and reprisals *strictu sensu* (i.e. the sequestration of properties for compensation) could be combined together, "but then any confiscation for breach of the blockade will be reprisal." (Westlake, *International Law* (above, n. 25), 17 fn. 2).

404 Thus, Mr Christie could warn the Brazilian Government not to retaliate or resist violently; otherwise, war would break out between both countries and bring unpleasant consequences. See Mr Christie to the Marquis of Abrantes, 30 December 1862: Great Britain, F. O., *BFSP 1863–1864* (above, n. 287), 774.

405 Thomas Alfred Walker, *A Manual of Public International Law* (Cambridge: CUP, 1895), 96. See also Paul Fauchille, *Du blocus maritime*: *Étude de droit international et de droit comparé* (Paris: Arthur Rousseau, 1882), 38–67, who strongly emphasised the illegality of pacific blockade as the abusive use of a right valid only in maritime warfare.

war was subject to severe criticisms.[406] Palmerston himself, who approved several times the establishment of such a coercive blockade while he was at the head of the Foreign Office, secretly confessed at the time of the Franco-British blockade of La Plata (1845–1847) that blockading the ports of another State was a belligerent right. Thus, if war was not declared between the blockading and the blockaded nations, the operation would be utterly illegal from the start.[407]

The first blockade short of war —a measure later labelled 'pacific blockade' in legal doctrine[408]—, instituted in a context of reprisals, was experimented under Palmerston's administration. This step was decided in response to the refusal by the New Granadan Government to give satisfaction for the allegedly false imprisonment of a British pro-consul and the ensuing violation of the British consulate of Panama City.[409] The blockade

---

406 See, e.g., Baron Brunnow to Viscount Palmerston, 22 January (O.S.)/8 February (N.S.) 1850: Great Britain, F. O., *BFSP 1849–1850. [2]* (above, n. 269), 503; Count Lavradio's memorandum, 27 May 1864: Great Britain, F. O., *Papers respecting the Renewal of Diplomatic Relations with Brazil* (above, n. 283), 3. Earl Malmesbury and Lord Chelmsford also drew the attention of the House of Lords on 19 June 1863 to the nature of blockade, namely an act of war. See Great Britain, Parliament, *Hansard's Parliamentary Debates* (above, n. 338), col. 1134 and 1160, respectively.

407 "The real truth is, though we had better keep the fact to ourselves, that the French and English blockade of the Plate has been from first to last illegal. Peel and Aberdeen have always declared that we have not been at war with Rosas [= Juan Manuel de Rosas, dictator of the Argentine Confederation]; but blockade is a belligerent right, and, unless you are at war with a state, you have no right to prevent ships of other states from communicating with the ports of that state —nay, you cannot prevent your own merchant ships from doing so. I think it important, therefore, in order to legalise retrospectively the operations of the blockade, to close the matter by a formal convention of peace between the two Powers and Rosas." (Viscount Palmerston to Lord Normanby, 7 December 1846: Henry Lytton Bulwer, *The Life of Henry John Temple, Viscount Palmerston: with Selections from his Correspondence*, 3rd vol. (3rd edn., London: Richard Bentley, 1874), 327). Cf. Sir William Scott's judgement in *The Fox and others*, pronounced on 30 May 1811, in which he concurred with the opinion that "a blockade, imposed for the purpose of obtaining a commercial monopoly for the private advantage of the state which lays on such blockade, is illegal and void on the very principle upon which it is founded." (Thomas Edwards, *Reports of Cases Argued and Determined in the High Court of Admiralty: Commencing with the Judgments of the Right Hon. Sir William Scott, Easter Term, 1808*, edited by George Minot (Boston: Little, Brown and Company, 1853), 320).

408 See Chapter Three.

409 See Great Britain, F. O., *BFSP 1837–1838* (26th vol.; London: Printed by Harrison and sons, 1855), 128–268.

of the whole New Granada coast began on 21 January and lasted till 2 February 1837 as the news of the pro-consul's liberation reached Commodore Peyton, anchored off Carthagena, and the Colombian general in charge of the defence of that place pledged the payment of the requested sum.[410]

The use of a blockade short of war proved to be efficient as a means of coercion since New Granada consented to provide redress. Indeed, statesmen had recognised the potent character of such a proceeding. Thus, already when reprisals were merely contemplated, the British diplomat stationed in Bogotá characterised such a blockade as compulsion not amounting to war.[411] In the context of the *Don Pacifico* affair of 1850, the MP for Sheffield also underlined the fact that a blockade could prevent war when instituted against weak nations. Still, he conceded that against a great nation, a blockade would not fail to be automatically treated as a declaration of war.[412] In the following years, the example set by Great Britain was soon to be imitated. For instance, France resorted to a similar kind of blockade against Mexico in 1838.

410 Commodore Peyton to Consul Kelly, 21 January 1837: Ibid., 256; the former to Mr Turner, 2 February 1837: Ibid., 263–5.
It is, however, unlikely that the whole coast was effectively blockaded since Commodore Peyton had only seven ships at his disposal. Carthagena was actually one of the only places blockaded. Cf. Falcke, *Le blocus pacifique* (above, n. 40), 49. Yet, President Francisco de Paula Santander claimed in his message to the New Granadan Congress on 1 March 1837 that the blockade "was done with so much rigour, that even Letters addressed to Granadan citizens and Authorities were intercepted." (Message of the President of the Republic of New Granada on the opening of the Congress, 1 March 1837: Great Britain, F. O., *BFSP 1836–1837* (25th vol.; London: James Ridgway, 1853), 1047).

411 Mr Turner to Admiral Halkett, 11 December 1836: Great Britain, F. O., *BFSP 1837–1838* (above, n. 409), 231–2.

412 "Now mark the curious mode of proceeding, and let us consider that with great nations a blockade is a declaration of war, and must of necessity be so; but in dealing with weak and comparatively powerless nations it is really a merciful and a useful mode of avoiding war to take the preliminary step of blockade—not reprisals, be it observed, as has been too often but most erroneously stated. This, I say, in dealing with weak nations, is far better than declaring war, and thereby risking the peace of the world." (Mr Roebuck, House of Commons, 24 June 1850: Great Britain, Parliament, *Hansard's Parliamentary Debates* (above, n. 274), col. 240).

Nevertheless, the legality of those blockades was very dubious. In fact, in the course of the blockade of New Granada, foreign vessels were detained and then released at the end.[413] Third States protested that outside a state of war the ingress and egress of their ships to any ports could not be impeded by a blockading force.[414] The Queen's Advocate, Sir John Dodson, also stated that, although Great Britain was entitled in that case to make reprisals by seizing ships and property of New Granadan citizens, only a state of war justified the blockade of ports and the interference with foreign merchant vessels. Therefore, he believed that Great Britain had actually been at war with New Granada.[415]

The same cause of complaint arose with the French blockade of Mexico. Indeed, according to the notification of the blockade, the so-called "neutral ships" could be detained if after special warning they attempted to break

413 See Commodore Peyton to Consul Turner, 23 January 1837: Great Britain, F. O., *BFSP 1837–1838* (above, n. 409), 257; Commodore Peyton to Mr Turner, 2 February 1837: Ibid., 263 and 265.

414 For instance, the Hanseatic towns stated the following: "En vain on feuillette les traités sur le droit des gens pour rencontrer le blocus dans l'énumération des moyens de terminer les différends nationaux sans avoir recours à la guerre. Certainement ils ne l'approuveraient guères dans une étendue qui fait souffrir d'autres nations que celle de laquelle ils [sic!] s'agit d'obtenir le redressement de quelque grief … En effet ce n'est guères [sic!] que la dernière nécessité qui jusqu'ici a justifié des mesures plus impérieuses à des tiers qu'aux belligérants. *Au moins dans un cas exceptionnel où d'autres mesures de fait ne paraissent pas applicables, le blocus diplomatique inconnu au droit des gens de nos pères devrait-il se distinguer par tous les ménagements pour la navigation des tiers qui ne le rendraient pas complètement illusoire.*" (Memorandum of the Hanseatic towns, 10 September 1838, quoted in Falcke, *Le blocus pacifique* (above, n. 40), 56 fn. 10 (emphasis in original)). Cf. the letter of the New York Chamber of Commerce to the U.S. Secretary of State John Forsyth, 5 September 1838: Martens, *Nouveau recueil de traités d'Alliance, de Paix, de Trêve, de Neutralité, de Commerce, de Limites, d'Echange etc. et de plusieurs autres actes servant à la connoissance des relations étrangères des Puissances et Etats de l'Europe tant dans leur rapport mutuel que dans celui envers les Puissances et Etats dans d'autres parties du globe depuis 1808 jusqu'à présent* (above, n. 267), 15th vol., 806–807.

415 P. R. O., F. O. 83–2254, 14 March 1837, quoted in Clive Parry, 'British Practice in Some Nineteenth Century Pacific Blockades', *ZaöRV* 8 (1938), 672–88, at 676. Sir John Dodson gave a similar opinion on the Anglo-French blockade of La Plata, to wit, that a blockade was altogether incompatible with a state of peace. See P. R. O., F. O. 83–2227, 25 July 1846, quoted in Ibid., 679.

the blockade.[416] Consequently, during the enforcement of the blockade that lasted seven months, 46 ships of third States were captured while 4 Mexican vessels were sequestrated.[417] The third States likewise protested against this proceeding.[418]

To make those coercive blockades acceptable, it was then imperative not to impede the free navigation of ships of third States. That is why the blockade that Great Britain established against Greece in 1850 confined its effects to ships under the Greek flag.[419] The same concern not to interfere with foreign shipping also appeared a decade later when Great Britain

---

416 Item 1 of the French notification of the blockade, 15 April 1838. Nevertheless, British packet boats used in mail service could freely ingress and egress the ports of Veracruz and Tampico (Item 3), and the vessels navigating under the flag of a third State had 15 days to leave the blockaded ports from the moment when the said blockade was established (Item 2). See Great Britain, F. O., *BFSP 1837–1838* (above, n. 409), 1100. According to Count Molé, these orders aimed to reach a balance between effective coercion and "the sincere desire to cause the least possible inconvenience to the navigation of neutral vessels." (Count Molé to Earl Granville, 1 June 1838: Ibid., 726f.).

417 Extract of Théobald de Lacrosse's report to the *Chambre des députés*, 21 June 1839: Martens, *Nouveau recueil de traités d'Alliance, de Paix, de Trêve, de Neutralité, de Commerce, de Limites, d'Echange etc. et de plusieurs autres actes servant à la connoissance des relations étrangères des Puissances et Etats de l'Europe tant dans leur rapport mutuel que dans celui envers les Puissances et Etats dans d'autres parties du globe depuis 1808 jusqu'à présent* (above, n. 267), 16th vol., 614.

418 After an American master rescued his schooner which had been captured by one of the French brigs of war blockading the Mexican ports, France asked the U.S. Government for the restitution of the vessel on 20 July 1838. But the Department of State did not accede to the demand on the grounds that "[t]he writers on international law have not enumerated blockade as one of the peaceable remedies to which an injured nation might resort, but have classed it among the usual means of direct hostility." Hence the applicable rules were those of belligerent blockade, what fell within the competence of the Judiciary but not of the Executive. See Moore, *A digest of international law* (above, n. 222), 135. However, months after the termination of the conflict, a French legislator asserted that a blockade as a coercive measure did not amount to war. See the extract of Théobald de Lacrosse's report to the *Chambre des députés*, 21 June 1839: Martens, *Nouveau recueil de traités d'Alliance, de Paix, de Trêve, de Neutralité, de Commerce, de Limites, d'Echange etc. et de plusieurs autres actes servant à la connoissance des relations étrangères des Puissances et Etats de l'Europe tant dans leur rapport mutuel que dans celui envers les Puissances et Etats dans d'autres parties du globe depuis 1808 jusqu'à présent* (above, n. 267), 16th vol., 614.

419 Consul Green to the Consular Body at Athens, 24 January 1850: Great Britain, F. O., *BFSP 1849–1850. [2]* (above, n. 269), 534. Besides, in order to avoid interfering with foreign commerce, Sir William Parker instructed a captain of his fleet that foreign merchants could within 24 hours produce the proof that the

blockaded the harbour of Rio de Janeiro in 1862–1863.[420] Regarding this latter incident, Earl Russell explained that the blockade had been intended to facilitate the capture of Brazilian ships. But he denied that it was equivalent to a wartime blockade because there had precisely been no effectual closing of the port of Rio de Janeiro against vessels of third States.[421]

2. Confusion between War and Peace

In the first half of the nineteenth century, a blockade short of war could still not claim a place amongst the lawful methods of coercion. In Clive Parry's own words, the cases of blockade show that at that time "there was either a state of war, real though undeclared, or a frankly illegal proceeding. [It] leads us to the conclusion that there was no such thing as pacific blockade in the sense of belligerent blockade bereft of belligerency in the time which later writers imagined to be the lusty childhood of the institution."[422] By extension, the same remark equally applies to other forceful measures like the bombardment of towns by way of reprisals.

---

cargo seized on a Greek ship belonged to them. See Vice-Admiral Sir W. Parker to Captain the Hon. F. Pelham, 26 January 1850: Ibid., 573–4. Only Greek property present on a Greek vessel could then be seized. See Mr Wyse to Viscount Palmerston, 25 January 1850: Ibid., 526. Yet, as Sir William Parker reported to the Secretary to the Admiralty, "[t]he cargoes of Greek vessels being chiefly the property of foreign merchants, many of them naturalised subjects of Turkey, Russia, and England, few vessels are to be met with whose cargoes and hulls can be identified as exclusively Greek, and we have been anxious not to give any cause of complaint by interfering with any foreign property." (Vice-Admiral Sir W. Parker to the Secretary to the Admiralty, 28 January 1850: Ibid., 573). Nonetheless, about 41 Greek vessels were being sequestrated on 18 February 1850 as it results from a despatch of Mr Wyse to Viscount Palmerston. See Ibid., 653. This led to the stinging commentary of Lord Stanley that the British step targeted "a weak, unoffending people, interrupting harmless commerce, and plundering wretched, half-pauper fishermen of their sole means of subsistence." (Lord Stanley, House of Lords, 17 June 1850: Great Britain, Parliament, *Hansard's Parliamentary Debates* (above, n. 274), col. 1321).

420 See Mr Christie to Acting Consul Hollocombe, 1 January 1869: Great Britain, F. O., *BFSP 1863–1864* (above, n. 287), 783.

421 Earl Russell to Count Lavradio, 10 October 1864: Great Britain, F. O., *Papers respecting the Renewal of Diplomatic Relations with Brazil* (above, n. 283), 10.

422 Parry, 'British Practice in Some Nineteenth Century Pacific Blockades' (above, n. 415), 682. See also August (von) Bulmerincq, 'Le blocus pacifique et ses effets sur la propriété privée', *Clunet* 11 (1884), 569–83, at 574.

Under such circumstances, the use of belligerent measures in time of peace could only create confusion between war and peace. In fact, the reprisal-taking countries never issued a declaration of war before resorting to armed reprisals.[423] It patently reveals that the great Powers did not want to assume the responsibility for declaring war or, at the very least, that they intended to delay the formality of a declaration of war as long as the inevitability of war could still be denied. And yet, a state of war could arise without a formal declaration of war by the attacking State.[424] Nonetheless, the distinction between peace and war was no easy thing to determine when armed reprisals were employed. The acts of armed reprisals were so ambiguous in character that only the subsequent events could help to classify them.

In 1831, i.e. the first known case of reprisals within the investigated period, France resolved to make reprisals against Portugal on account of the mistreatment of French citizens in the course of persecutions carried out by the self-proclaimed King of Portugal, Dom Miguel I, who sought to quell the unrest in his realm. Unlike Great Britain that successfully pressed the claims of the injured British nationals,[425] the consul of France failed in this attempt to obtain redress from the King. The French Government, thus, sent a squadron to the Tagus estuary to back up the consul's demands. Portuguese warships and merchant vessels were captured and then brought to France. Nevertheless, Dom Miguel's obstinacy compelled the French Government to dispatch a stronger naval force.[426] On 11 July 1831, an engagement between the French forces, on the one hand, and the Por-

---

423 Nonetheless, an examination of the cases shows that an ultimatum usually preceded the first acts of reprisals. The issuance of an ultimatum was sometimes strongly disapproved, e.g. by Count Nesselrode in 1850. See Lord Bloomfield to Viscount Palmerston, 12 February 1850: Great Britain, F. O., *BFSP 1849–1850. [2]* (above, n. 269), 612.

424 Parry, 'British Practice in Some Nineteenth Century Pacific Blockades' (above, n. 415), 680. See P. R. O., F. O. 83–2227, 25 July 1846, quoted in Ibid., 685.

425 In fact, Lord Palmerston had threatened to order the Naval Commander of the British squadron off Lisbon and Porto to take reprisals if the Portuguese Government did not accede to the demands within ten days. See Viscount Palmerston to R. B. Hoppner, 15 April 1831: Great Britain, F. O., *BFSP 1830–1831* (above, n. 267), 249.

426 Palmerston had actually warned the Portuguese diplomatic agent at London that "measures of more vigorous hostility" could supersede the acts of reprisals already made if France did not get immediate satisfaction from the Government of Portugal. See Viscount Palmerston to Viscount d'Asseca, 18 June 1831: Ibid., 380.

tuguese warships and coastal forts, on the other, took place. It ended in a decisive French victory. At last, the Portuguese Government yielded. A treaty was signed on 14 July by which Portugal gave full satisfaction to the French demands and committed to paying damages as well as a compensation for the naval expedition.[427]

The question of the existence of war had not been raised previously. It truly became of practical interest when Portugal raised the issue of the restitution of the ships captured on the day of the battle which took place on 11 July. Indeed, the Portuguese Government defended a legalistic approach to war, namely that in the absence of the formality of a preceding declaration, war could not exist *de jure*. Therefore, the ships in question could merely be detained by way of reprisals until satisfaction was given. On the other hand, France contended that the laws of war applied in the present case because there had been a war *de facto*. As a consequence, the ships should remain confiscated as good prizes of war.[428] It was obviously to France's advantage to claim the existence of a state of war despite the absence of a declaration.

When Portugal called the British Government to lend support in the controversy, the latter refused to back the Portugese claims by validating the French legal viewpoint.[429] As a matter of fact, French Admiral Roussin told the Portuguese foreign minister on 8 July that France would treat the rejection of the demands as an actual declaration of war.[430] On this basis, the King's Advocate Sir Herbert Jenner argued that, if it were not for Article 18 of the treaty of 14 July 1831 which provided the contrary, the French Government would have been entitled to retain even the ships captured since the beginning of the hostilities.[431] Yet, by referring to the terms

---

427 For a contemporary relation of the events, see Ulysse Tencé, *Annuaire historique universel pour 1831: Avec un Appendice contenant les actes publics, traités, notes diplomatiques, papiers d'états et tableaux statistiques, financiers, administratifs et nécrologiques; – une Chronique offrant les événements les plus piquants, les causes les plus célèbres, etc; et des notes pour servir à l'histoire des sciences, des lettres et des arts*, Nouvelle série (Paris: Thoisnier-Desplaces, 1833), 550–7. See also Great Britain, F. O., *BFSP 1830–1831* (above, n. 267), 43–341 and 341–440, for the diplomatic correspondence relative to the British and the French demands upon Portugal.

428 See Viscount de Santarem to Admiral Roussin, 11 August 1831: Ibid., 430–2.

429 See Viscount Palmerston to Viscount d'Asseca, 25 August 1831: Ibid., 427.

430 Admiral Roussin to Viscount de Santarem, 8 July 1831: Ibid., 407.

431 "This latter species of seizure [i.e. by way of reprisals] is resorted to, with the view of obtaining satisfaction for injuries alleged to have been received, and in order to prevent the necessity of having recourse to actual hostilities; and may

of the convention, Jenner failed to explain when and if hostilities, i.e. war, actually superseded reprisals.[432]

However, this case apart, the reprisal-taking Power generally asserted the uninterrupted state of peace and claimed that the means employed amounted to lawful coercion because of the absence of armed resistance or declaration of war by the target country. The only way for the latter to frustrate the former's contention consisted of issuing a clear statement of intention in the form of a declaration of war.

This happened in 1838 when France undertook reprisals against Mexico on account of a long list of offences against French nationals and their property over a span of thirteen years that had remained unredressed. On 21 March 1838, an ultimatum was issued: either the Mexican Government would comply with the demands it contained or France would blockade Mexican ports in order to cut the maritime custom revenues, in the same manner as an exasperated creditor would deal with a recalcitrant debtor.[433]

---

be looked upon as a provisional measure, the character of which is to be determined by subsequent events. If the reprisals should produce a satisfactory result, followed by a restoration of peace between the two Countries, the property seized would be considered as having been placed under temporary sequestrations only, and would be restored to the original proprietors. But, should hostilities once commence, the seizure would then assume an hostile character *ab initio*; so that those ships which were seized before, as well as those which were captured after, that event, would become the property of the capturing State, and the title of the former Owners be divested." (The King's Advocate to Viscount Palmerston, 9 August 1831: Ibid., 421–2). This opinion actually echoed the teaching of Sir William Scott's judgement in *The Boedes Lust* case (see *supra*, fn. 255).

432 Thereupon, Colbert rightly pointed out some flaws in Jenner's opinion. Firstly, it is quite doubtful that Admiral Roussin was actually accredited, without producing his instructions, to declare his country at war with the target country in the case of the latter's failure to comply with the demands. Secondly, Jenner did not clarify if any forceful resistance to reprisals should be regarded as an implicit acceptance of the challenge of war unless the intention to resort to counter-reprisals was clearly announced. See Colbert, *Retaliation in international law* (above, n. 6), 97f. But cf. Sir William Scott's view in the judgement of 11 June 1799 in *The Maria*, which dealt with the question of the forcible resistance of a neutral vessel to the belligerent party's right of visit and search. The judge of the High Court of Admiralty considered in this case that resistance to lawful force did not constitute a right in time of peace but was allowed only in a state of war. See Robinson, *Reports of Cases Argued and Determined in the High Court of Admiralty* (above, n. 255), 1st vol., 360.

433 See the ultimatum in Clercq & Clercq, *Recueil des traités de la France* (above, n. 269), 4th vol., 403–416.

On 16 April, the blockade began.[434] This blockade, which was enforced pacifically against the sole harbour of Veracruz, did not lead to hostilities until 27 November, when the French shelled the fort of San Juan de Ulúa and landed troops to occupy the town.[435] Although France justified the capture of the fort as a pledge,[436] the Mexican Government thwarted this plan by declaring war on 30 November.[437] The hostilities lasted till 9 March 1839 with the signature of an armistice, a peace treaty and a convention for the settlement of claims between France and Mexico.[438]

---

434 See the notification of the blockade to third Powers by the French foreign minister, 31 May 1838: Martens, *Nouveau recueil de traités d'Alliance, de Paix, de Trêve, de Neutralité, de Commerce, de Limites, d'Echange etc. et de plusieurs autres actes servant à la connoissance des relations étrangères des Puissances et Etats de l'Europe tant dans leur rapport mutuel que dans celui envers les Puissances et Etats dans d'autres parties du globe depuis 1808 jusqu'à présent* (above, n. 267), 15th vol., 803.

435 Falcke, *Le blocus pacifique* (above, n. 40), 55–8.

436 "Si M. le Contr'-Amiral Baudin, [...], se rendait maître du Château d'Ulloa, cette position, qui ne serait dans nos mains qu'un simple nantissement, serait évacuée le jour même où nous aurions obtenu du Mexique la satisfaction qui nous est due." (Count Molé to Earl Granville, 19 September 1838: Great Britain, F. O., *BFSP 1837–1838* (above, n. 409), 897). However, it is reported that Rear Admiral Baudin wrote on 27 November that his peace errand having failed, it was consequently time for war. See Falcke, *Le blocus pacifique* (above, n. 40), 57.

437 See the declaration in Great Britain, F. O., *BFSP 1837–1838* (above, n. 409), 1123.

438 See Martens, *Nouveau recueil de traités d'Alliance, de Paix, de Trêve, de Neutralité, de Commerce, de Limites, d'Echange etc. et de plusieurs autres actes servant à la connoissance des relations étrangères des Puissances et Etats de l'Europe tant dans leur rapport mutuel que dans celui envers les Puissances et Etats dans d'autres parties du globe depuis 1808 jusqu'à présent* (above, n. 267), 16th vol., 607–611.
One question left to arbitration related to the lot of the Mexican vessels seized in the course of the blockade and after the beginning of the hostilities. See Art. 2 of the Convention for the settlement of claims, 9 March 1839: Ibid., 16th vol., 610f. The young Queen Victoria agreed to arbitrate this issue and ruled on 1 August 1844 that, owing to the existence of a state of war, France had retroactively acquired the ships detained since the establishment of the blockade. See the arbitral award in Clercq & Clercq, *Recueil des traités de la France* (above, n. 269), 5th vol., 194. This decision corresponds with Jenner's opinion in 1831 and the teaching of Sir William Scott's judgement in the *Boedes Lust* case (see *supra*, fn. 255). According to John Westlake, the arbitral award conveyed the British opinion regarding the blockades short of war, namely that the ships of the blockaded country could merely be sequestrated unless war broke out. See John Westlake, 'Pacific Blockade', *The Law Quarterly Review* 25 (1909), 13–23, at 17.

So, unless the target country declared war, the operation of reprisals allegedly did not interrupt the state of peace between both parties involved. However, the nature of the action remained in most cases open to interpretation. For example, the official statements made at the time of the British reprisals against New Granada in 1837 indicate the existence of an undefined state of affairs, a twilight zone mid-way between 'perfect' peace and 'perfect' war. Indeed, New Granadan President Francisco de Paula Santander, although being careful not to speak of war or overtly declare it, seemed to regard the contemplated British proceeding as unwarrantable hostilities which suspended the friendly relations between both countries.[439] In the same vein, the British naval commander's turn of phrase that the blockade "materially assisted the pacification" also hints that the 'perfect' state of peace between the parties had been disrupted.[440] For the Queen's Advocate, there was little doubt, though, that the establishment of a blockade always entailed a state of war.[441] Nevertheless, in the absence of an express declaration of war, this case has been regarded hitherto as an instance of reprisals.

During the first half of the nineteenth century, a switch regarding the concept of war happened. It was no longer the nature of the acts exercised that allowed the assessment of the existence of a state of war, but the intent of the parties to the conflict: *non ex re sed ex nomine*. The Judiciary then had power neither to proclaim the existence of war nor to apply the corresponding effects, even though the reprisal action could oddly resemble war to all appearances.[442] The consequence was that all the acts which were not followed by a declaration or recognition of the existence of a status of war

---

439 See the proclamation of the President of New Granada to the Nation, 12 December 1836: Great Britain, F. O., *BFSP 1837–1838* (above, n. 409), 236–8. In his message to the New Granadan Congress after the termination of the incident, he referred to the British blockade as either a measure of coercion or an act of hostility. He stated too that "an arrangement being entered into, the Blockade was raised, *and the relations of the 2 countries replaced upon their former footing.*" (Message of the President of the Republic of New Granada on the opening of the Congress, 1 March 1837: Great Britain, F. O., *BFSP 1836–1837* (above, n. 410), 1047f. (emphasis added)).

440 Commodore Peyton to Mr Turner, 2 February 1837: Great Britain, F. O., *BFSP 1837–1838* (above, n. 409), 263.

441 Parry, 'British Practice in Some Nineteenth Century Pacific Blockades' (above, n. 415), 676.

442 This is what the U.S. Court of Claims pointed out in a case involving a French national who sought compensation for the destruction of her property following the bombardment of Greytown in 1854: "The claimant's case must necessar-

were presumed to remain within the limits of peace.[443] This reasoning led the *Conseil d'État*, the supreme administrative court of France, to decide in the *Comte de Thomar* case that goods seized on a neutral vessel could not be condemned as contraband when a blockade was instituted outside the time of war.[444]

---

ily rest upon the assumption that the bombardment and destruction of Greytown was illegal and not justified by the law of nations. […]. [The questions raised] are international political questions, which no court of this country in a case of this kind is authorized or empowered to decide. They grew out of and relate to peace and war, and to the relations and intercourse between this country and foreign nations. *They are political in their nature and character, and under our system belong to political departments of the government to define, arrange, and determine*. And when the questions arise incidentally in our courts the judiciary follow and adopt the action of the executive and legislative departments, whatever they may be." (*Marie Louise Perrin and Trautman Perrin, her husband, v. The United States* (1868): Charles C. Nott and Samuel H. Huntington, *Cases decided in the Court of Claims of the United States: at the December Term for 1868. With the Acts of Congress relating to the Court*, 4th vol. (Washington, D. C.: W. H. & O. H. Morrison, [1868]), 547 (emphasis added)). Lord Macnaghten maintained a similar opinion in *Janson v. Driefontein Consolidated Mines* (1902): "In every community it must be for the supreme power, whatever it is, to determine the policy of the community in regard to peace and war." (Pollock & Stone, *The Law Reports or The Incorporated Council of Law Reporting. House of Lords, Judicial Committee of the Privy Council, and Peerage Cases* (above, n. 33), 497).

443 In *Stephen Bishop et al. v. Jones & Petty* (1866), the Supreme Court of Texas stated that "though reprisals and embargoes are forcible measures of redress, yet they do not, *per se*, constitute war. Even hostile attacks and armed invasions, although accompanied by destruction of life and property, and made by the authorized officers of one government on the soil or jurisdiction of another, do not inevitably inaugurate war; for it may be that they will be atoned for and adjusted without war ensuing. War, in its legal sense, has been aptly defined to be "the state of nations between whom there is an interruption of all pacific relations, and a general contestation of arms authorized by the sovereigns."" (George W. Paschal, *Reports of cases argued and decided in the Supreme Court of the State of Texas, during the Austin session, 1866*, 28th vol. (Washington, D.C.: W. H. & O. H. Morrison, 1869), 295).

444 On Mr Guizot's own admission, the blockade of the Río de la Plata did not amount to a declared war between France and the Argentine Government. See *Chambre des pairs*, 8 February 1841 (*Le Moniteur universel*, 9 February 1841, 316). Before the *Conseil d'État*, both the Ministers of the Navy and of Foreign Affairs asserted that a state of war could not exist in the absence of a declaration of war. Yet, the same effects towards neutral shipping applied in the case of a blockade short of war as in the case of a belligerent one, in order to not deprive the measure of its efficacy. On the other hand, the ship-owners' counsel argued that there was a distinction to be made between a belligerent blockade and a "sim-

3. A Right in Vertical Power Relations

Since the criterion of *animus* was used to differentiate peace from war, no material test was thus available. Hence, the confusion between the two activities was greater because acts of war could be exercised abusively, with complete impunity, in time of peace if the target country did not dare to declare war.[445] This state of affairs worked to the advantage of the great Powers when conducting reprisals against weak countries. As a result, the category of reprisals came to encompass a wide variety of so-called measures short of war.

However, the resort to armed reprisals was inconceivable when the dispute involved two nations of equal strength or when the target country was a great Power. Forbearance, indeed, was required because their use

---

ple" one; the latter kind should be recognised as producing legal effects more advantageous to third States. See Antoine-Auguste Carette, '[Commentary on the decision *Le Comte de Thomar*]', in Jean-Baptiste Sirey, L.-M. Devilleneuve, and Antoine-Auguste Carette (eds.), *Recueil général des lois et des arrêts, en matière civile, criminelle, administrative et de droit public. 2e série. – An 1848.* (Paris: [s'adresser à M. Bachelier], 1848), 2nd part, col. 510–512, here at 511–512. In the end, the *Conseil d'État* confirmed that the capture of contraband of war found on a neutral ship was permitted only in time of war. See *Comte de Thomar*, Conseil d'État, 25 March 1848: Jean-Baptiste Sirey, L.-M. Devilleneuve, and Antoine-Auguste Carette (eds.), *Recueil général des lois et des arrêts, en matière civile, criminelle, administrative et de droit public: 2e série. – An 1848.* (Paris: [s'adresser à M. Bachelier], 1848), 2nd part, col. 511. Hence, some legal scholars were quick to regard this decision as an authoritative opinion that acknowledged the compatibility of pacific blockade with peace, although, in actual fact, the *Conseil d'État* did not conclude on the legality of the measure *per se*. For example, a French commentator argued that the establishment of a 'simple' blockade was a kind of reprisals that should be preferred because it was milder than the *ultima ratio* of war. He considered that the establishment of such blockades opened an intermediary state between peace and war since 'neutral' vessels were held to respect it insofar as a special notification was given and recorded in the logbook. See Mr Teyssier-Desfarges, 'Revue critique de la jurisprudence du conseil d'État.', *RDFE* 5 (1848), 368–76. Cf. Achille Morin, *Les lois relatives à la guerre selon le droit des gens moderne, le droit public et le droit criminel des pays civilisés*, 2nd vol. (Paris: Imprimerie et librairie générale de jurisprudence Cosse, Marchal et Billard, 1872), 109–10.

445 The reasons are quite obvious: a declaration of war on a great Power could wreak havoc, with the loss of many lives and property, in addition to the fact that a defeat might lead to subjugation, the transfer of territories or adverse peace terms imposed by the victor. Cf. Colbert, *Retaliation in international law* (above, n. 6), 94 and 98f.

would not fail to provoke generalised hostilities.[446] An illustrative example of this postulate is the following quarrel between the United States and France in 1834/35.

Between 1800 and 1817, American citizens were victims of spoliations committed by authority of the French Government. The United States pressed insistently for reparation until a treaty was signed in 1831 by which France acknowledged the claims. It fixed the French indebtedness to 25.000.000 francs and provided that the payment would spread over six annual instalments with an interest of four per cent.[447] Yet, notwithstanding the ratification and the promise of the French Government, the French Chambers neglected and later rejected the adoption of implementation measures for the assignment of money.[448]

Out of patience, U.S. President Andrew Jackson urged the Congress in December 1834 to pass a law authorising the seizure of French property by way of reprisals. He argued that the right of reprisals was a long-established institution of international law which did not bring about war. As a recent precedent, he cited the French reprisals against Portugal that took place in 1831 "under circumstances less unquestionable."[449] Nevertheless, he was aware of the danger that the proclamation of reprisals against such a strong opponent posed. Therefore, he invited France to put pride aside and acknowledge the validity of the claims. The legitimacy of reprisals was irrefutable. That is why he warned France that it would incur discredit in

---

446 The Earl of Malmesbury summed up quite well this idea during the debates in the House of Lords, following the British reprisals exercised in the *Prince of Wales* case against Brazil: "Reprisals are a most serious thing; for, mark you, they can only be practically made by a strong country against a weak one. That is a very great objection to reprisals. If they are made by a strong country against one as strong, or nearly as strong, that is war—there must be war, because they will not be suffered." (House of Lords, 19 June 1863: Great Britain, Parliament, *Hansard's Parliamentary Debates* (above, n. 338), col. 1135).

447 See Art. 1 of the Convention as to Claims and Duties on Wines and Cotton, in: William M. Malloy, *Treaties, Conventions, International Acts, Protocols and Agreements between the United States of America and Other Powers, 1776–1909*, 1st vol. (Washington: GPO, 1910), 524.

448 For a detailed account, see President Jackson, Sixth Annual Message, 2 December 1834: Andrew Jackson, *Messages of Gen. Andrew Jackson*: *With a short sketch of his life* (Concord, New Hampshire: John F. Brown and William White, 1837), 278ff. See also Moore, *A digest of international law* (above, n. 222), 123–4.

449 Sixth Annual Message, 2 December 1834: Jackson, *Messages of Gen. Andrew Jackson* (above, n. 448), 286–7.

the eyes of the civilised world if it chose to treat the measure as a menace and to undertake hostilities.[450]

However, the U.S. Senate Committee on Foreign Relations considered that the passing of such a law was ill-timed. It advocated patience since France had agreed by the treaty of 1831 to pay reparations. Besides, the recourse to reprisals would raise the question of the amount to be seized: either the whole debt or just up to the sum of the first due instalments. But the Committee mainly rejected the Bill because there was always a serious risk of slipping into a war when the target country was in position to resist. Albeit reprisals did not produce a state of war in itself, the Committee pointed out that a strong target country like France would not hesitate over retaliating, leading inevitably to war.[451] On the contrary, it stressed that the French reprisals against Portugal in 1831 were an ill-suited precedent for the present case. Indeed, the Committee believed that the acts of reprisals did not give rise to a state of war because Portugal, being weaker than France, had felt compelled to surrender.[452]

450 "Such a measure ought not to be considered by France as a menace. Her pride and power are too well known to expect any thing from her fears, and preclude the necessity of the declaration that nothing partaking of the character of intimidation is intended by us. She ought to look upon it as the evidence only of an inflexible determination on the part of the United States to insist on their rights. [...]. If she should continue to refuse that act of acknowledged justice, and, in violation of the law of nations, make reprisals on our part the occasion of hostilities against the United States, she would but add violence to injustice, and could not fail to expose herself to the just censure of civilized nations, and to the retributive judgments of Heaven." (Sixth Annual Message, 2 December 1834: Ibid., 287f.).

451 "When [reprisals] are accompanied with an authority from the Government which admits them, to employ force, they are believed invariably to have led to war in all cases where the nation against which they are directed is able to make resistance. It is wholly inconceivable that a powerful and chivalrous nation, like France, would submit, without retaliation, to the seizure of the property of her unoffending citizens, pursuing their lawful commerce, to pay a debt which the popular branch of her legislature had refused to acknowledge and provide for. It cannot be supposed that France would tacitly and quietly assent to the payment of a debt to the United States, by a forcible seizure of French property which, after full deliberation, the Chambers had expressly refused its consent to discharge. Retaliation would ensue, and retaliation would inevitably terminate in war." (quoted in Wharton, *A digest of the international law of the United States*, (above, n. 46), 92).

452 See the Committee's resolution: Ibid., 91–93.

Yet, the harm was already done. Jackson's speech caused resentment in France, where the suggestion of reprisals was deemed a threat and an insult to the national honour. France, thus, decided to suspend the diplomatic relations with the United States.[453] Furthermore, the French House of Deputies made the payment of the claims conditional on satisfactory explanations of Jackson's message.[454] In addition, the French Government asked for an official apology, too.[455] As a result, the situation worsened as the U.S. Chargé d'Affaire was recalled and news arrived in the United States that French naval forces might be dispatched to U.S. waters. And still, Jackson did not help to ease tensions as he enjoined the Congress, on the one hand, to prohibit the importation of French products and the entry of French vessels as peaceful coercive measures, and, on the other hand, to order the preparation of the navy and coastal defence.[456] Fortunately, the British who had much to lose in a war between two great allies offered mediation.[457] So, the issue was finally settled peacefully.[458]

Although U.S. President Jackson initially contemplated just non-forcible reprisals, i.e. the seizure of French property, the whole extent of the dispute shows that reprisals against a great Power (all the more so when they involved the use of armed force) were utterly impossible without giving rise to a state of war. In fact, the French indignation at the mere suggestion of reprisals in President Jackson's message and the ensuing rapid escalation of tension between both States, teetering on the verge of public war, clearly evidence that the exercise of the right of reprisals could only remain within the boundaries of peace when the reprisal-taking country was a Power enjoying a position of manifest superiority over the target country.

453 President Jackson, Seventh Annual Message, 7 December 1835: Jackson, *Messages of Gen. Andrew Jackson* (above, n. 448), 323. See the diplomatic correspondence: Great Britain, F. O., *BFSP 1833–1834* (above, n. 269), 964–93; Great Britain, F. O., *BFSP 1834–1835* (above, n. 269), 1295–341; Great Britain, F. O., *BFSP 1835–1836* (24th vol.; London: James Ridgway and sons, 1853), 1086–156.

454 President Jackson, Seventh Annual Message, 7 December 1835: Jackson, *Messages of Gen. Andrew Jackson* (above, n. 448), 324f.

455 President Jackson's message to the Congress, 15 January 1836: Ibid., 359.

456 President Jackson's message to the Congress, 15 January 1836: Ibid., 360–1.

457 See Grenville's Journal, 10–11 December 18[3]5, quoted in Wharton, *A digest of the international law of the United States,* (above, n. 46), 96–97. See also Great Britain, F. O., *BFSP 1835–1836* (above, n. 453), 1156–65.

458 Wharton, *A digest of the international law of the United States,* (above, n. 46), 96.

V. *Interim Conclusion*

During the three decades of 1831–1863, Great Britain and France took advantage of their superiority to shape armed reprisals into an informal privilege which concretely allowed them to resort to belligerent measures while simultaneously claiming the benefits of peace.

Factually, the great Powers made abusive use of reprisals against small countries to assert their influence and control on them. But since the target countries were militarily too weak to fight back, the great Powers could deny the outbreak of a war when it suited them. This had a vicious effect because they could thus exercise an overwhelming, though questionable, amount of force in order to obtain satisfaction to their demands without giving rise to a state of war. As a result, reprisals ceased to refer merely to acts of seizure and progressively came to cover a wide variety of measures short of war.

At the same time, the great Powers justified their deeds by pointing out the lack of respectability and responsibility of the target countries. This discourse gave them not only a reason for action, but also the authority to challenge and elude the rules which might have governed the use of reprisals. For instance, the disproportionate amount of force was explained by the stubbornness of the target countries, and the irrelevance of denial of justice as a requirement for reprisals was accounted for by the unreliability of their judiciary system. Of course, it was sheer opportunism guided by considerations of national policy and commercial interests. But it provided the great Powers with the authority to be the judge in their own case and to shape the practice of reprisals.

It is, therefore, unsurprising that the legal aspects of reprisals did not receive clarification and that the idea of establishing binding limitations on armed reprisals was not even contemplated.

Chapter Three. Legal Doctrine confronting State Practice, 1848–1912

I. Introduction

The first half of the nineteenth century provided a large number of cases of armed reprisals. However, it was not before the mid-nineteenth century that the State practice became a topic of discussion in legal doctrine. The purpose of the present chapter is to understand the role played by the legal doctrine in the maintenance of grey zones in international law regarding armed reprisals.

The time period under scrutiny stretches between 1848 (the year when the first thorough studies about the contemporary State practice of armed reprisals, more precisely pacific blockade, were published) and 1912 (the year when the Institute of International Law decided to postpone the examination of a proposal aiming at an international convention restricting the use of measures short of war).

It is argued in the course of this chapter that lawyers lacked the will and failed in the opportunity to deal with the issue of armed reprisals fully and that they might have made the situation even more burning.

II. Precursors of the Doctrinal Debate on Armed Reprisals: Wurm and Hautefeuille

During the first half of the nineteenth century, legal scholars did not pay much heed to the modern practice of reprisals. Their contribution to the law of reprisals was negligible.[459] The international law treatises of that period usually spoke of reprisals in historical terms. Indeed, only the pre-

459 For example, the German publicist Johann Ludwig Klüber developed the distinction between 'positive' and 'negative' reprisals. The former class referred to the refusal by the aggrieved State to fulfil a legal obligation or the act of withholding something owed to the wrongdoing State. The latter class related to the acts of reprisals involving the taking of something belonging to the target country. See Jean Louis Klüber, *Droit des gens moderne de l'Europe*, 2nd vol. (Stuttgart: J. G. Cotta, 1819), 371f. fn. c). For the sake of simplicity, it can be said that positive reprisals encompassed the positive acts of coercion while the negative kind

nineteenth-century practice (treaties, cases and opinions like those of Grotius, Vattel or Valin) and theory (in a manner reminiscent of Bartolus de Saxoferrato's *Tractatus*) were spelt out.[460] As Neff rightly points out, "[the] various changes in the character of reprisals came about largely as a matter of state practice, with legal doctrine (as so often) lagging behind. Indeed, a number of legal writers largely ignored the changes and treated reprisals entirely in the traditional fashion."[461] During the period 1815–1870, lawyers disdained the study of international law as a fully fledged discipline.[462]

Some legal scholars, however, showed a better understanding of the new evolution of reprisals by the 1840s. For instance, August Wilhelm Heffter, German writer on international law, appears to have been aware of the occurring changes. Indeed, he wrote in the first edition of his book *Das europäische Völkerrecht der Gegenwart* (1844) that the coercive maritime blockade could be deemed a legitimate means of reprisals which entailed the same rights and duties for third States as in neutrality.[463] U.S. jurist and diplomat Henry Wheaton also underlined that reprisals "seem[ed] to ex-

---

covered non-forcible reprisals. See Westlake, 'Reprisals and War' (above, n. 256), 132; Arrigo Cavaglieri, 'Règles générales du droit de la paix', *RdC* 26/I (1929), 315–585, at 575. However, this distinction was considered utterly useless for it did not lead to separate regimes of rules. See, e.g., Friedrich Fromhold von Martens, *Traité de droit international*, traduit du russe par Alfred Léo, 3rd vol. (Paris: Librairie Marescq ainé, 1887), 160; Amos S. Hershey, *The Essentials of International Public Law* (New York: The Macmillan Company, 1919), 344 fn. 4.

460 See, e.g., Saalfeld, *Handbuch des positiven Völkerrechts* (above, n. 221), 185–7; Manning, *Commentaries of the law of nations* (above, n. 240), 106ff.; Bello, *Principios de derecho internacional* (above, n. 12), 126–7; Antonio Riquelme, *Elementos de derecho público internacional: con esplicacion de todas las reglas que, segun los tratados, estipulaciones, leyes vigentes y costumbres, constituyen el derecho internacional español*, 1st vol. (Madrid: D. Santiago Saunaque, 1849), 258–263; Richard Wildman, *Institutes of International Law*, 1st vol. (London: William Benning & Co., 1849), 186–198. See also Archer Polson, *Principles of the Law of Nations: With Practical Notes and Supplementary Essays on the Law of Blockade, and on Contraband of War.* To Which is Added, *Diplomacy*, by Thomas Hartwell Horne, B. D. (Philadelphia: T. & J. W. Johnson & Co., 1860), 36–7; Agustín Aspiazu, *Dogmas del derecho internacional*, Obra impresa bajo la protección del coronel Agustín Morales (Nueva York: Hallet & Breen, 1872), 144–6.

461 Neff, *War and the Law of Nations* (above, n. 2), 227.

462 See Koskenniemi, *The Gentle Civilizer of Nations* (above, n. 80), 28ff.

463 August Wilhelm Heffter, *Das Europäische Völkerrecht der Gegenwart* (Berlin: E. H. Schroeder, 1844), 194.

tend to every species of forcible means for procuring redress, short of actual war".[464]

Two publicists, in particular, demonstrated clear-sightedness. Their names were Christian Friedrich Wurm, a German political author, and Laurent-Basile Hautefeuille, a French maritime law expert. While Wurm's contribution to the topic of reprisals has, hitherto, passed largely unnoticed, Hautefeuille is better known in legal history because he is credited with coining the term 'pacific blockade' to describe a coercive blockade or blockade short of war.[465]

In 1848, Wurm published an entry in *Das Staats-Lexikon* —an encyclopedia of public law edited by Karl von Rotteck and Carl Welcker— about self-help in international law. In this contribution, he expressed serious concern about the recent confusion between peace and war. Indeed, real acts of war were committed under the garb of reprisals, and yet the diplomatic relations between both countries were not severed. The too recurrent use of armed force not followed by the admission of a state of war led to blurring the line between peace and war for want of tangible criteria.[466] For Wurm, the reason why, in his time, some countries preferred to exercise 'pretended reprisals' rather than to declare war ensued from the serious inexpediency of war under modern conditions; namely, the enormous scale and costs of modern warfare, the fragility of credit, the need of production sale and, more generally, of trading. On the contrary, reprisals im-

464 Henry Wheaton, *Elements of international law* (3rd edn., Philadelphia: Lea and Blanchard, 1846), 340.

465 Laurent-Basile Hautefeuille, *Des droits et des devoirs des nations neutres en temps de guerre maritime*, 3rd vol. (1st edn., Paris: Au comptoir des imprimeurs-unis, 1849), 176. Amongst the authors who regarded Hautefeuille as the father of that expression, see, e.g., Ernest Nys, *La guerre maritime: Étude de droit international* (Bruxelles/Leipzig: C. Muquardt, Merzbach et Falk, 1881), 68; Thomas Barclay, 'Les blocus pacifiques', *RDILC* 29 (1897), 474–90, at 477; Westlake, 'Pacific Blockade' (above, n. 438), 19; Parry, 'British Practice in Some Nineteenth Century Pacific Blockades' (above, n. 415), 685; Brownlie, *International Law and the Use of Force by States* (above, n. 45), 223 fn. 5; Grewe, *Epochen der Völkerrechtsgeschichte* (above, n. 24), 619 fn. 11. However, the present Writer found the first use of the term 'pacific blockade' ("*Friedensblokade*" [sic!] in German) in Wurm, 'Selbsthilfe (völkerrechtliche)' (above, n. 292), 132; that being, one year before the publication of Hautefeuille's third volume containing this phrase.

466 Indeed, Wurm noted that "[e]in Hauptzug dieser neueren internationalen Politik ist die Geläufigkeit eines sehr ausgedehnten Begriffes von Repressalien und die Anwendung von Zwangsmaßregeln, um einer Unterhandlung Gewicht zu geben, welche sich auf streitige Rechte oder Interessen bezieht." (Ibid., 129). Cf. Vattel's comment about 'pretended reprisals' *supra*, Chapter One III.2.(c).

posed a lesser burden on the whole nation and, for passing more easily unnoticed, made the Government's course of action less subject to enquiry. The consequence was that injustices were more likely to be committed by way of reprisals. That is why Wurm refused to regard the use of reprisals as proof of moderation in comparison to war since they were usually employed in cases where the justice and relevance of the demands were more than dubious.[467]

Ten years later, in an article published in the *Deutsche Vierteljahrs-Schrift*, Wurm addressed the issue of armed reprisals again and criticised the lack of scholarly involvement in this topic.[468] He first acknowledged the fact that self-help was, in principle, a lawful remedy in international law because of the absence of a superior authority acting as a judge. Consequently, independent States were entitled to have recourse to such a proceeding in time of peace in order to protect their nationals living abroad. Yet, in his opinion, the resort to acts of war by way of reprisals could not be treated as lawful coercion in peacetime. Not only such acts —like pacific blockade— had adverse effects on third States, but they also did not really prevent the occurrence of war. Turning then his attention to the instances of the past thirty years, he observed that the resort to armed reprisals had just been the practice of strong Powers against weak and small nations in a very questionable and abusive manner. This observation made him wonder whether the institution of reprisals had actually not become an abuse in itself.[469] In such circumstances, he could not therefore concur with the opinion that the state of peace remained unaltered when armed reprisals were exercised. Thus, Wurm advocated the recourse to amicable means of settlement of international disputes like arbitration instead of the use of force.[470]

---

467 Ibid., esp. 111 and 128–132.

468 The recent publication of some documents in the *Aves Island* affair —a case in which the United States had contemplated for years whether reprisals should be made against Venezuela— prompted Wurm's new reflection.

469 "Auch solche Mißbräuche heben allerdings den Gebrauch nicht auf. Aber wir geben anheim, ob nicht das Institut der Repressalien durch seine, man darf sagen, ausschließliche Anwendung auf schwächere Staaten gehässig geworden, und fast in den Ruf gekommen, es sey selbst ein Mißbrauch? ferner: ob nicht auf dem Wege der Repressalien fast unbemerkt und ohne die öffentliche Meinung aufzuregen, Forderungen durchgeführt sind, die man nach Inhalt und Form auf dem Wege des Krieges durchzuführen nicht unternommen haben würde?" (Wurm, 'Selbsthülfe der Staaten in Friedenszeiten.' (above, n. 355), 83).

470 Ibid.

As for Hautefeuille, he did not address the issue of armed reprisals as a whole. He only looked into the phenomenon of pacific blockade following the *Conseil d'État*'s sentence of 25 March 1848 in the case of the *Comte de Thomar*, which, in his opinion, was erroneous and hence required a clarification.[471] He thus became the first legal scholar to ever deal at length with this new measure short of war.

For Hautefeuille, the establishment of a blockade clearly implied the existence of a status of war between the parties directly involved because the right of blockade derived from the belligerent right of conquest. It was rightly this taking of control of a portion of the territory or territorial sea of the attacked country that entitled the aggressor to impede ships of third States from navigating from and to the blockaded ports. Any attempt to run a blockade could then be punished by the capture and condemnation of the ship and cargo, whereas normally trade had to remain unhindered in time of peace. So, only war could impose obligations on third States, pursuant to the law of neutrality. It is from this angle that Hautefeuille challenged the legality of pacific blockade, precisely because it might have effects on vessels flying the flag of third States. He concluded then that either a blockade entailed a state of war or it was resorted to as an illegal proceeding in time of peace. Therefore, pacific blockade could not be recog-

471 Hautefeuille, *Des droits et des devoirs des nations neutres en temps de guerre maritime* (above, n. 465), 13. On this judgement, see *supra*, at 146 fn. 444. Indeed, the judgement of the *Conseil d'État* has sometimes been regarded as a landmark decision for pacific blockade. Calvo, e.g., called it a major precedent (Calvo, *Le droit international théorique et pratique* (above, n. 224), 538 (§ 1840)). However, other legal scholars after Hautefeuille also challenged the importance placed on this judgement as the judicial recognition of pacific blockade. See, e.g., Pistoye and Duverdy, *Traité des prises maritimes* (above, n. 223), 376–377; Gessner, *Le droit des neutres sur mer* (above, n. 234), 235–6. In fact, the judgement raises more questions than answers and it should be stressed that the *Conseil d'État* did not declare pacific blockade consistent with peace. As a matter of fact, it confirmed several condemnations of neutral ships pronounced by prize commissions during the same blockade of the Río de La Plat. See the judgements of the *Conseil d'État* collected by Pistoye and Duverdy, *Traité des prises maritimes* (above, n. 223), 382–390, and principally the decision in *La Louisia*. In the *Comte de Thomar*, the *Conseil d'État* quashed the decision of the prize commission of Montevideo solely because the Brazilian neutral ship did not receive a special warning. In other words, the question whether the blockade was instituted in wartime or in time of peace had absolutely no relevance on the outcome of the decision. The result of the judgement in the *Comte de Thomar* appears then as "un acte de munificence et de liberalité, bien plus qu'un acte juridique" (Ibid., 1st vol., 391). Cf. Fauchille, *Du blocus maritime* (above, n. 405), 43–4.

nised as a legitimate means of the law of nations, notwithstanding the fact that the great Powers, i.e. France and Great Britain, might well defend the institution of pacific blockade for allowing them to spare their own shipping and for being a powerful tool of coercion at a lower cost than war.[472]

In summary, both Wurm and Hautefeuille warned against the confusion between peace and war. They argued for a strict separation between wartime measures and acts of reprisals consistent with peace. However, instead of facing condemnation, the recent State practice denounced by Wurm and Hautefeuille was about to receive confirmation by the legal doctrine.

III. Building the Legal Theory of Pacific Blockade

1. Rising Interest and Controversy, 1849–1887

Of all the forms of armed reprisals, the most employed by the great Powers and hence the most studied in legal doctrine was the pacific blockade. Indeed, in Hautefeuille's wake, legal scholars started taking a keen interest in this anomalous measure. The name itself, built on an oxymoron, sparked off reactions.[473] Yet, the idea of a blockade bereft of belligerency intrigued them to the point where every publicist had his say on the subject. During about forty years from Hautefeuille's first analysis in 1849 till the Heidelberg session of the Institute of International Law in 1887, the legal scholar community addressed the 'burning issue' of pacific blockade without benchmarks.

The first step for studying the measure thus consisted of gathering the potential cases where a pacific blockade had been applied. In this regard, Hautefeuille identified the blockade of Navarino Bay as the first historical instance of a blockade allegedly established in time of peace. He narrated that, in order to come to the Greek insurgents' aid, Great Britain, France

472 Hautefeuille, *Des droits et des devoirs des nations neutres en temps de guerre maritime* (above, n. 465), 176–194.

473 Indeed, the authors almost unanimously deplored the name of the measure. See, e.g., Henry Bargrave Deane, *The Law of Blockade: Its History, Present Condition, and Probable Future. An International Law Essay, 1870* (London: Longmans, Green, Reader, and Dyer; Wildy & sons, 1870), 48f.; Fauchille, *Du blocus maritime* (above, n. 405), 48; Piédelièvre, *Précis de droit international public ou droit des gens* (above, n. 56), 94. Nevertheless, no other denomination succeeded in prevailing. See Falcke, *Le blocus pacifique* (above, n. 40), 9 fn. 1, and 247 fn. 8.

and Russia together closed the entrance of the bay of Navarino where the Ottoman fleet was anchored. A naval battle ensued on 20 October 1827 that saw the near total destruction of the Muslim fleet. Nevertheless, the three allied European Powers vigorously denied being at war with the Sublime Porte.[474]

This incident became the first case of pacific blockade on most authors' list.[475] All the subsequent blockades not preceded by a declaration of war were then added to the enumeration, regardless of the nature of the action. The result was a large variety of cases which revealed the heterogeneous pattern of execution of these so-called pacific blockades.

As a matter of fact, the resort to pacific blockade occurred either in cases of reprisals or intervention.[476] On the one hand, pacific blockade up to 1863 was often carried out to enforce reprisals, e.g. the British blockade of

---

474 Hautefeuille, *Des droits et des devoirs des nations neutres en temps de guerre maritime* (above, n. 465), 177–178. As evidence of the European Powers' peaceful intentions, see the common instructions sent to the commanding officers in chief in the Levantine Sea, 12 July 1827: Great Britain, F. O., *BFSP 1829–1830* (17th vol.; London: James Ridgway, 1832), 15. Their behaviour, however, led the Turkish Reis Effendi to exclaim: "Leur conduite présente à la fois l'exemple du pour et du contre. C'est absolument comme si, cassant la tête d'un homme, je l'assurerais en même tems [sic!] de mon amitié." (Report of the dragomans of France, Great Britain and Russia, 4 November 1827: Martens, *Nouveau recueil de traités d'Alliance, de Paix, de Trêve, de Neutralité, de Commerce, de Limites, d'Echange etc. et de plusieurs autres actes servant à la connoissance des relations étrangères des Puissances et Etats de l'Europe tant dans leur rapport mutuel que dans celui envers les Puissances et Etats dans d'autres parties du globe depuis 1808 jusqu'à présent* (above, n. 267), 12th vol., 146).

475 Nevertheless, some authors attempted to present earlier occurrences of pacific blockade. See, e.g., Smith and Sibley, *International law as interpreted during the Russo-Japanese War* (above, n. 240), 356; Nils Söderqvist, *Le blocus maritime: Étude de droit international* (Stockholm: Centraltryckeriet, 1908), 60–4. The former even believed that an extract from Sir William Scott's judgement in the *Staadt Embden* (1796) set the root of pacific blockade (Smith and Sibley, *International law as interpreted during the Russo-Japanese War* (above, n. 240), 203). The passage in question reads: "an auxiliary fleet is not of itself sufficient to make its government a principal in a war," (Robinson, *Reports of Cases Argued and Determined in the High Court of Admiralty* (above, n. 255), 1st vol., 30). But, in truth, this discussion about the birthday of pacific blockade was quite sterile.

476 The suppression of insurrection was regarded sometimes as a subcategory of pacific blockade, too. This is especially the view that Charles Sumner, Senator for Massachusetts, sustained at the time of the debates in the U.S. Senate relating to the ratification of the Seward-Johnson treaty which pursued the settlement of the famous Alabama Claims. He, indeed, argued that President Abraham Lincoln's proclamation of a blockade of the ports of the Confederate States on

the ports of New Granada in 1837 or the French blockade of Mexico in 1838. On the other hand, interventionist reasons also motivated some of those blockades bereft of belligerency. For example, the blockade of Navarino pursued a humanitarian goal, i.e. the prevention of bloodshed.[477] Between 1845 and 1850, France and Great Britain likewise interfered in the Uruguayan Civil War by blockading the entrance to the Río de La Plata in order to re-establish trade relations and ensure the protection of their nationals.[478]

Furthermore, in all these cases, the ships under flags of third States were differently affected by the blockade. They were sometimes driven away, merely sequestrated or even confiscated.[479] However, in other instances like the British blockades against Greece in 1850 and Brazil in 1862–1863 —which were both clear cases of reprisals, the former being a watershed in

---

19 April 1861 was merely an act of sovereignty, of internal police. Therefore, Great Britain was not allowed to recognise the Southern Confederacy as a belligerent Power. See Executive Session of the U.S. Senate, 13 April 1869: Sumner, *The works of Charles Sumner* (above, n. 54), 13th vol., 58–64, esp. 63–64. See also Thomas Erskine Holland, *Studies in international law* (Oxford: Clarendon Press, 1898), 132 and 138–140. But for a dissenting opinion, see Oppenheim, *International Law* (above, n. 25), 43 fn. 1.

477 See the preamble of the Treaty signed on 6 July 1827 between them for the Pacification of Greece: Great Britain, F. O., *BFSP 1826–1827* (14th vol.; London: Printed by J. Harrison and son, 1828), 632–3.

478 For an account of this intervention, see Auguste Bourguignat, *Question de La Plata: Les traités Leprédour. Notice au point de vue du droit international* (Paris: Imprimerie centrale de Napoléon Chaix et Cie, 1849); José Luis Bustamante, *Los cinco errores capitales de la intervención en el Plata* (Montevideo: Imprenta uruguayana, 1849); John Le Long, *Intervention de la France dans le Rio-de-La-Plata: Motifs et moyens. L'Opposition de l'Angleterre à une intervention armée pourrait-elle aller jusqu'à poser un casus belli?* (Paris: Imprimerie de Madame de Lacombe, 1849); Falcke, *Le blocus pacifique* (above, n. 40), 75–86; Graham-Yooll, *Imperial Skirmishes* (above, n. 47), 75–89.

479 Some authors, mainly French, denounced the confiscation by Great Britain of the vessels of third States for breach of a pacific blockade. On the contrary, they pointed out that France solely confined itself to sequestrating them. See, i.a., Hautefeuille, *Des droits et des devoirs des nations neutres en temps de guerre maritime* (above, n. 465), 191f.; Gessner, *Le droit des neutres sur mer* (above, n. 234), 240; Fauchille, *Du blocus maritime* (above, n. 405), 51; Barès, *Le blocus pacifique* (above, n. 81), 143–4; Ducrocq, *Représailles en temps de paix* (above, n. 81), 74; Despagnet, *Cours de droit international public* (above, n. 27), 787. However, this statement seems to rest on no serious foundations. Cf. Falcke, *Le blocus pacifique* (above, n. 40), 225; Parry, 'British Practice in Some Nineteenth Century Pacific Blockades' (above, n. 415), 682.

the practice of pacific blockade—,[480] the blockading Power refrained from interfering with foreign shipping and enforced the blockade exclusively against the ships of the target country.

Therefore, the question of the legality of pacific blockade raised much controversy in legal doctrine.

The vast majority of lawyers denied pacific blockade the character of an institution of international law. They maintained that the measure actually was an act of war, purely and solely inconsistent with a state of peace. In fact, they often put forward the indictment that the past instances did not give rise to a state of war only because the target countries were always too weak to forcefully resist against the stronger reprisal-taking Powers, i.e. almost exclusively France and Great Britain. The truth was that the resort to a belligerent blockade outside wartime was illegal at any rate. Besides, they argued that the practice of pacific blockade rested upon no treaty or rule of domestic law, and was too recent to have already entered customary international law. Finally, last but not least, they strove to demonstrate the illegality of the measure by laying great emphasis, like Hautefeuille, on the interference with the shipping of third States.[481]

480 Cf. Falcke, *Le blocus pacifique* (above, n. 40), 225; Washburn, 'The Legality of the Pacific Blockade' (above, n. 41), 458; Wolfgang Schumann, *Die Friedensblockade* (Das geltende Seekriegsrecht in Einzeldarstellungen, 9; Frankfurt am Main: Alfred Metzner, 1974), 65.

481 Cf. Pistoye and Duverdy, *Traité des prises maritimes* (above, n. 223), 376–377; Gregorio Perez Gomar, *Curso elemental de Derecho de Gente: Precedido de una Introduccion sobre el derecho natural*, 2nd vol. (Montevideo: Imprenta de El Pueblo, 1866), 135–6; Heinrich Bernhard Oppenheim, *System des Völkerrechts* (2nd edn., Stuttgart & Leipzig: A. Kröner, 1866), 255; William de Burgh, *The Elements of Maritime International Law: With a Preface on Some Unsettled Questions of Public Law* (London: Longmans, Green, and Co., 1868), 121–122 fn. 2; Theodore Dwight Woolsey, 'The Alabama Question.', *The New Englander* 28 (1869), 575–619, at 587–593; Ignacio de Negrin, *Tratado elemental de derecho internacional marítimo: Con varios apéndices que contienen la legislacion interior, los tratados de España y otros documentos nacionales y extranjeros referentes al asunto*, Obra de texto en la Escuela Naval Flotante y Academias del Cuerpo Administrativo de la Armada (Madrid: Miguel Ginesta, 1873), 133 fn. 1; Gabriel Massé, *Le droit commercial dans ses rapports avec le droit des gens et le droit civil*, 1st vol. (3rd edn., Paris: Guillaumin et Cie, 1874), 260; Raffaele Schiattarella, *Il diritto della neutralità nelle guerre marittime* (Sassari: Tipografia Sociale, 1874), 129–33; Guiseppe Carnazza Amari, *Trattato sul diritto internazionale pubblico di pace* (Corso di diritto internazionale, 1; 2nd edn., Milano: V. Maisner e compagnia, 1875), 904–7; Antenor Arias, *Lecciones de Derecho Maritimo: Dictadas en la Facultad de ciencias politicas y administrativas de la Universidad Mayor de San Marcos* (Lima: Imprenta del Estado, 1876), 431–3; Gessner, *Le droit des neutres sur mer* (above, n. 234),

Some publicists, on the other hand, resolutely insisted on the recognition of pacific blockade. In their view, the limited scale of the operation made the proceeding more humane than an all-out war. The measure, thus, was commendable for its restraint and because it could prevent war. With this in mind, they considered as a small but necessary drawback the right for the blockading Power to interfere with the ships of third States, insofar as the former abode by the rules governing wartime blockades (namely, i.a., the notification of the blockade to neutrals, the use of a sufficient force for an effective blockade and the special notice given to every approaching ship).[482] That is why the French publicist Eugène Cauchy and the Belgian lawyer Gustave Rolin-Jaequemyns regarded pacific blockade as introducing an intermediary state between war and peace.[483]

234–41; Leopold Neumann, *Grundriss des heutigen europäischen Völkerrechtes* (2nd edn., Wien: Wilhelm Braumüller, 1877), 92; Nys, *La guerre maritime* (above, n. 465), 69; Fauchille, *Du blocus maritime* (above, n. 405), 47–55; Henry Glass, *Marine International Law: Compiled from various sources* (Proceedings of the United States Naval Institute, 11, No. 3; Annapolis, Md.: The United States Naval Institute, 1885), 102–4; Carlos Testa, *Le droit public international maritime: Principes généraux. – Règles pratiques*, Traduction du portugais annotée et augmentée de documents nouveaux, touchant la contrebande de guerre, la neutralisation des mers et des fleuves et la décision de la conférence africaine (1885) en matière de droit maritime suivie d'une table alphabétique et analytique par Adolphe Boutiron (Bibliothèque internationale & diplomatique, 18; Paris: A. Durand et Pedone-Lauriel, 1886), 228–9; Funck-Brentano and Sorel, *Précis du droit ges gens* (above, n. 36), 408; Karl Gareis, *Institutionen des Völkerrechts* (Gießen: Emil Roth, 1888), 189f.

482 Cf. Eugène Cauchy, *Le droit maritime international considéré dans ses origines et dans ses rapports avec les progrès de la civilisation*, 2nd vol. (Paris: Guillaumin et Cie, 1862), 426–428; Carlos Calvo, *Le droit international théorique et pratique: Précédé d'un exposé historique des progrès de la science du droit des gens*, 2nd vol. (2nd edn., Paris: A. Durand et Pedone-Lauriel; Guillaumin et Cie; Amyot, 1872), 603f.; Gustave Rolin-Jaequemyns, '[Book Review: *Le droit des neutres sur mer.* By Ludwig Gessner]', *RDILC* 8 (1876), 165–6, at 166; Arthur Desjardins, *Traité de droit commercial maritime*, 1st vol. (Paris: A. Durand et Pedone-Lauriel, 1878), 30–31.

483 Cauchy, *Le droit maritime international considéré dans ses origines et dans ses rapports avec les progrès de la civilisation* (above, n. 482), 426; Rolin-Jaequemyns, '[Book Review: *Le droit des neutres sur mer.* By Ludwig Gessner]' (above, n. 482), 166. This assertion was strongly criticised by some opponents. See, e.g., Hautefeuille, *Des droits et des devoirs des nations neutres en temps de guerre maritime* (above, n. 465), 194; Woolsey, 'The Alabama Question.' (above, n. 481), 593; Carnazza Amari, *Trattato sul diritto internazionale pubblico di pace* (above, n. 481), 905; Fauchille, *Du blocus maritime* (above, n. 405), 48f.

However, several lawyers were willing to consent to the recognition of pacific blockade insomuch as the use of this measure fell within the scope of legitimate reprisals. For example, the German-speaking international law expert August von Bulmerincq condemned the past instances of pacific blockade as being cases of either illegitimate intervention or reprisals disproportionate to the offence or merely motivated by the blockading Power's personal interests. He considered, indeed, that pacific blockade still lacked a legal basis in international law. Nevertheless, he admitted that this measure could have the character of reprisals, provided that there was a just cause. Under such conditions and as long as the rules on wartime blockade were observed, Bulmerincq agreed that the blockading Power could interfere with foreign shipping, on the one hand, by detaining the ships of the target country the time of the blockade and, on the other, by driving away those of third States.[484]

But Bulmerincq's view was not shared by all legal experts who were ready to acknowledge pacific blockade as a special form of reprisals. For instance, Johann Caspar Bluntschli and Friedrich Fromhold (von) Martens defended the opinion that third States should suffer no ill effects at all from a pacific blockade: the blockaded ports should then remain open to them.[485]

In other words, the recognition of pacific blockade in legal doctrine was not altogether excluded insomuch as the measure was given the character of reprisals. Such a classification implied that the proceeding in question could not affect the third States. Indeed, this aspect was the main objection to the legality of pacific blockade. On the contrary, legal scholars did not appear to have assigned much importance to the fact that the blockade being an act of war might give rise to a state of war between the parties directly involved. In other words, it was not so much the act itself that posed a challenge, but the impact that pacific blockade had on the shipping of third States.

484 Bulmerincq, 'Le blocus pacifique et ses effets sur la propriété privée' (above, n. 422). Cf. Jan Helenus Ferguson, *Manual of International Law: for the Use of Navies, Colonies and Consulates*, 2nd vol. (London: W. B. Whittingham & co., 1884), 240–241; Fiore, *Nouveau droit international public suivant les besoins de la civilisation moderne* (above, n. 54), 667–670.

485 Johann Caspar Bluntschli, *Das moderne Völkerrecht der civilisirten Staten: als Rechtsbuch dargestellt* (3rd edn., Nördlingen: C. H. Beck, 1878), §§ 506–507; Martens, *Traité de droit international* (above, n. 459), 176. Cf. Morin, *Les lois relatives à la guerre selon le droit des gens moderne, le droit public et le droit criminel des pays civilisés* (above, n. 444), 109–11.

2. Examination by the Institute of International Law

(a) First Contact at The Hague, 1875

During this period of intense controversy, the Institute of International Law —hereafter shortened 'the Institute'— addressed briefly and superficially the issue of pacific blockade.

As preliminary work for the session at The Hague in 1875, the eleven members composing the fifth commission on private property in maritime war were asked to answer a questionnaire. One of the questions submitted to them was whether pacific blockade was a legitimate coercive means recognised in international law that allowed the seizure and confiscation of ships attempting to break the blockade.[486] The rapporteur, Albéric Rolin, noted that the majority of the answers condemned pacific blockade. Indeed, Theodore Dwight Woolsey, American international law expert and President of Yale University, reaffirmed his opinion expressed in 1869 that pacific blockade was an unlawful extension of the belligerent right of blockade. The English scholar John Westlake concurred with this view and considered pacific blockade to be a shameful act committed under the veil of peace against a small country by a great Power that did not want to accept the negative consequences of war. Therefore, he argued that pacific blockade could not affect shipping and that no prize court could legally be established to order the confiscation of any ships, either of the blockaded country or third States. On the other hand, Albéric Rolin believed that pacific blockade could have the same effects as a blockade in wartime because it was, in fact, an authentic act of war. Only Bulmerincq called pacific blockade a means as lawful as any other act of war.[487]

It cannot be said, as some lawyers claimed, that the whole Institute decided against the legality of pacific blockade.[488] As a matter of fact, out of the eleven members of the fifth commission, solely six replied to the ques-

486 Institut de Droit International, 'Questionnaire adressé à MM. les membres de la commission. [Suite des Travaux préliminaires à la Session de La Haye. Vme Commission. – Propriété privée dans la guerre maritime]', *RDILC* 7 (1875), 553–7, at 555.

487 Institut de Droit International, 'Rapport de M. Albéric Rolin sur les observations présentées en réponse au questionnaire', *RDILC* 7 (1875), 603–18, at 611–612.

488 See, e.g., Fauchille, *Du blocus maritime* (above, n. 405), 46; Wharton, *A digest of the international law of the United States,* (above, n. 46), 408.

tionnaire.[489] Besides, the matter remained at the level of preliminary work and the question addressed only the impact of pacific blockade on shipping, namely whether confiscation was allowed. Still, this hints at the high expectations placed on the Institute to give a decision of high authority on such a burning issue.

(b) The Heidelberg Declaration of 1887

i) Triggering Event: The French Blockade of Formosa, 1884

Until the early 1880s, the doctrinal discussion of the legality of pacific blockade stagnated. The vast majority of legal scholars condemned the measure, while some called for its acceptance. The absence of breakthrough in the debate resulted from the fact that all the instances of so-called pacific blockade occurred in the second quarter of the first half of the nineteenth century. That means that during a period of at least thirty years since the *Don Pacifico* affair in 1850 the practice of pacific blockade had been dormant, with the major exception of the British blockade of the bay of Rio de Janeiro in 1862/63.

However, the legal issue acquired new relevance in 1884 with a French blockade of the Chinese island of Formosa (now known as Taiwan).[490] This incident was the triggering event that revived the discussion.

At the root of the incident were France's colonial ambitions in Indochina. It all started when, at the outcome of a *de facto* war, China had been forced to recognise the territorial claims of France over Annam and Tonkin.[491] Yet, French forces on their way to occupy military places in Tonkin were allegedly attacked on 23 June 1884 by regular Chinese soldiers in violation of the peace treaty, resulting in several deaths and injuries.[492] Remonstrances were addressed to the Chinese Government but

489 See Institut de Droit International, 'Rapport de M. Albéric Rolin sur les observations présentées en réponse au questionnaire' (above, n. 487), 605.

490 F. von Martitz, 'Über Friedensblockaden', *ZVölkR* 9 (1920), 610–21, at 610.

491 See Preliminary Convention of Peace between France and China, 11 May 1884: Great Britain, F. O., *BFSP 1883–1884* (75th vol.; London: William Ridgway, 1891), 1110–1.

492 General Millot to Vice admiral Peyron, June 1884: France and Louis Renault, *Archives diplomatiques: Recueil mensuel international de diplomatie et d'histoire*, 13th vol. (2nd ser.) (Paris: Féchoz, 1885), 168.

remained vain.[493] Thus, France demanded, in the form of an ultimatum, a compensation of 250 million francs and the immediate withdrawal of Chinese troops from Tonkin.[494] In the end, China agreed to comply with the withdrawal but disputed the principle of indemnity because the imputation of responsibility in the attack on 23 June was without proof.[495]

Nevertheless, even before the Chinese reply, the French Government had resolved to adopt preventive measures, although it wished to avoid the blame for breaking the peaceful relations with China.[496] Thus, Counter admiral Courbet received the instruction to take possession of two Chinese ports, to seize Chinese ships trying to run the blockade of the Min River

---

493 See Viscount de Sémallé to Mr Jules Ferry, 29 and 30 June 1884: Ibid., 169–70.

494 Mr Patenôtre to Mr Jules Ferry, 13 July 1884: Ibid., 180–1. However, Ferry confessed three weeks later that the amount of compensation was exaggerated and, therefore, reduced it to 50 millions francs. See Mr Jules Ferry to Mr Patenôtre, 3 August 1884 : France, Ministère des Affaires étrangères, *Affaires de Chine et du Tonkin: 1884–1885.* (Documents diplomatiques; Paris: Imprimerie nationale, 1885), 9.

495 Mr Jules Ferry to Mr Li-Fong-Pao, 18 July 1884: France and Renault, *Archives diplomatiques* (above, n. 492), 184–5; Mr Li-Fong-Pao to Mr Jules Ferry, 18 July 1884: Ibid., 185.

496 Mr Jules Ferry to Mr Patenôtre, 7 July 1884: Ibid., 175. Cf. "L'amiral Courbet voulait l'état de guerre déclarée, afin d'exercer tous les droits de belligérants, de visiter les navires neutres, de leur interdire le transport de la contrebande de guerre, et de faire, au besoin, des prises maritimes. Le Gouvernement préférait la continuation de la paix, qui n'était pas officiellement rompue. Du moins tenait-il à ne pas prendre l'initiative de la rupture. Une déclaration de guerre à la Chine aurait alarmé les intérêts étrangers, suscité les réclamations des neutres, indisposé les Puissances maritimes, provoqué des déclarations de neutralité. Sans doute, il était privé des droits de belligérants au regard des neutres; mais, par compensation, tous les ports étrangers lui restaient ouverts sur la route des Indes et de l'extrême Orient; ses bâtiments continuaient à y faire escale et à s'y ravitailler librement : condition précieuse pour ses expéditions incessantes entre la métropole, l'Indo-Chine et la Chine même. L'amiral semblait oublier qu'en cas de guerre, l'escadre ne pourrait plus s'approvisionner par l'intermédiaire des neutres. Du reste, si l'état de paix limitait notre action vis-à-vis des tiers, il ne nous privait, à l'égard de la Chine, d'aucun des droits utiles d'un belligérant. Nous pouvions, par la voie des représailles, tenter toutes les opérations nécessaires pour l'amener à composition, prendre des gages territoriaux, courir sus à sa marine de guerre, bombarder ses ports militaires, déclarer des blocus pacifiques, interdire le transport de la contrebande de guerre et même du riz dans les limites de ces blocus. C'était assez pour parvenir à nos fins. Il était donc préférable de s'abstenir d'une déclaration de guerre." ([Albert Billot], *L'affaire du Tonkin: Histoire diplomatique de l'établissement de notre protectorat sur l'Annam et de notre conflit avec la Chine. 1882–1885* (Paris: J. Hetzel, 1888), 248–9).

and to prevent war preparations by force if the ultimatum proved unsuccessful.[497] The occupation of the port of Keelung in northern Formosa responded to strategic considerations: few foreign merchants frequented the port, minimal force was sufficient to occupy the place and control the Formosa Strait, and nearby coal mines would ensure supply for the fleet in the event of the closing of neutral ports if a state of war ensued.[498]

Shortly after the end of the ultimatum's deadline, Keelung was bombarded. French troops then landed but failed to secure control.[499] Still, the French Government hesitated over the course of action to follow, which gave China time to make military preparations for war.[500] It eventually decided to destroy the forts and arsenals of the port of Fuzhou as well as the Chinese vessels anchored there before concentrating the fleet near Keelung and occupying the latter place.[501] These plans were put into execution, but in the face of Chinese resistance, a blockade of the west coast of Formosa had to be declared. According to the notification of the blockade, any ship attempting to break it was liable to be captured and condemned pursuant to the law of nations.[502]

Heretofore, there was officially no state of war between France and China. In fact, the French Government intended to maintain an effective blockade without war, as had been done in the past by Great Britain and France. It argued that to this end, the vessels of third States could be either driven away or captured for breach of the blockade. Nevertheless, it assured Great Britain that it would not assert the belligerent rights of visit and capture of neutral vessels on the high seas.[503]

497 Vice admiral Peyron to Counter admiral Courbet, 13 July 1884: France and Renault, *Archives diplomatiques* (above, n. 492), 181.

498 [Billot], *L'affaire du Tonkin* (above, n. 496), 216.

499 Ibid., 216–7.

500 "Des représailles, dont la légitimité n'était contestée par personne, finiront, à force d'être différées, par être considérées comme des actes d'agression. La Chine profite de nos délais pour se fortifier et dépense en achats d'armes des sommes considérables. [...]. Nos hésitations auront pour résultat final de nous obliger à une guerre en règle qu'un acte de vigueur accompli en temps opportun eût rendue inutile." Mr Patenôtre to Mr Jules Ferry, 12 August 1884: (France, Ministère des Affaires étrangères, *Affaires de Chine et du Tonkin* (above, n. 494), 34).

501 [Billot], *L'affaire du Tonkin* (above, n. 496), 222.

502 Notification of the blockade, *J.O.R.F.*, 23 October 1884, 5577.

503 Mr Waddington to Earl Granville, 5 November 1884: Great Britain, F. O., *BFSP 1884–1885* (above, n. 269), 425.

These explanations did not convince the British Government. Earl Granville, Great Britain's Secretary of State for Foreign Affairs, told the French ambassador that a pacific blockade certainly did not allow the capture and condemnation of ships of third States attempting to get through the blockade. Besides, the British Government supported the view that given the large scale of the operations, a state of war existed between France and China. Consequently and although it refrained from issuing a formal Proclamation of Neutrality, it instructed the governors of the British Eastern colonies to enforce the Foreign Enlistment Act which prohibited the equipping of any foreign vessels employed for military duties.[504]

For France, this decision entailed dire consequences since its warships could not restock with coal in British colonial ports. As a result, the resupplying had to come all the way from Marseille to Saigon for a cost of 700.000 francs per steamship.[505] Finally, left with no alternative, the French Government treated the enforcement of the Foreign Enlistment Act as tantamount to a formal declaration of neutrality. It, therefore, decided to exercise all the rights granted to belligerent nations against neutral vessels.[506]

In terms of reprisals, this case is enlightening. France did not want to confess the existence of a state of war. French Prime Minister Jules Ferry defended the view that the legal situation between France and China actually was a 'state of reprisals' unless the latter wished to declare war.[507] He explained in the *Chambre des députés* that France pursued, through the occupation of Keelung, what he euphemistically called "une politique des gages", i.e. a policy of material guarantees. He stressed then that this occupation was not a conquest but a pledge which a creditor could seize for

504 Cf. Earl Granville to Mr Waddington, 11 and 26 November 1884: Ibid., 426–427 and 429–430; Earl Granville to the Marquis Tséng, 26 November 1884: Ibid., 430–1.

505 Geffcken, 'La France en Chine et le droit international' (above, n. 33), 147.

506 Mr Waddington to Earl Granville, 29 January 1885: Great Britain, F. O., *BFSP 1884–1885* (above, n. 269), 432–3.

507 Mr Jules Ferry to Mr Patenôtre, 18 August 1884: France, Ministère des Affaires étrangères, *Affaires de Chine et du Tonkin* (above, n. 494), 44. Yet, Geffcken pointed out that international law did not know a so-called state of reprisals, but just acts of reprisals (Geffcken, 'La France en Chine et le droit international' (above, n. 33), 145).

payment.[508] Finally, Ferry argued after reciting a list of past instances of pacific blockade that this hostile measure did not require a declaration of war to be legal and produce all its effects.[509] Indeed, the French Prime Minister understood pacific blockade as a fully fledged belligerent blockade not preceded by a declaration of war. And such a way of waging war offered major advantages (*"il y avait de très grands avantages [...] à faire la guerre comme nous la faisons, sans recourir à une déclaration préalable."*).[510] The three reasons why the French Government opted to pacific blockade and reprisals in the present case were that (1) negotiations could be resumed at any time; (2) the existing treaties were to remain in force; and (3) quarrels with third States could be avoided.[511]

On this latter point, the protest of Great Britain proved him wrong. It is, in fact, the exercise of belligerent rights within the scope of a pacific blockade that raised serious concerns and pointed to the urgent need for a juridical elucidation of great authority about this measure. It is noteworthy, however, that statesmen did not challenge the fact that there was such a thing as pacific blockade, although they disagreed as to the legal effects attached to its establishment.

ii) The Work of the Institute

Directly in the wake of the pacific blockade of Formosa, the Institute of International Law decided in 1885 to look more closely into the situation of pacific blockade and fill the existing legal vacuum.[512] A commission was thus set up to solve the question of the legitimacy of pacific blockade and,

508 M. le président du conseil, *Chambre des députés*, 26 November 1884: *J.O.R.F.*, 27 November 1884, 2487–8. Albert Billot, French diplomat and lawyer by training, also justified the projected destruction of Fuzhou as a lawful act of reprisals which would not have broken peace. See [Billot], *L'affaire du Tonkin* (above, n. 496), 223–4.

509 M. le président du conseil, *Chambre des députés*, 26 November 1884: *J.O.R.F.*, 27 November 1884, 2487.

510 M. le président du conseil, *Chambre des députés*, 26 November 1884: Ibid.

511 M. le président du conseil, *Chambre des députés*, 26 November 1884: Ibid.

512 In fact, the reading of an essay about the Sino-French conflict by Geffcken triggered the Institute's interest in the matter. See Institut de Droit International, 'Conflit franco-chinois. – Lecture de M. Geffcken.', in Institut de Droit International (ed.), *Session de Bruxelles – September 1885* (Annuaire IDI, vol. 8; Bruxelles/Leipzig: Librairie européenne C. Muquardt, Merzbach & Falk, 1886), 289.

if it be so, laying down the rules that should govern the measure.[513] On 7 September 1887 in Heidelberg, in the presence of the Grand Duke of Baden and under Bulmerincq's chairmanship, the Institute examined this issue in plenary session.

Ferdinand Perels, a German maritime law expert and Commissioner of the Imperial German Admiralty, acted as rapporteur of the Institute's sixth commission. He endeavoured in his report to demonstrate that a blockade outside a state of war and not preceded by a declaration of war could lawfully be instituted by way of reprisals or intervention. For this fervent advocate of pacific blockade, the measure had to be studied *in abstracto*. He, indeed, deemed incorrect to combat the legality of pacific blockade on the basis of the assumption that a blockade could only be an act of war. In his opinion, pacific blockade was a lesser evil than war and, therefore, as lawful as any other coercive acts of force short of war. For that reason, he judged that pacific blockade could affect the navigation of third States. Still, he agreed that the confiscation of ships attempting to run the blockade would exceed the aim of the measure. He thus proposed that the ships flying flags of third States should just be turned away. As for the vessels of the blockaded Power, he supported their mere sequestration and their restitution without compensation after the end of the blockade. Moreover, Perels was of the opinion that the blockade had to be effective, notified and declared. Finally, sufficient time should allow the ships of third States to leave the blockaded ports.[514]

However, Perel's statement was followed by a counter-report submitted by a staunch opponent of pacific blockade: the German lawyer Friedrich Heinrich Geffcken. Working on the hypothesis that pacific blockade could, arguably, be regarded as a special kind of reprisals, he insisted on

513 See Institut de Droit International (ed.), *Session de Bruxelles – September 1885* (Annuaire IDI, vol. 8; Bruxelles/Leipzig: Librairie européenne C. Muquardt, Merzbach & Falk, 1886), 11 and 347; and the copy of the circular of the Bureau of the Institute, May 1887: Institut de Droit International (ed.), *Session de Heidelberg – Septembre 1887* (Annuaire IDI, vol. 9; Bruxelles/Leipzig: C. Muquardt, 1888), 275–6.

514 Ibid., 276–86. The report is also published in *RDILC* 19 (1887), 245–52, and in *Clunet* 14 (1887), 721–9. It should be pointed out that, a few years earlier, Perels used to defend a more stringent view regarding the legal effects of the enforcement of the blockade against third States. Indeed, he maintained that the ships flying the flag of third States could eventually be sequestrated until the end of the blockade. See Ferdinand Perels, *Manuel de droit maritime international*, traduit de l'allemand et augmenté de quelques documents nouveaux par L. Arendt (Paris: Guillaumin et Cie, 1884), 182.

the fact that reprisals were legitimate in international law as isolated acts, but could by no means constitute a state of reprisals allowing all kind of hostilities outside of war. More importantly, they could not affect the third States. For Geffcken, it was on this point that pacific blockade exceeded the scope of mere reprisals since a blockade intrinsically meant the closing of ports to navigation. It thus had adverse effects on third States. So, in Geffcken's view, a pacific blockade could only be an abuse of force by a strong Power taking advantage of its superiority to enforce a belligerent measure against a weaker and smaller country, while simultaneously refusing to assume the responsibilities arising from war. He regarded such a proceeding as obviously contrary to the principle of equality amongst States. For all these reasons, he called the members of the Institute to decide against pacific blockade.[515]

From there, the minutes of the session are quite succinct about the ensuing debate.[516] Geffcken and Neumann reiterated that pacific blockade was a genuine act of war or an illegal practice of reprisals in terms of international law. Yet, Perels contested Geffcken's objections by maintaining that pacific blockade should be regarded as an act of reprisals as valid as embargo or the sequestration of property. Besides, he argued that States were equal to the extent that they all had the right to establish a pacific blockade, although they did not have the same capacity to perform it.[517]

At the heart of the debate was the question of the enforcement of the blockade against the ships of third States. Perels provided at Section 4 of his draft that the ships flying foreign flags could be driven away by the blockader. This opinion had the support of Gustave Koenig, professor of law at Bern, who looked upon pacific blockade as a measure of police whose efficacy depended on a strict closure of the blockaded ports to ships of third States. Others like Emilio Brusa, professor at the University of Turin, considered that only the ships carrying contraband could be impeded entrance into the blockaded ports. The reason he put forward was that

515 Institut de Droit International (ed.), *Session de Heidelberg – Septembre 1887* (above, n. 513), 286–95. Also published in: Friedrich Heinrich Geffcken, 'Le blocus pacifique. Réponse aux conclusions du rapport de M. Perels', *RDILC* 19 (1887), 377–83.

516 See Institut de Droit International (ed.), *Session de Heidelberg – Septembre 1887* (above, n. 513), 295–300.

517 Ibid., 295–296. Cf. Gerry J. Simpson, *Great Powers and Outlaw States: Unequal Sovereigns in the International Legal Order* (Cambridge Studies in International and Comparative Law; Cambridge: CUP, 2004), 44–5.

the right to resort to pacific blockade should be reserved to the Concert of the Great European Powers that could establish it by majority vote.[518]

However, it is the principle of the absolute free passage of ships under a foreign flag through the blockade line that prevailed. The unanimous vote of the Institute on this rule confirms that therein lied the key to the recognition of pacific blockade.

Apart from this matter, the thirty and more members present that day fairly quickly agreed on the text of a declaration despite various reformulations of Perels's draft. The result was the recognition of the validity and legality of pacific blockade by the Institute under certain conditions. The declaration reads as follows:

> "Declaration Voted by the Institute on Blockade in the Absence of a State of War
> The establishing of a blockade in the absence of a state of war should not be considered as permissible under the law of nations except under the following conditions:
> 1. Ships under a foreign flag shall enter freely in spite of the blockade.
> 2. Pacific blockade must be officially declared and notified, and maintained by a sufficient force.
> 3. The ships of a blockaded Power which do not respect such a blockade may be sequestrated. When the blockade is over, they shall be restored to their owners together with their cargoes, but without any compensation whatsoever."[519]

It must be noted that the declaration did not explain on what grounds pacific blockade could be resorted to. In other words, it did not say whether pacific blockade was a measure of reprisals or intervention or both. It is clear that during the session as well as in Perels's and Geffcken's reports, pacific blockade was addressed mainly in reference to reprisals. For instance, the Institute's secretary-general, Gustave Rolin-Jaequemyn, put to

---

518 This idea was shared by some authors. Cf. Eugène-Marie-Henri Rosse, *Guide international du commandant de bâtiment de guerre: Du droit de la force (D'après Calvo, Fauchille, Ortolan, Hautefeuille, etc.)* (Paris: Librairie militaire de L. Baudoin, 1891), 89; Albert Edmond Hogan, *Pacific blockade* (Oxford: Clarendon Press, 1908), 19f. But see Parry, 'British Practice in Some Nineteenth Century Pacific Blockades' (above, n. 415), 686–8.

519 Translation by Scott (ed.), *Resolutions of the Institute of International Law dealing with the Law of Nations* (above, n. 386), 69–70. See the original text in the French language in: Institut de Droit International (ed.), *Session de Heidelberg – Septembre 1887* (above, n. 513), 300–1.

discussion the requirement of a just cause for the legality of pacific blockade. He emphasised that, in the absence of a *justa causa*, this proceeding was nothing less than an act of war in the eyes of the target country. To which Bulmerincq added that as a measure of reprisals, pacific blockade always required a just cause in order not to amount to an arbitrary means. This amendment was turned down by a slight majority.[520]

Nevertheless, the so-called pacific blockade of Greece seems to have served as a model for the declaration. In many respects, that blockade contrasted diametrically with the one of Formosa. In 1886, the great European Powers, except France, resorted to this measure as a form of intervention in order to prevent Greece from waging war on Turkey. Only ships under Greek flag that did not carry foreign cargo were affected. A month after being established, the blockade was already lifted as Greece consented to lay the weapons down.[521] Lawyers applauded the *modus operandi* of this blockade, which manifestly contributed to the recognition of pacific blockade as a legitimate institution of international law.[522]

The conclusion to retain is thus that the Institute's declaration did not forbid resorting to pacific blockade either by way of intervention or of reprisals. It led Paul Heilborn, German international law expert and *Privatdozent* at the University of Berlin, to regard pacific blockade as a hybrid expedient, midway between reprisals and intervention.[523] Thereafter, pacific

520 See Ibid., 297–9.

521 About the whole incident, see Gustave Rolin-Jaequemyns, 'Chronique du droit international (1885–1886) [Troisième article]', *RDILC* 18 (1886), 591–626, esp. at 619–621.

522 See, i.a., Pradier-Fodéré, *Traité de droit international public européen et américain, suivant les progrès de la science et de la pratique contemporaines* (above, n. 36), 5th vol., 772; Antoine A. Rontiris, 'De l'évolution de l'idée de blocus pacifique', *Clunet* 26 (1899), 225–39, at 236–237. For the opinions of other authors, see Falcke, *Le blocus pacifique* (above, n. 40), 143–144 fn. 8.

523 "Die Friedensblockade […] ist eine einzelne Gewalthandlung; sie gehört begrifflich weder ausschliesslich zu den Repressalien, noch zu den Interventionshandlungen, noch ist sie eine dritte, besondere Art der Selbsthilfe; je nach den Umständen trägt sie den Charakter der Repressalie, der Interventionshandlung, ist sie rechtswidrig. Für die Beurteilung einer Friedensblockade kommt demnach – von der principiellen Frage abgesehen – in Betracht, ob der handelnde Staat interveniert oder zu Repressalien greift, ob ein Interventionsgrund bezw. ein Anlaß zu Repressalien vorliegt." (Paul Heilborn, *Das System des Völkerrechts entwickelt aus den völkerrechtlichen Begriffen* (Berlin: Julius Springer, 1896), 367). Cf. Hiller, 'Die Friedensblockade und ihre Stellung in Völkerrecht' (above, n. 45), 82–4.

blockade sometimes occupied an individual section, even chapter, apart from reprisals in international law manuals.[524]

As a final observation, it should be pointed out that the declaration barely concerned the relation between the blockading Power and the blockaded country. The last provision merely mentioned that the sequestrated ships of the latter State had to be restored at the end of the measure and without any compensation whatsoever. This succinctness regarding the relation between the blockaded and the blockading countries shows that the real concern of the members of the Institute was, in fact, the question of the adverse effects that might flow from a pacific blockade on the shipping of third States. Indeed, the Institute did not meet the accusation that pacific blockade was an oppressive measure used by major Powers against weak and small nations. This indictment was perhaps just a mere objection of principle that did not weight in comparison to the more severe issue of the free passage of ships of third States. It can even be said that by confirming the legitimacy of pacific blockade the Institute implicitly sanctioned the measure as a kind of prerogative of the great Powers.

(c) Reception of the Institute's Declaration

When in 1888 the German East Africa Company received the administration of a coastal territory from the Sultan of Zanzibar, the Arab slave traders who saw their interests compromised rose up in protest. A joint Brito-German blockade was then instituted on 2 December 1888 with the Sultan's consent. It aimed to put a stop to the slave trade in those waters and to quash the uprising by impeding the importation of arms. To this purpose, the blockading Powers reserved the right of visit and search against any ships.[525] One year later, on 1 October 1889, the blockade was

---

524 See, e.g., Oppenheim, *International Law* (above, n. 25), 43; Alexandre Mérignhac, *Traité de droit public international*, Tome premier de la 3ième partie (Paris: Librairie générale de droit & de jurisprudence, 1912), 60; Henry Bonfils, *Manuel de droit international public (droit des gens): Destiné aux étudiants des Facultés de Droit et aux aspirants aux fonctions diplomatiques et consulaires*, édition revue et mise au courant par Paul Fauchille (7th edn., Paris: Rousseau et Cie, 1914), 706.

525 See the declaration of the blockade and the notice of it by the German and British Rear-Admirals, 2 December and 29 November 1888 respectively: Great Britain, F. O., *BFSP 1888–1889* (81st vol.; London: Harrison and sons, [s.d.]), 97. On 5 December, Italy joined the blockade. See the extract from the Official Gazette of Italy, 19 December 1888: Ibid., 100. On the next day, Portugal decid-

lifted following the signature of a convention by which the Sultan abolished slavery and allowed Great Britain and Germany to visit and search the vessels of his subjects at any time.[526]

In this case, the Sovereign gave his consent to the blockade. So, the measure was a kind of legitimate intervention.[527] More accurately, scholars leaned towards a categorisation as a measure of police.[528] The blockade was, indeed, 'pacific' because of the absence of an official state of war.[529] Still, for Rolin-Jaequemyns, it could not be regarded as a pacific blockade *stricto sensu* since, he explained, a pacific blockade was an act of war in time of peace that required at least two belligerents, viz. two States or organised

---

ed to support this blockade by prohibiting the importation and exportation of arms in the Portuguese East African possessions. See the decree thereupon, 6 December 1888: Great Britain, F. O., *BFSP 1887–1888* (79th vol.; London: Harrison and sons, [s.d.]), 384–6. The French Government also consented to exceptionally grant the right of search on the occasion of this blockade. See The Marquis of Salisbury to Sir E. Malet, 5 November 1888: Ibid., 369.
The chancellor Prince von Bismark did not believe that the joint blockade could successfully abolish the slave trade. However, on his own admission, such a proceeding served German colonial policy by showing to African natives that Great Britain and Germany worked hand in hand in good harmony. See Reichstag, 26 January 1889: Deutsches Reich, *Stenographische Berichte über die Verhandlungen des Reichstags: VII. Legislaturperiode. IV. Session 1888/89*, 1st vol. (105th vol.; Berlin: Norddeutsche Buchdruckerei und Verlagsanstalt, 1889), 619 (A).

526 See the Agreement between Great Britain and Zanzibar, 13 September 1889: Great Britain, F. O., *BFSP 1888–1889* (above, n. 525), 1291; and the British notification of the raising of the blockade, 30 September 1889: Ibid., 132.

527 Cf. Bulmerincq, 'Le blocus pacifique et ses effets sur la propriété privée' (above, n. 422), 578.

528 See, e.g., Gustave Rolin-Jaequemyns, 'L'année 1888 au point de vue de la paix et du droit international', *RDILC* 21 (1889), 167–208, at 207–208; Rivier, *Principes du droit des gens* (above, n. 226), 198f. For Thomas E. Holland, this blockade was "a very anomalous [one]" within the category of blockades instituted without war that aimed to suppress rebellion (Holland, *Studies in international law* (above, n. 476), 139).

529 Nevertheless, a prize court was established at Zanzibar. Besides, Germany proclaimed the martial law for Dar es Salaam and other places, prohibited the importation of provisions and admitted the existence of a state of war. See the British Order in Council of 17 December 1888: Great Britain, F. O., *BFSP 1887–1888* (above, n. 525), 1336–7; the German Decree applying prize law to Zanzibar, 15 February 1889: *RGBl.*, 19 February 1889, 5–10; Colonel Euan-Smith to the Marquis of Salisbury, 27 February and 12 March 1889: Great Britain, F. O., *BFSP 1888–1889* (above, n. 525), 116 and 121; The Marquis of Salisbury to Mr Beauclerck, 9 March 1889: Ibid., 119.

forces. In addition, he specified that publicists had increasingly condemned pacific blockade.[530]

This last remark is quite surprising since Rolin-Jaequemyns was present and took an active part at the session of Heidelberg in 1887 where the Institute declared pacific blockade lawful. Of course, the blockade of Zanzibar was a peculiar one and, moreover, did not follow the rules laid down by the Institute. This deviation raises the question of the reception and authority of the Institute's declaration.

In general, legal scholars applauded the declaration, primarily because it offered a solution which spared the shipping of third States.[531] A notable exception is Ernest Nys, professor of international law at Brussels, who sarcastically pointed out that the Institute had preferred to find a compromise on the issue rather than to state the principles firmly, i.e. to condemn pacific blockade as an abuse.[532] Some years later, at the time of the French blockade against Siam in 1893, Thomas Gibson Bowles, MP for King's Lynn, came down against pacific blockade and attacked the Institute for having suggested its possibility. He disdainfully called the Institute's decision on this matter the work of "certain unauthorised persons in an unauthorised conference".[533]

On the other hand, some lawyers also criticised the declaration for not going far enough, for being lacunal or unsatisfactory. For example, Thomas E. Holland looked upon the Institute's declaration as "a well-considered expression of expert European opinion". He, however, argued that

530 Rolin-Jaequemyns, 'L'année 1888 au point de vue de la paix et du droit international' (above, n. 528), 206f.

531 See, e.g., Pradier-Fodéré, *Traité de droit international public européen et américain, suivant les progrès de la science et de la pratique contemporaines* (above, n. 36), 5th vol., 772; Calvo, *Le droit international théorique et pratique* (above, n. 224), 557 fn. 1 (§ 1859); Piédelièvre, *Précis de droit international public ou droit des gens* (above, n. 56), 105; Georges Bry, *Précis élémentaire de droit international public: mis au courant des progrès de la science et du droit positif contemporain à l'usage des étudiants des facultés de droit et des aspirants aux fonctions diplomatiques et consulaires* (3rd edn., Paris: L. Larose, 1896), 372.

532 Nys, *Le droit international* (above, n. 33), 93. Cf. Thomas Baty, 'The Institute of International Law on Pacific Blockade', *The Law Magazine and Law Review* 21 (4th ser.) (1895–96), 285–300, at 288; Kleen, *Lois et usages de la neutralité* (above, n. 230), 652 fn. 1.

533 Mr Gibson Bowles, House of Commons, 27 July 1893, Great Britain, Parliament, *The Parliamentary Debates authorised Edition: Fourth Series: Commencing with the Second Session of the Twenty-fifth Parliament of the United Kingdom of Great Britain and Ireland* (15th vol.; London: Eyre and Spottiswoode, 1893), col. 660.

the Institute treated pacific blockade as merely a species of reprisals and failed to sufficiently take into consideration the other natures of the measure. Thus, he supported the view that, in case of intervention or suppression of a rebellion, a pacific blockade ought to be directed against the ships under the flag of third Powers too, unlike the pacific blockades established by way of reprisals.[534] Finally, Léon Poinsard, secretary-general of the United International Bureaux for the Protection of Intellectual Property, criticised that the solution adopted by the Institute —which he did not name — consisting in excluding third States from the operation of pacific blockade deprived of its efficacy a measure that he regarded as an excellent alternative to war.[535]

Yet, apart from these few critical reactions, the rules laid down by the Institute in 1887 had received large approval from almost the entire international legal community and prevailed in diplomacy, according to Thomas Joseph Lawrence, lecturer in international law at Downing College of Cambridge University. Nonetheless, the latter author wished that a Hague convention sanctioned them officially.[536] As a matter of fact, the declaration did not lack authority as the Institute gathered the foremost international lawyers of the time. But for being a regulation enacted by a private institution, it had naturally no binding force upon Governments.[537]

3. Departing State Practice: The Blockades of Siam (1893) and Crete (1897–1898)

The Institute's declaration represents undoubtedly a landmark for the theory of pacific blockade given its positive reception amongst lawyers. However, it lacked binding force. That meant that the Governments did not have to abide by the rules laid down by the Institute. In fact, the instances of so-called pacific blockade after 1887 did not follow at all the Institute's declaration. This departing practice reveals a serious gap between State practice and legal theory.

534 Holland, *Studies in international law* (above, n. 476), 144–145 and 149–150.

535 Léon Poinsard, *Études de droit international conventionnel*, Première série (Paris: F. Pichon, 1894), 83. See Norman Wise Sibley, 'Pacific Blockade.', *The Westminster review* 147 (1897), 679–85, at 682, who concurred with Poinsard's view.

536 Lawrence, *The principles of international law* (above, n. 6), 342–3.

537 Washburn, 'The Legality of the Pacific Blockade' (above, n. 41), 57.

In addition to the peculiar blockade of Zanzibar, two significant cases of pacific blockade occurred during the period going from 1887 until the beginning of the twentieth century, namely the blockades of Siam in 1893 and Crete in 1897–1898.

The first instance happened in the context of the French colonial enterprise in Southeast Asia and a border dispute with the Kingdom of Siam —currently, Thailand— that caused the killing of a French police inspector and the capture of a French officer. The crisis worsened as two French gunboats, which attempted to reach the port of Bangkok notwithstanding the interdiction of the Siamese Government, were fired at by the defence line. The gunboats responded and eventually succeeded to arrive in Bangkok.[538] The French Government, thus, decided to send an ultimatum written in terms that would justify the making of reprisals in case of failure to comply with the demands.[539] It insisted on the recognition of territorial claims, satisfaction for the offence and compensation for damage.[540] Still, following Siam's insufficient reply,[541] parts of the Siamese coasts were blockaded on 26 July 1893.[542]

The French Minister of Foreign Affairs, Jules Develle, justified the course of action as a lawful pacific blockade.[543] However, three days were given to friendly vessels to leave the blockaded places, and blockade runners were liable to capture and condemnation. That is why the announce-

---

538 See the French Foreign Minister's account of the events read before the *Chambre des députés* on 18 July 1893: France and Louis Renault, *Archives diplomatiques: Recueil mensuel international de diplomatie et d'histoire*, 47th vol. (2nd ser.) (Paris: F.-J. Féchoz, 1893), 73–8.

539 That is why the ensuing blockade was regarded —e.g. by Emanuel von Ullmann, *Völkerrecht* (Das öffentliche Recht der Gegenwart, 3; 2nd edn., Tübingen: J. C. B. Mohr (Paul Siebeck), 1908), 458— as an instance of pacific blockade by way of reprisals.

540 See the French demands in France and Renault, *Archives diplomatiques* (above, n. 538), 79; and the telegraph of Captain Jones to the Earl of Rosebery, 20 July 1893: Great Britain, F. O., *BFSP 1894–1895* (87th vol.; London: Her Majesty's Stationery Office, 1900), 262–3.

541 See the Siamese reply: France and Renault, *Archives diplomatiques* (above, n. 538), 80–1.

542 See the First Notification and Second Declaration of Blockade, 26 and 29 July 1893 respectively: Great Britain, F. O., *BFSP 1894–1895* (above, n. 540), 351–2.

543 "[…] la mesure dont il s'agit constitue, en réalité, un moyen de contrainte auquel un État est fondé à recourir, sans rompre la paix, pour rappeler une autre Puissance à l'observation de ses devoirs internationaux." In support of this statement, Develle cited past examples of pacific blockade and asserted that the British Government did not dispute the rights invoked by France at the time of

ment of the French blockade of Siam raised concerns in Great Britain and led to question the 'pacific' character of the blockade.[544] The British Government then seriously considered to treat the blockade as giving rise to a state of war, and thence to apply the law of neutrality.[545] Nevertheless, the blockade was lifted not long after its establishment as the Siamese Government quickly resolved to accede to the demands of France.[546]

---

the blockade of Formosa in 1884, but merely issued a few reservations. See Mr Develle to the Marquess of Dufferin, 3 August 1893: Ibid., 297–8.

544 See, e.g., The Marquess of Dufferin to Mr Develle, 28 July 1893: Ibid., 284. Another example is George Curzon, MP for Southport, who declared the following while addressing the Under-Secretary of State for Foreign Affairs, Sir Edward Grey: "[…] although it is, I believe, a recognised principle of International Law that a pacific blockade does not apply to ships flying the flag of another Power, France is, in spite of that, on the verge of establishing a blockade which would have that effect, and which would not so much injure Siam as British trade and shipping." (House of Commons, 27 July 1893: Great Britain, Parliament, *The Parliamentary Debates authorised Edition* (above, n. 533), col. 660).

545 See The Earl of Rosebery to the Marquess of Dufferin, 28 July 1893: Great Britain, F. O., *BFSP 1894–1895* (above, n. 540), 282. In the House of Commons, the MP for King's Lynn, Thomas Gibson Bowles, reproached the British Government for not protesting strongly enough against the so-called pacific blockade of Siam whereas a British steamer had been seized, according to him. He also took the opportunity to reiterate that pacific blockade was an invention that aimed to legitimate the abuse of force by powerful States against weak and inferior countries without proceeding to all the extremities of war. For him, a blockade could only be an act of war. The pretended pacific blockade could thus not claim a place as an institution of international law. See Mr Gibson Bowles, House of Commons, 2 August 1893: Great Britain, Parliament, *The Parliamentary Debates authorised Edition* (above, n. 533), col. 1147–1150. See also Mr Gibson Bowles, House of Commons, 27 July 1893: Ibid., col. 660, where he peremptorily stated that pacific blockade did not have the support of any international lawyers. Sir William Vernon Harcourt who served then as Chancellor of the Exchequer agreed with Gibson Bowles that a blockade which interfered with the ships under the flags of third Powers was a belligerent blockade. Nevertheless, he stressed that pacific blockade was a lawful species of reprisals insomuch as it did not apply to ships of third countries. See The Chancellor of the Exchequer (Sir W. Harcourt), House of Commons, 2 August 1893: Ibid., col. 1151–1152. In fact, Harcourt's opinion was not insignificant. He was, indeed, considered an authority in international law during his lifetime as he held the chair of Whewell professor of International Law in the University of Cambridge from 1869 until 1887. See Alfred George Gardiner, *The Life of Sir William Harcourt*, 1st vol. (London/Bombay/Sydney: Constable & Company, 1923), 194.

This pretended pacific blockade evokes in many respects the blockade of Formosa. Indeed, the French Government claimed in both cases the existence of a 'state of reprisals' in order to institute these blockades.[547] The claims, however, were rather dubious and could not hide the French colonial ambitions in the background.

As to the blockade of Crete in 1897–1898, the Concert of Europe established it in order to preserve peace. As a matter of fact, in spite of the great Powers' injunction to withdraw troops and naval forces, Greece persisted in trying to annex Crete by providing military support to the islanders' uprising against Ottoman rule.[548] So, the blockade began on 21 March 1897 and aimed to prevent reinforcement. It was directed against all the ships flying the Greek flag. The vessels under other flags could enter the blockaded ports unless they carried supplies for the insurgents or troops. Therefore, the blockading Powers reserved the right of visit.[549] Despite these measures, war officially broke out between Greece and the Sublime Porte.[550] The great Powers, nevertheless, maintained the blockade so that Crete remained outside of the theatre of war.[551] It was only a year after the signature of a peace treaty between the warring nations that the blockade was ultimately lifted.[552]

---

546 See Prince Vadhana to Mr Develle, 29 July 1893: Great Britain, F. O., *BFSP 1894–1895* (above, n. 540), 288; and the Notification of Raising of Blockade, 3 August 1893: Ibid., 353. See also the Peace Treaty between France and Siam, 3 October 1893: Ibid., 187–9.

547 See the Second Declaration of Blockade, 29 July 1893: Ibid., 352.

548 See the great Powers' note presented to the Greek Government, 2 March 1897: Great Britain, F. O., *BFSP 1898–1899* (91st vol.; London: His Majesty's Stationery Office, 1902), 175–6; and Mr Métaxas to the Marquess of Salisbury, 10 March 1897: Ibid., 174–5.

549 See the British Notification of the Blockade of the Island of Crete, 19 March 1897: Great Britain, F. O., *BFSP 1896–1897* (89th vol.; London: His Majesty's Stationery Office, 1901), 446.

550 See the Greek Prime Minister's declaration in the Greek Chamber of Deputies, 6 [O.S.]/18 [N.S.] April 1897: Great Britain, F. O., *BFSP 1898–1899* (above, n. 548), 227–8.

551 Cf. The Marquess of Salisbury to Sir N. O'Conor, 20 April 1897: Ibid., 226; The Marquess of Salisbury to Sir Clare Ford, 20 April 1897: Ibid., 228; The First Lord of the Treasury, House of Commons, 26 April 1897: Great Britain, Parliament, *The Parliamentary Debates, authorised Edition. Fourth Series, Commencing with the Third Session of the Twenty-sixth Parliament of the United Kingdom of Great Britain and Ireland* (48th vol.; London: Waterlow & sons, 1897), col. 1076.

552 See Sir P. Currie to the Marquess of Salisbury, 4 December 1897: Great Britain, F. O., *BFSP 1898–1899* (above, n. 548), 465; British Notification raising the Blockade of the Island of Crete, 12 December 1898: Ibid., 113.

This blockade —similar in nature to the blockade of Greece in 1886— was not officially presented as a pacific blockade. George Curzon, the British Under-Secretary of State for Foreign Affairs, called it nothing more than a measure of police that did not amount to a state of war with either Greece or Turkey.[553] Nevertheless, a couple of weeks before the blockade effectively started, the MP for Sunderland asked the Attorney-General Sir Richard Webster whether the blockade would be belligerent or pacific. The latter did not know but emphasised the distinction between the two kinds. On the one hand, pacific blockade could be directed only against the ships of the target country. On the other, a belligerent blockade — which he also named blockade *jure gentium*— applied to all ships indistinctly and implied the existence of a state of war.[554]

Once established, the character of the blockade remained unclear. Nobody seemed willing or able to tell whether the blockade was pacific or belligerent.[555] That explains why, in view of the notification of the blockade, John Sherman, U.S. Secretary of State, "confined [himself] to […] not conceding the right to make such a blockade […], and reserving the consideration of all international rights and of any question which may in any way affect the commerce or interests of the United States."[556]

Thus, it clearly appears that the declaration adopted by the Institute in 1887 failed to dictate the conduct of the blockading Power in both cases (as well as in the blockade of Zanzibar). However, the legality of the said

---

553 Mr Curzon, House of Commons, 25 March 1897: Great Britain, Parliament, *The Parliamentary Debates authorised Edition*: *Fourth Series, Commencing with the Third Session of the Twenty-sixth Parliament of the United Kingdom of Great Britain and Ireland* (47th vol.; London: Waterlow & sons, 1897), col. 1311.

554 The Attorney General, House of Commons, 9 April 1897: Great Britain, Parliament, *The Parliamentary Debates, authorised Edition* (above, n. 551), col. 861.

555 For instance, three weeks after the beginning of the blockade, Harcourt —now Leader of the Opposition— asked the British Government who were the neutrals and the belligerents in the issue since the notification of the blockade explicitly used the term "neutral Powers". See Sir W. Harcourt, House of Commons, 12 April 1897: Ibid., col. 984. Arthur Balfour taunted him by responding that he was not as well-versed in international law as Harcout who could surely teach the House about pacific blockade. See The First Lord of the Treasury, House of Commons, 12 April 1897: Ibid., col. 999. Balfour's derision does not say whether the British Government truly believed that the blockade of Crete was 'pacific'.

556 Mr Sherman to Sir Julian Pauncefote, 26 March 1897: United States, Department of State, *Papers relating to the foreign relations of the United States, with the annual message of the President transmitted to Congress, December 6, 1897.* (Washington: GPO, 1898), 255.

pacific blockades was seriously challenged. This calling into question may support the view that the Institute succeeded, after all, in making pacific blockade become recognised as a lawful measure of self-help in international law, provided the shipping of third States remained unaffected.

4. A Custom of International Law?

(a) "Mais si la doctrine proteste, la politique agit"[557]

With these words written in 1896, Alphonse Rivier, Swiss lawyer and Nys's predecessor at the chair for public international law in Brussels, wanted to stress that he saw evidence in the repeated State practice that pacific blockade had indisputably gained a place amongst the lawful remedies of international law. He noted that a strong party amongst legal scholars vigorously opposed this measure for being an act of war that really disrupted the state of peace. Nevertheless, he gave to understand that pacific blockade now came under customary law.[558]

This assertion is rather peremptory. In fact, two elements were needed to form an international custom: a *repetitio facti* and the *opinio juris*.[559] Rivier seemed to consider the first component sufficient. So, he confined him-

557 The whole sentence is: "Mais si la doctrine proteste, la politique agit, et il n'est plus guère possible aujourd'hui de dénier au blocus le caractère d'une institution du droit des gens actuel." (Rivier, *Principes du droit des gens* (above, n. 226), 198).

558 Ibid., 198–199. Yet, he observed that the absence of interference with the shipping of third Powers achieved a compromise in legal doctrine that gave pacific blockade the recognition as a species of reprisals.
Other authors, like Rivier, viewed in the repeated occurrences of pacific blockade the existence of a legal institution. See, e.g., Poinsard, *Études de droit international conventionnel* (above, n. 535), 83; Heilborn, *Das System des Völkerrechts entwickelt aus den völkerrechtlichen Begriffen* (above, n. 523), 36; Söderqvist, *Le blocus maritime* (above, n. 475), 137; Hershey, *The Essentials of International Public Law* (above, n. 459), 345. But cf. Walker, *A Manual of Public International Law* (above, n. 405), 99: "Whether Pacific Blockade in any form has established its title to international recognition as a legal measure of coercion falling short of war is a question of historic fact. At present, *in view of the paucity of instances*, the divergence in the character of the actual operations in those instances and the disputes which arose thereon, we must be content to say that the title is not yet practically established." (emphasis added).

559 E. Chauveau, *Le droit des gens ou Droit international public: Introduction (notions générales – historique – méthode)* (Paris: Arthur Rousseau, 1891), no. 47.

self to enumerating the instances of blockade bereft of belligerency. In other words, he did not appear to have looked critically at each case individually.

However, a close examination of the cases of so-called pacific blockade does not show a consistent practice. There was undoubtedly a recurrence of instances of blockade short of war after 1887, but they barely bore resemblance, except for the absence of an overt state of war between the blockading and the blockaded States. Besides, the blockade of Siam was the only example that was called 'pacific' by the blockading Power, namely here the French Government. The other instances were either a measure of police by great Powers or a belligerent blockade. Still, many lawyers classified those cases as instances of pacific blockade, but without referring to the criteria set out in the Institute's declaration. In fact, those so-called pacific blockades were hardly permissible since at least one of the conditions was missing.

Those controversial cases, nevertheless, rekindled the debate about pacific blockade in legal doctrine. As a consequence, the study of this topic enjoyed a revival of interest that is observable in the variety of works —often doctoral theses— dealing fully or partially with the institution of pacific blockade.[560]

(b) Dialogue of the Deaf

Far from all lawyers shared Rivier's view. For example, in 1888, Émile Acollas, a French professor of law who is remembered as one of the founders of the League of Peace and Freedom, viewed pacific blockade as a concealed way of waging war. That is why he deplored that some publi-

560 See, i.a., Barès, *Le blocus pacifique* (above, n. 81); Ducrocq, *Représailles en temps de paix* (above, n. 81); Hogan, *Pacific blockade* (above, n. 518); Söderqvist, *Le blocus maritime* (above, n. 475); Hermann Staudacher, *Die Friedensblockade: Ein Beitrag zur Theorie und Praxis der nichtkriegerischen Selbsthilfe* (Staats- und völkerrechtliche Abhandlungen, 7/3; Leipzig: Duncker & Humblot, 1909); Teyssaire, *Le blocus pacifique* (above, n. 81); Falcke, *Le blocus pacifique* (above, n. 40); Hiller, 'Die Friedensblockade und ihre Stellung in Völkerrecht' (above, n. 45); Ho, 'Pacific blockade with special reference to its use as a measure of reprisal' (above, n. 81).

cists gave their approval to the measure merely because the great European Powers had repeatedly resorted to such a blockade.[561]

Despite its short duration and geographical remoteness, the blockade of Siam in 1893 reopened the discussion of the legality of pacific blockade as more voices were heard refusing to consider this measure a legitimate institution of international law. For example, an Italian publicist named Oreste Da Vella called to ban pacific blockade from international law and harshly condemned lawyers who corrupted the role of science by trying to legitimise a revolting practice introduced for mere political purposes. According to him, a blockade could only be an act of war that had to be preceded by a declaration of war and could then apply against neutral shipping. That is why he disagreed with the Institute's view that pacific blockade could be deemed a lawful coercive measure. Furthermore, he believed that non-forcible means like good offices, mediation and arbitration were better suited to prevent war than a pacific blockade. He applauded, therefore, the severe censure of Great Britain on the occasion of the blockade of Siam and hoped that this protest might pave the way to a general declaration by the neutral nations for the abolition of this deceitful practice.[562]

A couple of years after him, another lawyer also challenged the place of pacific blockade in international law. It was the young British lawyer Thomas Baty. Yet, unlike most authors, he attached little importance to the eventual impact of pacific blockade on the shipping of third States.

For Baty, pacific blockade could not be approved as a species of reprisals for being highly excessive and used to enforce dubious claims not always quantifiable in pecuniary terms. He believed that pacific blockade was not a lesser evil than war but actually amounted to war. In fact, he looked upon it as an insolent and one-sided measure because the target country alone felt the harshness of the blockade as long as it did not comply with the too-often frivolous demands of the blockading Power. Beyond that, what convinced Baty that pacific blockade meant war was the unacceptable dilemma that it posed for the target country. Either the blockaded State denounced pacific blockade as war or submitted. The first alternative was no option because, if so, the target country would incur the wrath of the international community for disturbing the peace and because it would suffer the calamities of war since its enemy —who was stronger— would already

561 Émile Acollas, *Le droit de la guerre* (Le droit mis à la portée de tout le monde; Paris: Librairie Ch. Delagrave, 1888), 34f.

562 Oreste Da Vella, 'Il blocco dei porti del Siam e i blocchi pacifici', *Nuova Antologia di Scienze, Lettere ed Arti* 47 (3rd ser.) (1893), 295–308.

be strategically in position to go on the offensive. So, the submission was the only way. However, this did not mean that the assailed State consented not to treat the blockade as war. Therefore, Baty strongly urged to regard such blockades in time of peace as a fully fledged war. He viewed it as necessary, too, on account of the crucial imperative to draw a clear and sharp line between war and peace, at a time when war no longer required a formal proclamation to commence. For Baty, the conclusion was straightforward: pacific blockade could not be considered an institution of international law since it was deprived of intrinsic righteousness.[563]

Nonetheless, it was the blockade of Crete —geographically closer to the main authors on international law— that generated the most reactions in legal doctrine. A large number of lawyers kept defending the institution of pacific blockade. Two authors in particular —Thomas Barclay, British international law expert, and Antoine A. Rontiris, Greek law professor at Athens— both noted that the past instances of pacific blockade were mainly of dubious legality and that the course of action, especially towards the shipping of third States, varied from case to case. Nonetheless, they gave their approval to pacific blockade, particularly in the form adopted by the Institute, since it was a mild alternative to war. Indeed, Rontiris judged that this measure fulfilled the new expectations of civilisation which demanded the settlement of disputes without the recourse to war. That is why, unlike Barclay who was less bold to take a categorical stance, he did not question the place of pacific blockade in international law.[564]

However, according to Lawrence, "[the great Powers'] proceedings have thrown the whole law of Pacific Blockade back into obscurity."[565] Lawrence expressed bewilderment because the blockading Powers did not comply with the condition laid down by the Institute that a pacific blockade could not have an impact on the ships of third States.[566] The two British legal scholars Frederick Edwin Smith (later titled Earl of Birkenhead) and Norman Wise Sibley also reached the conclusion that the block-

---

563 Baty, 'The Institute of International Law on Pacific Blockade' (above, n. 532). He understood that great Powers obviously preferred resorting to pacific blockade in order to resolve difficulties flowing from war: the question of prestige of waging war against a smaller State, some constitutional restrictions, the uncertainty of the outcome of war, the onus of beginning war, etc.

564 Cf. Barclay, 'Les blocus pacifiques' (above, n. 465); Rontiris, 'De l'évolution de l'idée de blocus pacifique' (above, n. 522).

565 Thomas Joseph Lawrence, *The principles of international law* (3rd edn., Boston: D. C. Heath & Co., 1900), 298 fn. 3.

566 Ibid.

ade of Crete destroyed the consensus by which pacific blockade became acceptable in international law. In fact, they identified that the great Powers were striving to fully assimilate pacific blockade to belligerent blockade with all its attendant consequences. They, thus, predicted future conflicts between blockaders and neutrals.[567]

In a condensed version of his previous article, Baty restated his views in 1898 and severely criticised Barclay's argument that political usages create international practices. He believed that legal scholars had, in fact, a substantial role to play in making an objective and impartial judgement upon those political usages, i.e. acting as a filter rather than merely registering them.[568]

Georgios Streit, another professor of law at Athens, condemned pacific blockade for being a measure utterly incompatible with a state of peace since it affected the independence and equality between States. He argued that pacific blockade went beyond lawful reprisals because it allowed the ships of the blockading Power to infringe on the sovereign territory of the target country. Besides, only strong States made use of this measure against smaller and weaker countries. Therefore, he could not agree with Perels that all States had the right to establish a pacific blockade but not the same capacity to enjoy it. This reflection inspired him with the remark that the resort to pacific blockade actually constituted a privilege of the great Powers. For him, such a situation could not be tolerable in international law.[569]

---

567 Smith and Sibley, *International law as interpreted during the Russo-Japanese War* (above, n. 240), 362–3. Cf. Teyssaire, *Le blocus pacifique* (above, n. 81), 82.

568 Thomas Baty, 'Les blocus pacifiques', *RDILC* 30 (1898), 606–9, at 609.

569 See Georges Streit, 'La question crétoise au point de vue du droit international', *RGDIP* 7 (1900), 301–69, at 347–356, esp. 350–351. "Mais, si la possibilité de la réalisation d'un droit n'existe en principe que pour une catégorie de personnes – à savoir pour les forts vis-à-vis des faibles, – n'est-on pas conduit à dire que le droit lui-même n'existe que pour cette catégorie et devient dès lors un *privilège*? M. Perels ne saurait certainement admettre que le droit international reconnaît aux États forts des privilèges vis-à-vis des États faibles." (at 351, emphasis in original).

(c) Opinio Juris

As it stood at the turn of the nineteenth century, the debate in legal theory was somehow exhausted. The divergence of opinions crystallised and seemed irreconcilable. Yet, the fact was that a shift in legal doctrine appeared to have taken place in favour of the recognition of pacific blockade since the Heidelberg declaration. There were still some legal scholars who categorically refused to admit that pacific blockade had entered international law. But many of those who entertained such a view were actually concerned by the adverse effects on the navigation of third States.[570] On the other hand, pacific blockade received the support of the majority of lawyers because it was viewed as a special measure of reprisals of lesser evil than war. That is why most of them fell in with the decision of the Institute that pacific blockade had to be directed only against vessels belonging to the target country, although some still held the view that it could interfere with the shipping of third States.[571] As a result, Westlake could say on

570 Cf. Kleen, *Lois et usages de la neutralité* (above, n. 230), 644–655; Gaston Compin, *Essai sur le blocus maritime en temps de guerre*, Thèse pour le doctorat de la Faculté de droit de l'Université de Paris (Paris: Arthur Rousseau, 1899), 2–3; Despagnet, *Cours de droit international public* (above, n. 27), 788–9; Bonfils, *Manuel de droit international public (droit des gens)* (above, n. 524), 708f. See also John Shuckburgh Risley, *The Law of War* (London: A. D. Innes & Co., 1897), 60 and 62, who noted that pacific blockade exceeded mere reprisals pursuing compensation. Nevertheless, he did not seem to challenge the measure beyond that.

571 Cf. José Joaquín Larrain y Zañartu, *Nociones de derecho internacional marítimo segun los mas recientes progresos de la ciencia: Adaptacion a las leyes i preceptos de Chile, i como testo de la Escuela Naval i libro de consulta para los oficiales de la Marina de Guerra, del testo de A. Lemoine, capitan de fragata i Licenciado en Derecho en Francia* (Santiago de Chile: Imprensa Nacional, 1892), 119–20; Piédelièvre, *Précis de droit international public ou droit des gens* (above, n. 56), 103; John M. Gover, 'Current notes on international law', *The Law Magazine and Law Review* 22 (4th ser.) (1896–97), 182–94, at 182–8; Letter of 5 March 1897: Holland, *Letters to "The Times" upon War and Neutrality (1881–1920)* (above, n. 26), 11–3; Manuel J. Mozo, *Tratado elemental de derecho de gentes y marítimo internacional: con varios apéndices que contienen documentos nacionales y extranjeros referentes al asunto* (Madrid: A. Avrial, 1898), 303–4; Antoine Pillet, *Les Lois actuelles de la Guerre* (Paris: Arthur Rousseau, 1898), 142–3; George Grafton Wilson and George Fox Tucker, *International law* (New York/Boston/Chicago: Silver, Burdett and Company, 1901), § 93; Albert Zorn, *Grundzüge des Völkerrechts* (Webers Illustrierte Katechismen, 79; 2nd edn., Leipzig: J. J. Weber, 1903), 243–4; Moore, *A digest of international law* (above, n. 222), 135; Söderqvist, *Le blocus maritime* (above, n. 475), 132–9; Westlake, 'Pacific Blockade' (above, n. 438), 21–2; Teyssaire, *Le blocus pacifique* (above, n. 81), 93–6; Luigi Olivi, *Manuale di dirit-*

the eve of World War One that "[...] pacific blockade as against the quasi-enemy is too well established as a recognised institution to be longer attacked with serious hope of success."[572]

As a matter of fact, the topic of pacific blockade became a burning issue because the measure raised serious objections. However, the jurists are mainly to blame for this. They literally invented pacific blockade by giving their approval to an illegal proceeding of the great Powers. In very few cases, those blockades bereft of belligerency were called 'pacific' by diplomats and statesmen themselves. Still, it was rather the work of publicists who characterised them so, irrespective of the lack of common features between the cases. Therefore, as the list of pretended cases grew, so the impression that pacific blockade was an admitted practice was reinforced. This vicious circle went on until the legality of pacific blockade became an undeniable state of affairs. In addition, the Institute's declaration represented a significant milestone in this process.

The result was, thus, that pacific blockade entered international law willy-nilly, although the applicable rules, in particular to third States, remained undefined. However, the protests of third States at the time of the blockades of Formosa, Siam and Crete reveal that Great Britain and the United States recognised pacific blockade only under the terms spelt out in the Institute's declaration of 1887, i.e. as long as a pacific blockade did not impact foreign shipping. They are indicative of an *opinio juris*.

At around the same time, pacific blockade was taken into account in diplomatic circles as a legitimate institution of international law. For instance, Article 1 Paras. 2 and 3 of the Constantinople Convention of 1888 provided the free navigation of the Suez maritime canal in time of both war and peace as well as the ban on blockading it in any way. During the discussion, the Italian jurist Augusto Pierantoni pointed out that a pacific

to internazionale pubblico e privato (Piccola biblioteca scientifica, 8; 2nd edn., Milano: Società editrice libraria, 1911), 488–91.
It must not be lost sight of the fact that pacific blockade was also admitted by some as a form of intervention or a measure of police. Cf., e.g., Wagner, *Zur Lehre von den Streiterledigungsmitteln des Völkerrechts. Eine historisch-kritische und thetische Untersuchung* (above, n. 36), 80–1; Oppenheim, *International Law* (above, n. 25), 43; Ullmann, *Völkerrecht* (above, n. 539), 458; Hershey, *The Essentials of International Public Law* (above, n. 459), 345 fn. 9. For his part, Franz von Liszt, *Das Völkerrecht: systematisch dargestellt* (Berlin: O. Haering, 1898), 206, looked upon pacific blockade just as a sort of intervention.

572 Westlake, *International Law* (above, n. 25), 17.

blockade fell within the scope of this stipulation.[573] Another example is the arbitration treaty of 23 January 1905 between Spain and Sweden-Norway —concluded pursuant to Article 19 of the convention (I) for the peaceful settlement of international disputes signed on 29 July 1899 at the First Hague Conference— which explicitly stipulated that the parties ought to submit any pecuniary claim stemming from a pacific blockade to the Permanent Court of Arbitration and ought not oppose the exception of vital interests and independence.[574]

During the work of the fourth commission of the Second Hague Conference in 1907, dealing with maritime warfare, the Dutch delegate, Willem Hendrik de Beaufort, maintained that the commission should limit itself to the study of the rules applicable to blockade in time of war and examine neither the question of the admissibility of pacific blockade nor of its conditions.[575] Then, at the London Naval Conference of 1909 where a Declaration concerning the Laws of Naval War was drafted, pacific blockade was expressly mentioned as being not covered by that declaration.[576]

573 See Tobias Michel Karel Asser, 'La convention de Constantinople pour le libre usage du canal de Suez', *RDILC* 20 (1888), 529–58, at 536–537.

574 See Art. 3: Ramón de Dalmau y de Olivart, *Tratados y documentos internacionales de España: publicados en la Revista de derecho internacional y política exterior bajo la dirección del Marqués de Olivart*, 1st vol. (Madrid: Estab. tipográfico de los hijos de R. Álvarez á cargo de Arturo Menéndez, 1905), 26.

575 See the eleventh meeting of the fourth commission on 2 August 1907: France, Ministère des Affaires étrangères, *Deuxième conférence internationale de la paix. La Haye 15 juin – 18 octobre 1907. Actes et documents.*, 3rd vol. (La Haye: Imprimerie nationale, 1907), 893. For a translation, see James Brown Scott, *The Proceedings of the Hague Peace Conferences: Translation of the Official Texts*, prepared in the Division of International Law of the Carnegie Endowment for International Peace, 5 vols. (Publications of the Carnegie Endowment for International Peace: Division of International Law (Washington); New York: OUP, 1920–1921), Conference of 1907, 3rd vol., 884.

576 France, Ministère des Affaires étrangères, *Conférence navale de Londres: 1908–1909* (Documents diplomatiques; Paris: Imprimerie nationale, 1909), 13. For a translation, see James Brown Scott, *The Declaration of London, February 26, 1909: A collection of official papers and documents relating to the international naval conference held in London, December, 1908–February, 1909*, with an introduction by Elihu Root (New York: OUP, 1919), 135. Thereupon, Gibson Bowles said that "while the Declaration narrows, trammels, restricts, and ties up by the minutest regulations that blockade in war which is as lawful as justifiable, it leaves untouched in anything that blockade in peace which is as unlawful as it is unjustifiable." He regarded this fact as a proof of the falseness of the signatory Powers which claimed to be motivated by feelings of humanity, civilisation, justice, etc. See Thomas Gibson Bowles, *Sea law and sea power as they would be affected by*

So, although pacific blockade never was the subject of a binding international agreement, these sporadic references show that the diplomats acknowledged the existence of the measure and took it into consideration in their negotiations. Hence, the place of pacific blockade in international law could hardly be disputed.[577]

IV. *The Larger Issue of Armed Reprisals*

1. Twilight Zone

(a) Variety of Armed Reprisals

Throughout the nineteenth century, pacific blockade was the main form of armed reprisals and, therefore, the most studied. It was, indeed, as a measure of reprisals that pacific blockade secured recognition in international law. Nevertheless, there were also other acts of force resorted to by way of reprisals.

In the narrow sense, reprisals still meant until the end of that century the seizure and sequestration of property or ships belonging to the target country and found on the high seas or in the ports of the reprisal-taking Power.[578] This concept of seizure and sequestration of property, however, had received a broader meaning which led to include in the category of reprisals the occupation of territory or custom houses of the wrongdoing State. This is what Jules Ferry, French President of the Council, actually called in 1884 a "politique des gages" because the occupation of the island

---

recent proposals; with reasons against those proposals (London: John Murray, 1910), 189.

577 Indeed, James Brown Scott, 'The Declaration of London of February 26, 1909', *AJIL* 8 (1914), 274–329, at 286, regarded pacific blockade as "a recent comer in international law, but destined, it would seem, to stay."

578 See, e.g., Rivier, *Principes du droit des gens* (above, n. 226), 194–195. There were examples of such reprisals still until the outbreak of World War One. In 1872, e.g., the German corvette *Vineta* captured two warships in the harbour of Port-au-Prince in response to the Haitian Government's refusal of paying Germany compensation. See Perels, *Manuel de droit maritime international* (above, n. 514), 178–9; Liszt, *Das Völkerrecht* (above, n. 571), 205. Another instance is the capture of two Venezuelan gunboats by the Netherlands in 1908. See Lawrence, *The principles of international law* (above, n. 6), 336f. On this crisis, see further Embert J. Hendrickson, 'Root's Watchful Waiting and the Venezuelan Controversy', *The Americas* 23 (1966), 115–29, at 121–126.

of Formosa —more precisely, the territory around Keelung— was contemplated only as a pledge until satisfaction was given.[579]

This latter form of reprisals was chiefly employed in the last quarter of the nineteenth century and the first decades of the next one.[580] For instance, in 1895 Great Britain occupied the Nicaraguan town of Corinto to seek redress for the incarceration of the British vice-consul.[581] In 1901, France took control of Mytilene and its custom houses by way of reprisals against the Ottoman Empire.[582] In 1914, the United States occupied the Mexican town of Veracruz as well as the custom house.[583] According to a French professor of public international law at Cairo, such a course of ac-

579 M. le président du conseil, *Chambre des députés*, 26 November 1884: *J.O.R.F.*, 27 November 1884, 2487–8.

580 Earlier cases of occupation of territory by way of reprisals can be identified retrospectively like, e.g., the French conquest of Algeria that officially began on the pretext of obtaining satisfaction for an insult to a French diplomat. See Neff, *Justice among Nations* (above, n. 266), 335. Cf. Wurm, 'Selbsthülfe der Staaten in Friedenszeiten.' (above, n. 355), 91.

581 See United States, Department of State, *Papers Relating to the Foreign Relations of the United States, with the Annual Message of the President, transmitted to Congress, December 2, 1895*, Part II (Washington: GPO, 1896), 1025–34; and also Hannis Taylor, *A treatise on international public law* (Chicago: Callaghan & Company, 1901), 441–2; Louter, *Le droit international public positif* (above, n. 51), 203; Abbot Lawrence Lowell, 'The Council of the League of Nations and Corfu', *League of Nations* 6 (1923), 169–75, at 170. But Smith and Sibley, *International law as interpreted during the Russo-Japanese War* (above, n. 240), 359f., just referred to a pacific blockade.

582 See Maurice Moncharville, 'Le conflit franco-turc de 1901', *RGDIP* 9 (1902), 677–700. Cf. Raymond Robin, *Des Occupations militaires en dehors des Occupations de Guerre (étude d'histoire diplomatique et de droit international)*, avec une Préface de M. Louis Renault (Paris: Libraire de la société du Recueil Sirey, 1913), 583–4.

583 See Editorial Comment, 'Mediation in Mexico', *AJIL* 8 (1914), 579–85; Walther Schoenborn, *Die Besetzung von Veracruz: (Zur Lehre von den völkerrechtlichen Selbsthilfeakten)*, mit einem Anhang: Urkunden zur Politik des Präsidenten Wilson gegenüber Mexiko (Berlin: W. Kohlhammer, 1914); Charles Cheney Hyde, *International law chiefly as interpreted and applied by the United States*, 2nd vol. (Boston: Little, Brown, and Company, 1922), 177–179. Falcke, *Le blocus pacifique* (above, n. 40), 205–6, told that the cabinet of U.S. President Woodrow Wilson contemplated the establishment of a pacific blockade. However, the plan was dropped because the U.S. Government did not deem effective enough a blockade that would apply only to U.S. and Mexican vessels. Indeed, the United States had held the view since at least the blockade of Venezuela in 1902–1903 that a pacific blockade could not affect the navigation of third States. So, it was decided instead to occupy the town and custom house of Veracruz with the

tion, especially when it targeted custom houses, had the advantage of not impacting third States, unlike pacific blockade.[584]

Finally, the bombardment or destruction of towns or villages was sometimes treated also as an operation of reprisals, although it does not look different from a punitive expedition at all.[585] An example is the shelling of Greytown in 1854 by the U.S.S. *Cyane*.[586]

So, in the broad sense, reprisals had "come to cover, and it is the only term which does cover generically, an indeterminate list of unfriendly acts [...] to which resort is had in order to obtain redress from an offending State without going to war with it."[587]

---

aim of preventing the importation of arms carried by a German steamship from reaching the Mexican President Huerta. The ship was detained but almost immediately released with apologies owing to the absence of war that made such detention illegal. On this incident, see Thomas Baecker, 'The Arms of the *Ypiranga*. The German Side', *The Americas* 30 (1973), 1–17.

584 Moncharville, 'Le conflit franco-turc de 1901' (above, n. 582), 699f.

585 Neff, *War and the Law of Nations* (above, n. 2), 229. As a matter of fact, the burning of villages was often carried out against primitive tribes or lawless nations. See the references mentioned in Colbert, *Retaliation in international law* (above, n. 6), 80 fn. 62; and Neff, *War and the Law of Nations* (above, n. 2), 229 fn. 49. Such expeditions (punitive or of reprisals) were usually viewed as mere measures of police. Cf. Thomas Joseph Lawrence, *Essays on Some Disputed Questions in Modern International Law* (2nd edn., Cambridge: Deighton, Bell and Co., 1885), 274; Annual message of President Theodore Roosevelt to the Congress, 3 December 1901: United States, Department of State, *Papers relating to the foreign relations of the United States, with the annual message of the President transmitted to Congress, December 3, 1901.* (Washington: GPO, 1902), XXXVI. Such was, e.g., the U.S. Government's opinion about Greytown. See President Pierce's annual message, 4 December 1854, quoted in Moore, *A digest of international law* (above, n. 222), 115.

586 See *supra*, at 134.

587 Letter of 26 December 1908: Holland, *Letters to "The Times" upon War and Neutrality (1881–1920)* (above, n. 26), 19. See also Wheaton, *Elements of international law* (above, n. 464), 340; Ferguson, *Manual of International Law* (above, n. 484), 227–229; Nys, *Les origines du droit international* (above, n. 61), 62; Lawrence, *The principles of international law* (above, n. 6), 337.
However, Bluntschli and Clavo tried to draw up a list of lawful acts of reprisals. They only named measures not involving any use of force, i.e. the so-called negative reprisals, like the sequestration of property belonging to the wrongdoing State or its nationals and found in the territory of the reprisal-taking country; the interruption of commercial, postal, telegraphic relations; the termination of treaties; etc. But unlike Calvo, Bluntschli did not consider the enumeration exhaustive. Cf. Bluntschli, *Das moderne Völkerrecht der civilisirten Staten* (above, n. 485), 280; Carlos Calvo, *Dictionnaire de droit international public et privé*,

(b) The Uncertain Dividing Line between Peace and War

The use of belligerent measures by way of reprisals (even in a milder form, like pacific blockade when it did not impede the navigation of third States) raised serious issues of compatibility with a state of peace. In general, reprisals were considered as not giving rise to a state of war and all its attendant consequences.[588] Thus, their employment did not cause the abrogation of the existing treaties or the suspension of the diplomatic relations; the proceeding terminated without a peace treaty; and third States were supposedly not affected by the measures taken. Moreover, the acts of reprisals, unlike war, were limited in scope and localised.[589] These effects flowed directly from a clear-cut distinction between reprisals and war.

However, the resemblance between the acts of armed reprisals and their belligerent equivalents made a distinction resting on objective criteria impossible. The differentiation of armed reprisals from war then relied exclusively on a 'subjective' test which consisted of sounding out the intent of the Powers immediately concerned.[590] So, although the unilateral use of force implied *prima facie* the existence of a state of war between the parties, the absence of *animus belligerendi*, viz. the intention of waging war, meant that the acts fell within the class of reprisals and did not set up a state of war.[591]

The difficulty, nevertheless, lied precisely in finding out the intention of the assailing country in order to distinguish between war *de facto* and bare reprisals. Hence, the continuance of peaceful relations or the outbreak of war depended largely on the attitude of the target country. Indeed, it took

---

2nd vol. (Berlin: Puttkammer & Mühlbrecht, 1885), 161–162. In fact, Thomas E. Holland did not recommend drafting a definite list because it would restrict the reprisal-taking country's freedom of action. See Letter of 26 December 1908: Holland, *Letters to "The Times" upon War and Neutrality (1881–1920)* (above, n. 26), 20.

588 See, e.g., Liszt, *Das Völkerrecht* (above, n. 571), 203.

589 Cf. M. le président du conseil, *Chambre des députés*, 26 November 1884: *J.O.R.F.*, 27 November 1884, 2487; Sainte-Croix, *Étude sur l'exception de dol en droit romain/La déclaration de guerre et ses effets immédiats; Étude d'histoire et de législation comparée* (above, n. 44), 228–9; Letter of 26 December 1908: Holland, *Letters to "The Times" upon War and Neutrality (1881–1920)* (above, n. 26), 19; Lawrence, *The principles of international law* (above, n. 6), 337. See further Arnold D. McNair, 'La terminaison et la dissolution des traités', *RdC* 22/II (1928), 463–537, at 512–513.

590 See Lawrence, *The principles of international law* (above, n. 6), 334.

591 Cf. Hall, *A treatise on international law* (above, n. 46), 382–383; 391.

two to make a war, according to Lassa Oppenheim's definition of war as the contention between at least two States through the application of armed force. This meant that the use of unilateral acts of force did not imply a state of war unless the target country fought back or decided to treat them as acts of war.[592] From this standpoint, the onus of beginning war fell on the assailed State. The attacking State had to do little more than to deny any intention of making war. As a result, flagrant acts of extreme violence like the occupation of territory or bombardments were professedly committed by way of reprisals without officially breaking the state of peace.

Such a theory was denounced by Baty as untenable. As already set out in an article of 1895–1896 about pacific blockade,[593] he underlined the distress of the target country that had, in the end, no other option than submitting to an overwhelming force. Indeed, armed reprisals were done almost exclusively by strong Powers against small and weak States. That is why the subjective test presented a serious threat to the target country's independence. Furthermore, it gave the strong Powers "a two-edged weapon" to settle their disputes with weak countries because it imposed upon the latter the alternative between the outbreak of war and the compliance with the demands. It, thus, allowed a powerful State to resort to forcible proceedings by betting on the target country's weakness. In this way, the reprisal-taking Power did not need the ascent of the national parliament and supported neither the onus of declaring war nor the risks associated with war. Therefore, against such "conditional war", Baty advocated for treating any act of violence exerted in time of peace as amounting purely and simply to war.[594]

592 Oppenheim, *International Law* (above, n. 25), 56–57. See also Articles 704 and 714 of David Dudley Field, *Draft. Outlines of an International Code* (New York: Baker, Voorhis & Company, 1872), 467 and 473. In case law, the U.S. Court of Claims, e.g., stated in 1909 that "[w]hile reprisals are acts of war in fact it is for the state affected by them to determine for itself whether the relation of actual war is intended." (*The Schooner Endeavor*, in Charles C. Nott and Archibald Hopkins, *Cases decided in the Court of Claims of the United States: At the Term of 1908–9, With Abstracts of Decisions of the Supreme Court in Appealed Cases, From October, 1908, to May, 1909*, 44th vol. (Washington: GPO, 1910), 243).

593 See Baty, 'The Institute of International Law on Pacific Blockade' (above, n. 532), 294–5.

594 Thomas Baty, 'Conditional War.', *LMR* 24 (1898–1899), 436–40.

Baty was not alone to share this view. Many lawyers regarded this proceeding as a real abuse of force by a major State against an inferior Power. Therefore, they argued that the use of armed reprisals involved the existence of a state of war, regardless of whether the target country attempted to resist or not.[595] War, in this context, was understood as the prosecution of a nation's rights by force.[596]

Against such a controversial background, some authors advocated the adoption of the formality of a declaration of war in order to distinguish armed reprisals from war.[597] The first Article of the III Hague Convention of 1907 provided precisely that the opening of hostilities had to be preceded by a declaration of war or, at least, an ultimatum.[598] Westlake explained the term 'hostilities' in this convention as not covering the acts of armed reprisals. A reprisal-taking State did not have then to fulfil the requirement of a declaration of war. Yet, the difficulty to separate reprisals from war remained. Now, Westlake believed that neither the objective test nor the subjective test was adequate in this respect. On the one hand, the acts of armed reprisals could not be distinguished objectively from those of war.

---

595 See, e.g., Funck-Brentano and Sorel, *Précis du droit ges gens* (above, n. 36), 229–30; Acollas, *Le droit de la guerre* (above, n. 561), 30 and 32–33 fn. 1; Articles 512 and 518 Para. 3 of E. Duplessix, *La Loi des Nations: Projet d'institution d'une Autorité internationale Législative, Administrative et Judiciaire. Projet de Code de Droit international public*, Ouvrage couronné par le Bureau international de la Paix (Concours 1905–1906 – 1er Prix) (Paris: Libraire de la société du Recueil J.-B. Sirey et du Journal du Palais, 1906), 171–3; Nys, *Le droit international* (above, n. 33), 88–9; Despagnet, *Cours de droit international public* (above, n. 27), 782–3; Article 385 of Epitacio Pessôa, *Projecto de Codigo de Direito Internacional Publico* (Rio de Janeiro: Imprensa Nacional, 1911), 160.

596 See, e.g., Despagnet, *Cours de droit international public* (above, n. 27), 782. In 1846, Sir John Dodson, the British Queen's Advocate, defined war in the same way. See P. R. O., F. O. 83–2227, 25 July 1846, quoted in Parry, 'British Practice in Some Nineteenth Century Pacific Blockades' (above, n. 415), 678.

597 See, e.g., Nicolas Bruyas, *De la déclaration de guerre: Sa justification. – Ses formes extérieures* (Lyon: A. Rey, 1899), 104–5; Maurel, *De la Déclaration de Guerre* (above, n. 27), 139.

598 "The contracting Powers recognize that hostilities between themselves must not commence without previous and explicit warning, in the form either of a reasoned declaration of war or of an ultimatum with conditional declaration of war." (James Brown Scott, *The Hague Conventions and Declarations of 1899 and 1907: accompanied by Tables of Signatures, Ratifications and Adhesions of the Various Powers, and Texts of Reservations* (Carnegie Endowment for International Peace: Division of International Law; New York: OUP, 1915), 96). About the III Hague Convention of 1907, see Ellery C. Stowell, 'Convention Relative to the Opening of Hostilities', *AJIL* 2 (1908), 50–62.

On the other hand, the effectiveness of the rule laid down by the Second Hague Peace Conference could not depend on an obscure criterion, because the Government exercising acts of force could deny too easily any *animus belligerendi* in order to evade the new obligation. Hence, Westlake argued that the distinction could only lie in the inequality of strength. So, if the Powers immediately concerned were of equal strength, the prospect of resorting to reprisals without causing the outbreak of war was so unlikely that a declaration of war needed to precede the use of force. Otherwise, i.e. when inequality of strength existed to the assailant's advantage, the acts would merely amount to reprisals and would not fall within the scope of the III Hague Convention.[599] By saying that, Westlake seemed to carelessly confirm the employment of armed reprisals as a privilege of the great Powers.

(c) State of Reprisals

Since, however, the existence of a state of war did not depend on a previous declaration of war,[600] it can actually be said that the line dividing armed reprisals from war was blurred to a large extent on account of the absence of an adequate criterion for distinguishing the two types of activity.

Thomas E. Holland warned against this confusion between war and armed reprisals in the light of the blockade of Venezuela established by Germany, Great Britain and Italy. He indeed regarded armed reprisals as not being inconsistent with a state of peace. So, the steps undertaken by way of reprisals prior to 20 December 1902 had not interrupted the peace.

599 Westlake, 'Reprisals and War' (above, n. 256).
It must be noted that during the works in commission, the Chinese delegate at the Hague Conference of 1907 called for a definition of the concept of 'war'. As he explained, his country had been by the past victim of military operations that were not named war (Colonel Ting, third meeting of the second commission's second subcommission on 12 July 1907: Scott, *The Proceedings of the Hague Peace Conferences* (above, n. 575), The Conference of 1907, 3rd vol., 169). Ellery C. Stowell, one of the members of the U.S. delegation, wrote thereupon that the Governments present at The Hague deliberately avoided defining 'war' because they found it "convenient for reasons of domestic and foreign policy to resort to measures of war while maintaining that no war exists." (Stowell, 'Convention Relative to the Opening of Hostilities' (above, n. 598), 55).

600 See Article 2 of the III Hague Convention of 1907. Cf. Söderqvist, *Le blocus maritime* (above, n. 475), 135.

However, he was not sure whether the establishment of the blockade on that day gave rise to an actual state of war. He stressed that it was neither preceded by any declaration of war nor followed by the announcement of neutrality by a third State. Besides, the settlement of the whole issue through an exchange of protocols provided for the restitution of the ships captured. Finally, he noted that the allies limited peculiarly and localised their action to a mere blockade *jure gentium*. Altogether, being unable to tell whether there had been a war or not, he preferred to call the state of affairs between the conflicting parties a state of "war *sub modo*".[601]

This ambiguous state of affairs regarding the commencement of war when armed reprisals were exercised had sometimes been called a 'state of reprisals', notably by Jules Ferry, French Prime Minister at the time of the blockade of Formosa in 1884.[602] At the same time, the French Councillor of State Léon Béquet argued that a state of reprisals was a state of uncertainty, a twilight zone, during which acts of violence were committed in peacetime but without knowing whether war might break out. For Béquet, the acts *per se* could not set up a state of war. Whereas reprisals pursued redress, war aimed to cause as much damage as possible to the enemy. Hence, the state of peace legally remained unbroken as long as the target country did not consent to provide satisfaction or none of the parties decided to declare war.[603]

601 Holland, 'War *Sub Modo*' (above, n. 35). In a study of pacific blockade, Hogan said that "it is sometimes extremely difficult to decide whether a blockade is warlike or pacific, and one of the strongest arguments that can be raised against the practice is that it tends to blur that clear line of demarcation which for the general good of the body of states should be drawn between peace and war. [...] although its rules are undoubtedly a compromise between those of war and peace, yet every blockade must of necessity be either peaceful or warlike." (Hogan, *Pacific blockade* (above, n. 518), 27). Cf. Teyssaire, *Le blocus pacifique* (above, n. 81), 81–2.

602 Mr Jules Ferry to Mr Patenôtre, 18 August 1884: France, Ministère des Affaires étrangères, *Affaires de Chine et du Tonkin* (above, n. 494), 44.

603 Léon Béquet, 'L'état de représailles', *Le Temps*, 31 August 1884, 1. Cf. with *The Boedes Lust* (*supra*, fn. 255). Also, Lord Macnaghten in *Janson v. Driefontein Consolidated Mines* (1902): "[...] if and so long as the Government of the State abstains from declaring or making war or accepting a hostile challenge there is peace—peace with all attendant consequences—for all its subjects." (Pollock & Stone, *The Law Reports or The Incorporated Council of Law Reporting. House of Lords, Judicial Committee of the Privy Council, and Peerage Cases* (above, n. 33), 498).

This idea that the use of armed reprisals opened an intermediate state between war and peace was not new. Already in the early days of the theory of pacific blockade, it was sometimes told that the said measure presented all the features of a *status mixtus*.[604] However, most international lawyers refused to abandon the peace/war dichotomy and to acknowledge the existence of a third, intermediary status. There were only acts of reprisals which fell either within a state of war or a state of peace.[605]

In order to remove the existing ambiguity between reprisals and war, it had been suggested from time to time to make obligatory a 'declaration of reprisals' which would clarify whether the acts resorted to were intended, or not, to be warlike.[606] Nevertheless, the proposal remained at the level of a doctrinal idea.

It should be noted that the uncertainty created a factual situation that benefited the great Powers. Indeed, they could evade war while forcefully coercing weaker target countries. The former, thus, enjoyed a real privilege since reprisals allowed them to elude war while achieving their ends. But the same proceeding applied against a State of equal strength would ineluctably lead to the outbreak of war.

---

604 See *supra*, at 162 fn. 483.

605 See, e.g., Geffcken, 'La France en Chine et le droit international' (above, n. 33), 145f.; Rivier, *Principes du droit des gens* (above, n. 226), 197; Kleen, *Lois et usages de la neutralité* (above, n. 230), 652 fn. 1; Ducrocq, *Représailles en temps de paix* (above, n. 81), 46–7; Nys, *Le droit international* (above, n. 33), 89. Sometimes though, voices were heard in favour of the abandonment of the dichotomy peace–war and the recognition of an intermediate state. This is, for example, what Prof. de Montmorency urged in 1925 in reaction to a paper read by McNair before the Grotius Society. See Arnold D. McNair, 'The Legal Meaning of War, and the Relation of War to Reprisals', *TGS* 11 (1925), 29–51, at 51.

606 See, e.g., Letter of 26 December 1908: Holland, *Letters to "The Times" upon War and Neutrality (1881–1920)* (above, n. 26), 20. Cf. Hautefeuille, *Des droits et des devoirs des nations neutres en temps de guerre maritime* (above, n. 230), 412.

2. The Blockade of Venezuela (1902–1903) as Breaking Point

(a) Background

The confusion between armed reprisals and war reached a critical point with the already mentioned blockade of Venezuela in 1902–1903.[607] This incident led to question not only the institution of pacific blockade but the employment of armed reprisals in general.

For several years, both Germany and Great Britain had had serious causes of complaint against Venezuela on account of ill-treatment of all kinds against their subjects as well as pecuniary claims owed to British and German companies.[608] And yet, the representations and threats of taking action failed to secure apology and redress from the Venezuelan Government of Cipriano Castro.

Already in December 1901, the German Government thought fit to inform the United States that it contemplated establishing a pacific blockade enforceable against any ship, including those of third States which would merely be turned away, "[i]n the same manner European States have proceeded on such occasions, especially England and France."[609] Nevertheless, the idea of a joint action by Great Britain and Germany was soon laid on the table.[610] Around mid-November 1902, both aggrieved countries agreed to issue an ultimatum to Castro and to resort to coercion by seizing the Venezuelan gunboats, in the event of refusal. This joint execution of coercive measures would be carried out until a satisfactory settlement was reached for both of them.[611] Their plan was communicated to the U.S. Secretary of State John Hay who, albeit regretting such a step, answered that the United States would not stand against the use of force by European Powers against Central and South American countries, providing that no

---

607 On this blockade, see esp. Hood, *Gunboat Diplomacy, 1895–1905* (above, n. 47).

608 See the British memorandum of 20 July 1902 and the German one communicated by Count Metternich on 13 November 1902: Great Britain, F. O., *BFSP 1901–1902* (above, n. 281), 1064–1068 and 1083–1084, respectively.

609 German pro memoria, 20 December 1901: United States, Department of State, *Papers relating to the foreign relations of the United States, with the annual message of the President transmitted to Congress, December 3, 1901.* (above, n. 585), 196.

610 See, e.g., The Marquess of Lansdowne to Mr Buchanan, 28 July 1902: Great Britain, F. O., *BFSP 1901–1902* (above, n. 281), 1069.

611 The Marquess of Lansdowne to Mr Buchanan, 11 November 1902: Ibid., 1083.

acquisition of territory was intended.[612] Hay's statement was the implicit reassertion of the Monroe Doctrine.

Despite Germany's insistence to institute a pacific blockade which would have effects against the shipping of third Powers, the British Government categorically refused to concede such an extension of the theory of pacific blockade.[613] So, the ships of third States could be neither sequestrated nor driven away. However, a blockade bereft of enforcement against third States lacked effectiveness. That is why, in order to avoid instituting a blockade *jure gentium*, viz. a belligerent blockade, that inevitably created a state of war, Great Britain suggested resorting to other coercive measures like the seizure of custom houses and the temporary military occupation of Venezuelan ports.[614] On this point, the British memorandum added the following remark:

> "The various measures mentioned are, no doubt, all of them, in essence acts of war; if Venezuela chose so to treat them, she would be justified in taking that course. It is, however, plainly in her interests not to regard them in this light, and they form a convenient *mitior usus* which is suitable to the case of a recalcitrant petty State in controversy with Great Powers of overwhelming strength, who, while desiring to obtain proper redress, are unwilling to dismember or destroy a puny antagonist."[615]

In this passage, the British Government tacitly admitted that the use of armed reprisals was a real privilege of the great Powers. Indeed, since the target country was in a position of manifest weakness in comparison to the reprisal-taking State and, therefore, had no interest to treat these acts as being tantamount to war, the state of peace would not be interrupted —to the advantage of the great Powers. In this context, the latter did not need

612 Sir M. Herbert to the Marquess of Lansdowne, 13 November 1902: Ibid., 1084. Cf. W. L. Penfield, 'The Anglo-German Intervention in Venezuela', *NAR* 177 (1903), 86–96, at 87.

613 See the two documents unearthed by Lothar Kotzsch in the British Record Office (P. R. O., F. O. 80/446/17), transcribed in Kotzsch, 'Die Blockade gegen Venezuela vom Jahre 1902 als Präzedenzfall für das moderne Kriegsrecht' (above, n. 28), 420–5.

614 According to the British note, other measures such as the seizure of merchant ships or property would be unavailing against Venezuela since that country's commerce and shipping was too insignificant (Memorandum for Communication to Count Metternich, 29 November 1902, reproduced in Ibid., 423).

615 Memorandum for Communication to Count Metternich, 29 November 1902, reproduced in Ibid., 423 (emphasis in original).

to have recourse to war in order to achieve their goals. Armed reprisals presented a convenient and expedient way of compelling a weaker nation without proceeding to war. This extract clearly shows, too, the prevailing of the subjective test, i.e. war does not break out as long as either party does not resolve to express an *animus belligerendi*.[616]

Finally, the ultimatum was issued but failed to produce results.[617] Reprisals, thus, began with the seizure of Venezuelan ships of war in the port of La Guaira.[618] Nevertheless, the measures did not succeed to break the obstinacy of Castro who, in retaliation, arrested British and German nationals.[619] The necessity to institute a blockade then imposed itself.[620] However, the situation escalated as a British and German squadron shelled two Venezuelan forts and troops were landed to dismantle the artillery.[621] As a consequence, the Venezuelan Government proposed to settle the dispute through arbitration.[622] Great Britain and Germany agreed in principle but not for all claims.[623] Therefore, the coercive measures were not sus-

---

616 Yet, Great Britain defended the opinion that pacific blockade had to be considered from an objective or material point of view: if a blockade impacted on the shipping of third Powers, it could only mean a belligerent blockade. The subjective test did not prevail here. It shows that the priority was to spare third States at any cost because they could declare the existence of a state of war between the parties involved in the conflict if their interests were directly affected by the blockade. Cf. Kotzsch, *The concept of war in contemporary history and international law* (above, n. 69), 131–41.

617 See The Marquess of Lansdowne to Mr Haggard, 2 December 1902: Great Britain, F. O., *BFSP 1901–1902* (above, n. 281), 1099–101; Mr Haggard to the Marquess of Lansdowne, 7 December 1902: Ibid., 1108.

618 Mr Haggard to the Marquess of Lansdowne, 7 December 1902: Ibid., 1110. Cf. the German memorandum communicated to the U.S. Government, 18 December 1902: United States, Department of State, *Papers relating to the foreign relations of the United States, with the annual message of the President transmitted to Congress, December 7, 1903.* (Washington: GPO, 1904), 422–3.

619 See for more details the correspondence of 10 and 11 December 1902: Great Britain, F. O., *BFSP 1901–1902* (above, n. 281), 1110–2.

620 The Marquess of Lansdowne to Mr Buchanan, 11 December 1902: Ibid., 1112–3.

621 Commodore Montgomerie to Admiralty, 16 December 1902: Ibid., 1119–20.

622 Mr White to the Marquess of Lansdowne, 13 December 1902: Ibid., 1116.

623 See The Marquess of Lansdowne to Sir F. Lascelles, 18 December 1902: Ibid., 1124–5.

pended, and a blockade of the coasts of Venezuela commenced on 20 December 1902 with the participation of Italy.[624]

In the end, Castro yielded to "superior force" and consented to recognise the claims of the assailing Powers.[625] Separate protocols of agreement were signed between the parties on 13 February 1903 and, on the next day, the blockade was raised.[626] Venezuela had consented to immediately pay Germany, Great Britain and Italy a sum of 5.500£ each to satisfy the first-rank claims while the other claims should be referred to a Mixed Commission. It also was decided that any other unsettled questions that might arise would fall under the jurisdiction of the Permanent Court of Arbitration. As for the captured Venezuelan ships, they should be restored without any indemnity whatsoever.[627]

It is unclear whether the whole proceeding gave rise to a state of war or not.

On the one hand, the separate protocols signed with Venezuela carefully avoided speaking of a state of war between the parties. The protocol signed with Great Britain even confirmed the continuation of all the bilateral treaties, "*inasmuch as it may be contended* that the establishment of a blockade of Venezuelan ports by the British naval forces has, *ipso facto*, created a state of war between Great Britain and Venezuela, and that any Treaty existing between the two countries has been thereby abrogated".[628] Besides the absence of a declaration of war, it is worth mentioning that the provision regarding the restitution of all the captured Venezuelan ships also seems to echo one of the conditions laid down by the Institute of International Law in 1887 for a pacific blockade to be lawful.[629] Altogether, the

624 See the British, German and Italian notifications of the blockade: Ibid., 425–7. Italy had previously expressed the wish to join in the effort. See Sir R. Rodd to the Marquess of Lansdowne, 3 December 1902: Ibid., 1101; The Marquess of Lansdowne to Sir R. Rodd, 5 December 1902: Ibid., 1107–8; The Marquess of Lansdowne to Mr Buchanan, 9 December 1902: Ibid., 1109.

625 See Mr White to the Marquess of Lansdowne, 1 January 1903: Great Britain, F. O., *BFSP 1902–1903* (96th vol.; London: His Majesty's Stationery Office, 1906), 439.

626 The Marquess of Lansdowne to Sir M. Herbert, 14 February 1903: Ibid., 506.

627 See the separate protocols of 13 February 1903: Ibid., 99–101, 803–805 and 1172–1174.

628 Art. 7 of the Protocol between Great Britain and Venezuela, 13 February 1903: Great Britain, F. O., *BFSP 1902–1903* (above, n. 625), 100 (emphasis added).

629 Viz. "The ships of a blockaded Power which do not respect such a blockade may be sequestrated. When the blockade is over, they shall be restored to their owners together with their cargoes, but without any compensation whatsoever."

operation against Venezuela had to all appearances the character of reprisals.[630]

On the other hand, there are various elements which contradict the assumption that the blockade might have been only 'pacific'. As a matter of fact, the U.S. Government strongly protested against any extension of the theory of pacific blockade in a way that might impact on the shipping of third Powers.[631] Great Britain acquiesced with the United States and pressed Germany to come around to this view.[632] Although the blockading

630 Such was the opinion of Jules Basdevant, a young French scholar later destined to become President of the International Court of Justice between 1949 and 1952. He was convinced that the blockade of Venezuela was an act of reprisals, which was called war blockade only to satisfy "des subtilités de juriste." For his part, he supported the view that pacific blockade could apply against the shipping of third States too. See Jules Basdevant, 'L'action coercitive anglo-germano-italienne contre le Vénézuéla (1902–1903)', *RGDIP* 11 (1904), 362–458, at 420–425. See also Walther Schücking, 'Rückblick auf den Streit mit Venezuela', *DJZ* 8 (1903), 157–60, at 158–159. But for a contrary view, see Theodore Salisbury Woolsey, 'The passing of pacific blockade', *YaleRev* 11 (May. 1902, to Feb. 1903), 340–6.

631 Mr Hay to Mr Tower, on the one hand, and to Mr White, on the other, 12 December 1902: United States, Department of State, *Papers relating to the foreign relations of the United States, with the annual message of the President transmitted to Congress, December 7, 1903.* (above, n. 618), 420 and 452. Before the Permanent Court of Arbitration, the U.S. counsels acting on behalf of Venezuela at The Hague believed that the proceeding of the great Powers indisputably constituted a state of war. Indeed, they put forward that a pacific blockade could only be directed against the ships of the target country according to "all the authorities upon international law" (Case of Venezuela: United States, Senate, *The Venezuelan arbitration before The Hague Tribunal, 1903: The protocols between Venezuela and Great Britain, Germany, Italy, United States, Belgium, France, Mexico, the Netherlands, Spain, Sweden and Norway, signed at Washington, May 7, 1903* (Washington: GPO, 1905), 157). According to W. L. Penfield, solicitor to the Department of State and one of the members of the U.S. delegation before the PCA, the United States helped to adjust the theory of pacific blockade by obtaining from "the three leading maritime Powers of the world" the repudiation of the idea that pacific blockade could extend its effects to vessels flying foreign flags. Under these conditions, Penfield agreed to regard pacific blockade as a legitimate species of reprisals milder than open war. See Penfield, 'The Anglo-German Intervention in Venezuela' (above, n. 612), 86; 89–96.

632 Mr Tower to Mr Hay, 14 December 1902: United States, Department of State, *Papers relating to the foreign relations of the United States, with the annual message of the President transmitted to Congress, December 7, 1903.* (above, n. 618), 421.

Powers considered superfluous to declare war, the blockade would, nevertheless, be warlike and affect neutral countries.[633]

In any case, the assailing Powers did not want to wage an all-out war against Venezuela. That is why Germany and Great Britain assured the U.S. Government that they would not act beyond a warlike blockade.[634]

Germany did not want to institute a belligerent blockade because, according to Article 11 Para. 2 of the German Imperial Constitution, the consent of the *Bundesrat* was required. See Mr White to Mr Hay, 17 December 1902: Ibid., 454. However, as the *Reichskanzler* Bernhard von Bülow explained to the Emperor, this step was necessary to give Great Britain the assurance that they were on the same page. See Graf von Bülow to Kaiser Wilhelm II, 12 December 1902: Johannes Lepsius, Albrecht Mendelssohn Bartholdy, and Friedrich Thimme (eds.), *Die Wendung im Deutsch-Englischen Verhältnis*, herausgegeben im Auftrage des Auswärtigen Amtes (Die Grosse Politik der Europäischen Kabinette 1871–1914, 17; Berlin: Deutsche Verlagsgesellschaft für Politik und Geschichte, 1924), 258. See also Freiherr von Richthofen to Graf von Metternich, 5 December 1902: Ibid., 257.

633 See Mr Tower to Mr Hay, 18 December 1902: United States, Department of State, *Papers relating to the foreign relations of the United States, with the annual message of the President transmitted to Congress, December 7, 1903.* (above, n. 618), 423; The Marquess of Lansdowne to Sir R. Rodd, 26 December 1902: Great Britain, F. O., *BFSP 1901–1902* (above, n. 281), 1133. Cf. Admiralty to Vice-Admiral Sir A. Douglas, 11 December 1902: Ibid., 1113–5.
For the British Government, the establishment of a blockade automatically gave rise to a state of war. This was, indeed, the opinion of Balfour, Prime Minister of the United Kingdom. That is why he sarcastically responded the following to an MP who wondered whether war had broken out with Venezuela: "Does the hon. and learned gentleman suppose that without a state of war you can take the ships of another Power and blockade its ports?" (Mr A. J. Balfour, House of Commons, 17 December 1902: Great Britain, Parliament, *The Parliamentary Debates: (authorised edition), fourth series. Third session of the twenty-seventh Parliament of the United Kingdom of Great Britain and Ireland* (116th vol.; London: Wyman and sons, 1902), col. 1490–1491). In the Reichstag, the German Secretary of State for Foreign Affairs Freiherr von Richthofen expressed on 23 January 1903 the same view: "Mit Eröffnung der Blockade war der Kriegszustand zwischen uns und Venezuela geschaffen, […]." (Deutsches Reich, *Stenographische Berichte über die Verhandlungen des Reichstags: X. Legislaturperiode. II. Session 1900/1903.*, 8th vol. (186th vol.; Berlin: Norddeutsche Buchdruckerei und Verlagsanstalt, 1903), 7511 (B)).

634 Mr Tower to Mr Hay, 14 December 1902: United States, Department of State, *Papers relating to the foreign relations of the United States, with the annual message of the President transmitted to Congress, December 7, 1903.* (above, n. 618), 421.

(b) The Venezuelan Preferential Claims

All the factors seem to confirm that the use of armed reprisals amounted to a privilege in the hands of the great Powers that could evade the negative consequences associated with war while exercising forcible pressure upon the target country during peacetime. In this regard, the joint blockade of Venezuela in 1902–1903 can also be deemed an example of such a privilege, albeit it had to be called on paper a belligerent blockade in order to meet the objections of third States. In fact, the allied Powers achieved their ends without overtly commencing war.

In the three separate protocols ending the conflict, a clause provided that 30 % of the custom revenues of the two most prosperous Venezuelan ports firmly under governmental control were assigned to the settlement of claims and payable in monthly instalments.[635] The redaction of this stipulation, however, posed a problem because it entitled all the other creditor States of Venezuela —namely Belgium, France, Mexico, the Netherlands, Spain, Sweden-Norway and the United States of America— to also receive a share of the reserved custom incomes.[636] It raised the question of whom amongst all the creditors should receive priority of payment.

Arduous negotiations ensued. The blockading Powers naturally contended that they should be paid first.[637] Nevertheless, prior to the blockade, France and Belgium had already drawn the attention of Great Britain to their right over a portion of Venezuela's custom receipts.[638] In addition, they (as well as Spain and the United States) invoked the most favoured nation clause with Venezuela that should allegedly guarantee them the most beneficial mode of payment for their claims.[639] In fact, the claim of the blockading Powers was coldly met by Herbert Wolcott Bowen, U.S. minister at Caracas, who acted in representation of Venezuela. He demurred that (1) a preferential treatment would be inequitable and illegal towards the other creditor States; (2) it would urge the latter to have re-

635 Article 5 of the separate protocols, 13 February 1903: Great Britain, F. O., *BFSP 1902–1903* (above, n. 625), 99f., 804 and 1173. See also Sir M. Herbert to the Marquess of Lansdowne, 28 January 1903: Ibid., 489–90.

636 Sir M. Herbert to the Marquess of Lansdowne, 25 January 1903: Ibid., 492.

637 Cf. The Marquess of Lansdowne to Sir F. Lascelles, 29 January 1903: Ibid., 496–7.

638 Memorandum of the French ambassador to London, 28 November 1902: Great Britain, F. O., *BFSP 1901–1902* (above, n. 281), 1098; Mr Grénier to the Marquess of Lansdowne, 14 December 1902: Ibid., 1117.

639 Mr Delcassé to Mr Cambon, 18 December 1902: Ibid., 1125–6.

course to force for the collection of their claims, too; and (3) the allied Powers had never asked for preferential treatment since the beginning.[640]

Faced with dogged determination on both sides, the issue was submitted to the Permanent Court of Arbitration at The Hague.[641] The arbitral panel, appointed by the Tsar of Russia, was formed by the Russians Nikolay Valerianovich Muraviev and Friedrich Fromhold Martens as well as the Austrian Heinrich Lammasch.[642]

Before the PCA, Bowen's remarks found an echo in the argumentation presented by the creditor third States. The case of the French delegation led by Louis Renault addressed the subject of the unilateral use of force. The French jurisconsults, indeed, neither criticised the use of force in general nor in the present case. They admitted that a Government could be driven to apply force in order to obtain redress. Still, they challenged the claim that the use of force against the debtor conferred upon the allied Powers a preferential treatment over the other creditor States. The French delegation argued that such treatment would actually be contrary to the principle of equality between States, here the creditors of Venezuela. Moreover, from the perspective of equity, the concession of a preferential treatment would have the following consequence:

> "If, according to the contention of the allied Powers, it be recognized by a judicial decision, whose authority will be unquestionable, that the mere fact by one or more States of exerting a violent coercion against another State, affords to the promoters of the said violence a privileged situation as against the States standing outside the conflict, it may be said that it involves the early end of any regular and patient transaction, as well as of any pacific arrangement for such States whose solvency is doubtful."[643]

---

640 Sir M. Herbert to the Marquess of Lansdowne, 29 January 1908: Great Britain, F. O., *BFSP 1902–1903* (above, n. 625), 495–6.

641 Article 1 of the agreement between Great Britain and Venezuela, 7 May 1903: Ibid., 102.

642 See the recitals of the award of the tribunal, 22 February 1904: James Brown Scott (ed.), *The Hague Court Reports: Comprising the awards, accompanied by syllabi, the agreements for arbitration, and other documents in each case submitted to the permanent court of arbitration and to commissions of inquiry under the provisions of the conventions of 1899 and 1907 for the pacific settlement of international disputes* (Carnegie Endowment for International Peace: Division of International Law; New York: OUP, 1916), 57.

643 Case of the French Republic: United States, Senate, *The Venezuelan arbitration before The Hague Tribunal, 1903* (above, n. 631), 886.

The French jurisconsults insisted that a judicial decision in favour of the allied Powers would encourage the use of force by creditor States, despite the recent progress related to the pacific settlement of international disputes like the I Hague Convention of 1899. But more than that, it would prompt the creditors to act forcibly fast in order to get served first: "a premium to speed."[644]

For Wayne MacVeagh, counsel of both the United States and Venezuela, the matter had to be approached from an ethical perspective. He then submitted to the PCA the argument that at the present stage of development of international law with the recent achievements of the First Hague Peace Conference, the allied Powers had a moral obligation to first exhaust the amicable means of settlement like mediation and arbitration before resorting to force.[645]

However, the allied Powers hid behind the argument that they exercised their sovereign right of force. They also pointed out that this employment of force concretely helped to obtain the recognition of their claims.[646] Therefore, they regarded the complaints of the creditor third States as a manoeuvre "to reap the benefit from such action without in the least exposing them or incurring any risk consequent upon war operations."[647]

On 22 February 1904, the PCA announced its decision. The arbitrators considered that the question of the character or nature of the military operations undertaken by the allied Powers fell outside their jurisdiction. They also thought that they did not have to examine the argument of the mandatory exhaustion of amicable methods of settlement prior to the use of force. As a matter of fact, the PCA confined itself to interpreting the protocols and, on this basis, ruled in favour of the three blockading Powers.[648]

644 See the Case of the French Republic: Ibid., 881–887, here quotation at 887.

645 Wayne MacVeagh, 'The Value of the Venezuelan Arbitration', *NAR* 177 (1903), 801–11.

646 *The New York Times* indirectly quoted Augusto Pierantoni, the Italian jurisconsult in this case, as saying that "the objections to the employment of force were purely sentimental, [...]. The blockade had excellent results, as it forced Venezuela to recognize her responsibility for damages resulting from the civil war." (from *The New York Times*, 8 November 1903, p. 4, quoted in Becker Lorca, *Mestizo International Law* (above, n. 273), 145). See also the observations of the British counsel, Sir Robert Finlay, during the meeting of 6 November 1903: United States, Senate, *The Venezuelan arbitration before The Hague Tribunal, 1903* (above, n. 631), 1238–9.

647 Counter case on behalf of Italy: Ibid., 1024. See further Ibid., 1022–5.

648 Scott (ed.), *The Hague Court Reports* (above, n. 642), 56–61, esp. 58–59.

Walther Schücking —German professor of international law at Marburg an der Lahn, later called to play a role at the Versailles Peace Conference in 1919 and to become a judge of the PCIJ— had already anticipated this award. He explained that for want of norms in international law which might justify an adverse decision, the PCA could only decide on the basis of the nature of things, which gave the blockading Powers in the present case a decisive advantage.[649] Many years later, this point of view was shared by Hersch Lauterpacht who rightly pointed out that the PCA could not fill the gap *de lege ferenda* since international law allowed the resort to war and reprisals for dispute settlement. Therefore, the PCA could not have decided differently in this case, even if its decision gave the impression that the States which made use of force were rewarded to the detriment of the other creditor States which for their part abstained from such military operations. In his opinion, the very reputation of arbitration had been at stake.[650]

On the other hand, the French legal scholar André Mallarmé believed that this award did not serve the cause of peace and arbitration. In fact, he argued that it rather set a dangerous precedent for minor States because they were particularly likely to be targeted, given their high dependency on monetary assistance and their unreliable public institutions with regard to the protection of aliens.[651]

(c) The Drago-Porter Convention of 1907

i) Previous Efforts of Prevention of Armed Reprisals in International Law

At the time of the arbitral award of the PCA, the use of force was mostly unrestricted in international law. Indeed, it was not conditional on the previous exhaustion of pacific methods of settlement, contrary to what

649 Schücking, 'Rückblick auf den Streit mit Venezuela' (above, n. 630), 159.

650 Lauterpacht, *The Function of Law in the International Community* (above, n. 264), 89–91. Cf. Rudolf Dulon, 'The Venezuelan Arbitration Once More. Facts and Law.', *The American Law Review* 38 (1904), 648–61, at 660–661. Indeed, during the meeting on 6 November 1903, Sir Robert Finlay stated that "nothing more fatal to arbitration could be conceived than any attempt to ignore the legitimate consequences of war." (United States, Senate, *The Venezuelan arbitration before The Hague Tribunal, 1903* (above, n. 631), 1239).

651 André Mallarmé, 'L'arbitrage vénézuélien devant la Cour de La Haye (1903–1904)', *RGDIP* 13 (1906), 423–500, at 496–500.

MacVeagh asserted. The aggrieved State had the sole and entire discretion to judge whether the diplomatic negotiations had failed and then whether it was expedient to make use of force and to what extent.[652]

Nevertheless, more and more authors in the nineteenth century had called for the creation of an international tribunal with mandatory jurisdiction to settle the conflicts between States or supported the idea of arbitration.[653] According to Oppenheim, the science of international law had the task to prevent the resort to reprisals or war by promoting arbitration or even by seeking a way to compel sovereign States to submit their disputes to arbitration.[654] This movement in favour of arbitration often went hand in hand with the project of a code of international law. In many cases, the legal scholars who drafted such a code provided a mandatory procedure of dispute resolution before commencing war or armed reprisals. For example, the American lawyer David Dudley Field imagined that if the negotiations between the parties in conflict failed, ten States making up a Joint High Commission would mediate in the dispute. The next step would be arbitration conducted by a High Tribunal of Arbitration with binding decision. Field included the obligation for all the adherents to his Code to combine forces together against the assailant that did not respect the procedure.[655]

As a matter of fact, between 1815 and 1914, arbitration grew in importance as a mode of settlement of disputes.[656] Many conflicts which might have led to reprisals were settled through some methods of pacific settlement.[657] As the U.S. minister to Spain said to the Spanish minister of State

652 Cf. Pasquale Fiore, 'L'organisation juridique de la société internationale', *RDILC* 31 (1899), 105–126 & 209–242, at 105–106; George Winfield Scott, 'International Law and the Drago Doctrine', *NAR* 183 (1906), 602–10, at 604.

653 See, e.g., Émile de Laveleye, *Des causes actuelles de guerre en Europe et de l'arbitrage* (Bruxelles: C. Muquardt, 1873); Edgar Rouard de Card, *L'arbitrage international dans le passé, le présent et l'avenir* (Paris: A. Durand et Pedone-Lauriel, 1877); Leonid Kamarowsky, 'De l'idée d'un tribunal international', *RDILC* 15 (1883), 44–51.

654 Lassa Oppenheim, 'The Science of International Law. Its Task and Method', *AJIL* 2 (1908), 313–56, at 322–323.

655 Field, *Draft. Outlines of an International Code* (above, n. 592), 369–373 (Art. 532–537) and 473 (Art. 716). See also Duplessix, *La Loi des Nations* (above, n. 595), 170 (Art. 504–506). Cf. Fiore, 'L'organisation juridique de la société internationale' (above, n. 652), 239–41.

656 Cornelis G. Roelofsen, 'International Arbitration and Courts', in Bardo Fassbender and Anne Peters (eds.), *The Oxford Handbook of the History of International Law* (Oxford: OUP, 2012), 145–69, at 162–166.

657 See Colbert, *Retaliation in international law* (above, n. 6), 69 fn. 30.

Práxedes Mateo-Sagasta following the seizure of American vessels and injuries sustained by American citizens during the hostilities in Cuba in 1869/70, "it was the better practice of modern times, instead of resorting to reprisals, to refer the questions at issue to an international tribunal for final adjustment."[658]

On 29 July 1899, the First Hague Peace Conference adopted a convention that instituted the Permanent Court of Arbitration.[659] Pursuant to Article 19 of this Convention for the Pacific Settlement of International Disputes, many States concluded bilateral treaties with the aim of binding them to refer some of their disputes to mandatory arbitration, unless the vital interests, the national independence or the honour of the contracting parties were affected.[660]

Despite those improvements, the situation of the small countries still remained vulnerable. The great Powers were in no way compelled to prefer arbitration over the use of force. That is why the blockade of Venezuela and the subsequent decision of the PCA shone light on the urgent need to fill the legal lacuna and make the use of force depend on the exhaustion of pacific methods.

ii) The Drago Doctrine as Corollary of the Monroe Doctrine

The blockade of Venezuela caused great consternation amongst the American nations.[661] Indeed, amongst the various classes of claims that the three great European Powers had against Venezuela, there was "the collection of the deferred interest on the foreign public debt, outstanding in the form of

658 John Bassett Moore, *History and digest of the international arbitrations to which the United States has been a party, together with appendices containing the treaties relating to such arbitrations, and historical and legal notes on other international arbitrations ancient and modern, and on the domestic commissions of the United States for the adjustment of international claims*, 2nd vol. (Washington: GPO, 1898), 1039.

659 Articles 20–29: Scott, *The Hague Conventions and Declarations of 1899 and 1907* (above, n. 598), 57–63.

660 See Editorial Comment, 'Treaties of Arbitration since the First Hague Conference', *AJIL* 2 (1908), 823–30.

661 Luis María Drago, 'State Loans in Their Relation to International Policy', *AJIL* 1 (1907), 692–726, at 692. This article was also published in French: Luis María Drago, 'Les emprunts d'Etat et leurs rapports avec la politique internationale', *RGDIP* 14 (1907), 251–87.

bonds issued by the Venezuelan government".[662] This particular demand worried the Argentinian lawyer and, at the time, Minister of Foreign Affairs: Luis María Drago. In a note of 29 December 1902, he laid down the rule that default on public debt could not give rise to an armed intervention against any debtor American State or the military occupation of the latter's territory by European Powers. He grounded this doctrine on the Monroe doctrine and the principles of state sovereignty and equality between States, yet without exonerating Governments from responsibility for "bad faith, disorder, and deliberate and voluntary insolvency."[663]

Drago crafted his doctrine as a corollary of the Monroe doctrine. Indeed, the U.S. President Theodore Roosevelt set forth the Monroe doctrine in his annual message to the United States Congress on 3 December 1901 as allowing no acquisition of territory in the Americas by any non-American Power. With this reservation, European States could, nevertheless, adopt forcible measures against recalcitrant American countries.[664] Now, Roosevelt's definition of the Monroe doctrine had a relatively narrow meaning because it only prohibited the *acquisition* of territory.[665] Hence, the Drago doctrine supplemented the Monroe doctrine as it also aimed to prevent the *control* of territory through an alleged temporary occupation under the pretext of bankruptcy.[666]

---

662 Drago, 'State Loans in Their Relation to International Policy' (above, n. 661), 692.

663 See Luis María Drago, *Cobro coercitivo de deudas públicas* (Buenos Aires: Coni Hermanos, 1906), 9–26. The quotation is from the English translation of the letter in United States, Department of State, *Papers relating to the foreign relations of the United States, with the annual message of the President transmitted to Congress, December 7, 1903.* (above, n. 618), 1–5, here at 2.

664 United States, Department of State, *Papers relating to the foreign relations of the United States, with the annual message of the President transmitted to Congress, December 3, 1901.* (above, n. 585), XXXVIf. For a study of the Monroe doctrine from this period, see John Brooks Henderson, *American Diplomatic Questions* (New York/London: The Macmillan Company, 1901), 289–448.

665 According to Redslob, *Histoire des grands principes du droit des gens* (above, n. 53), 466, the Monroe doctrine did not impede the use of reprisals. It was thus an implicit recognition of the lawfulness of reprisals.

666 Basdevant, 'L'action coercitive anglo-germano-italienne contre le Vénézuéla (1902–1903)' (above, n. 630), 450–2; Henri-Alexis Moulin, 'La doctrine de Drago', *RGDIP* 14 (1907), 417–72, at 460–467. A striking example of such control was the "temporary" and "provisional" occupation of Egypt by Great Britain which precisely proceeded from the former country's bankruptcy (A Jeffersonian Democrat, 'The Venezuela Affair and the Monroe Doctrine', *NAR* 176 (1903), 321–35, at 329–330). See further on Egypt's bankruptcy Clinton E.

The events in Venezuela urged Roosevelt to rectify his definition, thus endorsing the Drago doctrine implicitly. He recognised that the enforcement of contractual obligations by a European Power against an American country presented a severe threat to peace as a temporary occupation might turn permanent. He, therefore, said in his annual message to the Congress on 5 December 1905 that it was the duty of the United States to interpose between the parties to a dispute, in order to bring about some arrangement suitable for them and the other creditors. He argued that the case of the Dominican Republic provided good proof of success of this foreign policy. That country went through serious internal disturbances and was burdened with a large external debt. Only the appointment of American officials by the U.S. Government to administer the Dominican custom houses averted a foreign intervention.[667]

iii) From Political Policy to Norm of International Law

The Drago doctrine was initially just the formulation of a policy regarding the international relations in the western hemisphere. It had no ambition to become a universal principle of international law.[668] However, because it condemned the recourse to armed force for the very specific purpose of the recovery of contractual debts, the Drago doctrine pertained to the gen-

---

Dawkins, 'The Egyptian Public Debt', *NAR* 173 (1901), 487–507; Heimbeck, *Die Abwicklung von Staatsbankrotten im Völkerrecht* (above, n. 47), 63–142. But Alejandro Álvarez, 'Latin America and International Law', *AJIL* 3 (1909), 269–353, at 334–5, refuted this opinion that the Drago doctrine was a corollary of the Monroe doctrine.

667 United States, Department of State, *Papers relating to the foreign relations of the United States, with the annual message of the President transmitted to Congress, December 5, 1905.* (Washington: GPO, 1906), XXXIII–XXXVII. However, albeit Roosevelt's custom receivership prevented a European intervention, it entangled the United States from then on in the Dominican affairs. About the U.S. campaign that led to military occupation of that Republic following internal disturbances, see Max Boot, *The Savage Wars of Peace: Small Wars and the Rise of American Power* (revised edn., New York: Basic Books, 2014), 167–81.

668 See Drago's speech in Buenos Aires in August 1906 during Elihu Root's visit through Latin America: United States, *Report of the delegates of the United States to the Third International Conference of the American States* (Washington: GPO, 1907), 13.

eral discussion of the use of force in time of peace.[669] As a result, it quickly drew the attention of many legal scholars, some of whom acknowledged its legal dimension.[670] Nevertheless, this doctrine was imperfect and defective for being limited just to the American continent and for not making the recourse to armed force subject to a previous arbitral award.[671] As a consequence, legal scholars amended the Drago doctrine in this direction.

Friedrich Fromhold Martens, one of the three arbitrators in the *Venezuelan Preferential Claims*, conferred legal significance upon the Drago doctrine, which he regarded as being distinct from the controversial and political Monroe doctrine. Indeed, he concurred with the conclusions that Drago reached and used them as a starting point to question the unilateral use of force. His own observations actually led him also to recognise the arbitrariness of reprisals. In his opinion, they were too often abusively resorted to by great Powers only against small countries and for the enforcement of exaggerated claims, although he did not want to shirk the responsibility of the Latin American States. The problem was then how to conciliate the protection of nationals abroad while averting abuses. In this respect, he believed that diplomatic interposition and forcible coercion were inappropriate solutions because, with such methods, the examination of claims by the aggrieved country was generally partial, shallow and self-interested. Therefore, he maintained that the most reliable solution should be the exhaustion of the local remedies and that, in the event of any doubt or objection, the PCA might be seized.[672] Martens's conclusions were largely shared by

669 Prior to the Drago doctrine, the Argentine international law expert Carlos Calvo formulated a doctrine of wider scope, known as the 'Calvo doctrine'. Indeed, Calvo condemned any form of intervention, either diplomatic or armed, for the enforcement of private claims of pecuniary nature or resulting from wrongs following a civil war, insurrection or riot. He argued that this violent practice of the European States based upon mere force reflected a colonial tradition and their contempt for the nations of the New World. Therefore, Calvo advocated the exhaustion of local remedies before any such intervention. See Amos S. Hershey, 'The Calvo and Drago Doctrines', *AJIL* 1 (1907), 26–45; Edwin Montefiore Borchard, *The diplomatic protection of citizens abroad or the law of international claims* (New York: The Banks Law Publishing Co., 1925), 309–10.

670 See, e.g., the written reactions of some members of the Institute of International Law to the Drago doctrine: [Various], 'La doctrine de Monroë. – Une note diplomatique du Gouvernement argentin. – Consultations et avis.', *RDILC* 35 (1903), 597–623.

671 Álvarez, 'Latin America and International Law' (above, n. 666), 334–5.

672 Friedrich Fromhold von Martens, *Par la Justice Vers la Paix*: *Annexe : Doctrine de Drago ou Note diplomatique du Gouvernement Argentin du 29 Décembre 1902* (Paris: Henri Charles-Lavauzelle, [1904]), passim.

Henri-Alexis Moulin, professor of public international law at Dijon, who even suggested that the debtor State could request arbitration and that the creditor State had then to accept before making use of force.[673]

At the Third Pan-American Conference at Rio de Janeiro from 23 July to 26 August 1906, several American nations expressed the wish that the Drago doctrine entered the field of law as a conventional principle consistent with the respect of the sovereignty of the debtor countries.[674] This topic was not only the most absorbing at Rio[675] but the most delicate.[676]

On the one hand, some American republics encouraged the adoption of a rule of law at Rio. On the other hand, a group of States led by the United States defended the point of view that the question should be presented at the next Hague Conference.[677] The U.S. Government actually did not object to a discussion at Rio about the forcible collection of public debts, but only as preparation for the Second Hague Peace Conference which the American nations were to attend for the first time.[678] The instructions sent to the U.S. delegation at Rio were unambiguous on this point. Elihu Root, Hay's successor as Secretary of States, explained that the U.S. Government concurred with the content of the Drago doctrine which forbade the use of force for the collection of public debts. Such a proceeding generally turned into an act of oppression and bullying by strong Powers. Thus, a solution needed to be found in order to reassert the sacrosanct principle of the independent sovereignty of States, especially in situations where the weak

---

673 Moulin, 'La doctrine de Drago' (above, n. 666), 440–60.

674 See, e.g., the exposition of the Argentine delegation, 21 August 1906: International American Conference, *Third International American Conference. 1906: Minutes. Resolutions. Documents.* (Rio de Janeiro: Imprensa Nacional, 1907), 224–6. On that occasion, the Drago doctrine was detached from the Monroe doctrine because of the distrust of many American States regarding the latter policy which was viewed as a threat to their independence, but also because the United States did not want to assume all the consequences which might arise from the incorporation of the Drago doctrine into the Monroe doctrine. See Jules Basdevant, 'La conférence de Rio-de-Janeiro de 1906 et l'union internationale des républiques américaines', *RGDIP* 15 (1908), 209–70, at 262.

675 United States, *Report of the delegates of the United States to the Third International Conference of the American States* (above, n. 668), 12.

676 México, *Boletín Oficial de la Secretaría de Relaciones Exteriores*: *Mayo a octubre de 1906*, 22nd vol. (México: Tipografía de la viuda de Francisco Díaz de León, 1906), 338.

677 See Ibid., 339.

678 See Mr Root to Committee on Programme for the Third International of the American Republics, 22 March 1906: Drago, *Cobro coercitivo de deudas públicas* (above, n. 663), 153–157 and esp. 156–157.

debtor country was *bona fide* and momentarily unable to fulfil its obligations. Yet, Root believed that the sister republics of the American continent were not qualified to create a rule of law of such nature and scope, owing to the fact that most of them were debtor nations of creditor European Powers. The decision could then only be taken at The Hague where debtor and creditor States were to convene.[679]

The United States probably did not want to be held responsible by the European Powers for the adoption at Rio of a norm of international law which would bind all the creditor States —the United States included— and limit their capacity of action. Therefore, it was wiser to submit the issue to the Hague Conference.[680]

In any case, the Third Pan-American Conference came round to the opinion defended by the United States and resolved that any American State could invite the next Hague Conference "to examine the question of the compulsory collection of public debts, and, in general, means tending to diminish between Nations conflicts having an exclusively pecuniary origin."[681] Thus, the scope of this resolution was wider than the original Drago doctrine as it also encompassed conflicts arising from an exclusively pecuniary origin.

iv) Second Hague Peace Conference, 1907

The programme of the Second Hague Peace Conference initially did not include the study of the Drago doctrine.[682] Nonetheless, Root reserved the right to bring to the attention of the gathered Powers further subjects for discussion. One of them was the limitation of force for the collection of

679 Instructions to the delegates of the United States to the Third International Conference of American States, 18 June 1906: United States, *Report of the delegates of the United States to the Third International Conference of the American States* (above, n. 668), 41–2. Cf. Root's speech in Buenos Aires in August 1906: James Brown Scott, *The Hague Peace Conferences of 1899 and 1907: A Series of Lectures delivered before the Johns Hopkins University in the Year 1908*, 2 vols. (Baltimore: The Johns Hopkins Press, 1909), 1st vol., 421–422.

680 Cf. Basdevant, 'La conférence de Rio-de-Janeiro de 1906 et l'union internationale des républiques américaines' (above, n. 674), 262 fn. 1.

681 International American Conference, *Third International American Conference. 1906* (above, n. 674), 605.

682 See the circular sent by the Russian Government in March–April 1906 to the invited Governments: Scott, *The Proceedings of the Hague Peace Conferences* (above, n. 575), The Conference of 1907, 1st vol., 1.

ordinary public debts arising out of contracts; a small topic that he considered capable of restricting the *ius ad bellum* and leading to an agreement on compulsory arbitration.[683] Accordingly, the U.S. delegates at The Hague submitted this matter for consideration.[684] The examination of the proposition was entrusted to the first subcommission of the first commission dealing with the pacific settlement of international disputes.[685]

On 16 July 1907, the U.S. delegate Horace Porter provided explanations in support of the proposition. He first denounced the fact that unscrupulous speculators, who concluded contracts with foreign Governments, were generally behind the employment of force for the recovery of pecuniary claims. Porter was convinced that those claims were too often dubious and exaggerated, on the one hand, because of the cursory and biased examination of the claims by the national's foreign office and, on the other, because of the significant reduction of the amount claimed in all cases when the issue was referred to arbitration or a mixed commission. But besides, such claims involved considerable costs for the speculator's State. Porter mentioned the past example of a U.S. contractor demanding an indemnity of about 90.000$ for the cancellation of a contract with a foreign Government. Over sixteen years, the United States pressed the case and, at one point, even sent a fleet of nineteen warships. The result was the spending of more than 2.500.000$ by the U.S. Government. Porter argued, therefore, that the State of the speculator had no obligation at all to take up his case, mainly since the issue entailed no question of prestige and na-

683 Root's note, 6 June 1906: Scott, *The Hague Peace Conferences of 1899 and 1907* (above, n. 679), 1st vol., 104.

684 See the instructions to the U.S. delegates to the Hague Conference, 31 May 1907: Ibid., 2nd vol., 188–189; Horace Porter, second plenary meeting on 19 June 1907: Scott, *The Proceedings of the Hague Peace Conferences* (above, n. 575), The Conference of 1907, 1st vol., 55.

685 First meeting of the first commission on 22 June 1907: Ibid., The Conference of 1907, 2nd vol., 8. The first paragraph of the proposition read as follows: "For the purpose of avoiding between nations armed conflicts of a purely pecuniary origin, arising from contract debts, which are claimed as due to the subjects or citizens of one country by the Government of another country, and in order to guarantee that all contract debts of this nature which it may have been impossible to settle amicably through the diplomatic channel shall be submitted to arbitration, it is agreed that there cannot be recourse to any coercive measure involving the employment of military or naval forces for the recovery of such contract debts, until an offer of arbitration has been made by the creditor and refused or not answered by the debtor, or until arbitration has taken place and the debtor State has failed to comply with the award made." (Annexe 48: Ibid., The Conference of 1907, 2nd vol., 906).

tional honour. He then stressed the adverse effects that coercive collections had on the solvency of the debtor State, which sometimes went through great calamities (insurrections, floods, etc.). Finally, he noted that third States were also affected in their trade since the non-recognition of pacific blockade often led to the establishment of a belligerent blockade. That is why, for all those reasons, mandatory arbitration had to be the solution. Porter insisted on the fact that the gathering of both creditor and debtor nations made it timely to agree on a general treaty on the subject.[686]

However, while the delegations of the great European Powers unreservedly approved the text of the U.S. proposition, many delegations —in particular, Latin American countries, to Porter's surprise— made reservations.[687] The concerns were twofold: the scope was too limited, and the wording made clear that the use of force after arbitration was made lawful.

Regarding the scope, the Dominican Republic regarded the term "contract debts" of the proposition as not only vague —"to the grave and manifest detriment of small States"— but also narrow. That is why it introduced an amendment aiming to extend the proposal to include any pecuniary claims, regardless of whether they resulted from damages, losses, contracts or public loans.[688]

Not going as far as the delegation of the Dominican Republic, Luís M. Drago, present at The Hague, expounded on the central difference between contract debts and public loans. On the one hand, the local remedies had to be exhausted in case of ordinary contract claims (just like for claims arising from torts). On this point, he noted that it was even possible in most South American countries to sue the Government without its con-

686 General Porter, fifth meeting of the first commission's first subcommission on 16 July 1907: Ibid., The Conference of 1907, 2nd vol., 226–232. About Porter's assertion that claims submitted to arbitration or mixed commission were invariably reduced, cf. Philip C. Jessup, 'The United States and Treaties for the Avoidance of War', *IntlConciliation* 12 (1928–1929), 179–207, at 189–191.
It must be noted that Porter, as well as other diplomats, generally spoke of armed 'intervention' as an umbrella term for any use of force, including armed reprisals.

687 Cf. George Winfield Scott, 'Hague Convention Restricting the Use of Force to Recover on Contract Claims', *AJIL* 2 (1908), 78–94, at 87; Karl Strupp, 'L'intervention en matière financière', *RdC* 8 (1925), 5–124, at 99.

688 See Annexes 51 and 57: Scott, *The Proceedings of the Hague Peace Conferences* (above, n. 575), The Conference of 1907, 2nd vol., 908 and 910–912, here quotation at 912. See also the address of Francisco Henriquez i Carvajal, delegate of the Dominican Republic, seventh meeting of the first commission's first subcommission, 23 July 1907: Ibid., The Conference of 1907, 2nd vol., 271–272.

sent. However, if a denial of justice were confirmed through arbitration, nothing would impede the plaintiff State to have recourse to other means of its choice. On the other hand, the situation regarding state loans was radically different and, hence, deserved the adoption of guarantees because the issuance of bonds and the payment of the debt were acts of sovereignty. Besides, there was no contract between the issuing Government and the purchaser, which meant that bonds were easily transferable. Bondholders were better protected anyway than investors in a joint-stock company who could lose everything following a bankruptcy. In fact, it was only a matter of time before the insolvent State could regain solvency and pay off its debts. In the light of these observations, Drago held the view that the employment of force for the collection of state loans should be declared by the Hague Conference utterly forbidden, even after arbitration. Otherwise, it would amount to the recognition of war as a legal remedy.[689]

As a matter of fact, many delegations understood the U.S. proposition as the legitimisation of force after the failure of the procedure of arbitration.[690] The Swedish delegate Knut Hjalmar Hammarskjöld even withdrew his support for the proposition on this ground.[691] The opinion of the Colombian delegate Santiago Pérez Triana was even sharper on this aspect. He endorsed the idea to have recourse to arbitration because this institution was equitable and often reduced the exorbitant claims of creditors. However, he criticised that the proposition omitted or forgot to consider the situation of a debtor State which might be unable to pay its debts owing to circumstances beyond its control like revolutions, bad harvests, natural cataclysms, etc. In such cases, the debtor's failure to conform to the

689 Luis M. Drago, sixth meeting of the first commission's first subcommission on 18 July 1907: Ibid., The Conference of 1907, 2nd vol., 246–251. But see Scott, 'Hague Convention Restricting the Use of Force to Recover on Contract Claims' (above, n. 687), 90–3; Scott, *The Hague Peace Conferences of 1899 and 1907* (above, n. 679), 1st vol., 417–418; Borchard, *The diplomatic protection of citizens abroad or the law of international claims* (above, n. 669), 321–2; Strupp, 'L'intervention en matière financière' (above, n. 687), 106–8.

690 This position was, of course, not shared by all the countries, even amongst Latin American nations. For instance, the delegate of Brazil contended that the proposition did not legitimise the resort to war but merely recognised a factual situation: the regrettable, but unfortunately, unavoidable existence of war as a last resort. See Ruy Barbosa, seventh meeting of the first commission's first subcommission on 23 July 1907: Scott, *The Proceedings of the Hague Peace Conferences* (above, n. 575), The Conference of 1907, 2nd vol., 283–285.

691 Eighth meeting of the first commission's first subcommission on 27 July 1907: Ibid., The Conference of 1907, 2nd vol., 309.

arbitral award would give licence to the creditor State to recover debts by force, thereby implying that the debtor country acted with bad faith. This idea was intolerable for Pérez who suspected that the existence of this gap in the proposition was actually intentional in order to meet "exigencies of international politics in which absolute truth cannot have its place."[692]

Despite all this, the U.S. proposal was adopted by the first subcommission on 27 July 1907 with 36 votes in favour and 8 abstentions.[693] Still, Porter introduced soon thereafter a revised version of the proposition in order to meet the criticisms that too much importance was given to the use of force. Indeed, the first paragraph of the new draft stipulated the renunciation of the recourse to arms altogether. The second paragraph neither allowed the use of force explicitly after the failure of arbitration but specified that the debtor State would lose the benefit of the renunciation if it opposed arbitration.[694]

It is that new wording which prevailed and formed Article 1 of the II Hague Convention respecting the limitation of the employment of force for the recovery of contract debts, signed on 18 October 1907. It reads:

> "The contracting Powers agree not to have recourse to armed force for the recovery of contract debts claimed from the Government of one country by the Government of another country as being due to its nationals.
>
> "This undertaking is, however, not applicable when the debtor State refuses or neglects to reply to an offer of arbitration, or, after accepting the offer, prevents any *compromis* from being agreed on, or, after the arbitration, fails to submit to the award."[695]

Nevertheless, this Convention failed to pass unanimously. The Bolivian delegate, e.g., justified his country's refusal to assent to the draft by explaining that the Convention under discussion meant the legitimisation of a class of *wars* by a *Peace* Conference.[696] Furthermore, notwithstanding the

692 Sixth meeting of the first commission's first subcommission on 18 July 1907: Ibid., The Conference of 1907, 2nd vol., 259–262, here quotation at 261.

693 Eighth meeting of the first commission's first subcommission on 27 July 1907: Ibid., The Conference of 1907, 2nd vol., 310.

694 Scott, *The Hague Peace Conferences of 1899 and 1907* (above, n. 679), 1st vol., 415.

695 Scott, *The Hague Conventions and Declarations of 1899 and 1907* (above, n. 598), 89.

696 Claudio Pinilla, eighth meeting of the first commission on 9 October 1907: Scott, *The Proceedings of the Hague Peace Conferences* (above, n. 575), The Conference of 1907, 2nd vol., 140 (with Pinilla's emphasis).

adoption of the Convention, many signatory Powers —almost exclusively Latin American States— entered a reservation in the signature. Two main aspects were expressed: (1) the exhaustion of all local remedies before referring the issue to arbitration; (2) the absolute renunciation of the right to resort to arms for the collection of debts, particularly those arising from public loans.[697] In other words, the Latin American States wanted a complete ban on the use of force, whereas the Convention solely provided a limitation. Their disappointment was so high that almost twenty years later, most of them had still not ratified the Convention.[698]

The final result shows that many debtor States frequently targeted by operations of armed reprisals pursuing the collection of debts felt that the Convention was not ambitious enough but, instead, aligned with the interests of the creditor Powers. Indeed, the latter did not wave their right to use force, but only restricted it. It may be argued that for the great Powers, this achievement was actually a masterstroke because they displayed a spirit of conciliation, and yet did not yield their right.

v) Mixed Impact of the Second Hague Conference on Armed Reprisals

Considered as one of Latin America's major contributions to the development of international law,[699] the Drago doctrine and the subsequent II Hague Convention of 1907 (also known as the Drago-Porter Convention) introduced a new stage in the history of reprisals, marked by the progressive prohibition of force in peacetime.[700] Indeed, the Drago-Porter Convention provided an important restriction on the employment of

---

697 See the reservations in Scott, *The Hague Conventions and Declarations of 1899 and 1907* (above, n. 598), 92–5.

698 See Strupp, 'L'intervention en matière financière' (above, n. 687), 104.

699 Francisco-José Urrutia, 'La codification du droit international en Amérique', *RdC* 22/II (1928), 85–233, at 118; Wolfgang Benedek, 'Drago-Porter Convention (1907)', in Rüdiger Wolfrum (ed.), *The Max Planck Encyclopedia of Public International Law*, published under the auspices of the Max Planck Institute for comparative public law and international law, 3rd vol. (Oxford: OUP, 2012–2013; <http://www.mpepil.com>, accessed 18 August 2017), 234–6, here at no. 9.

700 Partsch, 'Repressalie' (above, n. 62), 103; Ruffert, 'Reprisals' (above, n. 10), no. 5. The contemporary legal scholar James Brown Scott even argued that the Convention sounded the death knell of pacific blockade against American nations. See James Brown Scott, 'The Work of the Second Hague Peace Conference', *AJIL* 2 (1908), 1–28, at 14; and also Maxime Chrétien, 'La « guerre totale » du Japon en Chine', *RGDIP* 46 (1939), 229–303, at 276–277.

armed reprisals.[701] The failure by the creditor State to offer arbitration made any recourse to this measure utterly illegal.[702] But when the debtor State rejected the offer of arbitration, prevented the conclusion of an arbitration agreement or failed to comply with the award, this renunciation of force disappeared.

The small States undeniably revealed their growing weight at The Hague by speaking loudly against the Western practice of resorting to measures of self-help.[703] However, a closer look at the Convention shows that there were still many loopholes regarding the use of armed reprisals. As a matter of fact, the Drago-Porter Convention did not cover claims arising from tort or resulting from a contract between two States or two individual persons. Only contract debts owed to nationals of one State by the Government of another State fell under its scope.[704]

---

701 Yet, the Drago-Porter Convention did not affect the use of non-forcible reprisals. See Strupp, 'L'intervention en matière financière' (above, n. 687), 110; Müller, *Wandlungen im Repressalienrecht* (above, n. 21), 82; Elagab, *The legality of non-forcible counter-measures in international law* (above, n. 14), 26f.
Neff, *War and the Law of Nations* (above, n. 2), 239 fn. 87, maintains that this Convention restricted only the resort to armed reprisals but not the recourse to war. However, Neff's view stands in contradiction with the spirit of the said Convention. Indeed, the represented States clearly sought to limit the existing *ius ad bellum*, as can been seen in the proceedings of the Second Hague Peace Conference. They actually referred indistinctly to war, recourse to arms, armed intervention. Moreover, the term "armed force" used in the Drago-Porter Convention do not permit to draw a distinction between armed reprisals and actual war.

702 Randall Lesaffer, 'Peace through law. The Hague Peace Conferences and the rise of the *ius contra bellum*', in Maartje Abbenhuis, Christopher Ernest Barber, and Annalise R. Higgins (eds.), *War, Peace and International Order? The Legacies of the Hague Conferences of 1899 and 1907* (Routledge Studies in Modern History; Abingdon, Oxon/New York: Routledge, 2017), 31–51, at 46.

703 Cf. Grewe, *Epochen der Völkerrechtsgeschichte* (above, n. 24), 621 fn. 16; Francis Anthony Boyle, *Foundations of World Order: The Legalist Approach to International Relations, 1898–1922* (Durham/London: Duke University Press, 1999), 81; O. Thomas Johnson, Jr. and Jonathan Gimblett, 'From gunboats to BITs. The evolution of modern international investment law', *Yearbook on International Investment Law and Policy* (2010–2011), 649–92, at 657; Lesaffer, 'Peace through law. The Hague Peace Conferences and the rise of the *ius contra bellum*' (above, n. 702), 45.

704 Müller, *Wandlungen im Repressalienrecht* (above, n. 21), 82–3; Elagab, *The legality of non-forcible counter-measures in international law* (above, n. 14), 26.

The Drago-Porter Convention could by no means be regarded as a victory of compulsory arbitration because it did not impose an obligation to submit a dispute about contract debts to arbitration. As the International Court of Justice stressed in 1957 in the *Case of Certain Norwegian Loans*, "[t]he only obligation imposed by the Convention is that an intervening Power must not have recourse to force before it has tried arbitration."[705] This obligation was incumbent on the creditor State.[706] For its part, the debtor country was under no obligation to accept the offer of arbitration, although a sword of Damocles hung over it in the event of rejection or a lack of commitment to the procedure of arbitration.[707] The debtor country could, of course, suggest the settlement of the dispute through arbitration, but this would not bind the creditor State.[708] It can thus be said that the Drago-Porter Convention had the result to pacify the relations between creditor and debtor States, and yet it made the inequality between them more blatant.[709] The problem of armed reprisals as a privilege right of the great Powers had, therefore, not seriously been attacked by the Drago-Porter Convention.

There was, in addition, no agreement on compulsory arbitration at The Hague in 1907.[710] The Swedish delegation, nevertheless, had introduced a proposition to declare arbitration obligatory for some pecuniary claims to

705 International Court of Justice, *Case of Certain Norwegian Loans (France v. Norway)*, Judgement of 6 July 1957, I.C.J. Reports (1957), 9–28, at 24.

706 Henri-Alexis Moulin, *La doctrine de Drago* (Questions de droit des gens et de politique internationale; Paris: A. Pedone, 1908), 324; Stanislas Dotremont, *L'arbitrage international et le Conseil de la Société des Nations: Le Pacte, les progrès tentés et réalisés depuis, les progrès réalisables* (Bruxelles: Maurice Lamertin, 1929), 60.

707 Strupp, 'L'intervention en matière financière' (above, n. 687), 108–9; Dotremont, *L'arbitrage international et le Conseil de la Société des Nations* (above, n. 706), 60.

708 Heimbeck, 'Legal Avoidance as Peace Instrument. Domination and Pacification through Asymmetric Loan Transactions' (above, n. 73), 126. But see Borchard, *The diplomatic protection of citizens abroad or the law of international claims* (above, n. 669), 328.

709 Heimbeck, 'Legal Avoidance as Peace Instrument. Domination and Pacification through Asymmetric Loan Transactions' (above, n. 73), 126.

710 See Scott, *The Hague Peace Conferences of 1899 and 1907* (above, n. 679), 1st vol., 330–385. The U.S. representative at The Hague, Joseph Hodges Choate, made the following response to the delegations, e.g. Germany's, which preferred the conclusion of special treaties of obligatory arbitration rather than a general agreement. His remark does not lack interest: "Now as to the question of the reservation of the right or the purpose to resort to force, which is the only other reason that I can conceive of for declining to join in a general arbitration agree-

which the exceptions of vital interests or independence could not be opposed, such as those arising from "so-called pacific blockade, the arrest of foreigners or the seizure of their property."[711] As Hammarskjöld explained to Porter, the Swedish proposition did not overlap the U.S. proposal on the limitation of the employment of force for the recovery of contract debts because it related only to disputes between States.[712]

In conclusion, the situation regarding armed reprisals had not really been impacted by the Second Hague Peace Conference, except for the cases falling under the scope of the Drago-Porter Convention. That is why there were high hopes to see the legal loophole regarding armed reprisals plugged at the next Hague Conference, which would have taken place in 1915 if World War I had not broken out in the meantime.[713] Indeed, in preparation for this Third Peace Conference, the Institute of International

---

ment on the part of those who are ready to accomplish the same thing by individual treaties. The idea of the opposition, as I understand it, is that we should maintain our right to select our own company, and not be compelled to admit all the nations into a general agreement with us. But suppose you do agree with twenty nations and conclude such treaties with that limited number, either separately or jointly, what do you mean to do with regard to the twenty-five other nations whom you will have refused to admit into your charmed circle of arbitral accord? You must reserve, must you not, you must mean to reserve the right to resort to war against the twenty-five non-signatory States, when differences with them cannot be settled by diplomatic means? *Those are the two alternative ways—arbitration or force. And if you will not agree to arbitration, it must be because you reserve the right, if not the intent, to resort to force with them*. But, gentlemen, empires and kingdoms, as well as republics, must sooner or later yield to the imperative dictates of the public opinion of the world. Every power, great or small, must submit to the overwhelming supremacy of the public will, which has already declared and will hereafter declare, more and more urgently, that every unnecessary war is an unpardonable crime, and that every war is unnecessary when a resort to arbitration might have settled the dispute. These are the two alternatives between which the opponents of our project must finally choose." (Mr Choate, fifth meeting of the first commission on 5 October 1907: Scott, *The Proceedings of the Hague Peace Conferences* (above, n. 575), Conference of 1907, 2nd vol., 75 (emphasis added)).

711 See Article 18, esp. Para. 3, of Annexe 22: Ibid., Conference of 1907, 2nd vol., 878; Mr Hammarskjöld, fifth meeting of the first commission's first subcommission on 16 July 1907: Ibid., The Conference of 1907, 2nd vol., 237–239.

712 Eleventh meeting of the committee of examination A of the first commission's first subcommission on 23 August 1907: Ibid., Conference of 1907, 2nd vol., 488.

713 See the text of the Final Act of the Hague Conference of 1907 recommending the assembly of a Third Peace Conference more or less eight years later: Scott, *The Hague Conventions and Declarations of 1899 and 1907* (above, n. 598), 29–30.

Law decided at its sitting of Paris in 1910 to set up a preparatory commission.[714] John Westlake was appointed rapporteur of the special commission dealing with the project of extension of the III Hague Convention of 1907 relative to the Opening of Hostilities to all coercive measures such as pacific blockade, occupation, etc.[715]

The choice of Westlake was not innocent. As a matter of fact, the Whewell professor of international law argued in a paper published the previous year that armed reprisals did not fall under the obligation laid down in Art. 1 of the III Hague Convention of 1907, viz. to issue a declaration of war or an ultimatum before commencing the hostilities.[716] Westlake maintained that there was a distinction between armed reprisals and war resting on the inequality of power between, on the one hand, the strong reprisal-taking State and, on the other, the small target country. Nevertheless, he acknowledged that this situation could lead to abuses. As a remedy, Westlake suggested on the model of Art. 1 of the Drago-Porter Convention that the resort to armed reprisals should be made conditional on an offer of arbitration. This proposal, which he intended to submit to the next Peace Conference, aimed to cover all classes of claims: the recovery of contract debts claimed by Governments on behalf of themselves or nationals, and the enforcement of non-contractual claims.[717]

Westlake's project did not aspire to the prohibition of armed reprisals. He merely sought to confine them within reasonable limits. Still, as much as a regulation on this topic was needed, he knew the temperament of the reprisal-taking Powers and feared their resistance:

714 Extract from the minutes of the meeting on 1 April 1910: Institut de Droit International (ed.), *Session de Paris – Mars-Avril 1910* (Annuaire IDI, vol. 23; Paris: A. Pedone, 1910), 498. See more generally about the preparation of the Third Hague Conference in Otfried Nippold, 'Die gegenwärtige Stand der Vorarbeiten für die dritte Haager Friedenskonferenz', *ZVölkR* 7 (1913), 286–307.

715 See Louis Renault and Édouard Rolin, 'Rapport fait à l'Institut de Droit International au nom de la Commission spéciale constituée en vue de la prochaine conférence de la paix', in Institut de Droit International (ed.), *Session de Christiana – Août 1912* (Annuaire IDI, vol. 25; Paris: A. Pedone, 1912), 23–40, at 29, 31 and 36.

716 See *supra*, at 195–196.

717 Westlake, 'Reprisals and War' (above, n. 256), 134–7. See Lawrence's positive reception of this proposal: Lawrence, *The principles of international law* (above, n. 6), 344. Cf. with Strupp's draft convention improving the Drago-Porter Convention: Strupp, 'L'intervention en matière financière' (above, n. 687), 111–20.

"We may be sure that all Governments, including our own, will strive to retain as much as possible of their powers of action. They desire to exercise those powers for the good of their respective nations, and there is little use in appealing to altruistic sentiment in those nations. If there is to be much improvement in international law, and especially in so much of that law as tends to restrict the powers of Governments, each nation must be convinced that, even for its own good, it is better to rely on well-considered general law than on particular measures taken to meet particular occasions."[718]

Unfortunately, Westlake's project did not materialise. By 1912, the IIL had to postpone the consideration of the subject owing to the absence of report.[719] The following year, Westlake died on 14 April. Finally, the First World War broke out in summer 1914, putting an end to the hope of seeing a general agreement on armed reprisals.

V. Interim Conclusion

At a time when international law grew in importance as a discipline, the contemporary practice of armed reprisals raised the question of compatibility regarding the use of force in peacetime. Thus, the attention of legal scholars was drawn to this matter, concerning in particular the unprecedented custom of resorting to a blockade in time of peace.

However, between 1848 and 1912, lawyers failed to significantly contribute to the clarification of the law of armed reprisals because of their unease about this measure. This was a period of tension. Legal doctrine had to position itself in relation to State practice: either it remained a passive observer consigning the State practice or it decided to play an active role and condemn the abuses.

---

718 Letter to *The Times* of 19 December 1908: John Westlake, *The Collected Papers of John Westlake on Public International Law* (Cambridge: CUP, 1914), 571. That is why Lawrence, who shared the view of a limitation of armed reprisals rather than their ban, suggested the creation of "a strong public opinion against their use on slight provocation, or for a manifestly unjust cause." (Lawrence, *The principles of international law* (above, n. 6), 344).

719 Morning meeting of the Institute's sitting at Christiania (Oslo), 27 August 1912: Institut de Droit International (ed.), *Session de Christiana – Août 1912* (Annuaire IDI, vol. 25; Paris: A. Pedone, 1912), 580f.

The first and main battleground was the question of pacific blockade which divided the legal community. At the session of Heidelberg in 1887, the Institute of International Law reached a consensus on the issue by which pacific blockades were recognised as a legitimate measure bereft of belligerency. This solution reveals the permissiveness towards the bullying practice of the great Powers as well as the timid attempt to limit the adverse effects of pacific blockades on the shipping of third States.

But the legal community was quickly overwhelmed by the State practice trying to extend the theory of pacific blockade. At the same time, the blockade of Venezuela of 1902/03 exposed the blurring of the thin line between war and peace and brought out the serious lacuna in international law regarding the use of force in peacetime, as the Permanent Court of Arbitration had to admit that the blockading Powers deserved a preferential treatment over the other creditor States as a result of their armed operation. The legal scholars' response was confused. The initiative had then to come from the Latin American countries with the Drago doctrine, which eventually gave birth to a Hague Convention of 1907 restricting partially armed reprisals.

Lawyers clearly missed the opportunity during the period 1848–1912 to firmly condemn the State practice of armed reprisals by adequately assessing and addressing the issue.

Chapter Four. Culmination of Antagonism: Peace-Building and Armed Reprisals in the Interwar Period

I. Introduction

The First World War highlighted the horrors of modern warfare and the pressing need to organise the international community in order to prevent the resurgence of conflicts of the same scale. The League of Nations was then created and aimed at the preservation of peace. However, while all efforts were directed towards the restriction of the *ius ad bellum*, the question of the limitation of the use of force in peacetime had mostly been neglected, if not deliberately avoided. It engendered situations where the international community was caught unprepared and unable to handle the case of military acts of reprisals adequately. In fact, by exploiting the loopholes of treaties and conventions, the reprisal-taking Powers could, in most cases, argue their way out of responsibility.

The present chapter intends to explain why the burning issue of armed reprisals failed to receive an adequate response despite the objectives of peace-building of the epoch. It is maintained here that, unlike the permissiveness that they demonstrated prior to WWI, the international lawyers condemned with one voice the practice of armed reprisals as being utterly incompatible with the legal documents of the time such as the Covenant of the League of Nations. Nevertheless, legal doctrine had not enough weight to dictate conduct to the great Powers which, for occupying a dominant position in the international community, opposed resistance against any initiative seeking to limit their right to armed reprisals.

II. State of Mind: The Peace Treaty of Versailles and Reprisals

1. Enforcement of War Reparations: The Ruhr Occupation, 1923–1925

After World War I, efforts at Versailles aimed at peace-building. It was within this frame of mind that the States present laid the foundations for an international organisation to preserve peace in future, viz. the League of Nations. However, beyond these lofty sentiments, the Allied Powers, especially France, also wanted to make Germany pay for initiating the war as well as prevent its quick recovery. Indeed, the French Prime Minister Georges Clemenceau feared that Germany's recovery would present a new threat to France and culminate in another all-out war. Therefore, he urged to dictate hard terms to Germany.[720] That is why John Maynard Keynes accurately called the Peace Treaty of Versailles signed on 28 June 1919 a "Carthaginian Peace".[721]

With the Treaty of Versailles, reprisals reappeared in a major European peace treaty after their omission since the end of the eighteenth century.[722] Paragraph 18 of Annexe II to Part VIII (Article 231ff.) about war reparations read as follows:

> "The measures which the Allied and Associated Powers shall have the right to take, in case of voluntary default by Germany, and which Germany agrees not to regard as acts of war, may include economic and financial prohibitions and reprisals and in general such other measures as the respective Governments may determine to be necessary in the circumstances."[723]

This stipulation provided the Allied Powers with the necessary instruments to lawfully coerce Germany if it failed to perform its obligations to repair war damage.

As a matter of fact, between 1920 and 1921, the Allied Powers threatened the latter country five times to occupy its territories militarily and twice this menace was carried out as Germany was found in default. Thus, in March 1920 France occupied Frankfort and Darmstadt, and then in March 1921 the towns of Duisburg, Ruhrort and Düsseldorf were occupied by France, Great Britain and Belgium.[724] The Governments of the Allied Powers asserted that the invasion of the German right bank of the

720 See John Maynard Keynes, *The Economic Consequences of the Peace* (New York: Harcourt, Brace and Howe, 1920), 32–5.

721 Ibid., 35.

722 Müller, *Wandlungen im Repressalienrecht* (above, n. 21), 80.

723 Charles Irving Bevans, *Treaties and other international agreements of the United States of America, 1776–1949*, 2nd vol. ([Washington]: [U.S. Department of State], 1969), 148.

724 John Maynard Keynes, *A Revision of the Treaty: being a Sequel to the Economic Consequences of the Peace* (New York: Harcourt, Brace and Howe, 1922), 57–8. Cf. Frederick M. Allemés and Ernest Joseph Schuster, 'The Legality or Illegality of the Ruhr Occupation', *TGS* 10 (1924), 61–87, at 64; Arnold D. McNair, 'The Legality of the Occupation of the Ruhr', *BYIL* 5 (1924), 17–37, at 32.

Rhine was justified by the treaty in case of Germany's failure to fulfil any of its obligations.[725]

Therefore, when on 26 December 1922 and on 9 January 1923 the Reparation Commission declared Germany in voluntary default regarding timber and coal deliveries,[726] the French Government immediately sent a missive the following day to the German ambassador at Paris that announced the taking of measures pursuant to Paragraph 18 of Annexe II to Part VIII of the Treaty of Versailles.[727] Thus began the controversial Franco-Belgian occupation of the Ruhr region —Germany's economic lung— which lasted from January 1923 till August 1925.

For the French Government, it was clear that § 18 allowed the temporary occupation of Germany. Already at the Conference of London on 13 February 1920, Alexandre Millerand, the then French Prime Minister, defended this interpretation and pointed out that in any event such a step was authorised in international law given some precedents such as the British occupation of Corinto in 1896 or the French occupation of Mytilene in 1901.[728] Yet, France did not claim to act on the basis of the term 'reprisals' because the French wording of § 18, unlike the English ver-

---

725 Keynes, *A Revision of the Treaty* (above, n. 724), 58.

726 On 26 December 1922, the Reparation Commission unanimously noted that Germany had not executed all its obligations. As a result, it declared by a majority (the British delegate voting against) that this non-execution constituted a default. See Points 53–57 of the minutes of the meeting on 26 December 1922: Allied Powers and Reparation Commission, *Report On the Work of the Reparation Commission from 1920 to 1922* (London: His Majesty's Stationery Office, 1923), 260.
McNair, 'The Legality of the Occupation of the Ruhr' (above, n. 724), 20, argued that the first point was a pure question of fact and, hence, required merely the majority, while the second amounted to a question of interpretation and, thus, imposed a unanimous vote. See Paragraph 13 Sec. 3(*f*) and 4 of Annexe II to Part VIII of the Peace Treaty of Versailles. For a contrary opinion, see Allemés and Schuster, 'The Legality or Illegality of the Ruhr Occupation' (above, n. 724), 70.

727 See extract of the missive quoted in Karl Strupp, 'Ruhreinmarsch, der französisch-belgische', in Karl Strupp (ed.), *Wörterbuch des Völkerrechts und der Diplomatie*, 2nd vol. (Berlin/Leipzig: Walter De Gruyter & Co., 1925), 404–7, at 404–5.

728 Mr Millerand, minutes of the Conference of London, 13 February 1920: France, Ministère des Affaires étrangères and Commission des archives diplomatiques, *1921: Annexes (10 janvier 1920 – 31 décembre 1921)* (Documents diplomatiques français, 6; Bruxelles: P.I.E.-Peter Lang, 2005), 47. Cf. Paul Fauchille, *Traité de droit international public*, 2 vols. (8th edn., Paris: Rousseau & Cie, 1921–1926), 2nd vol., 1051–1052.

sion,[729] strongly implied that the acts of reprisals had to be of economic or financial character.[730] That is why the French Government explained the occupation of the Ruhr valley as falling under the "other measures" referred to *in fine* since this expression allowed a broad interpretation and thus much leeway.[731]

Be that as it may, the occupation of the Ruhr was plainly an act of reprisals.[732] In fact, § 18 as a whole enshrined a right to reprisals.[733] It can even be argued that reprisals involving the use of force were actually permitted under the provision. Indeed, did not only the provision not exhaustively list all the measures which the Allied Powers might have recourse to —given the phrases "*may* include" and "*other* measures"—, but it also clearly specified that Germany agreed not to treat any such measures as acts of war.

However, this interpretation of § 18 was not unchallenged. Serious doubts regarding the legality of the Ruhr occupation were raised. It was contended that (1) France was not qualified to act unilaterally and (2) § 18 did not entitle a creditor State to occupy Germany's territory militarily.

---

729 According to Art. 440 Para. 3, both French and English were the authentic languages of the Peace Treaty of Versailles. See Bevans, *Treaties and other international agreements of the United States of America, 1776–1949* (above, n. 723), 233.

730 The relevant part of the provision read: "Les mesures [...] peuvent comprendre des *actes* de prohibitions et *de représailles économiques et financières* et, en général, telles autres mesures que les Gouvernements respectifs pourront estimer nécessitées par les circonstances." (*J.O.R.F.*, 11 January 1920, 485 (emphasis added)). See further George A. Finch, 'The Legality of the Occupation of the Ruhr Valley', *AJIL* 17 (1923), 724–33, at 724 fn. 2; McNair, 'The Legality of the Occupation of the Ruhr' (above, n. 724), 22.

731 M. le président du conseil, *Chambre des députés*, 11 January 1923: *J.O.R.F.*, 11 January 1923, 19. See also André Tardieu, *La paix*, Préface de Georges Clemenceau (Paris: Payot & Cie, 1921), 371.

732 Cf. Fauchille, *Traité de droit international public* (above, n. 728), 2nd vol., 1051.

733 Fernand De Visscher, *La Renonciation du Gouvernement britannique au Droit de Représailles sur les Biens des Particuliers allemands*, extrait de la *Revue de Droit international et de Législation comparée* (1920, n° 3–4) (Bruxelles: M. Weissenbruch, 1920), 9.

2. Question of the Legality of the Ruhr Occupation

(a) Right of Acting Unilaterally

The first objection is that § 18 did not authorise a creditor Power of Germany to act single-handedly because it stipulated that *the respective Governments* could determine the necessary measures "which *the Allied and Associated Powers* shall have the right to take".

Those 'respective Governments' were the *interested Powers* mentioned in § 17 of Annexe II to Part VIII of the Treaty of Versailles.[734] According to that stipulation,[735] the Reparation Commission —referred to in Article 233 and made up by the Allied Powers— was tasked with informing the *interested Powers*, i.e. the creditor States, of Germany's default and with recommending the best-suited course of action.[736] It then lied with this Commission to decide whether the non-execution by Germany of its obligations constituted a default, which, if so, would trigger the application of § 18.[737] At a meeting on 26 December 1922, the Reparation Commission

734 Allemés and Schuster, 'The Legality or Illegality of the Ruhr Occupation' (above, n. 724), 73; McNair, 'The Legality of the Occupation of the Ruhr' (above, n. 724), 23–4; Strupp, 'Ruhreinmarsch, der französisch-belgische' (above, n. 727), 406.

735 "In case of default by Germany in the performance of any obligation under this Part of the present Treaty, the Commission will forthwith give notice of such default to each of the interested Powers and may make such recommendations as to the action to be taken in consequence of such default as it may think necessary." (Bevans, *Treaties and other international agreements of the United States of America, 1776–1949* (above, n. 723), 147).

736 Ernest Joseph Schuster, KC, observed that the Reparation Commission failed to make recommendations in the present case, pursuant to § 17. Yet, he asserted that the Commission was not merely empowered to make recommendations, as the English text let it be understood ("*may* make recommendations"), but had, in fact, the obligation to do so according to the French version of the provision ("la Commission signalera immédiatement cette inexécution [...] *en y joignant* toutes propositions [...]."). That is why he maintained that the occupation of the Ruhr was illegal. See Allemés and Schuster, 'The Legality or Illegality of the Ruhr Occupation' (above, n. 724), 70.

737 Pursuant to § 12 Sec. 2 of Annexe II to Part VIII investing the Reparation Commission with the authority to interpret the provisions of this Part of the Treaty, the said Commission declared on 26 December 1922 that "default" in § 17 shared the same meaning as "voluntary default" in § 18. Yet, it did not give further explanation. See the formal interpretation of Paragraph 17, Point 1: Allied Powers and Reparation Commission, *Report On the Work of the Reparation Commission from 1920 to 1922* (above, n. 726), 263f. According to the French Gov-

interpreted the phrase 'interested Powers' as meaning Great Britain, France, Italy and Belgium.[738]

Pursuant to § 18, the respective Governments could determine the measures which they deemed necessary in the light of the circumstances surrounding a default by Germany. In other words, they had merely a right to propose some actions, while the Allied and Associated Powers were responsible for deciding which measures should be taken. For Karl Strupp, this decision then fell to all the twenty-six signatory parties of the Treaty of Versailles mentioned in the Preamble, except Germany.[739] However, since this interpretation lacked practical effect, the British international law expert Arnold D. McNair contended instead that the power to take the measures was entrusted to a common organ like the Supreme Council or the Reparation Commission.[740]

It, thus, appeared that § 18 contained a collective right of reprisals.[741] A parallel can be established between this conclusion and the statement of the Supreme Council of the Allies, following the occupation by Romania in August 1919 of Hungarian territory and the ensuing seizure of Hungarian assets, that no isolated actions were allowed to collect reparation.[742]

Nevertheless, the French Government defended the right to act unilaterally. In support of this opinion, the French Prime Minister Raymond Poincaré directed attention to Great Britain's unilateral renunciation of the right to seize German property found in the United Kingdom in case

---

ernment, a voluntary default existed "so long as Germany possessed any tangible assets". See Keynes, *A Revision of the Treaty* (above, n. 724), 58; and also Mr Millerand, minutes of the Conference of London, 13 February 1920: France, Ministère des Affaires étrangères and Commission des archives diplomatiques, *1921: Annexes (10 janvier 1920 – 31 décembre 1921)* (above, n. 728), 47. However, for Strupp, 'Ruhreinmarsch, der französisch-belgische' (above, n. 727), 405, it meant that the default had to be accompanied by Germany's specific intent to elude its treaty obligations. Cf. Keynes, *A Revision of the Treaty* (above, n. 724), 61.

738 Point 78 of the minutes of the meeting on 26 December 1922: Allied Powers and Reparation Commission, *Report On the Work of the Reparation Commission from 1920 to 1922* (above, n. 726), 263.

739 Strupp, 'Ruhreinmarsch, der französisch-belgische' (above, n. 727), 406.

740 McNair, 'The Legality of the Occupation of the Ruhr' (above, n. 724), 24.

741 Müller, *Wandlungen im Repressalienrecht* (above, n. 21), 81.

742 Cf. Allemés and Schuster, 'The Legality or Illegality of the Ruhr Occupation' (above, n. 724), 76f.; McNair, 'The Legality of the Occupation of the Ruhr' (above, n. 724), 24–5.

of default.[743] In fact, the Chancellor of the Exchequer stated on that occasion that the British Government took this decision on its own because "the words of the paragraph [§ 18] clearly leave it "to the respective Governments" to determine what action may be necessary under the paragraph."[744] He even explained a year and a half later that the British Government understood Paragraph 18 "as conferring upon the individual Governments the right to take action independently".[745] For Poincaré, this was the proof of Great Britain's admission that § 18 permitted isolated actions.[746] Therefore, some lawyers argued that the Chancellor's statements estopped the British Government from protesting against an isolated action by France.[747] In addition, the French Government opposed that France did not act alone since Belgium was also taking part in the occupation and Italy was participating by sending a body of engineers.[748]

So, on this aspect, the opinion of the 'interested Powers' that § 18 did not preclude isolated actions actually seemed to prevail over the objection of legal scholars.

---

743 Mr Raymond Poincaré to the Marquess of Crewe, 20 August 1923: France, Ministère des Affaires étrangères, *Diplomatic correspondence*: *Reply of the French Government to the note of the British Government of August 11, 1923 relating to reparations (August 20th, 1923)* (Paris: Imprimerie nationale, 1923), 12. See Great Britain, H.M. Government, 'Liability of German Property in the United Kingdom to Seizure under the Peace Treaty.', *The Board of Trade Journal and Commercial Gazette*, 21 October 1920, 479.

744 Mr Chamberlain, House of Commons, 28 October 1920: Great Britain, Parliament, *The Parliamentary Debates: Official Report. Second Session of the Thirty-First Parliament of the United Kingdom of Great Britain and Ireland. 11 George V. House of Commons* (133rd vol.; London: His Majesty's Stationery Office, 1920), col. 1922.

745 Mr Chamberlain, House of Commons, 24 May 1922: Great Britain, Parliament, *The Parliamentary Debates: Official Report*: *Fifth Session of the Thirty-First Parliament of the United Kingdom of Great Britain and Ireland. 12 & 13 George V. House of Commons* (154th vol.; London: His Majesty's Stationery Office, 1922), col. 1246W.

746 Cf. De Visscher, *La Renonciation du Gouvernement britannique au Droit de Représailles sur les Biens des Particuliers allemands* (above, n. 733), 9–14. But see Allemés and Schuster, 'The Legality or Illegality of the Ruhr Occupation' (above, n. 724), 75.

747 Finch, 'The Legality of the Occupation of the Ruhr Valley' (above, n. 730), 725–6; McNair, 'The Legality of the Occupation of the Ruhr' (above, n. 724), 32 and 37. See also, as a less explicit argument, Allemés and Schuster, 'The Legality or Illegality of the Ruhr Occupation' (above, n. 724), 67.

748 Mr Raymond Poincaré to the Marquess of Crewe, 20 August 1923: France, Ministère des Affaires étrangères, *Diplomatic correspondence* (above, n. 743), 12.

(b) Allowed Measures

Another contentious point concerned the measures allowed under § 18. Indeed, the German Government claimed that those measures could only have an economic and financial nature.[749] The British Government agreed that the provision in question did not cover the military occupation of territory.[750]

However, the Reparation Commission never made use of its power to interpret the said paragraph, due to the firm opposition from the French Government. As a matter of fact, the British delegate to the Reparation Commission, Sir John Bradbury, called on 26 December 1922 for "the definite and authoritative interpretation of that paragraph."[751] Yet, the Chairman, the Frenchman Louis Barthou, replied that the question of the interpretation of § 18 did not fall within the competence of the Reparation Commission.[752] Even though Barthou's assertion might not be accurate, it should actually be noted that in any case § 13 Sec. 3*(f)* of Annexe II to Part VIII required a unanimous decision on questions of interpretation. As an alternative, the British Secretary of State for Foreign Affairs suggested that the legal interpretation of § 18 should be referred either to the Permanent Court of International Justice or arbitration. But again, this proposal was met with the French Government's flat refusal.[753] Against this background, any attempt to interpret § 18 had remained in the realm of speculation.

---

749 Müller, *Wandlungen im Repressalienrecht* (above, n. 21), 81.

750 "The highest legal authorities in Great Britain have advised His Majesty's Government that the contention of the German Government is well founded, and His Majesty's Government have never concealed their view that the Franco-Belgian action in occupying the Ruhr, quite apart from the question of expediency, was not a sanction authorised by the Treaty itself." (The Marquess Curzon of Kedleston to Count de Saint-Aulaire, 11 August 1923: France, Ministère des Affaires étrangères, *Diplomatic correspondence* (above, n. 743), 36–37, here quotation at 36).

751 Point 38 of the minutes of the meeting on 26 December 1922: Allied Powers and Reparation Commission, *Report On the Work of the Reparation Commission from 1920 to 1922* (above, n. 726), 257.

752 Point 43 of the minutes of the meeting on 26 December 1922: Ibid.

753 The Marquess Curzon of Kedleston to Count de Saint-Aulaire, 11 August 1923: France, Ministère des Affaires étrangères, *Diplomatic correspondence* (above, n. 743), 36–7. An opinion shared by Allemés and Schuster, 'The Legality or Illegality of the Ruhr Occupation' (above, n. 724), 71.

The phrase "such other measures" in Paragraph 18 could thus be construed *ejusdem generis* to hold that such other measures had to belong to the same class of measures like the "economic and financial prohibition and reprisals" mentioned in the same provision.[754] A German lawyer, for instance, pointed out that the phrase used "*such* other measures" instead of 'all', hence implying a connection with the previously enumerated remedies.[755]

Nevertheless, the main argument put forward by those who denounced the illegality of the occupation of the Ruhr region rested on a reading of § 18 in conjunction with Article 430. In Part XIV (entitled 'Guarantees') of the Treaty of Versailles, Art. 428–430 dealt with the military occupation of Germany. On the one hand, Articles 428 and 429 provided the occupation of the German territory situated to the west of the Rhine by the Allied forces for a duration of fifteen years and their progressive withdrawal from the occupied areas every five years. On the other hand, Art. 430 allowed the *re*occupation of territories if Germany "refuses to observe the whole or part of her obligations under the present Treaty with regard to reparation". So, on the basis of Art. 430, the German and British Governments argued that the 'other measures' in § 18 permitted a reoccupation of the whole or part of the evacuated territory narrowly delimited in the Treaty but certainly not the occupation of a territory lying on the right side of the Rhine.[756] In addition to some lawyers,[757] the British economist John Maynard Keynes concurred with this view too, explaining that otherwise Art. 430 would be devoid of meaning if § 18 authorised the occupation of any territory on the right bank of the Rhine.[758]

On the other hand, a publicist named George A. Finch argued that the Treaty of Versailles pursued the payment of the full amount of the reparations. Therefore, § 18 could not be restricted by Part XIV of the Treaty, especially as Articles 248 and 252 specified that all the assets of Germany

754 See upon this rule of construction McNair, 'The Legality of the Occupation of the Ruhr' (above, n. 724), 25–7.

755 Müller, *Wandlungen im Repressalienrecht* (above, n. 21), 82.

756 The Marquess Curzon of Kedleston to Count de Saint-Aulaire, 11 August 1923: France, Ministère des Affaires étrangères, *Diplomatic correspondence* (above, n. 743), 37–8; Müller, *Wandlungen im Repressalienrecht* (above, n. 21), 81–2.

757 Allemés and Schuster, 'The Legality or Illegality of the Ruhr Occupation' (above, n. 724), 79–80; McNair, 'The Legality of the Occupation of the Ruhr' (above, n. 724), 30; Strupp, 'Ruhreinmarsch, der französisch-belgische' (above, n. 727), 407.

758 Keynes, *A Revision of the Treaty* (above, n. 724), 60.

were pledged to the payment of reparations. In other words, this meant that the assets and property outside the area described by Art. 428 and 429 might also be subject to seizure by the creditor States.[759] Moreover, it should be remarked that in January 1923, the first five-year time period had still not elapsed for the first evacuation of troops pursuant to Art. 429. Article 430 providing the reoccupation of the evacuated territories, thus, had no meaning. That is why Poincaré maintained that § 18 was complementary to Art. 430.[760]

The French Government also claimed that several precedents proved that the Allied Powers did not only threaten to occupy territories on the right bank of the Rhine by virtue of § 18 but actually did it. For France, the British Government was then precluded from raising such an objection since Great Britain had also participated in an occupation of German territories to the east of the Rhine.[761]

3. Outlook: The Unlikely Limitation of Armed Reprisals

It cannot be said with certainty that § 18 of the Peace Treaty of Versailles definitely permitted the employment of armed reprisals in the form of the occupation of the Ruhr region. There was, in fact, no unanimous and unequivocal interpretation of this provision. But the main great Power being interested in such a use of force, i.e. France, firmly opposed any narrow reading. The German Government, of course, could protest.[762] Still, the war guilt enshrined in Art. 231, the ensuing political isolation and the acceptance to pay reparations placed Germany —removed from the rank of great Power— in a position of inferiority which could be taken advantage of.[763] Indeed, the presence of such a stipulation in a peace treaty is not ano-

759 Finch, 'The Legality of the Occupation of the Ruhr Valley' (above, n. 730), 728–9.

760 Mr Raymond Poincaré to the Marquess of Crewe, 20 August 1923: France, Ministère des Affaires étrangères, *Diplomatic correspondence* (above, n. 743), 15. See also Finch, 'The Legality of the Occupation of the Ruhr Valley' (above, n. 730), 729.

761 Mr Raymond Poincaré to the Marquess of Crewe, 20 August 1923: France, Ministère des Affaires étrangères, *Diplomatic correspondence* (above, n. 743), 12–5. Cf. McNair, 'The Legality of the Occupation of the Ruhr' (above, n. 724), 31–7; Finch, 'The Legality of the Occupation of the Ruhr Valley' (above, n. 730), 730–1.

762 Cf. McNair, 'The Legality of the Occupation of the Ruhr' (above, n. 724), 36–7.

763 Cf. Colbert, *Retaliation in international law* (above, n. 6), 62.

dyne and reveals the intent of the victors to reserve the right to compel the loser to pay its debts.

Against this background, it appears clear that a limitation of armed reprisals was, for most of the Allied Powers, not on the agenda since it was a convenient and intimidating means of coercion. Nevertheless, the case of the Ruhr occupation highlighted the danger that the resort to armed reprisals against a prominent European nation presented for the peace of Europe.[764]

III. Loophole in the Ius ad Bellum Mechanism of the League of Nations

1. System of the Covenant

(a) Organisation of the League of Nations

During the whole incident of the occupation of the Ruhr, the French Government inflexibly refused to let the League of Nations examine the issue. It argued, indeed, that § 18 of Annexe II to Part VIII of the Treaty of Versailles presented a clear legal basis for such an action.[765] On the other hand, the British Government claimed that the French course of action presented a threat of war which might disturb international peace. That is why it encouraged the referral of the matter to the League's bodies for settlement.[766] Notwithstanding, France dismissed this option, thus preclud-

---

About the impact that the Plan Young should have had on the Allied Powers' right to use reprisals against Germany to secure the payment of reparations, see Pépy, 'Après les ratifications du Plan Young. Révision et Sanctions' (above, n. 23), 470–5; Müller, *Wandlungen im Repressalienrecht* (above, n. 21), 99–106.

764 The Marquess Curzon of Kedleston to Count de Saint-Aulaire, 11 August 1923: France, Ministère des Affaires étrangères, *Diplomatic correspondence* (above, n. 743), 41–2. See also the concern expressed by Sir John Bradbury that the interpretation of § 18 was of vital importance for the peace of Europe. See Point 38 of the minutes of the meeting on 26 December 1922: Allied Powers and Reparation Commission, *Report On the Work of the Reparation Commission from 1920 to 1922* (above, n. 726), 257.

765 Mr Raymond Poincaré to the Marquess of Crewe, 20 August 1923: France, Ministère des Affaires étrangères, *Diplomatic correspondence* (above, n. 743), 11.

766 The Marquess Curzon of Kedleston to Count de Saint-Aulaire, 11 August 1923: Ibid., 41–2.

ing the League from looking into the situation.[767] But could the League of Nations really avert the use of armed reprisals?

The League of Nations was an intergovernmental organisation founded in 1919 which pursued international peace and security as well as the prevention of the resort to war.[768] It was the Covenant, enshrined in Part I of the Treaty of Versailles, that acted as the legal charter which created the League and defined its actions.[769]

Various organs composed the League.

The Assembly (Art. 3) was the general body where all the Member States were represented and met on an equal footing as each had one vote. It was competent to deal with a wide range of issues, either falling "within the sphere of action of the League or affecting the peace of the world", according to Art. 3 Para. 3.

The Council (Art. 4) was in a way the League's executive body.[770] It was initially imagined to be composed exclusively of the great Powers, but the Council finally came to also include lesser Powers.[771] Nevertheless, while the five great Powers —Great Britain, France, Italy, Japan and the United States— were granted a permanent seat, Article 4 Para. 1 provided only four temporary seats so that the great Powers would remain in majority. But owing to the absence of the United States from the League and the addition of two non-permanent seats in 1922 pursuant to Art. 4 Para. 2, the great Powers had been in minority within the Council.[772] The Council shared the same competence as the Assembly (Art. 4 Para. 4). And like the Assembly, the basic rule of decision-making was unanimity (Art. 5 Para. 1). This meant that a decision could never be taken against a great Power's will.[773]

---

767 See Francis Paul Walters, *A History of the League of Nations* (London: OUP, 1952 [Reprint 1960]), 234–7.

768 See the Preamble of the Covenant of the League of Nations: Bevans, *Treaties and other international agreements of the United States of America, 1776–1949* (above, n. 723), 48.

769 Walters, *A History of the League of Nations* (above, n. 767), 40. Therefore, the date of birth of the League of Nations was on 28 June 1919 when the Peace Treaty of Versailles was signed. See Walther Schücking and Hans Wehberg, *Die Satzung des Völkerbundes* (2nd edn., Berlin: Franz Vahlen, 1924), 25.

770 Lassa Oppenheim, 'Le caractère essentiel de la Société des Nations', *RGDIP* 26 (1919), 234–44, at 235.

771 See Walters, *A History of the League of Nations* (above, n. 767), 45f.

772 Ibid., 46.

773 Cf. Frederick Pollock, *The League of Nations* (2nd edn., London: Stevens and sons, 1922), 106.

The Assembly and the Council were the two main bodies of the League of Nations. The League's founders probably conceived the Assembly as a form of parliament which could counterbalance the executive power of the Council. Nevertheless, the real centre of gravity of the League lied in the Council.[774] It was made a central actor in the procedure for the settlement of disputes and the prevention of war. Hence, it meant for Oppenheim that the success of the League would mostly depend on the goodwill of the great Powers.[775]

Two more organs of significance formed the machinery of the League of Nations. On the one hand, there was the Secretariat (Art. 6–7). It was in many respects an innovative body which acted as the League's administrative link between the Assembly and the Council.[776] On the other hand, there was the Permanent Court of International Justice which was established in 1921 on the basis of Art. 14 of the Covenant.[777]

(b) Dispute Settlement Procedure

The Covenant provided the League of Nations with an institutional structure that promoted international cooperation and discussion. Besides this organisation, the maintenance of peace also passed through a detailed procedure for the settlement of disputes.

Articles 10 and 11 specifically pursued the prevention of war. The former provision laid down the principle of respecting and preserving the territorial integrity and the political independence of all Member States against external aggression. The idea was to condemn the changing of territory, policy or government through the use of force, e.g. in the form of

---

774 Oppenheim, 'Le caractère essentiel de la Société des Nations' (above, n. 770), 236; Hans Kelsen, *Peace through law* (1st edn. of 1944, Clark, New Jersey: The Lawbook Exchange, 2008), 49–50.

775 Oppenheim, 'Le caractère essentiel de la Société des Nations' (above, n. 770), 244. Cf. Alfred Zimmern, *The League of Nations and the Rule of Law, 1918–1935* (London: Macmillan and Co., 1936), 285.

776 Pollock, *The League of Nations* (above, n. 773), 113; C. Howard-Ellis, *The origin, structure & working of the League of Nations* (London: George Allen & Unwin, 1928), 108.

777 Walters, *A History of the League of Nations* (above, n. 767), 53–4.

an armed intervention.[778] Each Member State had, therefore, a twofold obligation: on the one hand, a *negative* duty to refrain from undertaking anything against the territorial integrity or the existing political independence of a Member State; on the other, a *positive* duty to provide assistance against external aggression and to use all the necessary means to re-establish the situation prior to the aggression.[779] It was incumbent upon the Council to advise how each Member should fulfil its obligation when an external aggression was underway, threatened or feared. Notwithstanding the non-binding force of the recommendation, the Council had still to decide it unanimously.[780]

According to Art. 11 Para. 1, the League had a broad power to look into situations of war or threat of war and could decide a series of actions for the preservation of peace, irrespective of whether a Member of the League was directly involved or not. The Secretary General would then seize the Council at the request of any Member State. Art. 11 Para. 2 had a larger scope because it stipulated that any situation where the international peace or the good understanding between nations might be disturbed could be brought to the attention of either the Assembly or the Council by any Member State. Nevertheless, the role of the Council or the Assembly within the scope of Art. 11 was limited to propose solutions but in no case to impose them to the parties concerned.[781]

The *ius ad bellum* was thus not outlawed. Still, Articles 12 to 17 aimed to restrict the recourse to war. Pursuant to Art. 12, "any dispute likely to lead to a rupture" between Member States triggered for them the obligation to submit the issue either to arbitration, to judicial settlement or to the Council before resorting to war. The arbitrators or the PCIJ had reasonable time to examine the case and make the award or the judgement, whereas the Council had six months for issuing a report. Meanwhile, the parties had to refrain from resorting to war and were not allowed to claim that their honour or some vital interests were affected so as to prevent the settlement of the dispute.[782] Besides, after the award, decision or report was given, they

778 Cf. Pollock, *The League of Nations* (above, n. 773), 133; Miroslas Gonsiorowski, *Société des Nations et Problème de la Paix*, 2nd vol. (Paris: Rousseau & Cie, 1927), 281. The latter author also included acts of armed reprisals directed against the territorial integrity or the political independence.

779 Schücking and Wehberg, *Die Satzung des Völkerbundes* (above, n. 769), 458.

780 Pollock, *The League of Nations* (above, n. 773), 134; Gonsiorowski, *Société des Nations et Problème de la Paix* (above, n. 778), 288–290.

781 Ibid., 329–330.

782 Ibid., 342.

had to respect another moratorium of three months before waging war.[783] In this way, peace was given every chance to succeed.

The choice between a judicial body —a panel of arbitrators or the PCIJ — and the Council depended on the parties. In fact, they were not bound to refer their dispute of legal character to an international tribunal unless there was a binding treaty of arbitration between them or they both had agreed to refer disputes to the jurisdiction of the PCIJ in accordance with Art. 36 of the Statute of the PCIJ.[784] As a consequence, if the parties did not agree to submit the dispute to an international tribunal, one of them could bring it to the attention of the Council pursuant to Art. 15.[785] In other words, the Council, i.e. a political agency, could be called to settle any disputes of political character as well as legal disputes. This anomaly was obviously a serious flaw in the Covenant.[786]

According to Art. 15, the Council had to investigate the case and mediate between the parties so that they could reach a settlement. However, it could not examine the merits of the request, i.e. whether the dispute would likely lead to a rupture, or declare itself incompetent and refer the case to an international tribunal.[787] Either the conciliation worked, and the Council, in that case, had to make a public statement about the facts of the dispute and the terms of the settlement; or the settlement failed, and the Council then had to publish a report containing some recommendations. The consequences were different and depended on whether the report was adopted unanimously or by a majority vote. A resort to war was

783 It should be noted that the Covenant created in this way a distinction between just and unjust war from a formal point of view. If the party complied with the procedure, the resort to war after the moratorium would be licit. Only Art. 10 of the Covenant took the justness of the cause of war into account. See Ibid., 332–335.

784 Ibid., 346.
Art. 13 Para. 2 defined legal disputes as relating "to the interpretation of a treaty, [...] to any question of international law, [...] to the existence of any fact which if established would constitute a breach of any international obligation, or [...] to the extent and nature of the reparation to be made for any such breach".

785 Schücking and Wehberg, *Die Satzung des Völkerbundes* (above, n. 769), 588; Olof Hoijer, *Le Pacte de la Société des Nations: Commentaire théorique et pratique*, Préface de M. André Weiss (Paris: Spes, 1926), 266–7; Gonsiorowski, *Société des Nations et Problème de la Paix* (above, n. 778), 353.

786 See Hans Kelsen, 'The Old and the New League: The Covenant and the Dumbarton Oaks Proposals', *AJIL* 39 (1945), 45–83, at 58–59.

787 Schücking and Wehberg, *Die Satzung des Völkerbundes* (above, n. 769), 588–9; Hoijer, *Le Pacte de la Société des Nations* (above, n. 785), 267; Gonsiorowski, *Société des Nations et Problème de la Paix* (above, n. 778), 353–354.

formally forbidden against the Member State which complied with the recommendations when the report was unanimously agreed. If, on the contrary, the report was adopted by a majority, only the moratorium of three months prevented the immediate resort to war for both parties.

Comparing the judicial procedure with the procedure before the Council, it appears that the former naturally had the advantage that the award or judgement bound the parties to the result. According to Art. 13 Para. 4, the resort to war was therefore prohibited against the Member State that abode by the judicial decision. The same effect flowed from the report agreed unanimously by the Council. Yet, the difficulty to reach unanimity within the Council meant that the restraint of war was flawed. Moreover, the Council's recommendations had no binding nature and did not settle the dispute.[788] That is why a party to the dispute might prefer the procedure laid down in Art. 15 over the judicial procedure of Art. 13.

The Covenant heretofore focused on disputes between Member States. Article 17 addressed the situation when a dispute occurred between a Member of the League and a non-Member or between two non-Members.[789] In the former case, the non-Member State received an invitation to accept the obligations of membership of the League. Either the obligations were accepted, and hence Articles 12 to 16 of the Covenant applied in order to settle the dispute, or the invited State refused. If the recourse to war against a Member of the League followed the refusal, the sanctions of Art. 16 applied.[790] However, if the dispute involved two non-Members and both refused to accept the obligations imposed by the Covenant, the

788 Kelsen, 'The Old and the New League: The Covenant and the Dumbarton Oaks Proposals' (above, n. 786), 59. Cf. Gonsiorowski, *Société des Nations et Problème de la Paix* (above, n. 778), 346–347.

789 Till its admission in 1926, Germany was not a Member of the League. Any dispute between Germany and the Allied Powers arising from the Treaty of Versailles and not touching upon the payment of war reparations were thus liable to bring into operation Art. 17 of the Covenant. See Keynes, *A Revision of the Treaty* (above, n. 724), 61–3. However, the invitation in this provision had to be agreed unanimously, according to Gonsiorowski, *Société des Nations et Problème de la Paix* (above, n. 778), 392. So, France, with its permanent seat on the Council, could prevent the sending of an invitation to Germany at the time of the occupation of the Ruhr region. Of course, pursuant to Art. 11, any Member State could bring the dispute to the attention of either the Council or the Assembly. But again, unanimity would have stood here in the way of the adoption of recommendations.

790 Paradoxically, the sanctions provided in Art. 16 would not apply against the Member State that resorted to war against the non-Member which refused the invitation. See Ibid., 394.

Council remained competent to take measures and make recommendations in order to prevent the outbreak of hostilities and to reach a settlement. This provision confirmed the role of the League as guardian of the world's peace.[791]

Finally, the League had at its disposal a system of sanctions against the Covenant-breaking States.[792] Article 16 aimed to prevent the resort to war and the aggrieved State taking the law into its own hands. That is why the violation of the Covenant was made a matter of general concern for all the Members of the League. Indeed, Art. 16 Para. 1 provided that a resort to war by a Member State in disregard to the obligations under Art. 12, 13 or 15 was *ipso facto* an act of war against all other Members. This circumstance compelled the latter to immediately throw a 'cordon sanitaire' around the Covenant-breaking State through a set of financial, commercial and isolationist measures. So, any relation of financial and commercial character with the assailant State had to be severed, prohibited and prevented and this applied as well for the intercourse that the nationals of the Member States and third States had with those of the Covenant-breaking State. Besides, Art. 16 Para. 2 allowed the taking of military sanctions, too.

However, the application of Art. 16 was not without raising practical questions.[793] In fact, the enforcement of the economic boycott provided in the first paragraph was imagined as a kind of pacific blockade.[794] Based on the report of an International Blockade Committee set up in 1921 to answer a series of questions,[795] the Assembly adopted guidelines for the application of Art. 16, amongst which Clause 18 recommended in support of

791 Cf. Thomas Joseph Lawrence, *Lectures on the League of Nations: delivered in the University of Bristol* (Bristol: J. W. Arrowsmith, 1919), 65.

792 See thereupon Henri Vauzanges, *Les Sanctions internationales dans la Société des Nations*, Thèse pour le doctorat de la Faculté de Droit de l'Université de Paris, présentée et soutenue le Vendredi 28 mai 1920 à 3 heures 1/2 (Paris: Jouve & Cie, 1920). See also Hindmarsh, 'Self-Help in Time of Peace' (above, n. 17), about the historical evolution from individual self-help through state coercive methods towards international sanctions.

793 See Hoijer, *Le Pacte de la Société des Nations* (above, n. 785), 304; John Fischer Williams, 'Sanctions under the Covenant', *BYIL* 17 (1936), 130–49, at 134.

794 Already in the nineteenth century, the Italian legal scholar Pasquale Fiore regarded pacific blockade as a form of coercion which an organised international society could decide against a wrongdoing State. See Fiore, 'L'organisation juridique de la société internationale' (above, n. 652), 241.

795 This Committee was composed of representatives of Cuba, Spain, Norway and Switzerland as well as of the four permanent Members of the Council, i.e. France, Great Britain, Italy and Japan. See League of Nations, Permanent Secretariat, 'Letter from the Secretary-General to the Members of the League con-

the economic measures the establishment of an effective blockade entrusted to some Member States.[796] A few years later, the Protocol for the Pacific Settlement of International Disputes specified that the cooperation mainly depended on the geographical position and the importance of the armed force of each Member State.[797] The leading naval powers were thus mostly responsible for the enforcement of this economic blockade.[798] There still remained some doubts regarding the enforcement of such a blockade against non-Member States.[799]

---

cerning the Obligations arising out of Article 16 of the Covenant.', *LNOJ* 2 (1921), 220–1; League of Nations, Permanent Secretariat, 'Circular letter from the Secretary-General to the Members of the International Blockade Committee.', *LNOJ* 2 (1921), 430–5, at 430–432.

796 League of Nations, Assembly, 'Resolutions and Recommendations adopted on the Reports of the Third Committee.', *LNOJ* 6 (1921), Special Supplement, 23–6, at 26. As remarked Williams, 'Sanctions under the Covenant' (above, n. 793), 145, "[…] such a blockade though economic in its effect is not purely economic in its methods."

797 Art. 11 Para. 2 of the Protocol for the Pacific Settlement of International Disputes adopted by the Fifth Assembly of the League of Nations on 2 October 1924.

798 See Amos E. Taylor, 'Economic Sanctions and International Security', *UPaLRev* 74 (1925), 155–68, at 168.

799 See Williams, 'Sanctions under the Covenant' (above, n. 793), 146–7. In Great Britain, members of the Government were of the opinion that, on the question of the establishment of a blockade as part of the collective peace system, the United States, for being the main third State of the time, should be consulted. See, e.g., Viscount Cecil of Chelwood, House of Lords, 5 December 1934: Great Britain, Parliament, *The Parliamentary Debates (Official Report): Fourth Session of the Thirty-Sixth Parliament of the United Kingdom of Great Britain and Northern Ireland. 25 George V. House of Lords* (95th vol.; London: His Majesty's Stationery Office, 1935), col. 135–136. Indeed, according to Viscount Cecil, "It is quite plain now, as I understand International Law, that *the doctrine of pacific blockade is exploded*, and that *if you wish to interfere with the free use of the sea in order to put pressure on another country, you must do it by virtue of belligerent rights*. Of course that is true of the League as it is true of individual countries, […]." (Ibid., col. 136 (emphasis added)). That is why the success of the economic sanctions was largely conditional on the attitude of the powerful economic third States like the United States. Cf. the British Government's statement, Sixth (Public) Meeting of the Council of the League, 12 March 1925: League of Nations, Council, 'Thirty-Third Session of the Council. Held at Geneva from Monday, March 9th, to Saturday, March 14th, 1925.', *LNOJ* 6 (1925), 429–628, at 447.
Yet, the Secretary-General considered in a report in 1927 that a pacific blockade instituted by the League could take three different ways: (1) third States might consent to the interference of the blockading Powers with their own ships; (2) the League might declare war in order to enjoy the rights of belligerents to-

(c) Deficiency Regarding Armed Reprisals

The Covenant of the League of Nations spoke of "war", "act of war", "resort to war", "threat of war", "external aggression" and "dispute likely to lead to a rupture". However, amongst this host of phrases, no mention was made of reprisals. And yet, the various drafts of the Covenant submitted by U.S. President Woodrow Wilson contained a provision which, although not referring explicitly to reprisals, precisely aimed to limit their use.[800] Indeed, if such a provision had been adopted, the resort to armed reprisals would have then brought about the application of sanctions against the Covenant-breaking State, in the same way as a recourse to war. Nevertheless, the stipulation was amended —purportedly an insignificant change— so that the "hostile step short of war" were omitted outright.[801]

---

wards ships under the flags of third States; or (3) third States might consider applicable the laws of neutrality without a declaration of war. The report added that in the last two possibilities the existence of a state of war would be acknowledged for the practical relationship between third States and the Covenant-enforcing States albeit the latter would not be at war with the Covenant-breaking State. See League of Nations, Secretary-General, 'Annex 964. Legal position arising from the enforcement in time of peace of the measures of economic pressure indicated in Article 16 of the Covenant, particularly by a maritime blockade. Report by the Secretary-General of the League submitted to the Council on June 15th, 1927 [C. 241. 1927 V]', *LNOJ* 8 (1927), 834–45, at 839. See further Appendix II, a study by Émile Giraud about pacific blockade prior to the foundation of the League of Nations: Ibid., 841–5.

800 Art. VII read: "If any Power shall declare war or begin hostilities, or take any hostile step short of war, against another Power before submitting the dispute involved to arbitrators as herein provided, or shall declare war or begin hostilities, or take any hostile step short of war, in regard to any dispute which has been decided adversely to it by arbitrators chosen and empowered as herein provided, the Contracting Powers hereby bind themselves not only to cease all commerce and intercourse with that Power but also to unite in blockading and closing the frontiers of that power to commerce or intercourse with any part of the world or to use any force that may be necessary to accomplish that object." (David Hunter Miller, *The drafting of the Covenant*, With an introduction by Nicholas Murray Butler, 2nd vol. (New York/London: G. P. Putnam's sons, 1928), 14, 101 and 149).

801 Schwarzenberger, 'Jus Pacis Ac Belli? Prolegomena to a Sociology of International Law' (above, n. 33), 476.

Did it mean that the lack of restrictive limitation allowed the legitimate use of armed reprisals under the system of the Covenant?[802]

Before the creation of the League, the unilateral resort to self-help was justified by the existing anarchy in international relations.[803] Indeed, Bartolus de Saxoferrato explained the need for reprisals from the absence of a superior authority.[804] However, with the League of Nations, the body of the civilised States was structured, and the *ius ad bellum* was drastically restricted. Against this background and in the light of the spirit of the Covenant, the resort to armed reprisals by a single Member State without the League's consent seemed, at least, morally reprehensible.[805]

In fact, the Covenant as a whole also imposed on the Member States the duty to prefer the procedure governing the settlement of disputes over war and reprisals.[806] Besides, some of the general terms used by the Covenant could possibly fill the lacuna left by the absence of an explicit legal provision limiting or outlawing armed reprisals. Thence, the use of armed reprisals might have been regarded as a threat of war in the light of Art. 11.[807]

The phrase "dispute likely to lead to a rupture" in Art. 12 provided perhaps a stronger argument. Insofar as the target country might respond to armed reprisals, what would lead to war, their resort was necessarily the consequence of a dispute likely to amount to a rupture.[808] Nevertheless, this reading depended on the meaning of "rupture". The framers' drafts of the Covenant originally spoke of disputes "which cannot be satisfactorily settled or adjusted by the ordinary processes of diplomacy".[809] In this light, a "dispute likely to lead to a rupture" might refer to a dispute which could not be settled through diplomatic means. The parties would then be bound to submit it to the League according to Article 12, and the resort to

802 See Alberto Guani, 'Les mesures de coercition entre membres de la Société des Nations envisagées spécialement au point de vue américain', *RGDIP* 31 (1924), 285–90, at 289.

803 Cf. Gonsiorowski, *Société des Nations et Problème de la Paix* (above, n. 778), 337.

804 See *supra*, at 51.

805 Gonsiorowski, *Société des Nations et Problème de la Paix* (above, n. 778), 335f. and 339.

806 Cf. Karl Strupp, *Das völkerrechtliche Delikt* (Handbuch des Völkerrechts, 3/3; Stuttgart: W. Kohlhammer, 1920), 222–3.

807 But see Elagab, *The legality of non-forcible counter-measures in international law* (above, n. 14), 27.

808 Gonsiorowski, *Société des Nations et Problème de la Paix* (above, n. 778), 339.

809 See Miller, *The drafting of the Covenant* (above, n. 800), 100, 123, 135, 143, 147, 234, 267, 311 and 330.

war as well as the employment of reprisals would be forbidden in the meantime. On the other hand, if "rupture" were comprehended as the rupture of diplomatic relations, the provision of the Covenant would not affect the resort to armed reprisals since the parties to the dispute usually did not interrupt the conduct of diplomatic relations.[810]

Therefore, it can be said that the conformity of armed reprisals with the Covenant appeared dubious, although not unlikely for all that.[811]

2. Baptism of Fire for the Covenant: The Italian Bombardment and Occupation of Corfu, 1923

(a) The Facts

The question of the conformity of armed reprisals within the Covenant had, until 1923, only a theoretical interest. However, a few months after the French occupation of the Ruhr valley, another event gave it practical meaning: the Italo-Greek dispute.[812]

In the context of the redrawing of the borders in the Balkans after World War One, the Conference of Ambassadors —an authority representing the Principal Allied and Associated Powers signatory of the Peace Treaties— assigned a commission led by the Italian general Tellini to delineate the Greek-Albanian frontier.[813] At the end of August 1923, the bodies of General Tellini and his Italian staff were found assassinated on Greek territory nearby Ioannina, yet close to the Albanian border.

---

810 Cf. Olof Hoijer, *La solution pacifique des litiges internationaux avant et depuis la Société des Nations: Étude de Droit International et d'Histoire Diplomatique* (Paris: Spes, 1925), 401.

811 Non-forcible reprisals, on the other hand, did not raise issues since they were less likely to lead to a rupture. See Charles De Visscher, 'L'interprétation du pacte au lendemain du différend italo-grec', *RDILC* 51 (1924), 213–230 & 377–396, at 385–6; Guani, 'Les mesures de coercition entre membres de la Société des Nations envisagées spécialement au point de vue américain' (above, n. 802), 286; Gonsiorowski, *Société des Nations et Problème de la Paix* (above, n. 778), 339–400; Elagab, *The legality of non-forcible counter-measures in international law* (above, n. 14), 27–8.

812 For a historical account of the incident, see James Barros, *The Corfu incident of 1923: Mussolini and the League of Nations* (Princeton, New Jersey: PUP, 1965).

813 See Hoijer, *La solution pacifique des litiges internationaux avant et depuis la Société des Nations* (above, n. 810), 418–20.

Eager to confirm Italy's place amongst the leading nations of the world, the answer of Mussolini was not long in coming.[814] Greece was held entirely responsible for the crime. An ultimatum was addressed to the Greek Government. The Italian Government demanded redress in the form of official apologies, a criminal investigation supervised by an Italian agent, the culprits' condemnation to death, and the payment of an indemnity of 50 million lira.[815] However, the Greek Government was not disposed to accept the conditions altogether but consented to express official regrets, honour the victims, salute the Italian flag as well as pay equitable damages to the victims' family. However, it rejected the other demands on the grounds that it would be a dishonour and an infringement on the sovereignty of Greece.[816]

Mussolini did not deem the reply satisfactory. He, thus, ordered the bombardment of Corfu and its temporary occupation as a pledge until the fulfilment of the demands contained in the ultimatum.[817] The Greek Government, therefore, seized both the Conference of Ambassadors and the Council of the League of Nations.[818]

(b) Discussion in the Council

The Greek Government brought the issue to the attention of the Council by virtue of Art. 15 of the Covenant. Before the Council, Greek international law expert Nicolas Politis, who represented his Government, men-

814 See Barros, *The Corfu incident of 1923* (above, n. 812), 33–4. Nevertheless, the relations between Greece and Italy had been marked since 1912 by suspicion and hostility. This mutual animosity may explain why the incident raised much indignation in Italy and was seen as an insult to its national prestige. See David Jayne Hill, 'The Janina-Corfu Affair', *AJIL* 18 (1924), 98–104, at 99–100.

815 See extract of the Italian demands reproduced in Hoijer, *Le Pacte de la Société des Nations* (above, n. 785), 288.

816 Ibid., 288–9. See further Nicolas Politis's explanations before the Council: Eighth Meeting of the Council of the League, 4 September 1923: League of Nations, Council, 'Twenty-Sixth Session of the Council. Held at Geneva from Friday, August 31st, to Saturday, September 29th, 1923.', *LNOJ* 4 (1923), 1261–513, at 1284.

817 Hoijer, *Le Pacte de la Société des Nations* (above, n. 785), 289. Nevertheless, Corfu was at the time a neutralised territory. See thereupon Quincy Wright, 'The Neutralization of Corfu', *AJIL* 18 (1924), 104–8.

818 Hoijer, *La solution pacifique des litiges internationaux avant et depuis la Société des Nations* (above, n. 810), 421.

tioned the application of the sanctions provided in Article 16 because the case might lean towards it. Indeed, he maintained that acts of violence should be appraised objectively without considering how the assailant State described them, viz. *non ex nomine sed ex re*. That is why he strongly implied that Italy had committed acts of war in defiance of the obligations imposed by the Covenant.[819]

Antonio Salandra, the Italian delegate who was also a legal scholar, considered the allusion to Art. 16 offensive because Italy had not intended to commit an act of war. He asserted that there was neither a danger of war nor a suspension of diplomatic relations, notwithstanding that Italy had been compelled to act forcibly. For Salandra, the taking of a pledge by Italy had been necessary since Greece was an unreliable State. Indeed, he called the assassination of Tellini's staff an offence against the prestige and national honour of Italy as well as a serious violation of international law. He, thus, accused the Greek Government of being trying to shift the public opinion's attention from this crime to the acts of violence in Corfu. Italy had had, therefore, the right to take guarantees and to act for the defence of its national honour. In fact, he argued that the League of Nations membership did not imply a renunciation of such a right; otherwise, no State would like to join the League. Finally, Salandra denied the competence of the Council to examine the issue since it clearly fell within the jurisdiction of the Conference of Ambassadors.[820]

819 Sixth (Private) Meeting of the Council of the League, 1 September 1923: League of Nations, Council, 'Twenty-Sixth Session of the Council. Held at Geneva from Friday, August 31st, to Saturday, September 29th, 1923.' (above, n. 816), 1277–8. Politis published an article in the *RGDIP* in which he clarified his theory of the incompatibility of armed reprisals with the Covenant. He supported the view that there would be, i.a., a paradox if the reprisal-taking State could resort to violent measures while professing to have peaceful intent. In such a case, the target country might be liable to the sanctions provided in Art. 16 of the Covenant if it resisted and war ensued. Thus, he contended that armed reprisals should be assimilated to acts of war in the light of the Covenant on the basis of an objective criterion. See Politis, 'Les représailles entre Etats membres de la Société des Nations' (above, n. 19). About Politis's legal views regarding war and aggression, see Nicholas Tsagourias, 'Nicolas Politis' Initiatives to Outlaw War and Define Aggression, and the Narrative of Progress in International Law', *EJIL* 23 (2012), 255–66.

820 Sixth (Private) Meeting of the Council of the League, 1 September 1923: League of Nations, Council, 'Twenty-Sixth Session of the Council. Held at Geneva from Friday, August 31st, to Saturday, September 29th, 1923.' (above, n. 816), 1278–9; Ninth (Public) Meeting of the Council of the League, 5 September 1923: Ibid., 1287–8.

Politis responded that the Greek Government was ready to accept in advance the decision of the Council but disclaimed responsibility in the absence of proof to the contrary. He laid great emphasis then on the importance for the League to come up to the world's expectations by settling the issue. The League had set up a procedure that made the seizure of guarantees unnecessary. Hence, no interested party to a dispute could evade its duties under the Covenant by putting forward the League's incompetence. He insisted that the future success of the League would depend on the decision of the Council in the present case.[821]

As a matter of fact, this issue was seen from the outset as a power struggle between a great Power and a weak State. Therefore, the minor European Powers challenged the permissive interpretation of the Covenant asserted by the Italian delegation. That is why Hjalmar Branting, Sweden's representative on the Council and co-recipient of the Nobel Peace Prize in 1921, acted as the champion of the small European Powers when he told that "These States have a vital interest in ensuring that a breach of the provisions of the Covenant should not be allowed to pass without protest and without energetic steps being taken."[822] On that occasion, they could enjoy the support of Great Britain. British representative Lord Cecil of Chelwood agreed with this view that both great and small Powers were to abide by the obligations flowing from the Covenant.[823] However, Salandra denied that Italy had acted as a great Power against a little State with the aim of obtaining something from the latter. He confined himself to concurring with the statement that all Member States were equal regardless of their respective strength.[824]

The small Powers insisted that the Council was competent to settle the dispute.[825] Yet, Salandra's persistent refusal to recognise the jurisdiction of the League on a matter involving a Member's national honour and dignity

821 Ninth (Public) Meeting of the Council of the League, 5 September 1923: Ibid., 1288–90.

822 Sixth (Private) Meeting of the Council of the League, 1 September 1923: Ibid., 1280.

823 Sixth (Private) Meeting of the Council of the League, 1 September 1923: Ibid., 1279.

824 Sixth (Private) Meeting of the Council of the League, 1 September 1923: Ibid., 1281.

825 See the opinions expressed by the representatives of Great Britain, Belgium, Sweden and Uruguay who considered that the League was competent. Tenth (Public) Meeting of the Council of the League, 6 September 1923: Ibid., 1298–300.

paralysed the action of the League.[826] Indeed, all the elements indicate that Italy did not want to lose control over the issue, just like France refused a few months earlier to refer the dispute with Germany to the League. So, the Italian argument that the Conference of Ambassadors was competent patently aimed to prevent the interference of other countries, especially of small Powers which within the Council had their say in the matter.[827] Moreover, a settlement of the dispute through the Conference of Ambassadors had several advantages.[828] Firstly, the Italian Government would not run the risk of being subject to sanctions. Secondly, the issue would be settled between peers. Finally, the meetings of the Conference of Ambassadors were not public, unlike the discussions in the Council where private meetings were hardly justifiable given the significance of the case.

As a result, the dispute was settled by the Conference of Ambassadors in September 1923. Although the members of the Council applauded the solution and credited the Council with the settlement,[829] Branting remarked that the competence of the Council had actually been denied and that the bombardment and occupation of Corfu had not been punished. He argued that the confidence in the League's work had consequently been shaken and Italy's example might set a dangerous precedent.[830] Regarding this latter comment, Salandra contended that Italy did not act differently from past examples of France and Great Britain. Besides, he mentioned Schücking and Wehberg's authoritative commentary on the Covenant to assert that armed reprisals were a recognised institution of international law and

---

826 See Tenth (Public) Meeting of the Council of the League, 6 September 1923: Ibid., 1299.

827 In fact, Salandra claimed that "as small nations, they [Belgium and Sweden] have no interest in the question." According to him, this was because Belgium and Sweden were countries where political assassination did not exist. See Tenth (Public) Meeting of the Council of the League, 6 September 1923: Ibid., 1300. This argument is quite flimsy and evidently shows that Italy feared a coalition of small Powers against Italy.

828 Cf. Nicolas N. Petrascu, *Les Mesures de Contrainte Internationale qui ne sont pas la Guerre entre États Membres de la Société des Nations*, Thèse pour le doctorat de la Faculté de Droit de l'Université de Paris présentée et soutenue le mardi 24 mai 1927, à 2 heures (Paris: Jouve & Cie, 1927), 160–1.

829 See Thirteenth (Public) Meeting of the Council of the League, 17 September 1923: League of Nations, Council, 'Twenty-Sixth Session of the Council. Held at Geneva from Friday, August 31st, to Saturday, September 29th, 1923.' (above, n. 816), 1305–10.

830 Thirteenth (Public) Meeting of the Council of the League, 17 September 1923: Ibid., 1306.

remained allowed for want of a provision in the Covenant that forbade them.[831]

However, Salandra's explanations did not convince Branting for whom armed reprisals were no longer permissible under the new international law introduced by the Covenant, which had superseded the old one.[832]

From a general point of view, it can be said that the Council overcome by hypegiaphobia preferred to act out of deference to Italy, lest it withdrew from the League, and thence let, at the cost of its prestige, the Conference of Ambassadors decide upon the case.[833] This incident proved the Council's ineptitude to settle conflicts involving a great Power.[834] Furthermore, the Council clearly failed to adopt a firm stance on the use of armed force.

In fact, it is argued that Italy, with the support of France, obviously tried to prevent "any authoritative criticism of coercive measures short of war in view of the Corfu and Ruhr occupations."[835] It is also likely that they actually pursued more than just the censure of their recent conduct: they probably wanted to protect in the long run their prerogative as great Powers to make use of armed reprisals. As a matter of fact, when Salandra justified before the Council the bombardment and occupation of Corfu by way of reprisals against Greece, he said that "Italy, who has recently taken her place in world history, has merely followed illustrious examples [i.e. those

831 Fourteenth (Public) Meeting of the Council of the League, 18 September 1923: Ibid., 1313–1314, here quotation at 1314. Salandra referred to the first edition of Schücking and Wehberg's work. In the second edition published after the Corfu incident, the two German legal scholars did no longer support such a view. Cf. Schücking and Wehberg, *Die Satzung des Völkerbundes* (above, n. 769), 508–10.

832 Fourteenth (Public) Meeting of the Council of the League, 18 September 1923: League of Nations, Council, 'Twenty-Sixth Session of the Council. Held at Geneva from Friday, August 31st, to Saturday, September 29th, 1923.' (above, n. 816), 1316.

833 Cf. Hill, 'The Janina-Corfu Affair' (above, n. 814), 103; Ciriaque Georges Ténékidès, 'L'évolution de l'idée des mesures coercitives et la Société des Nations', *RDILC* 53 (1926), 398–418, at 402; Brownlie, *International Law and the Use of Force by States* (above, n. 45), 221.

834 But for a contrary view, see Manley O. Hudson, 'How the League of Nations Met the Corfu Crisis', *League of Nations* 6 (1923), 176–98, at 196–198.

835 Quincy Wright, 'Opinion of Commission of Jurists on Janina-Corfu Affair', *AJIL* 18 (1924), 536–44, at 538.

of France and Great Britain]."[836] More or less, he made explicitly the connection between the employment of armed reprisals and the status of great Power. Moreover, Mussolini instructed him to warn the French and British representatives in private against the consequences that the Council's enquiry into the case might bring about: the automatic submission to that organ of all the affairs involving national honour and prestige.[837] Mussolini's instruction meant that the great Powers should strive together to retain a privileged position within the League and prevent reprehension for their doings. Indeed, if the League could examine any case where a great Power made resort to armed reprisals, it would signify the end of their privilege.

836 Fourteenth (Public) Meeting of the Council of the League, 18 September 1923: League of Nations, Council, 'Twenty-Sixth Session of the Council. Held at Geneva from Friday, August 31st, to Saturday, September 29th, 1923.' (above, n. 816), 1314.
To justify the legality of the bombardment and occupation of Corfu, Italy rested its argumentation, i.a., on precedents. See Barros, *The Corfu incident of 1923* (above, n. 812), 101–2. This justification aimed perhaps to speak to the great Powers and to remind them of the privilege they had. But the reference to precedents predating the signature of the Covenant actually did not produce the effect expected on the Council because Italy failed to demonstrate that the League's charter did not make a clean slate of the old international law. Moreover, the mention by Italy of the U.S. occupation of Veracruz in 1914 irritated the United States that refused to see any parallel between that incident and the Italo-Greek conflict. See Ibid., 102 fn. 65. In juristic writings, the precedents were viewed as irrelevant on account of the new international situation. Even the U.S. international legal scholar Manley Ottmer Hudson, who regarded the settlement of the whole issue as a success on the part of the League though, wrote that "it is […] clear that the action was a jeopardizing of the peace of the world; *that the precedents antedating the establishment of the League did not justify it*; […]." (Hudson, 'How the League of Nations Met the Corfu Crisis' (above, n. 834), 185 (emphasis added)). See also Hill, 'The Janina-Corfu Affair' (above, n. 814), 98, calling for the repudiation of precedent in international affairs.

837 Barros, *The Corfu incident of 1923* (above, n. 812), 99f.

(c) Armed Reprisals Questioned

i) Interpretation of the Covenant by the Special Commission of Jurists

The incident had shown the loophole in the Covenant. In consequence, the Council unanimously resolved on 20 September 1923 to submit some controversial questions to a group of legal experts.[838] It, however, took some time before the members of the Council agreed on the phrasing of the questions as the Italian delegate did not consent to a wording referring even slightly to the Greco-Italian dispute.[839] A Committee of Jurists was then tasked to draft the questions. One of them —the question about the conformity of reprisals with the Covenant— was rephrased as follows:

> "IV. Are measures of coercion which are not meant to constitute acts of war consistent with the terms of Articles 12 to 15 of the Covenant when they are taken by one Member of the League of Nations against another Member of the League without prior recourse to the procedure laid down in these articles?"[840]

The wording did not raise any serious objection.[841] However, the members of the Council disagreed on whom should answer the questions. On the one hand, Great Britain and most of the small Powers wanted to submit the questions to the PCIJ for an advisory opinion which would enjoy high moral authority. On the other hand, Italy and France considered that the fourth question relating to reprisals was unsuitable for an examination by the PCIJ since the question was not entirely legal but actually contained a

838 Fifteenth (Public) Meeting of the Council of the League, 20 September 1923: League of Nations, Council, 'Twenty-Sixth Session of the Council. Held at Geneva from Friday, August 31st, to Saturday, September 29th, 1923.' (above, n. 816), 1317.

839 See Sixteenth (Private) Meeting of the Council of the League, 22 September 1923: Ibid., 1320–5. In the course of the discussion, Salandra explained that the acts of reprisals allowed were not listed and hence "all that international law has done is to classify the various attitudes taken up by States." (Ibid., 1324). However, Lord Cecil pointed out that a school of jurists challenged the legality of the coercive measures short of war (Ibid., 1323).

840 Eighteenth (Private) Meeting of the Council of the League, 26 September 1923: Ibid., 1328.

841 See Eighteenth (Private) Meeting of the Council of the League, 26 September 1923: Ibid., 1329–30.

significant amount of political character.[842] Thus, it was decided to submit all the questions to a Special Commission of Jurists.[843]

On 24 January 1924, this Commission communicated the replies. The answer to Question IV read:

> "Coercive measures which are not intended to constitute acts of war may or may not be consistent with the provisions of Articles 12 to 15 of the Covenant, and it is for the Council, when the dispute has been submitted to it, to decide immediately having due regard to all the circumstances of the case and to the nature of the measures adopted, whether it should recommend the maintenance or the withdrawal of such measures."[844]

---

842 See Eighteenth (Private) Meeting of the Council of the League, 26 September 1923: Ibid., 1330–2. Cf. Frances Kellor and Antonia Hatvany, *Security against war*, 2nd vol. (New York: The Macmillan Company, 1924), 637–639.

843 See Twentieth (Private) Meeting of the Council of the League, 27 September 1923: League of Nations, Council, 'Twenty-Sixth Session of the Council. Held at Geneva from Friday, August 31st, to Saturday, September 29th, 1923.' (above, n. 816), 1338–45; Twenty-Second (Private) Meeting of the Council of the League, 28 September 1923: Ibid., 1349–52. This Special Commission of Jurists was composed by Adatci (Japan), Lord Buckmaster (Great Britain), Buero (Uruguay), de Castelo Branco Clark (Brazil), Fromageot (France), van Hamel (Director of the Legal Section of the Secretariat of the League of Nations), Rolandi Ricci (Italy), Undén (Sweden), Marquis de Villaurrutia (Spain), De Visscher (Belgium).

844 Sixth (Public) Meeting of the Council of the League, 13 March 1924: League of Nations, Council, 'Twenty-Eight Session of the Council. Held at Geneva from Monday, March 10th, to Saturday, March 15th, 1924.', *LNOJ* 5 (1924), 495–744, at 524. Four other questions were asked about the application of Art. 15 of the Covenant and the responsibility of a State for a political crime. The Special Commission of Jurists gave the following answers: (1) The Council was not bound to examine whether a dispute submitted pursuant to Art. 15 was in fact "likely to lead to a rupture"; (2) Where a dispute was already referred to arbitration or judicial proceedings, the Council could not be seized; (3) Apart from Paragraph 8 of Art. 15, no exceptions could prevent the Council's examination of a dispute likely to lead to a rupture, not even the argument that the national honour or some vital interests were affected; (4) A State could be imputed the commission of a political crime within its national territory when it had failed to prosecute the culprits and had neglected to take the suitable preventive measures commensurate with the importance of the foreigner and the circumstances of his presence. See Sixth (Public) Meeting of the Council of the League, 13 March 1924: Ibid., 524. Regarding the latter answer to Question V, it is clear that when a State failed to its international obligations, it committed an international delinquency that justified the resort to reprisals. This was the only question that had nothing to do with the interpretation of the Covenant but

Although the Council adopted the replies unanimously, Branting and the Uruguayan representative on the Council (Alberto Guani) entered a reservation regarding the enigmatic answer to the fourth question. On behalf of their Government, they stated that they did not recognise the use of armed reprisals as being compatible with the Covenant.[845]

The answer of the Special Commission of Jurists to the fourth question was couched in puzzling terms which actually met Italy's expectations. Indeed, as the Greek lawyer Kuriakos Tenekidēs correctly stressed, the Commission did not condemn the resort to armed reprisals but left the Council a wide margin of appreciation to judge the lawfulness of coercive measures in relation to the Covenant, as far as they did not constitute acts of war. Still, the answer did not provide any relevant criterion to distinguish acts of war from coercive measures.[846] In addition to the examination of the legality of armed reprisals on a case-by-case basis, the Commission also recognised the competence of the Council to recommend the withdrawal or maintenance of such measures. This last aspect was a question of procedure mostly independent of the question of the compatibility of those measures short of war with the Covenant.[847]

---

dealt with a general principle of international law. See De Visscher, 'L'interprétation du pacte au lendemain du différend italo-grec' (above, n. 811), 388f. Strupp, who published in 1920 a study on international delinquency, entirely concurred with the Special Commission's answer on this point. See Karl Strupp, 'L'incident de Janina entre la Grèce et l'Italie', *RGDIP* 31 (1924), 255–84, at 280–1.

845 Sixth (Public) Meeting of the Council of the League, 13 March 1924: League of Nations, Council, 'Twenty-Eight Session of the Council. Held at Geneva from Monday, March 10th, to Saturday, March 15th, 1924.' (above, n. 844), 526. Guani who used to teach law at Montevideo expounded on his views in an article published in the *RGDIP*. Broadly similar to Politis's ideas, Guani also judged the recourse to military or naval force by way of reprisals as being tantamount to an act of war. See Guani, 'Les mesures de coercition entre membres de la Société des Nations envisagées spécialement au point de vue américain' (above, n. 802).

846 Ténékidès, 'L'évolution de l'idée des mesures coercitives et la Société des Nations' (above, n. 833), 403. Cf. Wright, 'Opinion of Commission of Jurists on Janina-Corfu Affair' (above, n. 835), 541–2, who believed that the coercive measures short of war could be legitimate under certain circumstances left to the appreciation of the Council. Nevertheless, Wright failed to provide the applicable criterion.

847 De Visscher, 'L'interprétation du pacte au lendemain du différend italo-grec' (above, n. 811), 388.

ii) Renewal of the Doctrinal Debate

International lawyers spoke out in large number against the sibylline answer to the fourth question, which entrusted a large discretionary power to the Council. Some even suspected that political considerations might have biased the answer of the Special Commission of Jurists.[848] For Petrascu, the answer of that Commission was evasive and transformed a question of principle into a matter dealt on a case-by-case basis. Under these circumstances, the fear that a State might take advantage of its close relationship with the Council to avoid condemnation for a resort to armed reprisals could not be allayed.[849] This observation was especially true as far as the great Powers were concerned since they were permanent members of the Council. So, the use of armed reprisals might actually remain unpunished when a great Power had recourse to them.

The answer to the fourth question was sharply criticised by one of the very own jurists of the said Commission. Indeed, Belgian international lawyer Charles De Visscher regarded as incomplete the first part of the answer because it did not provide the criterion for distinguishing between lawful and unlawful coercive measures short of war. Nevertheless, in his opinion, the employment of armed reprisals was, in every instance, hardly lawful. He argued in fact that the peaceful settlement procedure of Art. 12 to 15 had drastically restricted the *ius ad bellum*. In this context, armed reprisals were no longer a milder method than war to settle irreconcilable differences, and their use before the exhaustion of that procedure and the end of the moratorium would then amount to a violation of the Covenant. That is why he maintained that the criterion to apply could not be subjective —i.e., depending on the reprisal-taking State's *animus*— or contingent —i.e., whether the target country did not resist— but had to be purely objective. So, only the intrinsic nature of the acts had to be assessed. It was, thus, a question of principle which could not differ from case to case. Altogether, the Council had no power to declare lawful an act of armed reprisals.[850]

---

848 See, e.g., Schücking and Wehberg, *Die Satzung des Völkerbundes* (above, n. 769), 509.

849 Petrascu, *Les Mesures de Contrainte Internationale qui ne sont pas la Guerre entre États Membres de la Société des Nations* (above, n. 828), 188–90.

850 De Visscher, 'L'interprétation du pacte au lendemain du différend italo-grec' (above, n. 811), 377–88.

De Visscher's view should be regarded not as an authorised commentary but rather as a kind of separate opinion. Yet, the vast majority of legal scholars agreed with him that the use of armed reprisals was utterly incompatible with the Covenant and that a distinction between armed reprisals and acts of war on a subjective basis could only lead to abuses.[851] As a result, the view prevailed that armed reprisals should be assimilated to acts of war from a strictly objective standpoint devoid of subjective considerations.[852] A resort to military or naval force by way of reprisals should thus be treated as tantamount to war in the light of the League's charter.

The answer of the Special Commission of Jurists seemed to support such an interpretation as it was added that the Council ought "to decide immediately *having due regard* [...] *to the nature of the measures adopted*" whether the coercive measures short of war should be maintained or withdrawn. Although this part of the answer dealt with the expediency of the measures

851 Cf. Guani, 'Les mesures de coercition entre membres de la Société des Nations envisagées spécialement au point de vue américain' (above, n. 802); Politis, 'Les représailles entre Etats membres de la Société des Nations' (above, n. 19); Schücking and Wehberg, *Die Satzung des Völkerbundes* (above, n. 769), 508–10; Maccoby, 'Reprisals as a Measure of Redress Short of War' (above, n. 56), 71–3; Stéphan Ph. Nicoglou, *L'Affaire de Corfou et la Société des Nations*, Préface de M. Georges Scelle (Dijon: Libraire générale Félix Rey, F. Mettray et A. Dugrivel, 1925), 64–79, esp. 72–79; Hoijer, *Le Pacte de la Société des Nations* (above, n. 785), 218; André Nicolayévitch Mandelstam, 'La conciliation internationale d'après le Pacte et la jurisprudence du Conseil de la Société des Nations', *RdC* 14/IV (1926), 333–648, at 346–348; Ténékidès, 'L'évolution de l'idée des mesures coercitives et la Société des Nations' (above, n. 833), 410–2; Gonsiorowski, *Société des Nations et Problème de la Paix* (above, n. 778), 339–341; Petrascu, *Les Mesures de Contrainte Internationale qui ne sont pas la Guerre entre États Membres de la Société des Nations* (above, n. 828), 190.
Rafael Erich, international law professor at Helsinki and former Finnish Prime Minister, reached an analogous conclusion based on a broad interpretation of Art. 10 of the Covenant. This provision was for him the cornerstone of the League because it contained the ban on aggression and defined the protected interests of the Member States, namely their integrity and independence. Hence, the Council could not take into consideration the intent of the author of reprisals when one of these interests was affected. See Rafael Waldemar Erich, 'Quelques observations sur les mesures de coercition "pacifiques"', *RDI* 4 (1926), 16–9. Yet, according to Lowell, 'The Council of the League of Nations and Corfu' (above, n. 581), 171–2, the term 'aggression' in Art. 10 did not apply to acts of reprisals because nothing indicated that the framers of the Covenant meant to include them under this phrase.

852 Edouard Descamps, 'Le droit international nouveau. L'influence de la condamnation de la guerre sur l'évolution juridique internationale', *RdC* 31/I (1930), 399–559, at 518.

employed rather than their propriety, it strongly hints that the Council had to apply an objective test.[853]

It should be stressed that the authors did not necessarily condemn armed reprisals *per se* but merely their resort before the exhaustion of the remedies provided for in the Covenant and the moratorium of three months.[854] As a matter of fact, the Covenant did not outlaw war, but solely the early recourse to war. The same was true for armed reprisals.

Nevertheless, some authors challenged the opinion of the assimilation of armed reprisals to war because they claimed that the use of force was allowed in peacetime, too. Therefore, there was a clear-cut distinction to be drawn between these two activities, and the only criterion capable of keeping the demarcation unblurred was, in fact, the subjective test of *animus*. Indeed, British international lawyer Arnold McNair believed that, in the absence of *animus belligerendi* and a declaration of war, there was no state of war, unless the defendant State elected to regard the measures of reprisals as war. Yet, he understood the limits of this theory in the context of the Covenant. That is why McNair held the view that only the reprisal-taking State should be subject to the sanctions of the Covenant if the target country decided to resist forcibly. He also proposed amending the Covenant by substituting the term 'war' for the more general expression of 'recourse to force' used in the Drago-Porter Convention.[855]

853 Erich Kaufmann, 'Règles générales du droit de la paix', *RdC* 54/IV (1935), 313–620, at 583 fn. 1.

854 See, e.g., Hoijer, *La solution pacifique des litiges internationaux avant et depuis la Société des Nations* (above, n. 810), 430–1; Fauchille, *Traité de droit international public* (above, n. 728), 1st vol., Part. III, 696; Alfred Verdross, 'Règles générales du droit international de la paix', *RdC* 30/V (1929), 275–517, at 493–496.

855 McNair, 'The Legal Meaning of War, and the Relation of War to Reprisals' (above, n. 605), esp. 38–46. Cf. Cavaglieri, 'Règles générales du droit de la paix' (above, n. 459), 578–9; Scelle, 'Règles générales du droit de la paix' (above, n. 17), 677. Both authors also believed that armed reprisals could be differentiated from war by applying the subjective test. However, Cavaglieri used to defend in 1915 the opposite view, namely that armed reprisals were inherently acts of war and that the intent of the assailant State had no influence to define the action. See Arrigo Cavaglieri, 'Note critiche su la teoria dei mezzi coercitivi al difuori della guerra', *RivDirInt* 9 (1915), 23–49 & 305–342. Yet, his opinion shifted in the course of fourteen years because he considered that the subjective test of *animus* corresponded more precisely to international practice which permitted the use of coercion short of war as something compatible with a state of peace. Nevertheless, Scelle critically pointed out that strong Powers could easily pretext the absence of *animus belligerendi* to deny the existence of a state of war and thus take advantage of the fiction that peace was not broken.

Perhaps the most noteworthy opinion in this group was expressed by the prolific German international legal scholar Karl Strupp for whom a right to reprisals prevailed over the obligations imposed by the Covenant. Indeed, he explained that the resort to reprisals was the legitimate response of an aggrieved State to a wrongful act imputed to another country. For him, international delinquency justified derogation from Art. 10 of the Covenant. Moreover, he stressed that the resort to reprisals could not be conditional to the exhaustion of the procedure described in the Articles 12 and 15 because these provisions aimed, in his opinion, solely at the limitation of the recourse to war. The issue leading to some acts of reprisals could be referred anyway to the attention of the Council, but this did not justify any assimilation of armed reprisals to war. The answer of the Special Commission of Jurists to the fourth question should thus be read as asking whether the coercive measures short of war were justified or not by the right of reprisals —what would make them either licit or illicit.[856]

Still, with the notable exception of Strupp, lawyers mainly spoke with one voice against the resort to armed reprisals by way of derogation from the Covenant.

iii) Opinion of the Small Member States

Since the League's end was the preservation of peace, many Member States had believed until the Corfu incident that coercion was no longer allowed under the Covenant.[857] An author said: "With a League of Nations ready to inquire and adjudge in cases of grievance, there should be no reason why a large nation should be at liberty to resort to forcible measures of compulsion against a smaller one."[858] All the more so as the hegemons guaranteed the world peace.[859] However, the Corfu incident highlighted

856 Strupp, 'L'incident de Janina entre la Grèce et l'Italie' (above, n. 844), 280–4.

857 This was Politis's opinion before the Council when he said: "I thought that between Members of the League of Nations there was no longer any place for measures such as an ultimatum and coercion." (Sixth (Private) Meeting of the Council of the League, 1 September 1923: League of Nations, Council, 'Twenty-Sixth Session of the Council. Held at Geneva from Friday, August 31st, to Saturday, September 29th, 1923.' (above, n. 816), 1281).

858 Lowell, 'The Council of the League of Nations and Corfu' (above, n. 581), 174.

859 Hill, 'The Janina-Corfu Affair' (above, n. 814), 100.

the fact that the League's machinery did not apply to the great Powers in the same way as to the other Member States.[860]

The issue of the compatibility of armed reprisals with the Covenant was thus far more than just an academic topic. In fact, many minor countries expressed their concern and disapproval with the report of the Special Commission of Jurists. Faced with such an outcry, the Council was urged by the Assembly to invite all the Governments of Member States to send their criticisms.[861]

In the end, twenty-one Member States replied.[862] The split between great and small Powers was visible. On the one hand, the four permanent Members of the Council —Great Britain, France, Italy and Japan— did not present any observations; they unreservedly approved the Commission's answers.[863] On the other, twelve small Powers raised objections against the reply to the fourth question.[864] The number of replies and their extent, which sometimes took the form of a real memorandum, reveal that this aspect of the report was the most disputed and perhaps the most important for the Governments of small States, but arguably also for the future of the League.

The twelve Governments in question vehemently expressed their concern that considerations of expediency might govern the legality of coercive measures short of war because of the absence of standards which specified when measures of coercion short of war could be considered consistent with the Covenant. They feared that this lacuna might put them at risk of being abusively targeted by strong Powers. Thus, most of them unsur-

860 Cf. Ibid., 101.

861 Sixteenth (Public) Meeting of the Council of the League, 26 September 1925: League of Nations, Council, 'Thirty-Fifth Session of the Council. Held at Geneva from Wednesday September 2nd, to Monday, September 28th, 1925.', *LNOJ* 6 (1925), 1297–548, at 1393.

862 Most of them were European States, four American (Brazil, Cuba, Salvador, Uruguay), one African (South Africa) and one Asian (Siam).

863 For German international law scholar Erich Kaufmann, the approval by these nations —as well as Belgium, Brazil and Spain— was conclusive to raise the reply of the Special Commission of Jurists as a source of positive international law since they were the main actors in respect of coercion. See Kaufmann, 'Règles générales du droit de la paix' (above, n. 853), 583.

864 Viz. Denmark, Finland, Greece, Hungary, the Netherlands, Norway, Poland, Salvador, Siam, Sweden, Switzerland and Uruguay.

prisingly defended the inconsistency of the measures short of war with the letter and spirit of the Covenant.[865]

It was unprecedented that so many States simultaneously criticised the practice of armed reprisals with such severity.[866] Therefore, the Council could not turn a blind eye on the reactions of the Member States. It had a choice to make: either a new Committee should be appointed to formulate new answers, or the Council could simply take into consideration the replies of the Member States as a kind of guidance to read the answers of the Special Commission of Jurists. This latter option was preferred as the Japanese delegate specified that the Council had never intended to impose the Commission's answers as an authoritative statement of law.[867]

The Council, thus, succeeded in retaining a large margin of appreciation. The chief criticism of small States that the legality of coercive measures short of war could not be determined in advance due to the absence of criterion was not met at all by the Council. The Council was then free to choose between the subjective and the objective test in order to decide

865 See Annex 858: League of Nations, Council, 'Thirty-Eight (Extraordinary Meeting) and Thirty-Ninth Sessions of the Council. Held at Geneva on Friday, February 12th, 1926, at 3 p.m; and from Monday, March 8th, to Thursday, March 18th, 1926.', *LNOJ* 7 (1926), 491–642, at 597–612. In addition to the twelve Governments, the Polish Government also pointed out the deficiency of the answer of the Special Commission of Jurists to the fourth question on account of the absence of criteria. Yet, Poland considered that coercive measures involving armed force like the occupation of territory were not in itself incompatible with the Covenant. See the observations of the Polish Branch of the International Law Association, Annex 858: Ibid., 605.

866 Interestingly, around the same period, the adoption of a convention declaring the illegality of reprisals in peacetime was advocated, and the matter was even brought to the attention of the Council. See League of Nations, Permanent Secretariat, *Proposed Convention declaring the Illegality of Peace-Time Reprisals*, The President Secretary General of the International Federation of the League of Nations Societies, Brussels – Forward copy of a resolution adopted by the Representative Council of the International Federation of League of Nations Societies at Lausanne on 29 October drawing the attention of the League Council to the resolution adopted by the Federation in Warsaw in July 1925 recommending the drawing up of such a Convention (Geneva, 1925; <http://biblio-archive.unog.ch/detail.aspx?ID=224823>, accessed 13 November 2018). However, no such convention came to fruition.

867 Fifth (Public) Meeting of the Thirty-Ninth Session of the Council of the League, 17 March 1926: League of Nations, Council, 'Thirty-Eight (Extraordinary Meeting) and Thirty-Ninth Sessions of the Council. Held at Geneva on Friday, February 12th, 1926, at 3 p.m; and from Monday, March 8th, to Thursday, March 18th, 1926.' (above, n. 865), 519–20.

whether the resort to such measures amounted to a breach of the Covenant.[868] Moreover, the observations of small States had a non-binding character for the Council, which could thus assess freely on a case-by-case basis the compatibility of the measures employed with the Covenant.

As a result, the legal situation of armed reprisals in relation to the Covenant was not clarified at all despite the outcry against their use. This lacuna seemed to benefit the great Powers since they more than anyone else enjoyed a close relationship with the Council and could in this capacity persuade its members to waive the application of sanctions. This link obviously placed them in a privileged position in comparison to the other Member States.

3. The Spectre of Armed Reprisals Looming over the League

(a) The Greek-Bulgarian Incident, 1925

Following the Italian bombardment and occupation of Corfu, the League addressed the question of reprisals, but failed to lift a great deal of uncertainty regarding the resort to this measure in relation to the Covenant. In the years that followed, the opportunity to fill the lacuna was never to present itself again. And yet, the issue still remained highly relevant for the League as shown by the Greek-Bulgarian conflict of 1925 and the Japanese invasion and occupation of Manchuria in the early 1930s.

The former case occurred a bit more than a year after the settlement of the Italo-Greek conflict, during the period of time within which the Member States could communicate their observations on the report of the Special Commission of Jurists. On 22 October 1925, the Bulgarian Government appealed to the League following the outbreak of hostilities with Greece. Greek forces had invaded Bulgaria, taken control of several posts on the Bulgarian side of the frontier and even bombarded the town of Petrich. This military action was the consequence of a regrettable incident on the border between the two countries where a Greek sentry lost his life. Greece claimed the right to legitimate defence on account of a Bulgarian

868 Kotzsch, *The concept of war in contemporary history and international law* (above, n. 69), 160.

attack on Greek outposts.[869] However, in the light of the demands of the Greek Government, the whole operation can be viewed as partially having the character of reprisals, too. Indeed, Greece sent an ultimatum asking the Bulgarian Government for a formal apology, the punishment of those responsible and the payment of a large sum of money for redress.[870]

The Council immediately enjoined a ceasefire and the withdrawal of troops behind the respective national frontiers.[871] In private, the representatives of the great Powers contemplated the application of sanctions against Greece.[872] Nevertheless, both parties involved in the conflict complied with the Council's recommendation. A commission of enquiry was then set up by the Council to clarify the causes of the conflict and establish the responsibility of each Government.[873] This commission came to the conclusion that the responsibility was divided, but provided for substantial damages to be paid by Greece because of destructions and injuries resulting from the military invasion.[874]

Greece and Bulgaria approved the settlement. Yet, the Greek representative raised the question of the legitimacy of the coercive measures in the present case to compel the payment of reparations and force the withdrawal of the Bulgarian troops. Indeed, he contended that the resort to such

869 Cf. the telegrams sent by the Bulgarian and Greek Governments to the Secretary-General on 22 and 24 October 1925, read to the Council of the League, First (Public) Meeting, 26 October 1925: League of Nations, Council, 'Thirty-Sixth (Extraordinary) Session of the Council. Held at Paris from Monday October 26th, to Friday October 30th, 1925.', *LNOJ* 6 (1925), Part II, 1691–722, at 1696–1697; as well as the statement of the facts by Bulgarian representative Mr Marfoff and Greek representative Mr Carpanos at the Second (Public) Meeting of the Council of the League, 27 October 1925: Ibid., 1701–1704 and 1704–1706.

870 See Ténékidès, 'L'évolution de l'idée des mesures coercitives et la Société des Nations' (above, n. 833), 406.

871 See the First (Public) Meeting of the Council of the League, 26 October 1925: League of Nations, Council, 'Thirty-Sixth (Extraordinary) Session of the Council. Held at Paris from Monday October 26th, to Friday October 30th, 1925.' (above, n. 869), 1697–700.

872 James Barros, *The League of Nations and the Great Powers: The Greek-Bulgarian Incident, 1925* (Oxford: Clarendon Press, 1970), 78–81.

873 Fourth (Public) Meeting of the Council of the League, 29 October 1925: League of Nations, Council, 'Thirty-Sixth (Extraordinary) Session of the Council. Held at Paris from Monday October 26th, to Friday October 30th, 1925.' (above, n. 869), 1711–3.

874 See Annex 815: League of Nations, Council, 'Thirty-Seventh Session of the Council. Held at Geneva from Monday, December 7th, to Wednesday, December 16th, 1925.', *LNOJ* 7 (1926), 101–366, at 196–210.

measures had not been intended to constitute a violation of the Covenant.[875] Nevertheless, the Council confirmed the amount of the indemnity owed by Greece.[876]

While this affair presents parallels with the Corfu incident, there were also differences.[877] One of the most striking was the role played by the Council and the success of its intervention. Unlike in 1923, the executive body of the League did not tergiversate. It adopted recommendations at once and the application of Art. 16 of the Covenant was even on the table. In fact, the Council faced in this case neither serious legal and jurisdictional issues nor a question of high politics because only two small Member States were involved.[878]

But beyond that and most importantly, the Council did not display as much permissiveness towards the use of coercive measures short of war as at the time of the bombardment and occupation of Corfu. As a matter of fact, Greece was held responsible for the invasion of the Bulgarian territory and the shelling of Petrich, whereas, for the very same kind of violent acts, Italy did not suffer any consequences in 1923. Furthermore, the Council even adopted a report submitted by the representatives of Great Britain, Belgium and Japan, which laid down the principle that “where a territory is violated without sufficient cause, reparation is due, even if at the time of the occurrence it was believed by the party committing the act of violation that circumstances justified the action.”[879]

---

875 See the statement of Mr Rentis, First (Public) Meeting of the Council of the League, 7 December 1925: Ibid., 115.

876 Twelfth (Public) Meeting of the Council of the League, 14 December 1925: Ibid., 172–7.

877 For a comparison, see Ténékidès, ‘L'évolution de l'idée des mesures coercitives et la Société des Nations’ (above, n. 833), 408–10.

878 Walters, *A History of the League of Nations* (above, n. 767), 315. Cf. Schwarzenberger, *Power Politics* (above, n. 33), 363–9, who explained that the League of Nations was able to settle disputes between small States, providing that the great Powers mediated between the parties and the conflict was geographically close to them. But when these parameters were not met (e.g., the dispute between small States was not within their reach or two great Powers clashed), the League was powerless. As for conflicts like the Corfu incident between a great Power and a small one, the success of the League's action depended largely on the great Power's reasonableness and the attitude of the other great Powers.

879 Twelfth (Public) Meeting of the Council of the League, 14 December 1925: League of Nations, Council, ‘Thirty-Seventh Session of the Council. Held at Geneva from Monday, December 7th, to Wednesday, December 16th, 1925.’ (above, n. 874), 173. This statement of the Council was unmistakably related to the Treaty of Mutual Guaranteed recently signed at Locarno by Germany, Bel-

The Council's opinion was a clear condemnation of the use of force in peacetime, which some Member States saw as a reversal of jurisprudence.[880] Indeed, the Council seemed to have adopted the objective test in the present case. However, the answer of the Special Commission of Jurists to the fourth question allowed a case-by-case examination. So, it cannot be deduced that the Council ruled out the subjective test for good.[881]

---

gium, France, Great Britain and Italy. Indeed, Art. 2 of the said agreement provided that attacks, invasions or resorts to war were forbidden, with some exceptions though. Art. 3 contained too the undertaking to settle "by peaceful means" disputes "which it may not be possible to settle by the normal methods of diplomacy." (Locarno Treaty, 16 October 1925: League of Nations, Permanent Secretariat, *Publication of Treaties and International Engagements Registered with the Secretariat of the League of Nations* (LNTS 54; [Geneva]: [League of Nations], 1926–1927), 293). Thus, this treaty also had a restrictive effect on the resort to armed reprisals. Cf. Hans Wehberg, 'Le problème de la mise de la guerre hors la loi', *RdC* 24/IV (1928), 145–306, at 197; Müller, *Wandlungen im Repressalienrecht* (above, n. 21), 91–7.

880 In fact, the Greek and Swedish Governments stressed the departure of the Council from its previous attitude at the time of the Corfu incident in their reply to the Council's enquiry regarding the answers of the Special Commission of Jurists. They regarded it as evidence that the Council came around to the opinion of the incompatibility of the measures of coercion short of war with the provisions of the Covenant. See Annex 858: League of Nations, Council, 'Thirty-Eight (Extraordinary Meeting) and Thirty-Ninth Sessions of the Council. Held at Geneva on Friday, February 12th, 1926, at 3 p.m; and from Monday, March 8th, to Thursday, March 18th, 1926.' (above, n. 865), 600 and 607. T. P. Conwell-Evans, *The League Council in Action: A Study of the Methods employed by the Council of the League of Nations to prevent War and to settle International Disputes* (London: OUP, 1929), 89, concurred with the view that the experience of the Greco-Bulgarian conflict conferred from then on a narrow interpretation on the answer to the fourth question.

881 As a matter of fact, other bodies of the League still regarded the subjective criterion of *animus* as a valid test. For instance, the Secretary-General said about the coercive measures that the Member States could take under the sanctions Article of the Covenant: "It may be noted here that, from the legal point of view the existence of a state of war between two States depends upon their intention and not upon the nature of their acts. Accordingly measures of coercion, however drastic, which are not intended to create and are not regarded by the State to which they are applied as creating a state of war, do not legally establish a relation of war between the States concerned." (League of Nations, Secretary-General, 'Annex 964. Legal position arising from the enforcement in time of peace of the measures of economic pressure indicated in Article 16 of the Covenant, particularly by a maritime blockade. Report by the Secretary-General of the League submitted to the Council on June 15th, 1927' (above, n. 799), 834).

(b) Japan's Invasion of Chinese Manchuria

The Kellogg-Briand Pact of 1928 proclaimed the renunciation of war as an instrument of national policy (Art. 1) and enjoined the parties to settle their disputes solely through 'pacific means' (Art. 2).[882] However, peace was jeopardised again in the early 1930s.

In 1931, hostilities between Japan and China broke out in Manchuria.[883] Japanese troops marched into Manchuria in the night of 18 to 19 September 1931, attacked Chinese barracks and took control of the town of Mukden (now Shenyang). Japan justified the invasion by claiming self-defence as a result of the attack by Chinese fighters on a portion of train tracks be-

---

882 General Treaty for Renunciation of War as an Instrument of National Policy, 27 August 1928: League of Nations, Permanent Secretariat, *Publication of Treaties and International Engagements Registered with the Secretariat of the League of Nations* (LNTS 94; [Geneva]: [League of Nations], 1929), 63.
Most authors shared the view that while Art. 1 outlawed only war in the narrow sense, Art. 2 actually introduced a restriction of the use of armed reprisals. Cf. Axel Møller, 'The Briand-Kellogg Pact', *NordJIntLaw* 3 (1932), 94–107, at 95–98; Quincy Wright, 'When does war exist?', *AJIL* 26 (1932), 362–8, at 367–368; Müller, *Wandlungen im Repressalienrecht* (above, n. 21), 98–9; Quincy Wright, 'The Meaning of the Pact of Paris', *AJIL* 27 (1933), 39–61, at 52–53 and 55. German international lawyer Hans Wehberg, however, argued that the means of settlement referred to in Art. 2 were in fact *pacific* insofar as they did not *relate to war*. See Wehberg, 'Le problème de la mise de la guerre hors la loi' (above, n. 879), 258 fn. 2; and the concurring opinion of Pépy, 'Après les ratifications du Plan Young. Révision et Sanctions' (above, n. 23), 469–73. But cf. American Institute of International Law, 'Texts of Projects', *AJIL* 20/4 (1926), Supplement, 300–87, at 382–383; J. L. Brierly, 'International Law and Resort to Armed Force', *CLJ* 4 (1932), 308–19, at 314f.; Gottschalk, 'Die völkerrechtlichen Hauptprobleme des Mandschureikonflikts' (above, n. 74), 215–28. Still, Wehberg advocated that the outlawing of war should be accompanied concretely by the ban on measures involving military force in time of peace like the military occupations of territory (Wehberg, 'Le problème de la mise de la guerre hors la loi' (above, n. 879), 271–3).

883 The dispute between both countries in the region had deep roots. See Carl Walter Young, *Japan's Special Position in Manchuria: Its Assertion, Legal Interpretation and Present Meaning* (Japan's Jurisdiction and International Legal Position in Manchuria, 1; Baltimore: The Johns Hopkins Press, 1931); League of Nations, Commission of Enquiry into the Sino-Japanese Dispute, *Appeal by the Chinese Government: Report of the Commission of Enquiry* (Series of League of Nations Publications, VII. Political. 1932. VII. 12; [Geneva]: [s.n.], 1932), 13–61.

longing to a Japanese railway company.[884] That is why China made a formal appeal to the Council on 21 September, pursuant to Article 11 of the Covenant.[885]

The Commission of Enquiry set up by the Council submitted a report and concluded that the incident that night did not justify the Japanese military operations to be called measures of legitimate self-defence.[886] Indeed, the hostilities with China had continued to the point that Japan occupied the whole Manchuria and, as a consequence thereof, a new independent State called Manchukuo had been created.[887] However, because of the Council's indecisiveness, China asked for the transfer of the issue to the Assembly which quickly threw itself into the examination of the case wholeheartedly and ultimately adopted the report of the Commission of En-

---

884 See the Japanese statement of facts and plea: Ibid., 67–9; and Japanese Delegation to the League of Nations, *Japan's Case in the Sino-Japanese Dispute: As Presented Before the Special Session of the Assembly of the League of Nations. Geneva, 1933* ([s.l.]: [s.n.], [1933]), 11 and 43. On the Japanese international law discourse in the context of the Manchurian conflict, see further Urs Matthias Zachmann, *Völkerrechtsdenken und Außenpolitik in Japan, 1919–1960* (Studien zur Geschichte des Völkerrechts, 29; Baden-Baden: Nomos, 2013), 159–203.

885 League of Nations, Commission of Enquiry into the Sino-Japanese Dispute, *Appeal by the Chinese Government* (above, n. 883), 5. However, China imposed at the same time an economic boycott on Japanese trade by way of reprisals. This exacerbated the conflict. See League of Nations, Assembly, 'League of Nations Assembly Report on the Sino-Japanese Dispute', *AJIL* 27/3 (1933), Supplement: Official Documents, 119–53, at 145. About the legality of the measure, cf. Kenzo Takayanagi, 'On the Legality of the Chinese Boycott', *Pacific Affairs* 5 (1932), 855–62; Yuen-Li Liang, 'Some Legal Issues in the Sino-Japanese Controversy before the League Assembly.', *The China Law Review* 6 (1933), 213–24, at 220–224. The latter article was published in German too: Yuen-Li Liang, 'Rechtsprobleme des Mandschureikonflikts', *ZVölkR* 17 (1933), 1–12, at 8–12.

886 League of Nations, Commission of Enquiry into the Sino-Japanese Dispute, *Appeal by the Chinese Government* (above, n. 883), 6–10 and 71. See about the so-called Lytton report, Arthur K. Kuhn, 'The Lytton Report on the Manchurian Crisis', *AJIL* 27 (1933), 96–100.

887 League of Nations, Commission of Enquiry into the Sino-Japanese Dispute, *Appeal by the Chinese Government* (above, n. 883), 97. The creation of Japan's Manchurian puppet State was the event which prompted the U.S. Secretary of State Henry L. Stimson to lay down the principle of the non-recognition of territorial conquests —the so-called Stimson Doctrine. See thereupon Quincy Wright, 'The Stimson Note of January 7, 1932', *AJIL* 26 (1932), 342–8; David Turns, 'The Stimson Doctrine of Non-Recognition. Its Historical Genesis and Influence on Contemporary International Law', *Chinese JIL* 2 (2003), 105–43.

quiry, which caused the withdrawal of Japan from the League in March 1933.[888]

Japan's withdrawal represented a bitter failure for the League and heralded its end. In fact, the Council's reluctance to declare the existence of war in the Far East had weakened the League.[889] The confidence of many small Powers in the Covenant system had been shaken and led them to suspect that the Council and more precisely the great Powers had some sympathy with Japan's action.[890]

The conflict rekindled the issue around armed reprisals and more generally the use of force in peacetime.[891] Indeed, once again, the absence of formal war, i.e. in the legal or technical sense, prevented the application of sanctions against the Covenant-breaker.[892] Although the Japanese military operation in Manchuria was not an act of reprisals,[893] the employment of

888 See Walters, *A History of the League of Nations* (above, n. 767), 487–95.

889 See Elbridge Colby, 'Was There War in the East?', *GeoLJ* 21 (1932–1933), 315–26, at 323–326.

890 Walters, *A History of the League of Nations* (above, n. 767), 499.

891 On the question of the distinction between the use of force in time of peace and war, see, e.g., George Grafton Wilson, 'Use of Force and War', *AJIL* 26 (1932), 327–8; Kunz, *Kriegsrecht und Neutralitätsrecht* (above, n. 16), 7–11; Kappus, *Der völkerrechtliche Kriegsbegriff in seiner Abgrenzung gegenüber den militärischen Repressalien* (above, n. 16).

892 In fact, on the existence of war depended the automatic enforcement of Art. 16 of the Covenant. See Hersch Lauterpacht, '"Resort to War" and the Interpretation of the Covenant during the Manchurian Dispute', *AJIL* 28 (1934), 43–60, at 44–45. However, Japan avoided calling its action war and China refrained from declaring war lest it would be treated as being the Covenant-breaker. In addition, no third States openly considered that war had begun and made a declaration of neutrality. See Clyde Eagleton, 'The attempt to define war', *IntlConciliation* 15 (1933), 233–87, at 254–255. About the term 'aggression', see Quincy Wright, 'The Concept of Aggression in International Law', *AJIL* 29 (1935), 373–95. Nevertheless, the Lytton report strongly implied the existence of war: "It is a fact that, *without a declaration of war*, a large area of what was indisputably the Chinese territory has been forcibly seized and occupied by the armed forces of Japan [...]." (League of Nations, Commission of Enquiry into the Sino-Japanese Dispute, *Appeal by the Chinese Government* (above, n. 883), 127 (emphasis added)).

893 According to Crawford M. Bishop, the killing of Captain Nakamura by Chinese forces about 27 June 1931 might have justified the exercise of reprisals. Yet, not only did the Japanese action exceed mere reprisals, but also China acknowledged its responsibility for the crime and was willing to give redress without delay. See Crawford M. Bishop, 'International Law and the Manchurian Question', *GeoLJ* 21 (1932–1933), 306–14, at 308–310. Japan claimed instead to have acted in self-defence.

armed reprisals remained a dangerous method of waging war in disguise and thence evading the restrictions imposed by the Covenant and the Kellogg-Briand Pact.[894] In this context, the delegates of small States to the Assembly vigorously condemned the resort to armed force under the Covenant.[895]

Other conflicts around the same time also contributed to this general concern.[896] For example, in July 1932, the situation on the frontier between Bolivia and Paraguay in the strategic Chaco region worsened. Bolivian troops captured three Paraguayan frontier outposts by way of reprisals because of alleged Paraguayan attacks.[897] This event led to the outbreak of the Chaco War.[898]

---

894 Cf. Scelle, 'Règles générales du droit de la paix' (above, n. 17), 677; Kunz, *Kriegsrecht und Neutralitätsrecht* (above, n. 16), 8 fn. 37; Grewe, *Epochen der Völkerrechtsgeschichte* (above, n. 24), 735; Neff, *War and the Law of Nations* (above, n. 2), 296–7. See further Gottschalk, 'Die völkerrechtlichen Hauptprobleme des Mandschureikonflikts' (above, n. 74), 194–215.

895 See the statements of the delegates of Colombia, Sweden, Finland, Denmark, Switzerland, Czechoslovakia, Uruguay, Panama, Salvador, Haiti, Bolivia at the Second, Third, Fourth and Fifth Meetings of the General Commission, from 4 to 8 March 1932: League of Nations, Assembly, 'Records of the Special Session of the Assembly convened in virtue of Article 15 of the Covenant at the Request of the Chinese Government.', *LNOJ* (1932), Special Supplement No. 101, 1st vol., 48–50, 52–53, 55, 57, 66–67, 71–73 and 77. The great Powers, on the other hand, did not have the courage to challenge this view and hence remained silent. See Eagleton, 'The attempt to define war' (above, n. 892), 280.

896 The Leticia dispute between Peru and Colombia in 1932–1933 led to hostilities which were not justified as reprisals by either side. But see Kunz, *Kriegsrecht und Neutralitätsrecht* (above, n. 16), 8 fn. 34. Nevertheless, the absence of a declaration of war prior to the outbreak of the hostilities, the denial of the existence of a state of war by the parties involved and the failure of the League of Nations and other third States to qualify the conflict as war threw a veil of doubt over the reality of a clear-cut line demarcating peace from war. About the Leticia conflict, see L. H. Woolsey, 'The Leticia Dispute between Colombia and Peru', *AJIL* 27 (1933), 317–24; J.-M. Yepes, 'L'Affaire de Leticia entre la Colombie et le Pérou. Étude Historique et Juridique', *RDI* 11 (1933), 133–71.

897 Telegram from the Bolivian Government to the President-in-Office of the Council, 3 August 1932: League of Nations, Permanent Secretariat, 'Documentation concerning the Dispute between Bolivia and Paraguay', *LNOJ* 13 (1932), 1573–86, at 1578. Paraguayan representative Caballero de Bedoya, however, protested against this argumentation: "Private justice between States in the form of reprisals can hardly be justified, now the League of Nations exists, more particularly between two of its Members." (Sixth (Public) Meeting of the Council of the League, 3 February 1933: League of Nations, Council, 'Seventieth Session of the Council. Held at Geneva from Tuesday, January 24th, to Friday, Febru-

Those incidents provoked a reaction in legal doctrine. In fact, many authors contended that the use of force should be purely and simply identified with war, based on the objective test which erased the distinction between the two activities, for the sake of the provisions on the renunciation of war in the Covenant and the Kellogg-Briand Pact.[899] Even Strupp, who previously supported the subjective test of *animus*, rallied behind this view following the Sino-Japanese conflict in the Far East which made him realise that armed reprisals should be regarded as equivalent to the resort to war.[900]

---

ary 3rd, 1933.', *LNOJ* 14 (1933), 173–381, at 261). The same later declared: "In the present dispute, *Bolivia invaded our territory while carefully avoiding a declaration of war, upon the pretext of acts of armed coercion, reprisals and measures of military constraint carried out in time of peace*. These are illicit acts condemned by international law and, with still more reason, prohibited to the Members of the League. The Covenant has done away with this real international anarchy by withdrawing from the States the unusual right of taking justice into their own hands. *In order to bring that state of hypocrisy to an end, Paraguay had to declare war and thus she might once more appear, on a superficial examination, as the aggressor.*" (Fifth (Public) Meeting of the Council of the League, 20 January 1934: League of Nations, Council, 'Seventy-Eighth Session of the Council. (Part II). Held at Geneva from Monday January 15th, to Saturday, January 20th, 1934.', *LNOJ* 15 (1934), 237–71, at 248 (emphasis added)).

898 On the Chaco War, see Walther L. Bernecker and Florian B. Meister (eds.), *Der Kampf um die «grüne Hölle»: Quellen und Materialien zum Chaco-Krieg (1932–1935)*, unter Mitarbeit von Michael Herzig (Zürich: Chronos, 1993). See further Charles G. Fenwick, 'The Arms Embargo against Bolivia and Paraguay', *AJIL* 28 (1934), 534–8.

899 See Brierly, 'International Law and Resort to Armed Force' (above, n. 882), 314; John Fischer Williams, 'The Covenant of the League of Nations and War', *CLJ* 5 (1933), 1–21, at 14–17; Hindmarsh, 'Self-Help in Time of Peace' (above, n. 17), 325.

900 "Gerade der Ostasienkonflikt erleichtert eine Stellungnahme, ob unter der Herrschaft von Völkerbund und Kelloggpakt noch *kriegerische* (militärische) Repressalien als zulässig zu erachten sind. Unter *starker Ueberschätzung des Willens der in Betracht kommenden Staaten, der die Abgrenzung zwischen Krieg und Repressalie unzweifelhaft allein ermöglicht, habe ich bisher die kriegerischen Repressalien für zulässig angesehen. Ich vermag diese Auffassung nicht aufrechtzuerhalten: Das Kollektivinteresse und das Prinzip von Treu und Glauben erweisen sich heute als stärker*. Sie führen beide Gesamtinteresse der Staaten der Welt dahin, auch ohne daß ein besonderer neuer Rechtssatz notwendig wäre (so sehr er wünschenswert ist!), *Handlungen, die nach objektiven Gesichtspunkten als kriegerische erscheinen müssen* (wie dies unzweifelhaft im östlichen Konflikt der Fall ist), *als mit Geist und Inhalt von Völkerbunds- und Kelloggpakt unvereinbar und demgemäß als unzulässig erscheinen zu lassen*." (Karl Strupp, *Grundzüge des positiven Völkerrechts* (Der Staatsbürger: Sammlung zur Einführung in das öffentliche Recht, 2/3; 5th edn.,

However, the problem was chiefly terminological since the renunciation of war in the Covenant and the Kellogg-Briand Pact received a restricted interpretation. Indeed, the terms 'war' and 'resort to war' were understood as meaning war in the legal sense, viz. a state of war resulting from a declaration of war. This meaning then deprived these legal instruments of practically all value because armed reprisals and other *acts* of war fell outside their scope.[901] So, as U.S. law professor Clyde Eagleton rightly observed, either the existing rules should be amended by replacing the term 'war' by 'armed force', or it should be agreed on an enlarged and more precise definition of war. For him, the solution lied in the amendment of the existing treaties.[902]

On the other hand, Hersch Lauterpacht proposed a broader interpretation of 'resort to war' which he called "a constructive state of war". He, indeed, argued that the existence of a state of war could result not only from the express or implied *animus belligerendi* of the parties, but also from the recognition of belligerency by a third State. The blockade of Formosa in 1884 and the one of Venezuela in 1902–1903 were evidence in favour of this interpretation which, he believed, reconciled the letter of the Covenant with its spirit, without proceeding to an unwarranted extension of the meaning of the League's charter.[903]

Bonn/Köln: Ludwig Röhrscheid, 1932), 200 (emphasis in original)). See also Karl Strupp, 'Les règles générales du droit de la paix', *RdC* 47/I (1934), 263–595, at 571–572.

901 Cf. Edwin Montefiore Borchard, '"War" and "Peace"', *AJIL* 27 (1933), 114–7; Eagleton, 'The attempt to define war' (above, n. 892).

902 Ibid., 286–7. See also the similar opinion of the representative of El Salvador at the Fifth Meeting of the General Commission, 8 March 1932: League of Nations, Assembly, 'Records of the Special Session of the Assembly convened in virtue of Article 15 of the Covenant at the Request of the Chinese Government.' (above, n. 895), 1st vol., 71.

903 Lauterpacht, '"Resort to War" and the Interpretation of the Covenant during the Manchurian Dispute' (above, n. 892), esp. 51–55. Cf. Wright, 'When does war exist?' (above, n. 882); Eagleton, 'The attempt to define war' (above, n. 892), 265–273 and 283. However, reprisals could normally not affect third States at all, unlike war. See Cavaglieri, 'Règles générales du droit de la paix' (above, n. 459), 578–81.

IV. Involvement of the Institute of International Law

1. Session of Paris, 1934

Following the reopening of the discussion of the use of force in peacetime so much at an inter-state level as in legal doctrine, the Institute of International Law resolved to examine the compatibility of reprisals within the current international law and to determine the applicable rules as well as the *lex ferenda* on this topic.[904] Politis was appointed rapporteur to this end and the results of the preparatory work by the fourth commission were presented to the Institute at the session of Paris which took place in mid-October 1934.[905]

In a draft resolution, the fourth commission expressed the opinion that there was an urgent need to adapt the legal regime of reprisals to the new international state of affairs. Indeed, it pointed out that, while the resort to reprisals had in the past been justified by the deficiencies of international law and the absence of organisation of the international community, the recent improvements in the peaceful settlement of disputes and the limitation of war had made reprisals mostly undesirable.[906] Therefore, the commission submitted a draft regulation which aimed to fill the existing lacuna in international law and thereby prevent the arbitrariness of Governments.[907]

Articles 1 and 2 of the draft dealt with the scope. The first provision defined reprisals as illegal measures decided and taken by a State, yet exceptionally permitted in response to wrongful acts committed against it by another State, for the purpose of compelling the latter to return to legality. This return to legality could take the form of either reparation or the cessa-

---

904 Politis's preliminary report: Institut de Droit International (ed.), *Session de Paris, Octobre 1934* (above, n. 5), 23. But cf. "Der Jurist kann aber nur das geltende Recht darstellen, sowie kritisch auf Schwächen hinweisen; es ist aber nicht seines Amtes, noch steht es in seiner Macht, das Recht zu verbessern." (Kunz, *Kriegsrecht und Neutralitätsrecht* (above, n. 16), 11).

905 See Politis's preliminary report and questionnaire as well as the proposal of drafts and the responses of all the members of the fourth commission in Annexes I and II: Institut de Droit International (ed.), *Session de Paris, Octobre 1934* (above, n. 5), 23–161. That commission was formed by Sir Thomas Barclay, Maurice Bourquin, Yves de la Brière, Jacques-Louis-Eugène Dumas, Rafael Erich, Herbert Kraus, André Mandelstam, Henri Rolin, Karl Strupp, Östen Undén, Charles De Visscher, Bohdan Winiarski.

906 See Ibid., 3–6.

907 Concluding observation in Politis's report: Ibid., 22.

tion of the illegal conduct. As for Art. 2, it distinguished reprisals from other coercive measures like retorsion or self-defence.[908] In plenary session, the Institute adopted, after a long discussion, a slightly modified definition which removed the impression that reprisals were intended as acts of revenge, by substituting "respect for law" for the phrase "return to legality". Regarding the second Article, the Institute did not touch on the substance of the provision. It merely revised the form and added the international sanctions to the list of measures distinct from reprisals.[909]

Articles 3 to 5 can be regarded as forming the crux of the draft regulation. Indeed, Art. 4 forbade the resort to armed reprisals in the same conditions as war. According to the foregoing provision (Art. 3), armed reprisals were, unlike non-forcible reprisals, those which involved the use of force in any form whatsoever. Of course, Art. 4 did not contain a total ban on the resort to armed reprisals. Nevertheless, by making them subject to the same limitations as war and without making it necessary to list all the exceptions authorising them, the fourth commission hoped that States would judge the prohibition acceptable. Finally, Art. 5 made the general resort to reprisals, i.e. both armed and non-forcible reprisals, depend upon the failure of the peaceful means of dispute settlement. So, reprisals could not be employed unless no peaceful remedies remained available.[910]

The examination of Art. 3 by the Institute in plenary session gave rise to a discussion on the substance and the form of this provision. On the one hand, Greek jurist Stelio Seferiades contended that armed reprisals should not be merely assimilated with war but instead fully identified with it from a legal point of view. Indeed, since armed reprisals were in effect acts of war, they should then be assessed objectively. On the other hand, the members of the Institute disagreed with him and argued that a distinction actually existed between the two activities. War, in fact, aimed to bend another State to one's will through the destruction of its military forces while armed reprisals had a limited object, namely to coerce the target country into respecting the law. That is why the use of armed reprisals did not interrupt the diplomatic relations unlike war and thus pertained to a state of

908 See the commented draft regulation for both provisions: Ibid., 6–13.

909 See the minutes of the plenary session regarding Articles 1 and 2: Ibid., 629–58. The members of the Institute, however, stumbled over the distinction between reprisals and self-defence.

910 Ibid., 13–9.

peace. Furthermore, as Politis pointed out, no State would adhere to the regulation of the Institute if armed reprisals were identified to war.[911]

Apart from that, many members of the Institute questioned the definition of armed reprisals in Art. 3 as being too vague. So, suggestions were made to replace the expression "resort to force in any form whatsoever" with something such as "resort to violence", "resort to an act of war" or "resort to military means". Yet, Politis disagreed with these amendments and maintained instead that the phrase "resort to force" should be kept in order to harmonise the Institute's regulation with the other international texts like the joint declaration of 11 December 1932 where France, Great Britain, Germany and Italy reaffirmed that "they will in no circumstance attempt to resolve any present or future differences between the signatories by resort to force."[912] As he explained further, the term "resort to force" did not include the measures of police taken within a State's territory, e.g. forced eviction. Indeed, armed reprisals referred only to the use of "military, naval or aerial" force by a State against another State.[913]

---

911 Ibid., 659–62. About Seferiades, see Thomas Skouteris, 'The Vocabulary of Progress in Interwar International Law. An Intellectual Portrait of Stelios Seferiades', *EJIL* 16 (2006), 823–56.

912 Art. 3: United States, Department of State, *Papers Relating to the Foreign Relations of the United States: The Paris Peace Conference, 1919*, 13th vol. (Washington: U.S. GPO, 1947), 311. It is noteworthy that at the Conference for the Reduction and Limitation of Armaments held at Geneva several States wanted this declaration to be declared a universal principle, i.e. not limited to European States. Yet, Great Britain took a firm stand against such extension. See Acting Chairman of the American Delegation (Gibson) to the Secretary of State, 15 February and 2 March 1933: United States, Department of State, *Foreign Relations of the United States: Diplomatic Papers, 1933*, 1st vol. (Washington: U.S. GPO, 1950), 14–16 and 21. But when U.S. President Franklin D. Roosevelt promoted the adoption of a pact of non-aggression forbidding the use of armed force beyond the national boundaries the British Government worried that the sending of ships for the protection of British nationals abroad might from now on be interpreted as an aggression. See President Roosevelt's message to Various Chiefs of State, 16 May 1933: Ibid., 145; Chairman of the American Delegation (Davis) to the Secretary of State, 30 May 1933: Ibid., 175–6; Great Britain, H.M. Government, *Cabinet 38 (33). Conclusions of a Meeting of the Cabinet held at 10 Downing Street, on Wednesday, 31st May, 1933, at 11.0 a.m.* (1933; <http://filestore.nationalarchives.gov.uk/>, accessed 8 January 2019), at 141 and 145. The British reaction confirms that Great Britain regarded the use of force in peacetime as a great Power's privilege.

913 Institut de Droit International (ed.), *Session de Paris, Octobre 1934* (above, n. 5), 662–7.

After the adoption of the definition of armed reprisals, the fourth Article prohibiting their resort under the same conditions as war was voted without difficulty.[914] It was the central provision of the regulation.[915]

As to Article 5, a member of the Institute expressed concern that a State might claim the impossibility of reaching a settlement through peaceful means in order to resort to reprisals. Therefore, a new wording which had the merit of laying the onus of proof on the complaining State was proposed by Henri Rolin and adopted by the Institute.[916]

The draft regulation consisted of four more provisions which were passed with few modifications.[917] Article 6 laid down six conditions for reprisals to be lawful: (a) a final demand must be made to the wrongdoing State; (b) reprisals must be proportionate to the wrong; (c) the rights of third States and individuals must be spared as much as possible; (d) the laws of humanity and the dictates of public conscience must be respected; (e) the object of reprisals could not change during their employment; (f) reprisals must end as soon as the goal is achieved.[918]

Article 7 permitted the use of counter-reprisals only in the event of a breach of Art. 6 and providing the requirements enumerated in that provision were observed.[919]

---

914 Ibid., 667–8. At its thirty-eight conference held at Budapest a month earlier, the International Law Association agreed on an interpretation of the Kellogg-Briand Pact which condemned the resort to armed force for the settlement of issues: "Whereas by their participation in the Pact sixty-three States have abolished the conception of war as a legitimate means of exercising pressure on another State in the pursuit of national policy and have also renounced any recourse to armed force for the solution of international disputes:— […] (2) A signatory State which threatens to resort to armed force for the solution of an international dispute or conflict is guilty of a violation of the Pact." (International Law Association (ed.), *Report of the Thirty-Eighth Conference held at Budapest in the Hungarian Academy of Science, September 6th to 10th, 1934*, 38th vol. (London/Reading: The Eastern Press, 1935), 67). That is why German lawyer Walter Simons pointed out that Article 4 of the draft resolution was in line with the text of the International Law Association.

915 Institut de Droit International (ed.), *Session de Paris, Octobre 1934* (above, n. 5), 683.

916 Ibid., 668–75.

917 Ibid., 675–92.

918 Ibid., 19–20.

919 Ibid., 20–1. Cf. Verdross, 'Règles générales du droit international de la paix' (above, n. 854), 492–3.

Article 8 placed the use of reprisals under the supervision of the international community or the League of Nations when the issue involved Member States.[920] This article was viewed as a progressive step forward because it declared the use of reprisals a matter of international public order in the same way as war since the Kellogg-Briand Pact. For Politis, this provision was consistent with the evolution of international law of the last two decades.[921]

Finally, Article 9 stipulated that the Permanent Court of International Justice was competent to interpret the regulation unless the interested parties agreed to submit this interpretation to an arbitral tribunal.[922]

The resolution and regulation were passed by a clear majority of 53 in favour, 3 against and 6 abstentions.[923] It was the first time in a century and a half at least that a legal text which substantially restricted the employment of armed reprisals was adopted. This result was made possible mainly thanks to the rapporteur Politis who during the whole debate was a leading figure and refused amendments which might have diminished or altered the significance of the regulation.

2. Criticisms

The assimilation of armed reprisals with war when it came to their legality was, without doubt, the greatest success of the Institute's regulation. In 1935, in a contribution in a book honouring the Belgian international legal scholar Ernest Mahaim who presided the session of Paris, Strupp applauded the solution reached by the Institute as the only one in compliance with international morality, good faith and the spirit of both the Covenant of the League of Nations and the Kellogg-Briand Pact. He believed that this regulation would likely put an end to abuses and the

920 Institut de Droit International (ed.), *Session de Paris, Octobre 1934* (above, n. 5), 21–2.

921 See Ibid., 683–90. About Art. 8, Politis drew the attention of the Institute to Francisco de Vitoria who recognised for the subjects of a monarch the right to disobey him if the Sovereign decided to wage an unjust and unlawful war. For Politis, "[c]'est aller très loin, à une époque où le devoir d'obéissance des sujets envers leur souverain était entendu d'une manière particulièrement stricte. C'est aller beaucoup moins loin aujourd'hui que de demander à l'Institut de consacrer l'idée d'un contrôle international sur l'exercice des représailles." (Ibid., 689).

922 Ibid., 22.

923 Ibid., 694.

hypocrisy of States which were too frequent when armed reprisals were involved.[924]

However, not all of the authors shared this optimism. Right before the Institute put the regulation to the vote, Politis's fellow countryman Michel Stavro Kebedgy announced his abstention because it would be evincing too much optimism to believe that States would voluntarily abide by the law. He believed, indeed, that States followed their own interests and so would depart from the adopted rules while others would simply turn a blind eye on the latter's action. So, because of this persistent mentality, a detailed regulation of peacetime reprisals was for him as vain as any attempt to limit the right to use force.[925]

Kebedgy's opinion was shared by Thomas Baty, who also abstained. In an article ominously called 'The Threatened Chaos in the Law of Nations', he looked with apprehension at the recent innovations in the field of international law. He argued that in time of nationalism (when the existence and authority of international law were constantly questioned), legal scholars should proclaim the accepted principles rather than imply that no law existed at all. He illustrated his view with the IIL's regulation on reprisals. Indeed, he regarded armed reprisals as being (1) absurd since they blurred the line between war and peace, (2) dangerous because they encouraged States to resort to violence in dubious cases, and (3) unjust as strong Powers always exercised them against weaker nations. That is why he criticised the Institute for not having identified armed reprisals with war. He contended that the regulation of the Institute actually recognised armed reprisals, e.g. in the form of a bombardment or occupation of territories, as compatible with a state of peace, instead of reaffirming the sacred principle of territorial integrity of States.[926]

924 Strupp, 'Problèmes actuels du droit des représailles' (above, n. 1), 346–51.

925 Institut de Droit International (ed.), *Session de Paris, Octobre 1934* (above, n. 5), 693.

926 Thomas Baty, 'The Threatened Chaos in the Law of Nations', *The Contemporary Review* 148 (1935), 65–71. He believed that these innovations were doomed to be futile for "Every chancery in the world will make short work of these elaborate regulations, and the only consequence will be a demonstration of how far academic opinion is out of touch with reality." (Ibid., 67). But the fact that the Institute adopted a regulation which somehow approved armed reprisals really concerned him: "That an academic body of the highest distinction should unanimously accept a doctrine which leads straight to international anarchy is a disturbing sign of the times." (Ibid., 70). About Baty's opinion that the use of force against a State in breach of the principle of territorial integrity was inconsistent with a state of peace, see Thomas Baty, 'Abuse of Terms: "Recognition": "War"',

Baty's harsh criticism may be questionable. However, he was not alone to express disapproval of the rules adopted by the Institute which still permitted —in narrowly limited cases— the resort to armed reprisals. Others also called for the outright ban on armed reprisals.

Seferiades was one of those radical international lawyers who defended the identification of armed reprisals and war. In an article clarifying his opinion on the issue, he pointed out that several legal scholars, including Politis at the time of the Italian occupation of Corfu,[927] supported the same view. Yet, the regulation of the Institute confirmed the existence of a legal distinction between the two activities. It just assimilated armed reprisals to war as to the sanctions. This result meant that armed reprisals remained an available remedy falling short of war, i.e. being governed by the law of peace. The *ius in bello* did not then apply. Consequently, the inhabitants who would spontaneously take up arms to resist the occupation by way of reprisals of their territory could not be treated as belligerents in accordance with Article 2 of the Annexe to the Fourth Hague Convention respecting the Laws and Customs of War on Land. A bombardment by way of reprisals would likewise evade the provisions of the Fourth and Ninth Hague Conventions.

Another aspect that Seferiades developed was the absence of criteria enabling the distinction of armed reprisals from war. He stressed, for instance, that the diplomatic relations were not necessarily severed following the outbreak of war, whereas they are sometimes interrupted even in time of peace. Furthermore, he remarked that neither the goal of reprisals, viz. the return to respect for the law, nor their limited scope could serve to differentiate armed reprisals from war. On the one hand, the goal of both reprisals and a 'just' war was appreciated subjectively as being legitimate by the State resorting to the measure. On the other hand, the scope of armed reprisals could be said to be limited insofar as the target country was weaker than the reprisal-taking country and had then no choice but to capitulate when facing the latter's military. Nevertheless, as Seferiades observed, this was no legal criterion. So, he contended that no party to the conflict could characterise the measures as being of the nature of reprisals.

AJIL 30 (1936), 377–99, at 395–397 and more largely 381–397. Cf. Thomas Baty, 'Danger-Signals in International Law', *YaleLJ* 34 (1925), 457–79.

927 Politis wrote in 1924 that "Il est donc impossible de nier que les représailles violentes constituent incontestablement des actes de guerre". (Politis, 'Les représailles entre Etats membres de la Société des Nations' (above, n. 19), 14).

Otherwise, it would be (1) arbitrary;[928] (2) anti-legal since only the strong Powers could claim that the measures did not amount to war; and (3) dangerous that violent actions, thus, might evade the laws of war.

For all these reasons, the identification of armed reprisals and war was, in his opinion, the only acceptable solution. That is why he disapproved the IIL's Paris regulation, although he voted in favour of its adoption in 1934. He pointed out that the mission of the Institute as an independent scientific body consisted primarily of figuring out the *ius condendum* and formulating the principles corresponding to the legal conscience of the civilised world.[929]

However, while part of the legal scholars condemned what they regarded as the shortfall of the regulation, some States deemed the rules of the Institute too far-reaching because armed reprisals were assimilated with war. Indeed, the legal department of the French Ministry of Foreign Affairs maintained that the resolution of the IIL was no statement of current international law, and considered instead the answer of the Special Commission of Jurists to the fourth question at the time of the Corfu incident as the only valid rule of law, namely that measures short of war "may or may not" be consistent with the Covenant. Therefore, the note concluded the question of the illegality of armed reprisals as follows:

> "En fin de compte, on n'est pas sur un terrain très solide pour soutenir que les représailles armées sont toujours illicites…"[930]

This opinion might actually have been shared by the Governments of the other main reprisal-taking Powers. It evidences anyway the deep gulf existing between legal doctrine and State practice on such a subject: while the legal community hoped to fill a great lacuna in international law, the great Powers strove to retain the right to resort to armed reprisals.

---

928 Cf. "The legal designation applied by one or other of the interested Parties to the act in dispute is irrelevant […]." (Permanent Court of International Justice, *Case concerning certain German interests in Polish Upper Silesia (The Merits)*, judgement of 25 May 1926, Collection of Judgments. Publications of the Permanent Court of International Justice (1926), Series A – No. 7, at 22).

929 Stelio Sériadès, 'La question des représailles armées en temps de paix, en l'état actuel du droit des gens', *RDILC* 63 (1936), 138–64.

930 Note of 4 June 1937, reproduced in Alexandre-Charles Kiss, *Répertoire de la pratique française en matière de droit international public*, 6th vol. (Paris: Éditions du Centre National de la Recherche Scientifique, 1969), 9.

V. Epilogue

1. An Insoluble Issue?

On the eve of WWII, the employment of armed reprisals remained largely unrestricted in international law in spite of all the efforts of the legal community and many Governments of small States that tried to limit it or even ban it. Indeed, some lawyers still continued to regard reprisals as a legitimate measure of self-help.[931] Furthermore, the Institute's regulation did not put an end to armed reprisals in State practice. When, e.g., on 29 May 1937 —in the midst of the Spanish Civil War— Republican Spain launched an air raid against the German cruiser *Deutschland*, German warships shelled the Spanish port of Almería by way of so-called reprisals.[932] Nevertheless, this action should be instead categorised as an act of war, notwithstanding the absence of war between the two countries. In fact, it may be recalled that Germany did not recognise the Spanish Republican Government[933] and got involved in the Spanish Civil War since the early stages of the conflict in support of Franco's faction, which led to the infamous bombing of Guernica on 26 April 1937, just a month before the shelling of Almería.

The differentiation between pacific measures and acts of war was, indeed, quite delicate in the interwar period. For the German legal scholar Carl Schmitt, this ensued from the existence of an intermediate state between peace and war since the Versailles Peace Conference, whereas both concepts traditionally used to mutually exclude each other. So, what did not constitute war belonged to peace and vice versa, except for some rare anomalous situations lying halfway between war and peace like Thomas E. Holland's concept of 'war *sub modo*'. However, after WWI, the Allied Pow-

931 See, e.g., J.-P.-A. François, 'Règles générales du droit de la paix', *RdC* 66/IV (1938), 5–294, at 252–255.

932 See Mr Juan Negrín, Third (Private, then Public) Meeting of the Ninety-Eighth Session of the Council of the League, 16 September 1937: League of Nations, Council, 'Ninety-Eighth and Ninety-Ninth Sessions of the Council. Held at Geneva from Friday, September 10th, to Thursday, September 16th, 1937; and from Wednesday, September 29th, to Tuesday, October 5th, 1937.', *LNOJ* 18 (1937), 877–1324, at 914; Viktor Böhmert, 'Die Beschießung des befestigten Hafens Almeria, eine gerechte Selbsthilfemaßnahme', *ZVölkR* 21 (1937), 297–307; Brownlie, *International Law and the Use of Force by States* (above, n. 45), 222; Grewe, *Epochen der Völkerrechtsgeschichte* (above, n. 24), 735.

933 Brownlie, *International Law and the Use of Force by States* (above, n. 45), 222 fn. 1.

ers wishing to continue the war through other means drew up legal documents as the Peace Treaty of 1919, the Covenant of the League of Nations and the Kellogg-Briand Pact which provided them with a flexible legal basis to decide case-by-case if war or peace was involved. The result was the institutionalisation of an intermediate state where non-military acts like propaganda could achieve a high degree of hostility while, conversely, the *animus belligerendi* of some military acts could be denied. And yet, paradoxically, only the subjective test was really relevant to separate war from peace. Schmitt, thus, argued that such an intermediate state created chaos in international law because it emptied the fundamental concept of peace of any meaning. Therefore, he regarded the abrogation of the Peace of Versailles and its replacement with a new order genuinely dedicated to peace as the only way to get rid of that *status mixtus*.[934]

Schmitt appeared to have correctly understood the problem posed by armed reprisals as an act of force compatible with a state of peace. However, although he identified the existence of a legal lacuna in that regard, his response to the issue was manifestly inadequate.

The question of armed reprisals passed in the interwar years from trifling to extremely sensitive. As a result, the problem could not simply be removed by the adoption of a regulation by an academic body, even as prominent as the Institute of International Law might have been. It required a legal text. Nevertheless, right before the beginning of WWII, no solution appeared to efficiently address the burning issue of the resort to armed reprisals. In this sense, the epoch of the League of Nations can rightly be regarded as a period of transition.[935]

2. Prohibition of the Use of Force under the UN-Charter

This legal text finally came in 1945 in the form of the unambiguous ban on the use of any kind of force in peacetime. Article 2 Para. 4 of the UN-Charter —called by Judge Nabil Elaraby "the most important principle in

934 Schmitt, '„Inter pacem et bellum nihil medium"' (above, n. 33).

935 Cf. Politis, 'Les représailles entre Etats membres de la Société des Nations' (above, n. 19), 16; Gottschalk, 'Die völkerrechtlichen Hauptprobleme des Mandschureikonflikts' (above, n. 74), 209f.; Kotzsch, *The concept of war in contemporary history and international law* (above, n. 69), 162; Paddeu, *Justification and Excuse in International Law* (above, n. 5), 238–44.

contemporary international law to govern inter-State conduct" and "the cornerstone of the Charter"[936]— reads:

> "All Members shall refrain in their international relations from the threat or use of force against the territorial integrity or political independence of any state, or in any other manner inconsistent with the Purposes of the United Nations."

During the drafting of the Charter, no express reference was made to armed reprisals.[937] Nevertheless, the provision was drafted with the apparent intention of precluding any resort to force in time of peace.[938] That is why the view prevails in legal doctrine that the unilateral use or threat of armed reprisals is prohibited under this Article.[939] Indeed, the "peaceful

---

936 Dissenting Opinion of Judge Elaraby, International Court of Justice, *Oil Platforms (Islamic Republic of Iran v. United States of America)*, Judgement of 6 November 2003, I.C.J. Reports (2003), 290–305, at 291, Para. 1.1.

937 Shane Darcy, 'Retaliation and reprisal', in Marc Weller, Alexia Solomou and Jake William Rylatt (eds.), *The Oxford Handbook of the Use of Force in International Law* (Oxford handbooks; Oxford: OUP, 2015), 879–96, at 887.

938 See the statement of the Delegate of the United States during the Conference at San Francisco in 1945: "The intention of the authors of the original text was to state in the broadest terms as an absolute all-inclusive prohibition; the phrase "or in other manner" was designed to insure that there should be no loopholes." (Summary Report of Eleventh Meeting of Committee I/1, 4 June 1945, Doc. 784, I/1/27: United Nations, *Documents of the United Nations Conference on International Organization, San Francisco, 1945*, 6th vol. (London/New York: United Nations Information Organizations, 1945–1955), 335).

939 See, i.a., Philip C. Jessup, 'Force under a Modern Law of Nations', *ForeignAff* 25 (1946), 90–105, at 101; Philip C. Jessup, *A modern law of nations: An introduction* (New York: The Macmillan Company, 1948), 175; C. H. M. Waldock, 'The regulation of the use of force by individual States in international law', *RdC* 81 (1952), 451–517, at 493; Delbez, *La notion de guerre* (above, n. 46), 99; De Visscher, *Théories et réalités en droit international public* (above, n. 39), 350; Paul Guggenheim, *Traité de Droit international public*, avec la collaboration de Denise Bindschedler-Robert, 2nd vol. (Genève: Librairie de l'Université, Georg & Cie, 1954), 91; Stone, *Legal controls of International Conflict* (above, n. 58), 286–7; Kotzsch, *The concept of war in contemporary history and international law* (above, n. 69), 270; Derek William Bowett, *Self-defence in international law* (Manchester: Manchester University Press, 1958), 13 and 99; Constantine John Colombos, *The international law of the sea* (4th edn., London: Longmans, 1959), 409; Partsch, 'Repressalie' (above, n. 62), 104; Rosalyn Higgins, 'The Legal Limits to the Use of Force by Sovereign States United Nations Practice', *BYIL* 37 (1961), 269–319, at 314; Brownlie, *International Law and the Use of Force by States* (above, n. 45), 223 and 281; Kalshoven, *Belligerent Reprisals* (above, n. 9), 6–7; Falcon,

means" of dispute settlement, mentioned in Art. 2(3), do not seem to cover armed reprisals.[940]

The UN-Charter has successfully avoided making the same mistake as the Covenant of the League of Nations, which almost exclusively focused on war and, thus, left a gap in favour of the employment of armed reprisals.

However, there have been attempts to revive armed reprisals under Art. 51 of the UN-Charter —the only exception to the ban on the use of force in case of self-defence.[941] But all the UN organs have confirmed several times that armed reprisals fall within the scope of Art. 2(4).[942] It means

---

'Reprisals' (above, n. 71), 34; Ramón Paniagua Redondo, 'Las represalias en el derecho internacional. Perspectiva histórica', *RevJurCat* 83 (1984), 149–70, at 167; Zoller, *Peacetime unilateral remedies* (above, n. 23), 38f.; Guttry, *Le rappresaglie non comportanti la coercizione militare nel diritto internazionale* (above, n. 14), 10–1; Roberto Barsotti, 'Armed reprisals', in Antonio Cassese (ed.), *The Current legal restraints of the use of force* (Developments in International Law; Dordrecht: Martinus Nijhoff, 1986), 79–110, at 79; Michael J. Kelly, 'Time warp to 1945 – Resurrection of the reprisal and anticipatory self-defense doctrines in international law', *JTransnatLawPol* 13 (2003), 1–39, at 12; Neff, *War and the Law of Nations* (above, n. 2), 318; Mary Ellen O'Connell, *The Power and Purpose of International Law: Insights from the Theory and Practice of Enforcement* (Oxford: OUP, 2011), 163; Darcy, 'Retaliation and reprisal' (above, n. 937), 886–7; Math Noortmann, *Enforcing International Law: From Self-help to Self-contained Regimes* (London/New York: Routledge, 2016), 38.

940 Leland M. Goodrich and Edvard Hambro, *Charter of the United Nations: Commentary and Documents*, published under the auspice of the London Institute of World Affairs (The Library of World Affairs, 10; 2nd edn., London: Stevens & sons, 1949), 94f. and 102. Chapter VI of the Charter (Art. 33 to 38) deals in greater detail with the procedure for the pacific settlement of disputes while Chapter VII (Art. 39 to 51) relates to the sanctions that the UN can adopt in response to threats to the peace, breaches of the peace, and acts of aggression.

941 Cf. Bowett, 'Reprisals Involving Recourse to Armed Force' (above, n. 5); Tucker, 'Reprisals and Self-Defence. The Customary Law' (above, n. 5); Burton M. Leiser, 'The Morality of Reprisals', *Ethics* 1975 (1985), 159–63; Barsotti, 'Armed reprisals' (above, n. 939); Jeffrey Allen McCredie, 'The April 14, 1986 Bombing of Libya. Act of Self-Defense or Reprisal?', *CaseWResJIntlL* 19 (1987), 215–42, at 238–239; Kelly, 'Time warp to 1945 – Resurrection of the reprisal and anticipatory self-defense doctrines in international law' (above, n. 939).

942 The jurisprudence of these organs was always unequivocal. For the opinion of the General Assembly, see GA Res 2625 (XXV) (24 October 1970), Annexe; GA Res 36/103 (9 December 1981), Annexe: Art. 2 Sec. II(c). For the opinion of the Security Council, see SC Res 111, S/3538 (19 January 1956), Para. 4; SC Res 188 (9 April 1964), Para. 1. See Barsotti, 'Armed reprisals' (above, n. 939), 79–80, for

that the resort to armed reprisals in violation of the ban is to be treated as an act of aggression (but not as war).[943]

The only point which the Charter has not solved is the question of the differentiation between war and armed reprisals. In fact, they are technically still distinct from each other, albeit the division has lost part of its practical significance.[944] As a result, when the use of force is permitted, armed

further concurring opinion expressed by the Secretary-General and delegates of Member States.
The ICJ has also repeatedly condemned the employment of forcible self-help and more precisely armed reprisals under the Charter: *Corfu Channel Case (United Kingdom of Great Britain and Northern Ireland v. Albania)*, Judgement of 9 April 1949, I.C.J. Reports (1949), 4–169, at 35 (see also Dissenting Opinion of Judge Sergei Krylov, Ibid., 76–7. Cf. Olaoluwa Olusanya, *Identifying the Aggressor under International Law: A Principles Approach* (Bern: Peter Lang, 2006), 96, who tells that the judgement pronounced armed reprisals illegal); *Military and Paramilitary Activities in and against Nicaragua (Case Concerning Military and Paramilitary Activities in and against Nicaragua (Nicaragua v. United States of America)*, Judgement of 27 June 1986, I.C.J. Reports (1986), 14–150, at 101, Para. 191, and at 127, Para. 249; *Legality of the Threat or Use of Nuclear Weapons*, Advisory Opinion of 8 July 1996, I.C.J. Reports (1996), 226–67, at 246, Para. 46; Dissenting Opinion of Judge Elaraby, *Oil Platforms (Islamic Republic of Iran v. United States of America)*, Judgement of 6 November 2003, I.C.J. Reports (2003), 290–305, at 294–295, Para. 1.2; Separate Opinion of Judge Simma, Ibid., 324–61, at 331–332, Para. 12.
Finally, when working on the Draft Articles on the Responsibility of States for Internationally Wrongful Acts, the International Law Commission stated that armed reprisals were utterly forbidden, even under customary international law. See Roberto Ago, 1619th Meeting, 25 June 1980: United Nations, *Yearbook of the International Law Commission 1980: Summary records of the meetings of the thirty-second session 5 May-25 July 1980*, 1st vol. (New York: United Nations, 1981), 185, Para. 5; The Chairman Pemmaraju Sreenivasa Rao, 2424th Meeting, 21 July 1995: United Nations, *Yearbook of the International Law Commission 1995* (above, n. 9), 297 fn. 3, Para. 12. But see Nicholas Tsagourias, 'Necessity and the Use of Force. A Special Regime', *NYIL* 41 (2010), 11–44, at 26, who holds the view that armed reprisals remain lawful as a rule of customary international law.

943 Neff, *War and the Law of Nations* (above, n. 2), 318f. On the definition of aggression, see GA Res 3314 (XXIX) (14 December 1974).

944 Kunz, 'Sanctions in International Law' (above, n. 22), 331. In fact, "the UN Charter succeeded, at one fell swoop, in eliminating the legal relevance of the distinction between wars and forcible reprisals, which had so bedevilled lawyers in the interwar period." Neff, *War and the Law of Nations* (above, n. 2), 318. However, it is interesting to remark that if armed reprisals and war have to be distinguished anyway, no objective criteria could be used. As a consequence, the subjective test of the *animus* is the only criterion available. Cf. Delbez, *La notion*

reprisals can be preferable to war for being a lesser means of pressure to vindicate claims.[945]

In summary, the coming into force of the UN-Charter sounded the death knell for armed reprisals in peacetime.

VI. Interim Conclusion

During the period between the two World Wars, the issue of armed reprisals reached unprecedented proportions. Indeed, the resort to this measure blurring the thin line between war and peace seriously compromised the work of peace that was of such a great importance after WWI. The use of force in peacetime spread confusion as to the limits of the state of peace.

However, there was strong reluctance and resistance from the great Powers to waive their inherent privilege to resort to military acts, without incurring the liability and the consequences of committing an aggression or beginning war. In fact, the compromises that they made in favour of peace were not followed by their renunciation of the right to armed reprisals. This reluctance manifested within as well as outside the system of the League of Nations. For example, France justified the occupation of Germany's Ruhr valley as a means of reprisals allowed under the Treaty of Versailles as well as the general law of nations. Indeed, the great Powers exploited the loopholes in the Covenant of the League of Nations, the Treaty of Versailles and the other legal documents that they drafted, in order to evade the *ius ad bellum* restrictions. For instance, Italy did it to avoid the sanctions of the Covenant for the bombardment and occupation of the Greek island of Corfu by way of reprisals. The strategy of Italy in that case consisted of (a) challenging the jurisdiction of the League of Nations by preferring a settlement through the Conference of Ambassadors made up of peers, and (b) preventing the Council of the League from deciding on sanctions and laying down a general principle condemning armed reprisals. This last aspect was facilitated by the reply of a Special Commission of Jurists which conferred the power on the Council to decide on a

---

de guerre (above, n. 46), 97–8; Guggenheim, *Traité de Droit international public* (above, n. 939), 92; Venezia, 'La notion de représailles en droit international public' (above, n. 9).

945 Stone, *Legal controls of International Conflict* (above, n. 58), 288.

case-by-case basis the compatibility of acts of armed reprisals with the Covenant.

As a result, many small States and, more significantly, the legal community opposed their ambitions. The antagonism between legal theory and the opinion of the leading reprisal-taking States reached a breaking point. Legal scholars strove to see the employment of armed reprisals condemned in the same way as the resort to war. Some even supported the view that there was no difference at all between the two activities. However, all their efforts failed. Not due to a lack of will, but because their opinions did not receive approval in the highest political circles of the great Powers. Only the traumatic experience of WWII made the latter countries see the necessity to propose a collective security, purged of the flaws that marred the system of the Covenant. Therefore, the resort to armed reprisals is prohibited under the Charter of the United Nations, just like any unpermitted use of force in peacetime.

Conclusion

The present study seeks to shed light on the history of reprisals in international law by addressing the question of why the law of armed reprisals remained in a legal limbo of international law from the outset of the nineteenth century up to 1945.

The institution of reprisals arose in medieval times as a palliative to justice in an age when the free access to impartial justice was not necessarily ensured to aliens. The measure emerged outside the law as a form of private justice consisting of the forcible seizure of property belonging to the wrongdoer's countrymen in order to procure compensation to the aggrieved individual. At first, Sovereigns attempted to prohibit it within their realm because it encouraged brigandage and hampered commerce. However, given the fact that reprisals fulfilled an essential function of justice in cases where there was a cross-border element, a law of reprisals developed in medieval times as a necessity to prevent abuses. Thus, bilateral treaties and municipal law laid down rules limiting and controlling the use of reprisals. Initially, this newly-developed regulation was far from coordinated and harmonised. That is why Bartolus de Saxoferrato's treatise on the topic of reprisals can be viewed as the pinnacle of this regulation process. He formulated a sophisticated legal theory which not only justified reprisals as a legitimate measure, but also minutely dealt with every single aspect of the whole procedure.

This elaborate legal framework, nevertheless, did not resist the transformation of reprisals into a measure of the law of nations. In fact, since medieval reprisals served to protect private interests, the law aimed to provide the aggrieved individuals with a fair and predictable form of compensation under the supervision of the public authorities. But as the centralisation of power in the Sovereign's hands and the emergence of the modern State occurred, reprisals progressively began to be exclusively used in a State-to-State relation. In this context, political considerations often prevailed over the strict abidance by the rules governing reprisals. This phenomenon entailed a loss of standards in State practice, and hence the medieval regulation did no longer suitably respond to the new state of affairs.

During the period 1831–1863, the law of reprisals was even more in a state of dereliction as France and Great Britain —the great Powers at the time— began to resort to reprisals as a means of coercion against the small and weak States of the globe. Indeed, because they pursued an informal imperialism, war was a measure too disruptive in many ways. On the contrary, reprisals were governed by unclear and general standards. This malleability favoured the great Powers' use of excessive armed force by way of reprisals against the target countries, while simultaneously enabling the former to claim the benefits of peace. There was, in fact, no restriction on the amount of force which could be resorted to in peacetime. Besides, the military superiority of the great Powers, as well as their preponderance in other fields like commerce, made any resistance from the target countries quite illusory and unadvisable. It, therefore, allowed the great Powers to act forcibly with impunity and press —often dubious— demands, whereas a small Power could not hope to act likewise without incurring the consequences of war.

Nonetheless, to guarantee the free use of armed reprisals and evade criticism on the expediency and execution of this measure in each case, the great Powers adroitly invoked arguments depicting the target countries as irresponsible or disreputable members of the family of nations. Non-legal considerations were then put forward to explain and justify the necessity to act, but also the departure from standards which might have governed and limited armed reprisals. Machiavelli's phrase "the end justifies the means" took on here its full meaning.

For all these reasons, the second third of the nineteenth century saw the emergence of armed reprisals as the measure short of war par excellence in international law. The great Powers, more or less consciously, reshaped the concept of reprisals through their practice and, hence, made the employment of this measure an informal privilege attached to their supremacy. This privilege persisted beyond the nineteenth century for want of clear-cut rules restricting State practice.

Another factor which accounts for the lack of legal clarity over the topic of armed reprisals is the lawyers' failure to firmly condemn the State practice of armed reprisals by adequately assessing and addressing the issue during the period 1848–1912. As a matter of fact, they oscillated between permissiveness and utter disapproval. Legal scholars actually proved faint-hearted and hesitant about tackling the issue.

In the late 1840s, Christian Friedrich Wurm and Laurent-Basile Hautefeuille were the first authors to sound the alarm on the danger of armed reprisals, especially in the form of blockades short of war. At the beginning, most lawyers rallied around the view that the so-called pacific blockades were tantamount to war. When, however, the Institute of International Law looked into the topic at the session of Heidelberg in 1887, the legal community refrained from objecting to the practice of the great Powers through reaffirming the cornerstone principles of international law, such as the independence and equality of States. Lawyers, instead, agreed on a declaration which recognised pacific blockade as a rightful measure of international law as long as it did not impact third States. So, they preferred to generally treat armed reprisals as a better alternative to war.

However, later instances of armed reprisals between 1887 and 1912 — most notably the joint blockade of Venezuela in 1902/03 by Great Britain, Germany and Italy— highlighted the outrageous consequences of such an indulgent doctrine. Few like Thomas Baty called for the identification of armed reprisals with war, given their impact on the target country. But most legal scholars seemed overtaken until the adoption of the Drago-Porter Convention at the Second Hague Peace Conference in 1907 made them realise the importance of the issue and the need of a proper regulation for armed reprisals.

Finally, the interwar period witnessed the great Powers' obstruction to the attempts to limit the use of armed reprisals and, hence, their informal privilege. While the end of the First World War was supposed to augur a new era built on peace and cooperation between all the nations, the great Powers showed several times reluctance to yield the right to make use of force in peacetime, despite the growing efforts against war and violence in the international relations.

The year 1923 was fateful as acts of armed reprisals were exercised by France against Germany, on the one hand, and by Italy against Greece, on the other hand. Nevertheless, the respective situation was quite different. In the former case, France considered that it did not owe anybody an explanation because the reprisal provision in the Peace Treaty of Versailles and, more generally, international law offered a sufficient legal basis to justify the military occupation of the Ruhr valley. On the contrary, in the latter case, Italy walked a tightrope since the League of Nations felt entitled to intervene in a conflict involving two Member States, of which one — Italy— had a permanent seat on the Council. The Italian bombardment and occupation of Corfu raised criticism from the ranks of the small Member States. Nevertheless, Italy's strategy consisted of challenging the jurisdiction of the League in this affair and defending, due to the existing loophole in the Covenant, the legality of armed reprisals. On this point, Italy and the other great Powers proved to cling to their privilege as they prevented the League from laying down a clear and general principle condemning armed reprisals. In fact, they favoured an ambiguous answer, a solution that allowed a case-to-case examination more subject to political influence.

A great legal achievement was, however, the regulation adopted by the Institute of International Law in 1934, which explicitly banned the employment of armed reprisals in the same conditions as the resort to war. But in spite of the fact that the legal community tried to overcome the legal vacuum, the IIL had no authority over the States and, unsurprisingly, its regulation did not receive a warm welcome from the great Powers. The result was, therefore, the absence of rules in the form of a convention.

Since the beginning of the nineteenth century, the legal situation of armed reprisals had been unclear. It was only after the Second World War that the UN-Charter sanctioned the prohibition of the use of force as one of the core principles of the new era of international law. As a consequence, the recourse to armed reprisals is no longer authorised today.

Perhaps more than any other measures of international law, armed reprisals enjoyed a close connection with the great Powers which accounts for the remarkable longevity of the legal grey zone surrounding them. The result of the present historical investigation is to have captured the cynicism with which actors of international law, namely the great Powers, worked to keep armed reprisals in a legal twilight zone until 1945. This topic, thus, teaches a great deal about the use of international law as a tool of power strategy. Therefore, against such a background, a general ban on the use of force in peacetime under the UN-Charter was certainly the best solution to prevent the oppression of the weak by the strong because it conveys the idea that the settlement of disputes must be non-forcible. This solution favours the respect of the principle of the independence and equality of States, although modern counter-measures may perhaps, today, no longer efficiently fulfil their role of coercion and, thence, ensure the respect for international law.

Bibliography

Primary Sources

ADAMS, HENRY, *The Writings of Albert Gallatin*, 2nd vol. (Philadelphia: J.B. Lippincott, 1879).

ALLIED POWERS, and REPARATION COMMISSION, *Report On the Work of the Reparation Commission from 1920 to 1922* (London: His Majesty's Stationery Office, 1923).

AMERICAN INSTITUTE OF INTERNATIONAL LAW, 'Texts of Projects', *AJIL* 20/4 (1926), Supplement, 300–87.

BERNECKER, WALTHER L., and MEISTER, FLORIAN B. (eds.), *Der Kampf um die «grüne Hölle»: Quellen und Materialien zum Chaco-Krieg (1932–1935)*, unter Mitarbeit von Michael Herzig (Zürich: Chronos, 1993).

BERNIS, FRANÇOIS-JOACHIM de Pierre de, *Memoirs and letters of Cardinal de Bernis in two volumes*, with an introduction by C.-A. Sainte-Beuve. Translated by Katharine Prescott Wormeley. Illustrated with portraits from the original, 1st vol. (New York: P. F. Collier & Son, [1901]).

BEUGNOT, ARTHUR AUGUSTE, *Les Olim ou registres des arrêts rendus par la cour du roi sous les règnes de Saint Louis, de Philippe le Hardi, de Philippe le Bel, de Louis le Hutin et de Philippe le Long* (Collection de documents inédits sur l'histoire de France publiés par ordre du roi et par les soins du ministre de l'instruction publique. Première série: Histoire politique; Paris: Imprimerie Royale, 1839).

BEVANS, CHARLES IRVING, *Treaties and other international agreements of the United States of America, 1776–1949*, 2nd vol. ([Washington]: [U.S. Department of State], 1969).

BLUHME, FRIEDRICH, 'Edictus Langobardorum', in Georg Heinrich Pertz (ed.), *Monumenta Germaniae Historica. Inde ab anno Christi quingentesimo usque ad annum millesimum et quingentesimum*, Auspiciis Societatis aperiendis fontibus rerum germanicarum medii aevi (Hannover: Hahn, 1868), 1–225.

BULWER, HENRY LYTTON, *The Life of Henry John Temple, Viscount Palmerston: with Selections from his Correspondence*, 3rd vol. (3rd edn., London: Richard Bentley, 1874).

CAPMANY Y DE MONTPALAU, ANTONIO de, *Memorias históricas sobre la marina, comercio y artes de la antigua ciudad de Barcelona*, publicadas por disposicion y a expensas de la Real Junta y Consulado de Comercio de la misma ciudad, Real Junta y Consuldado de Comercio de Barcelona, 2nd vol. (Madrid: en la imprenta de don Antonio de Sancha, 1779).

CHOISEUL, ÉTIENNE-FRANÇOIS de, *An Historical Memorial of the Negotiation of France and England, From the 26th of March, 1761, to the 20th of September of the same Year*, With the Vouchers. Translated from the *French Original*, published at *Paris* by Authority (London: Printed for D. Wilson, and T. Becket and P. A. Dehondt in the Strand, 1761).

Clercq, Alexandre Jehan Henry de, and Clercq, Jules de, *Recueil des traités de la France*, publié sous les auspices de S. Exc. M. Drouyn de Lhuys, Ministre des Affaires Étrangères, 23 vols. (Paris: Amyot, 1864–1917).

Dalmau y de Olivart, Ramón de, *Tratados y documentos internacionales de España: publicados en la Revista de derecho internacional y política exterior bajo la dirección del Marqués de Olivart*, 1st vol. (Madrid: Estab. tipográfico de los hijos de R. Álvarez á cargo de Arturo Menéndez, 1905).

Deutsches Institut für Erforschung des Mittelalters, and Stürner, Wolfgang, *Monumenta Germaniae Historica: Inde ab anno Christi Quingentesimo usque ad annum millesimum et quingentesimum* (Legum sectio IV. Constitutiones et acta publica imperatorum et regum, 2 Suppl.; Hannover: Hahn, 1996).

Deutsches Institut für Erforschung des Mittelalters, and Weiland, Ludwig, *Monumenta Germaniae Historica: Inde ab anno Christi Quingentesimo usque ad annum millesimum et quingentesimum* (Legum sectio IV. Constitutiones et acta publica imperatorum et regum, 1; Hannover: Hahn, 1893).

Deutsches Reich, *Stenographische Berichte über die Verhandlungen des Reichstags: VII. Legislaturperiode. IV. Session 1888/89*, 1st vol. (105th vol.; Berlin: Norddeutsche Buchdruckerei und Verlagsanstalt, 1889).

——, *Stenographische Berichte über die Verhandlungen des Reichstags: X. Legislaturperiode. II. Session 1900/1903.*, 8th vol. (186th vol.; Berlin: Norddeutsche Buchdruckerei und Verlagsanstalt, 1903).

Dodsley, James, *The Annual Register: Or a View of the History, Politics and Literature, for the Year 1779*, 22nd vol. (London: Printed for J. Dodsley, 1780).

Dumont, Jean, *Corps universel diplomatique du droit des gens: Contenant un Recueil des Traitez d'Alliance, de Paix, de Treve, de Neutralité, de Commerce, d'Échange, de Protection & de Garantie, de toutes les Conventions, Transactions, Pactes, Concordats, & autres Contrats, qui ont été faits en Europe, depuis le Regne de l'Empereur Charlemagne jusques à présent; Avec les Capitulations Imperiales et Royales; les Sentences Arbitrales & Souveraines dans les Causes importantes; les Déclarations de Guerre, les Contrats de Mariage des Grands Princes, leurs Testamens, Donations, Renonciations, & Protestations; les Investitures des grands Fiefs; les Erections des grandes Dignités, celles des grandes Compagnies de Commerce, & en général de tous les Titres, sous quelque nom qu'on les désigne, qui peuvent servir à fonder, établir, ou justifier les droits et les interets des Princes et Etats de l'Europe; Le tout tiré en partie des Archives de la Tres-Auguste Maison d'Autriche, & en partie de celles de quelques autres Princes & Etats; comme aussi des Protocolles de quelques Grands Ministres; des Manuscrits de la Bibliotheque Royale de Berlin; des meilleures Collections, qui ont déjà paru tant en Allemagne, qu'en France, en Angleterre, en Hollande, & ailleurs; sur tout, des Actes de Rymer; & enfin les plus estimés, soit en Histoire, en Politique, ou en Droit*, 8 vols. (Amsterdam: P. Brunel, R. et G. Wetstein, les Janssons à Waesberge, L'Honoré et Chatelain, 1726–1731).

EDWARDS, THOMAS, *Reports of Cases Argued and Determined in the High Court of Admiralty: Commencing with the Judgments of the Right Hon. Sir William Scott, Easter Term, 1808*, edited by George Minot (Boston: Little, Brown and Company, 1853).

ELLIOT, JONATHAN, *The American Diplomatic Code, Embracing A Collection of Treaties and Conventions between the United States and Foreign Powers: From 1778 to 1834. With an Abstract of Important Judicial Decisions on Points connected with Our Foreign Relations. Also, A Concise Diplomatic Manual, containing a Summary of the Law of Nations, from the Works of Wicquefort, Martens, Kent, Vattel, Ward, Story, &c. &c. and Other Diplomatic Writings on Questions of International Law*, 2nd vol. (Washington: Printed by Jonathan Elliot, 1834).

FORD, PAUL LEICESTER, *The Works of Thomas Jefferson*, 12 vols. (New York/London: G. P. Putnam's sons, 1904–1905).

FRANCE, *Pétition des réclamans français contre le gouvernement napolitain adressée à MM. les membres de la Chambre des Députés* (Marseille: Imprimerie Ed. Buret et Co, 1845).

FRANCE, and RENAULT, LOUIS, *Archives diplomatiques: Recueil mensuel international de diplomatie et d'histoire*, 13th vol. (2nd ser.) (Paris: Féchoz, 1885).

——, *Archives diplomatiques: Recueil mensuel international de diplomatie et d'histoire*, 47th vol. (2nd ser.) (Paris: F.-J. Féchoz, 1893).

FRANCE, MINISTÈRE DES AFFAIRES ÉTRANGÈRES, *Affaires de Chine et du Tonkin: 1884–1885.* (Documents diplomatiques; Paris: Imprimerie nationale, 1885).

——, *Deuxième conférence internationale de la paix. La Haye 15 juin – 18 octobre 1907. Actes et documents*, 3rd vol. (La Haye: Imprimerie nationale, 1907).

——, *Conférence navale de Londres: 1908–1909* (Documents diplomatiques; Paris: Imprimerie nationale, 1909).

——, *Diplomatic correspondence: Reply of the French Government to the note of the British Government of August 11, 1923 relating to reparations (August 20th, 1923)* (Paris: Imprimerie nationale, 1923).

——, *Recueil des instructions données aux ambassadeurs et ministres de France depuis les traités de Westphalie jusqu'à la Révolution française*, 24th vol. (Paris: E. De Boccard, 1929).

FRANCE, MINISTÈRE DES AFFAIRES ÉTRANGÈRES, and COMMISSION DES ARCHIVES DIPLOMATIQUES, *1921: Annexes (10 janvier 1920 – 31 décembre 1921)* (Documents diplomatiques français, 6; Bruxelles: P.I.E.-Peter Lang, 2005).

GARDINER, SAMUEL RAWSON, *Letters and papers relating to the First Dutch War, 1652–1654* (Publications of the Navy Records Society, 13; [London]: Navy Records Society, 1899).

GREAT BRITAIN, *The Statutes of the Realm*, Printed by command of his majesty King George the Third. In pursuance of an address of the House of Commons of Great Britain. From Original Records and Authentic Manuscripts. 1st vol. (London: Dawsons of Pall Mall, 1810 [Reprinted 1963]).

GREAT BRITAIN, F. O., *British and Foreign State Papers: 1826–1827* (14th vol.; London: Printed by J. Harrison and son, 1828).

——, *British and Foreign State Papers: 1829,-1830* (17th vol.; London: James Ridgway, 1832).

——, *British and Foreign State Papers: 1830,-1831* (18th vol.; London: James Ridgway, 1833).

——, *British and Foreign State Papers: 1831,-1832* (19th vol.; London: James Ridgway, 1834).

——, *British and Foreign State Papers: 1833–1834* (22nd vol.; London: James Ridgway and sons, 1847).

——, *British and Foreign State Papers: 1834–1835* (23rd vol.; London: James Ridgway and sons, 1852).

——, *British and Foreign State Papers: 1835–1836* (24th vol.; London: James Ridgway and sons, 1853).

——, *British and Foreign State Papers: 1836–1837* (25th vol.; London: James Ridgway, 1853).

——, *British and Foreign State Papers: 1837–1838* (26th vol.; London: Printed by Harrison and sons, 1855).

——, *British and Foreign State Papers: 1839–1840* (28th vol.; London: Printed by Harrison and sons, 1857).

——, *British and Foreign State Papers: 1840–1841* (29th vol.; London: James Ridgway and sons, 1857).

——, *British and Foreign State Papers: 1841–1842* (30th vol.; London: James Ridgway and sons, 1858).

——, *British and Foreign State Papers: 1845–1846* (34th vol.; London: Harrison and sons, 1860).

——, *British and Foreign State Papers: 1846–1847* (35th vol.; London: Printed by Harrison and sons, 1860).

——, *British and Foreign State Papers: 1847–1848* (36th vol.; London: Harrison and sons, 1861).

——, *British and Foreign State Papers: 1848–1849* (37th vol.; London: Harrison and sons, 1862).

——, *British and Foreign State Papers: 1849–1850. (1)* (38th vol.; London: Harrison and sons, 1862).

——, *British and Foreign State Papers: 1849–1850. [2]* (39th vol.; London: Harrison and sons, 1863).

——, *British and Foreign State Papers: 1850–1851* (40th vol.; London: James Ridgway and sons, 1863).

——, *British and Foreign State Papers: 1851–1852* (41st vol.; London: William Ridgway, 1864).

——, *British and Foreign State Papers: 1855–1856* (46th vol.; London: William Ridgway, 1865).

——, *British and Foreign State Papers: 1856–1857* (47th vol.; London: William Ridgway, 1866).

——, *British and Foreign State Papers: 1857–1858* (48th vol.; London: William Ridgway, 1866).

——, *British and Foreign State Papers: 1859–1860* (50th vol.; London: William Ridgway, 1867).

——, *British and Foreign State Papers: 1861–1862* (52nd vol.; London: William Ridgway, 1868).

——, *British and Foreign State Papers: 1862–1863* (53rd vol.; London: William Ridgway, 1868).

——, *British and Foreign State Papers: 1863–1864* (54th vol.; London: William Ridgway, 1869).

——, *British and Foreign State Papers: 1883–1884* (75th vol.; London: William Ridgway, 1891).

——, *British and Foreign State Papers: 1884–1885* (76th vol.; London: William Ridgway, 1892).

——, *British and Foreign State Papers. 1887–1888* (79th vol.; London: Harrison and sons, [s.d.]).

——, *British and Foreign State Papers: 1888–1889* (81st vol.; London: Harrison and sons, [s.d.]).

——, *British and Foreign State Papers: 1894–1895* (87th vol.; London: Her Majesty's Stationery Office, 1900).

——, *British and Foreign State Papers: 1896–1897* (89th vol.; London: His Majesty's Stationery Office, 1901).

——, *British and Foreign State Papers: 1898–1899* (91st vol.; London: His Majesty's Stationery Office, 1902).

——, *British and Foreign State Papers: 1901–1902* (95th vol.; London: His Majesty's Stationery Office, 1905).

——, *British and Foreign State Papers: 1902–1903* (96th vol.; London: His Majesty's Stationery Office, 1906).

——, *Papers respecting the Renewal of Diplomatic Relations with Brazil* (London: Harrison and sons, 1866).

Great Britain, H.M. Government, 'Liability of German Property in the United Kingdom to Seizure under the Peace Treaty.', *The Board of Trade Journal and Commercial Gazette,* 21 October 1920, 479.

——, *Cabinet 38 (33). Conclusions of a Meeting of the Cabinet held at 10 Downing Street, on Wednesday, 31st May, 1933, at 11.0 a.m.* (1933; <http://filestore.nationalarchives.gov.uk/>, accessed 8 January 2019).

Great Britain, Parliament, *Documents and statements respecting the Sulphur Monopoly, constituting grounds for Parliamentary inquiry into the conduct of the Foreign Secretary.* (London: John Reid and Co., 1841).

——, *Hansard's Parliamentary Debates: Third Series, commencing with the accession of William IV.* (93rd vol.; London: G. Woodfall and son, 1847).

——, *Hansard's Parliamentary Debates: Third Series, commencing with the accession of William IV.* (109th vol.; London: Cornelius Buck, 1850).

——, *Hansard's Parliamentary Debates*: *Third Series, commencing with the accession of William IV.* (111th vol.; London: Cornelius Buck, 1850).

——, *Hansard's Parliamentary Debates*: *Third Series, commencing with the accession of William IV.* (112th vol.; London: Cornelius Buck, 1850).

——, *Hansard's Parliamentary Debates*: *Third Series. Commencing with the accession of William IV.* (149th vol.; London: Cornelius Buck, 1858).

——, *Hansard's Parliamentary Debates*: *Third Series. Commencing with the accession of William IV.* (169th vol.; London: Cornelius Buck, 1863).

——, *Hansard's Parliamentary Debates*: *Third Series. Commencing with the accession of William IV.* (171st vol.; London: Cornelius Buck, 1863).

——, *Hansard's Parliamentary Debates*: *Third Series, Commencing with the accession of William IV.* (172nd vol.; London: Cornelius Buck, 1863).

——, *Hansard's Parliamentary Debates*: *Third Series, Commencing with the accession of William IV.* (177th vol.; London: Cornelius Buck, 1865).

——, *The Parliamentary Debates authorised Edition*: *Fourth Series: Commencing with the Second Session of the Twenty-fifth Parliament of the United Kingdom of Great Britain and Ireland* (15th vol.; London: Eyre and Spottiswoode, 1893).

——, *The Parliamentary Debates authorised Edition*: *Fourth Series, Commencing with the Third Session of the Twenty-sixth Parliament of the United Kingdom of Great Britain and Ireland* (47th vol.; London: Waterlow & sons, 1897).

——, *The Parliamentary Debates, authorised Edition. Fourth Series, Commencing with the Third Session of the Twenty-sixth Parliament of the United Kingdom of Great Britain and Ireland* (48th vol.; London: Waterlow & sons, 1897).

——, *The Parliamentary Debates*: *(authorised edition), fourth series. Third session of the twenty-seventh Parliament of the United Kingdom of Great Britain and Ireland* (116th vol.; London: Wyman and sons, 1902).

——, *The Parliamentary Debates: Official Report. Second Session of the Thirty-First Parliament of the United Kingdom of Great Britain and Ireland. 11 George V. House of Commons* (133rd vol.; London: His Majesty's Stationery Office, 1920).

——, *The Parliamentary Debates: Official Report*: *Fifth Session of the Thirty-First Parliament of the United Kingdom of Great Britain and Ireland. 12 & 13 George V. House of Commons* (154th vol.; London: His Majesty's Stationery Office, 1922).

——, *The Parliamentary Debates (Official Report)*: *Fourth Session of the Thirty-Sixth Parliament of the United Kingdom of Great Britain and Northern Ireland. 25 George V. House of Lords* (95th vol.; London: His Majesty's Stationery Office, 1935).

Grewe, Wilhelm Georg, *Fontes historiae iuris gentium*, In Zusammenarbeit mit dem Institut für Internationales Recht an der Freien Universität Berlin, 2nd vol. (Berlin: Walter de Gruyter, 1988).

Harris, Earl of Malmesbury, James Howard, *Memoirs of an ex-minister*: *An autobiography*, 2nd vol. (3rd edn., London: Longmans, Green, and Co., 1884).

Harvard Research in International Law (ed.), *Drafts of conventions prepared for the codification of international law*: *I. Judicial Assistance, II. Rights and Duties of Neutral States in Naval and Aerial War, III. Rights and Duties of States in Case of*

Aggression, Under the Auspices of the Faculty of the Harvard Law School, *AJIL* 33 (1939), Suppl.

Hay, George, and Marriott, James, *Decisions in the High Court of Admiralty: During The Time of Sir George Hay, and of Sir James Marriott, Late Judges of That Court. Michaelmas Term, 1776, to Hilary Term, 1779*, 1st vol. (London: R. Bickerstaff, 1801).

Institut de Droit International, 'Questionnaire adressé à MM. les membres de la commission. [Suite des Travaux préliminaires à la Session de La Haye. Vme Commission. – Propriété privée dans la guerre maritime]', *RDILC* 7 (1875), 553–7.

——, 'Rapport de M. Albéric Rolin sur les observations présentées en réponse au questionnaire', *RDILC* 7 (1875), 603–18.

——, 'Conflit franco-chinois. – Lecture de M. Geffcken.', in Institut de Droit International (ed.), *Session de Bruxelles – September 1885* (Annuaire IDI, vol. 8; Bruxelles/Leipzig: Librairie européenne C. Muquardt, Merzbach & Falk, 1886), 289.

—— (ed.), *Session de Bruxelles – September 1885* (Annuaire IDI, vol. 8; Bruxelles/Leipzig: Librairie européenne C. Muquardt, Merzbach & Falk, 1886).

—— (ed.), *Session de Heidelberg – Septembre 1887* (Annuaire IDI, vol. 9; Bruxelles/Leipzig: C. Muquardt, 1888).

—— (ed.), *Session de Paris – Mars-Avril 1910* (Annuaire IDI, vol. 23; Paris: A. Pedone, 1910).

—— (ed.), *Session de Christiana – Août 1912* (Annuaire IDI, vol. 25; Paris: A. Pedone, 1912).

—— (ed.), *Session de Paris, Octobre 1934* (Annuaire IDI, vol. 38; Bruxelles: Goemaere, 1934).

International American Conference, *Third International American Conference. 1906: Minutes. Resolutions. Documents.* (Rio de Janeiro: Imprensa Nacional, 1907).

International Law Association (ed.), *Report of the Thirty-Eighth Conference held at Budapest in the Hungarian Academy of Science, September 6th to 10th, 1934*, 38th vol. (London/Reading: The Eastern Press, 1935).

Jackson, Andrew, *Messages of Gen. Andrew Jackson: With a short sketch of his life* (Concord, New Hampshire: John F. Brown and William White, 1837).

Japanese Delegation to the League of Nations, *Japan's Case in the Sino-Japanese Dispute: As Presented Before the Special Session of the Assembly of the League of Nations. Geneva, 1933* ([s.l.]: [s.n.], [1933]).

Jourdan, Athanase Jean Léger; Isambert, François André; Decrusy et al., *Recueil général des anciennes lois françaises: Depuis l'an 420 jusqu'à la Révoution de 1789*, 29 vols. (Paris: Belin-Leprieur, 1821–1833).

Kiss, Alexandre-Charles, *Répertoire de la pratique française en matière de droit international public*, 6th vol. (Paris: Éditions du Centre National de la Recherche Scientifique, 1969).

Laurière, Eusèbe Jacob de; Secousse, Denis-François; Villevaut, Louis-Guillaume de et al., *Ordonnances des Roys de France de la Troisième Race*, 21 vols. (Paris: Imprimerie Royale, 1723–1849).

League of Nations, Assembly, 'Resolutions and Recommendations adopted on the Reports of the Third Committee.', *LNOJ* 6 (1921), Special Supplement, 23–6.

——, 'Records of the Special Session of the Assembly convened in virtue of Article 15 of the Covenant at the Request of the Chinese Government.', *LNOJ* (1932), Special Supplement No. 101.

——, 'League of Nations Assembly Report on the Sino-Japanese Dispute', *AJIL* 27/3 (1933), Supplement: Official Documents, 119–53.

League of Nations, Commission of Enquiry into the Sino-Japanese Dispute, *Appeal by the Chinese Government: Report of the Commission of Enquiry* (Series of League of Nations Publications, VII. Political. 1932. VII. 12; [Geneva]: [s.n.], 1932).

League of Nations, Council, 'Twenty-Sixth Session of the Council. Held at Geneva from Friday, August 31st, to Saturday, September 29th, 1923.', *LNOJ* 4 (1923), 1261–513.

——, 'Twenty-Eight Session of the Council. Held at Geneva from Monday, March 10th, to Saturday, March 15th, 1924.', *LNOJ* 5 (1924), 495–744.

——, 'Thirty-Third Session of the Council. Held at Geneva from Monday, March 9th, to Saturday, March 14th, 1925.', *LNOJ* 6 (1925), 429–628.

——, 'Thirty-Fifth Session of the Council. Held at Geneva from Wednesday September 2nd, to Monday, September 28th, 1925.', *LNOJ* 6 (1925), 1297–548.

——, 'Thirty-Sixth (Extraordinary) Session of the Council. Held at Paris from Monday October 26th, to Friday October 30th, 1925.', *LNOJ* 6 (1925), Part II, 1691–722.

——, 'Thirty-Seventh Session of the Council. Held at Geneva from Monday, December 7th, to Wednesday, December 16th, 1925.', *LNOJ* 7 (1926), 101–366.

——, 'Thirty-Eight (Extraordinary Meeting) and Thirty-Ninth Sessions of the Council. Held at Geneva on Friday, February 12th, 1926, at 3 p.m; and from Monday, March 8th, to Thursday, March 18th, 1926.', *LNOJ* 7 (1926), 491–642.

——, 'Seventieth Session of the Council. Held at Geneva from Tuesday, January 24th, to Friday, February 3rd, 1933.', *LNOJ* 14 (1933), 173–381.

——, 'Seventy-Eighth Session of the Council. (Part II). Held at Geneva from Monday January 15th, to Saturday, January 20th, 1934.', *LNOJ* 15 (1934), 237–71.

——, 'Ninety-Eighth and Ninety-Ninth Sessions of the Council. Held at Geneva from Friday, September 10th, to Thursday, September 16th, 1937; and from Wednesday, September 29th, to Tuesday, October 5th, 1937.', *LNOJ* 18 (1937), 877–1324.

League of Nations, Permanent Secretariat, 'Circular letter from the Secretary-General to the Members of the International Blockade Committee.', *LNOJ* 2 (1921), 430–5.

——, 'Letter from the Secretary-General to the Members of the League concerning the Obligations arising out of Article 16 of the Covenant.', *LNOJ* 2 (1921), 220–1.

——, *Proposed Convention declaring the Illegality of Peace-Time Reprisals*, The President Secretary General of the International Federation of the League of Nations Societies, Brussels – Forward copy of a resolution adopted by the Representative Council of the International Federation of League of Nations Societies at Lausanne on 29 October drawing the attention of the League Council to the resolution adopted by the Federation in Warsaw in July 1925 recommending the drawing up of such a Convention (Geneva, 1925; <http://biblio-archive.unog.ch/detail.aspx?ID=224823>, accessed 13 November 2018).

——, *Publication of Treaties and International Engagements Registered with the Secretariat of the League of Nations* (LNTS 54; [Geneva]: [League of Nations], 1926–1927).

——, *Publication of Treaties and International Engagements Registered with the Secretariat of the League of Nations* (LNTS 94; [Geneva]: [League of Nations], 1929).

——, 'Documentation concerning the Dispute between Bolivia and Paraguay', *LNOJ* 13 (1932), 1573–86.

League of Nations, Secretary-General, 'Annex 964. Legal position arising from the enforcement in time of peace of the measures of economic pressure indicated in Article 16 of the Covenant, particularly by a maritime blockade. Report by the Secretary-General of the League submitted to the Council on June 15th, 1927 [C. 241. 1927 V]', *LNOJ* 8 (1927), 834–45.

Lebeau, Sylvain, *Nouveau code des prises: ou recueil des édits, déclarations, lettres patentes, arrêts, ordonnances, réglemens et décisions sur la Course et l'administration des Prises, depuis 1400 jusqu'au mois de mai 1789 (v. st.); suivi de toutes les lois, arrêtés, messages, et autres actes qui ont paru depuis cette dernière époque jusqu'à présent*, 1st vol. (Paris: Imprimerie de la République, an VII).

Lefèvre-Pontalis, Germain, *Correspondance politique de Odet de Selve, ambassadeur de France en Angleterre (1546–1549)*, publiée sous les auspices de la Commission des Archives Diplomatiques (Inventaire analytique des archives du Ministère des affaires étrangères; Paris: Félix Alcan, 1888).

Lepsius, Johannes; Mendelssohn Bartholdy, Albrecht, and Thimme, Friedrich (eds.), *Die Wendung im Deutsch-Englischen Verhältnis*, herausgegeben im Auftrage des Auswärtigen Amtes (Die Grosse Politik der Europäischen Kabinette 1871–1914, 17; Berlin: Deutsche Verlagsgesellschaft für Politik und Geschichte, 1924).

Macarel, Louis-Antoine, *Recueil des arrêts du Conseil, ou Ordonnances royales rendues en Conseil d'État, sur toutes les matières du contentieux de l'administration: Année 1823*, 5th vol. (Paris: Bureau d'administration du recueil, 1823).

——, *Recueil des arrêts du Conseil, ou Ordonnances royales rendues en Conseil d'État, sur toutes les matières du contentieux de l'administration: Année 1826*, 8th vol. (Paris: Bureau d'administration du recueil, 1826).

Malden, Henry Elliot, *The Cely papers: Selections from the correspondence and memoranda of the Cely family, merchants of the Staple; A.D. 1475–1488* (London: Longmans, Green, and Co., 1900).

Malloy, William M., *Treaties, Conventions, International Acts, Protocols and Agreements between the United States of America and Other Powers, 1776–1909*, 1st vol. (Washington: GPO, 1910).

MANNING, WILLIAM RAY, *Arbitration Treaties among the American Nations: To the Close of the Year 1910* (Publications of the Carnegie Endowment for International Peace: Division of International Law (Washington); New York: OUP, 1924).

MARSDEN, REGINALD GODFREY, *Documents relating to law and custom of the sea*, 2 vols. (Publications of the Navy Records Society, 49–50; London: Navy Records Society, 1915–1916).

MARTENS, GEORG FRIEDRICH von, *Nouveau recueil de traités d'Alliance, de Paix, de Trêve, de Neutralité, de Commerce, de Limites, d'Echange etc. et de plusieurs autres actes servant à la connoissance des relations étrangères des Puissances et Etats de l'Europe tant dans leur rapport mutuel que dans celui envers les Puissances et Etats dans d'autres parties du globe depuis 1808 jusqu'à présent*, 16 vols. (Göttingen: Dans la librairie de Dieterich, 1817–1842).

MÉXICO, *Boletín Oficial de la Secretaría de Relaciones Exteriores: Mayo a octubre de 1906*, 22th vol. (México: Tipografía de la viuda de Francisco Díaz de León, 1906).

MILLER, DAVID HUNTER, *Treaties and other international acts of the United States of America*, 2nd vol. (Washington, D. C.: GPO, 1931).

MURHARD, FRIEDRICH WILHELM AUGUST; MURHARD, KARL; PINHAS, J. et al., *Nouveau recueil général de traités, conventions et autres transactions remarquables, servant à la connaissance des relations étrangères des puissances et États dans leurs rapports mutuels. Continuation du grand Recueil de feu M. de Martens*, 20 vols. (Goettingue: Librairie de Dieterich, 1843–1875).

NOTT, CHARLES C., and HOPKINS, ARCHIBALD, *Cases decided in the Court of Claims of the United States: At the Term of 1908–9, With Abstracts of Decisions of the Supreme Court in Appealed Cases, From October, 1908, to May, 1909*, 44th vol. (Washington: GPO, 1910).

NOTT, CHARLES C., and HUNTINGTON, SAMUEL H., *Cases decided in the Court of Claims of the United States: at the December Term for 1868. With the Acts of Congress relating to the Court*, 4th vol. (Washington, D. C.: W. H. & O. H. Morrison, [1868]).

PARDESSUS, JEAN-MARIE, *Collection de lois maritimes antérieures au XVIIIe siècle*, 2nd vol. (Paris: Imprimerie Royale, 1831).

PASCHAL, GEORGE W., *Reports of cases argued and decided in the Supreme Court of the State of Texas, during the Austin session, 1866*, 28th vol. (Washington, D.C.: W. H. & O. H. Morrison, 1869).

PICKERING, DANBY, *The Statutes at Large: From Magna Charta To the End of the Eleventh Parliament of Great Britain, Anno 1761*, 32nd vol (Cambridge: Charles Bathurst, 1778).

PIGGOTT, FRANCIS TAYLOR, and OMOND, GEORGE WILLIAM THOMSON, *Documentary history of the armed neutralities, 1780 and 1800: together with selected documents relating to the war of American independence 1776–1783 and the Dutch war 1780–1784* ("Law of the Sea" Series, 1; London: University of London Press, 1919).

POLLOCK, FREDERICK, and STONE, A. P., *The Law Reports or The Incorporated Council of Law Reporting. House of Lords, Judicial Committee of the Privy Council, and Peerage Cases: 1902.* (London: William Clowes and sons, 1902).

PRUSSIA, *Allgemeines Landrecht für die Preussischen Staaten*, 4th vol. (2nd edn., Berlin: Pauli, 1794).

RICHTER, EMIL LUDWIG, and FRIEDBERG, EMIL, *Corpus Iuris Canonici: Editio Lipsiensis Secunda*, 2nd vol. (Graz: Akademische Druck- u. Verlagsanstalt, 1959).

ROBINSON, CHRISTOPHER, *Reports of Cases Argued and Determined in the High Court of Admiralty: Commencing with the Judgments of the Right Hon. Sir William Scott. Michaelmas Term, 1798*, 6 vols. (Boston: Little, Brown and Company, 1853).

ROSCOE, EDWARD STANLEY, *Reports of prize cases determined in the High Court of Admiralty, before the Lords Commissioners of Appeals in prize causes, and before the Judicial Committee of the Privy Council, from 1745 to 1859*, 1st vol. (London: Stevens and sons, 1905).

SANFORD, HENRY S., *The Aves Island Case: with the Correspondence Relating Thereto and Discussion of Law and Facts, Being the Official Documents published by Order of the Senate of the United States* (Washington: [s.n.], 1861).

SAWYER, EDMUND, *Memorials of Affairs of State in the Reigns of Q. Elizabeth and K. James I.: Collected (chiefly) from the Original Papers Of the Right Honourable Sir Ralph Winwood, Kt. Sometime one of the Principal Secretaries of State. Comprehending likewise the Negotiations of Sir Henry Neville, Sir Charles Cornwallis, Sir Dudley Carleton, Sir Thomas Edmondes, Mr. Trumbull, Mr. Cottington and other, At the Courts of France and Spain, and in Holland, Venice, &c. Wherein the Principal Transactions of those Times Are faithfully related, and the Policies and Intrigues of those Courts at large discover'd. The whole digested in an exact Series of Time. To which are added Two Tables: One of the Letters, the other of the Principal Matters*, 1st vol. (London: Printed by W. B. for T. Ward, 1725).

SCOTT, JAMES BROWN, *The Hague Conventions and Declarations of 1899 and 1907: accompanied by Tables of Signatures, Ratifications and Adhesions of the Various Powers, and Texts of Reservations* (Carnegie Endowment for International Peace: Division of International Law; New York: OUP, 1915).

—— (ed.), *Resolutions of the Institute of International Law dealing with the Law of Nations: With an Historical Introduction and Explanatory Notes*, Collected and translated under the supervision of and edited by James Scott Brown (Carnegie Endowment for International Peace: Division of International Law; New York: OUP, 1916).

—— (ed.), *The Hague Court Reports: Comprising the awards, accompanied by syllabi, the agreements for arbitration, and other documents in each case submitted to the permanent court of arbitration and to commissions of inquiry under the provisions of the conventions of 1899 and 1907 for the pacific settlement of international disputes* (Carnegie Endowment for International Peace: Division of International Law; New York: OUP, 1916).

——, *The armed neutralities of 1780 and 1800: A collection of official documents preceded by the views of representative publicists* (Carnegie Endowment for International Peace: Division of International Law; New York: OUP, 1918).

——, *The Declaration of London, February 26, 1909: A collection of official papers and documents relating to the international naval conference held in London, December, 1908–February, 1909*, with an introduction by Elihu Root (New York: OUP, 1919).

——, *The Proceedings of the Hague Peace Conferences: Translation of the Official Texts*, prepared in the Division of International Law of the Carnegie Endowment for International Peace, 5 vols. (Publications of the Carnegie Endowment for International Peace: Division of International Law (Washington); New York: OUP, 1920–1921).

Sirey, Jean-Baptiste; Devilleneuve, L.-M., and Carette, Antoine-Auguste (eds.), *Recueil général des lois et des arrêts, en matière civile, criminelle, administrative et de droit public: 2e série. – An 1848.* (Paris: [s'adresser à M. Bachelier], 1848).

Sumner, Charles, *The works of Charles Sumner*, 15 vols. (Boston: Lee and Shepard, 1875–1883).

Tencé, Ulysse, *Annuaire historique universel pour 1831: Avec un Appendice contenant les actes publics, traités, notes diplomatiques, papiers d'états et tableaux statistiques, financiers, administratifs et nécrologiques; – une Chronique offrant les événements les plus piquants, les causes les plus célèbres, etc; et des notes pour servir à l'histoire des sciences, des lettres et des arts*, Nouvelle série (Paris: Thoisnier-Desplaces, 1833).

——, *Annuaire historique universel pour 1836: Avec un Appendice contenant les actes publics, traités, notes diplomatiques, papiers d'états et tableaux statistiques, financiers, administratifs et nécrologiques; – une Chronique offrant les événements les plus piquants, les causes les plus célèbres, etc; et des notes pour servir à l'histoire des sciences, des lettres et des arts*, Nouvelle série (Paris: Thoisnier-Desplaces, 1837).

United Nations, *Documents of the United Nations Conference on International Organization, San Francisco, 1945*, 6th vol. (London/New York: United Nations Information Organizations, 1945).

——, *Yearbook of the International Law Commission 1980: Summary records of the meetings of the thirty-second session 5 May-25 July 1980*, 1st vol. (New York: United Nations, 1981).

——, *Yearbook of the International Law Commission 1995: Summary records of the meetings of the forty-seventh session 2 May-21 July 1995*, 1st vol. (New York/Geneva: United Nations, 1997).

——, *Materials on the Responsibility of States for Internationally Wrongful Acts* (United Nations Legislative Series, 25; New York: United Nations, 2012).

United States, *Report of the delegates of the United States to the Third International Conference of the American States* (Washington: GPO, 1907).

United States, Department of State, *Papers Relating to the Foreign Relations of the United States, with the Annual Message of the President, transmitted to Congress, December 2, 1895*, Part II (Washington: GPO, 1896).

——, *Papers relating to the foreign relations of the United States, with the annual message of the President transmitted to Congress, December 6, 1897.* (Washington: GPO, 1898).

——, *Papers relating to the foreign relations of the United States, with the annual message of the President transmitted to Congress, December 3, 1901.* (Washington: GPO, 1902).

——, *Papers relating to the foreign relations of the United States, with the annual message of the President transmitted to Congress, December 7, 1903.* (Washington: GPO, 1904).

——, *Papers relating to the foreign relations of the United States, with the annual message of the President transmitted to Congress, December 5, 1905.* (Washington: GPO, 1906).

——, *Papers Relating to the Foreign Relations of the United States: The Paris Peace Conference, 1919*, 13th vol. (Washington: U.S. GPO, 1947).

——, *Foreign Relations of the United States: Diplomatic Papers, 1933*, 1st vol. (Washington: U.S. GPO, 1950).

United States, Senate, *The Venezuelan arbitration before The Hague Tribunal, 1903: The protocols between Venezuela and Great Britain, Germany, Italy, United States, Belgium, France, Mexico, the Netherlands, Spain, Sweden and Norway, signed at Washington, May 7, 1903* (Washington: GPO, 1905).

Verein für Hansische Geschichte, and Höhlbaum, Konstantin, *Hansisches Urkundenbuch*, 1st vol. (Halle: Buchhandlung des Waisenhauses, 1876).

Wendell, John Lansing, *Reports of Cases Argued and Determined in the Supreme Court of Judicature and in the Court for the Trial of Impeachments and the Correction of Errors of the State of New-York*, 25th vol. (2nd edn., New-York: Published by the reporter, 1850).

Secondary Sources

[Anonymous], 'The law relating to letters of marque and reprisals.', *The Legal Observer, or Journal of Jurisprudence* 19 (1839–1840), 481–2.

[Billot, Albert], *L'affaire du Tonkin: Histoire diplomatique de l'établissement de notre protectorat sur l'Annam et de notre conflit avec la Chine. 1882–1885* (Paris: J. Hetzel, 1888).

A Jeffersonian Democrat, 'The Venezuela Affair and the Monroe Doctrine', *NAR* 176 (1903), 321–35.

Acollas, Émile, *Le droit de la guerre* (Le droit mis à la portée de tout le monde; Paris: Librairie Ch. Delagrave, 1888).

Allemés, Frederick M., and Schuster, Ernest Joseph, 'The Legality or Illegality of the Ruhr Occupation', *TGS* 10 (1924), 61–87.

Álvarez, Alejandro, 'Latin America and International Law', *AJIL* 3 (1909), 269–353.

——, *Le droit international américain: Son fondement – sa nature, d'après l'Histoire diplomatique des Etats du Nouveau Monde et leur Vie Politique et Économique* (Paris: A. Pedone, 1910).

AMERASINGHE, CHITTHARANJAN FELIX, *Local Remedies in International Law* (Cambridge Studies in International and Comparative Law; 2nd edn., Cambridge: CUP, 2004).

ARIAS, ANTENOR, *Lecciones de Derecho Maritimo: Dictadas en la Facultad de ciencias politicas y administrativas de la Universidad Mayor de San Marcos* (Lima: Imprenta del Estado, 1876).

ASPIAZU, AGUSTÍN, *Dogmas del derecho internacional*, Obra impresa bajo la protección del coronel Agustín Morales (Nueva York: Hallet & Breen, 1872).

ASSER, TOBIAS MICHEL KAREL, 'La convention de Constantinople pour le libre usage du canal de Suez', *RDILC* 20 (1888), 529–58.

AYALA, BALTHAZAR, *De Jure et Officiis Bellicis et Disciplina Militari Libri III*, 2 vols. (The Classics of International Law, 2; Washington, D.C.: The Carnegie Institution of Washington, 1912).

AZUNI, DOMENICO ALBERTO, *Droit maritime de l'Europe*, 2nd vol. (Paris: L'Auteur/ Ant. Aug. Renouard, 1805).

B. F., 'The International Law of Embargo and Reprisal', *The Law Magazine; Or Quarterly Review of Jurisprudence* 24 (1840), 73–9.

BAECKER, THOMAS, 'The Arms of the *Ypiranga*. The German Side', *The Americas* 30 (1973), 1–17.

BAENZIGER, JAKOB, *Die Repressalien im Völkerrecht*, Dissertation zur Erlangung der Würde eines Doktors beider Rechte vorgelegt der hohen juristischen Fakultät der Universität Freiburg in der Schweiz (Zug: J. Kündigs Erben, 1925).

BARCLAY, THOMAS, 'Les blocus pacifiques', *RDILC* 29 (1897), 474–90.

BARÈS, CHARLES, *Le blocus pacifique* (Toulouse: G. Berthoumieu, 1898).

BARROS, JAMES, *The Corfu incident of 1923: Mussolini and the League of Nations* (Princeton, New Jersey: PUP, 1965).

——, *The League of Nations and the Great Powers: The Greek-Bulgarian Incident, 1925* (Oxford: Clarendon Press, 1970).

BARSALOU, OLIVIER, 'The History of Reprisals Up to 1945. Some Lessons Learned and Unlearned for Contemporary International Law', *MLLWR* 49 (2010), 335–71.

BARSOTTI, ROBERTO, 'Armed reprisals', in Antonio Cassese (ed.), *The Current legal restraints of the use of force* (Developments in International Law; Dordrecht: Martinus Nijhoff, 1986), 79–110.

BASDEVANT, JULES, 'L'action coercitive anglo-germano-italienne contre le Vénézuéla (1902–1903)', *RGDIP* 11 (1904), 362–458.

——, 'La conférence de Rio-de-Janeiro de 1906 et l'union internationale des républiques américaines', *RGDIP* 15 (1908), 209–70.

BATY, THOMAS, 'The Institute of International Law on Pacific Blockade', *The Law Magazine and Law Review* 21 (4th ser.) (1895–96), 285–300.

——, 'Conditional War.', *LMR* 24 (1898–1899), 436–40.

——, 'Les blocus pacifiques', *RDILC* 30 (1898), 606–9.

——, 'Danger-Signals in International Law', *YaleLJ* 34 (1925), 457–79.

——, 'The Threatened Chaos in the Law of Nations', *The Contemporary Review* 148 (1935), 65–71.

——, 'Abuse of Terms: "Recognition": "War"', *AJIL* 30 (1936), 377–99.

Becker Lorca, Arnulf, *Mestizo International Law: A Global Intellectual History 1842–1933* (Cambridge Studies in International and Comparative Law, 115; Cambridge: CUP, 2014).

Bello, Andrés, *Principios de derecho internacional* (2nd edn., Caracas: J. M. de Rojas, 1847).

Benedek, Wolfgang, 'Drago-Porter Convention (1907)', in Rüdiger Wolfrum (ed.), *The Max Planck Encyclopedia of Public International Law*, published under the auspices of the Max Planck Institute for comparative public law and international law, 3rd vol. (Oxford: OUP, 2012–2013; <http://www.mpepil.com>, accessed 18 August 2017), 234–6.

Béquet, Léon, 'L'état de représailles', *Le Temps*, 31 August 1884, 1.

Bergbohm, Carl, *Die bewaffnete Neutralität, 1780–1783: Eine Entwicklungsphase des Völkerrechts im Seekriege* (Berlin: Puttkammer & Mühlbrecht, 1884).

Bishop, Crawford M., 'International Law and the Manchurian Question', *GeoLJ* 21 (1932–1933), 306–14.

Bluntschli, Johann Caspar, *Das moderne Völkerrecht der civilisirten Staten: als Rechtsbuch dargestellt* (3rd edn., Nördlingen: C. H. Beck, 1878).

Bodin, Jean, *Les six livres de la République* (Paris: Chez Iacques du Puys, Librairie Iuré, 1576).

Böhmert, Viktor, 'Die Beschießung des befestigten Hafens Almeria, eine gerechte Selbsthilfemaßnahme', *ZVölkR* 21 (1937), 297–307.

Boisset, Louis, 'Les conciles provinciaux français et la réception des décrets du IIe concile de Lyon (1274)', *RHEF* 69 (1983), 29–59.

Bonet, Honoré, *L'arbre des batailles*, publié par Ernest Nys (Bruxelles/Leipzig: C. Muquardt, Merzbach et Falk, 1883).

Bonfils, Henry, *Manuel de droit international public (droit des gens): Destiné aux étudiants des Facultés de Droit et aux aspirants aux fonctions diplomatiques et consulaires*, édition revue et mise au courant par Paul Fauchille (7th edn., Paris: Rousseau et Cie, 1914).

Bonnot de Mably, Gabriel, *Le droit public de l'Europe, fondé sur les traités: Précédé des principes de négociations, pour servir d'Introduction*, avec des Remarques Historiques, Politiques & Critiques par Mr. Rousset, 2nd vol. (2nd edn., Amsterdam/Leipzig: Arkstée & Merkus, 1773).

Boot, Max, *The Savage Wars of Peace: Small Wars and the Rise of American Power* (revised edn., New York: Basic Books, 2014).

Borchard, Edwin Montefiore, *The diplomatic protection of citizens abroad or the law of international claims* (New York: The Banks Law Publishing Co., 1925).

——, '"War" and "Peace"', *AJIL* 27 (1933), 114–7.

——, 'Reprisals on Private Property', *AJIL* 30 (1936), 108–13.

Bordwell, Percy, *The Law of War Between Belligerents: A History and Commentary* (Chicago: Callaghan & Co., 1908).

Bourguignat, Auguste, *Question de La Plata: Les traités Leprédour. Notice au point de vue du droit international* (Paris: Imprimerie centrale de Napoléon Chaix et Cie, 1849).

Bowett, Derek, 'Reprisals Involving Recourse to Armed Force', *AJIL* 66 (1972), 1–36.

Bowett, Derek William, *Self-defence in international law* (Manchester: Manchester University Press, 1958).

Boye, Thorvald, 'Quelques aspects du développement des règles de la neutralité', *RdC* 64/II (1938), 157–231.

Boyle, Francis Anthony, *Foundations of World Order: The Legalist Approach to International Relations, 1898–1922* (Durham/London: Duke University Press, 1999).

Bravard-Veyrières, Pierre, *Des prises maritimes d'après l'ancient et le nouveau droit tel qu'il résulte du traité de Paris et de la déclaration du 16 avril 1856*, avec des notes par P. Royer-Collard (Paris: Cotillon, 1861).

Bravo, Benedetto, 'Sulân. Représailles et justice privée contre des étrangers dans les cités grecques (*Étude du vocabulaire et des institutions*)', *Annali della Scuola Normale Superiore di Pisa. Classe di Lettere e Filosofia* 10 (3rd ser.)/3 (1980), 675–987.

Brière, Yves de la, 'Évolution de la doctrine et de la pratique en matière de représailles', *RdC* 22/II (1928), 237–94.

Brierly, J. L., 'International Law and Resort to Armed Force', *CLJ* 4 (1932), 308–19.

Brownlie, Ian, *International Law and the Use of Force by States* (Oxford: Clarendon Press, 1963).

Bruyas, Nicolas, *De la déclaration de guerre: Sa justification. – Ses formes extérieures* (Lyon: A. Rey, 1899).

Bry, Georges, *Précis élémentaire de droit international public: mis au courant des progrès de la science et du droit positif contemporain à l'usage des étudiants des facultés de droit et des aspirants aux fonctions diplomatiques et consulaires* (3rd edn., Paris: L. Larose, 1896).

Bulmerincq, August (von), 'Le blocus pacifique et ses effets sur la propriété privée', *Clunet* 11 (1884), 569–83.

Bulmerincq, August von, 'Die Staatsstreitigkeiten und ihre Entscheidung ohne Krieg.', in Franz von Holtzendorff (ed.), *Handbuch des Völkerrechts. Auf Grundlage Europäischer Staatspraxis*, 4th vol. (Hamburg: A.-G. (vormals J. F. Richter), 1889), 3–127.

Burgh, William de, *The Elements of Maritime International Law: With a Preface on Some Unsettled Questions of Public Law* (London: Longmans, Green, and Co., 1868).

Burlamaqui, Jean-Jacques, *Principes du droit politiques*, 2nd vol. (Bibliothèque de Philosophie politique et juridique: Textes et Documents; Caen [Amsterdam]: Centre de Philosophie politique et juridique de l'Université de Caen [chez Zacharie Chatelain], 1987 [1752]).

Bustamante, José Luis, *Los cinco errores capitales de la intervención en el Plata* (Montevideo: Imprenta uruguayana, 1849).

Butler, Geoffrey, and Maccoby, Simon, *The Development of International Law* (Contributions to international law and diplomacy; London: Longmans, Green and Co., 1928).

Bynkershoek, Cornelius van, *Traité du Juge Competent des Ambassadeurs, Tant pour le Civil, que pour le Criminel* (La Haye: Thomas Johnson, 1723).

——, *Quaestionum juris publici libri duo*, 2 vols. (The Classics of International Law, 14; [1st edn. of 1737], Oxford: Clarendon Press, 1930).

Cable, James, *Gunboat diplomacy: Political applications of limited naval force.* (Studies in International Security, 16; 3rd edn., Basingstoke: Palgrave Macmillan, 1994).

Caflisch, Lucius, 'Vattel and the peaceful settlement of international disputes', in Vincent Chetail and Peter Haggenmacher (eds.), *Vattel's International Law in a XXIst Century Perspective* (Graduate Institute of International and Development Studies, 9; Leiden/Boston: Martinus Nijhoff Publishers, 2011), 257–66.

Calvo, Carlos, *Le droit international théorique et pratique: Précédé d'un exposé historique des progrès de la science du droit des gens*, 2nd vol. (2nd edn., Paris: A. Durand et Pedone-Lauriel; Guillaumin et Cie; Amyot, 1872).

——, *Le droit international théorique et pratique: précédé d'un exposé historique des progrès de la science du droit des gens*, 3rd vol. (4th edn., Paris: Guillaumin et Cie, 1888).

——, *Dictionnaire de droit international public et privé*, 2nd vol. (Berlin: Puttkammer & Mühlbrecht, 1885).

Cançado Trindade, Antônio Augusto, 'Denial of justice and its relationship to exhaustion of local remedies in international law', *PhilipLJ* 53 (1978), 404–20.

Canis, Johannes Jacobus, 'De Represaliis', in Franciscus Zilettus (ed.), *Tractatus illustrium in utraque tum pontificii, tum cæsarei iuris facultate Iurisconsultorum, De Fisco, & eius Priuilegiis. Ex multis in hoc volumen congesti, additis plurimis, etiam nunquam editis, hac nota designatis; & multò, quàm antea, emendatiores redditi; Summariis singulorum Tractatuum locupletißimis illustrati. Indices accessere ita locupletes, ut omnes materiæ, quæ sparsim leguntur, facillimè distinctæ Lectoribus appareant*, 12th vol. (Venetiis: [s.n.], 1584), fol. 275r–fol 279r.

Carette, Antoine-Auguste, '[Commentary on the decision *Le Comte de Thomar*]', in Jean-Baptiste Sirey, L.-M. Devilleneuve, and Antoine-Auguste Carette (eds.), *Recueil général des lois et des arrêts, en matière civile, criminelle, administrative et de droit public. 2e série. – An 1848.* (Paris: [s'adresser à M. Bachelier], 1848), 510–512 (2nd part).

Carnazza Amari, Guiseppe, *Trattato sul diritto internazionale pubblico di pace* (Corso di diritto internazionale, 1; 2nd edn., Milano: V. Maisner e compagnia, 1875).

Cassiodorus, *The letters of Cassiodorus: being a condensed translation of the Variae epistolae of Magnus Aurelius Cassiodorus Senator*, With an Introduction by Thomas Hodgkin (London: Henry Frowde, 1886).

Castle, Edward James, *The law of commerce in time of war: with particular reference to the respective rights and duties of belligerents and neutrals* (London: William Maxwell & son, 1870).

Cauchy, Eugène, *Le droit maritime international considéré dans ses origines et dans ses rapports avec les progrès de la civilisation*, 2nd vol. (Paris: Guillaumin et Cie, 1862).

Cavaglieri, Arrigo, 'Note critiche su la teoria dei mezzi coercitivi al difuori della guerra', *RivDirInt* 9 (1915), 23–49 & 305–342.

——, 'Règles générales du droit de la paix', *RdC* 26/I (1929), 315–585.

Chast, Denyse, '[Book Review: *As Represalias. Estudo de historia do direito português sécs. XV e XVI*, by Ruy de Albuquerque]', *RID comp.* 28 (1976), 621–2.

Chauveau, E., *Le droit des gens ou Droit international public: Introduction (notions générales – historique – méthode)* (Paris: Arthur Rousseau, 1891).

Chavarot, Marie-Claire, 'La pratique des lettres de marque d'après les arrêts du parlement (XIIIe-début XVe siècle)', *Bibliothèque de l'école des chartes* 149 (1991), 51–89.

Choppin, René, *Trois livres du domaine de la couronne de France: Composez en latin [...]. Et traduits en langage vulgaire sur la derniere impression de l'an 1605. Avec une table alphabetique fort ample des matieres, & choses plus remarquables y contenuës.* (Paris: Chez Estienne Richer, 1634).

Chrétien, Maxime, 'La « guerre totale » du Japon en Chine', *RGDIP* 46 (1939), 229–303.

Clark, Grover, 'The English Practice with Regard to Reprisals by Private Persons', *AJIL* 27 (1933), 694–723.

Colbert, Evelyn Speyer, *Retaliation in international law* (New York: King's Crown Press, 1948).

Colby, Elbridge, 'Was There War in the East?', *GeoLJ* 21 (1932–1933), 315–26.

Colombos, Constantine John, *The international law of the sea* (4th edn., London: Longmans, 1959).

Compin, Gaston, *Essai sur le blocus maritime en temps de guerre*, Thèse pour le doctorat de la Faculté de droit de l'Université de Paris (Paris: Arthur Rousseau, 1899).

Conwell-Evans, T. P., *The League Council in Action: A Study of the Methods employed by the Council of the League of Nations to prevent War and to settle International Disputes* (London: OUP, 1929).

Corbett, Julian Stafford, *England in the Seven Years' War: A Study in Combined Strategy*, 1st vol. (London: Longmans, Green, and Co., 1907).

Covarrubias y Leyva, Diego de, *Opera omnia: in duos tomos divisa* (Genève: Gabriel de Tournes & filiorum, 1724).

Curtis, Roy Emerson, 'The Law of Hostile Military Expeditions as Applied by the United States', *AJIL* 8 (1914), 224–55.

Cussy, Ferdinand de, *Phases et causes célèbres du droit maritime des nations*, 2 vols. (Leipzig: F. A. Brockhaus, 1856).

Da Vella, Oreste, 'Il blocco dei porti del Siam e i blocchi pacifici', *Nuova Antologia di Scienze, Lettere ed Arti* 47 (3rd ser.) (1893), 295–308.

Darcy, Shane, 'The Evolution of the Law of Belligerent Reprisals', *MilLRev* 175 (2003), 184–251.

——, 'Retaliation and reprisal', in Marc Weller, Alexia Solomou and Jake William Rylatt (eds.), *The Oxford Handbook of the Use of Force in International Law* (Oxford handbooks; Oxford: OUP, 2015), 879–96.

Dareste, Rodolphe, *Nouvelles études d'histoire du droit* (Paris: Librairie de la société du recueil général des lois et des arrêts, 1902).

Dawkins, Clinton E., 'The Egyptian Public Debt', *NAR* 173 (1901), 487–507.

De Cecco, Marcello, 'The Italian Economy Seen from Abroad', in Gianni Toniolo (ed.), *The Oxford Handbook of the Italian Economy Since Unification* (Oxford: OUP, 2013), 134–54.

De Visscher, Charles, 'L'interprétation du pacte au lendemain du différend italogrec', *RDILC* 51 (1924), 213–230 & 377–396.

——, 'Le déni de justice en droit international', *RdC* 52/II (1935), 369–442.

——, *Théories et réalités en droit international public* (Paris: A. Pedone, 1953).

De Visscher, Fernand, *La Renonciation du Gouvernement britannique au Droit de Représailles sur les Biens des Particuliers allemands*, extrait de la *Revue de Droit international et de Législation comparée* (1920, n° 3–4) (Bruxelles: M. Weissenbruch, 1920).

Deane, Henry Bargrave, *The Law of Blockade: Its History, Present Condition, and Probable Future. An International Law Essay, 1870* (London: Longmans, Green, Reader, and Dyer; Wildy & sons, 1870).

Del Vecchio, Alberto, and Casanova, Eugenio, *Le rappresaglie dei comuni medievali e specialmente in Firenze: Saggio storico* (Bologna: Nicola Zanichelli (Cesare e Giacomo Zanichelli), 1894).

Delbez, Louis, *La notion de guerre: Essai d'analyse dogmatique* (Paris: A. Pedone, 1953).

Derrett, J. Duncan M., 'Withernam. A Legal Practice Joke of Sir Thomas More', *CathLaw* 7 (1961), 211–222 & 242.

——, 'Withernam. A Postscript', *CathLaw* 9 (1963), 124–37.

Des Marez, G., 'La lettre de foire au XIIIe siècle. Contribution à l'étude sur les origines des papiers de crédit.', *RDILC* 31 (1899), 533–44.

Descamps, Edouard, 'Le droit international nouveau. L'influence de la condamnation de la guerre sur l'évolution juridique internationale', *RdC* 31/I (1930), 399–559.

Desjardins, Arthur, *Traité de droit commercial maritime*, 1st vol. (Paris: A. Durand et Pedone-Lauriel, 1878).

Despagnet, Frantz, *Cours de droit international public* (4th edn., Paris: Libraire de la société du Recueil Sirey, 1910).

Díaz Borrás, Andrés, 'Marca, arte de la mercadería y protorganización de la estructura recaudatoria en la Valencia del trescientos', *Anuario de Estudios Medievales* 41 (2011), 3–29.

Dotremont, Stanislas, *L'arbitrage international et le Conseil de la Société des Nations: Le Pacte, les progrès tentés et réalisés depuis, les progrès réalisables* (Bruxelles: Maurice Lamertin, 1929).

Drago, Luis María, *Cobro coercitivo de deudas públicas* (Buenos Aires: Coni Hermanos, 1906).

——, 'Les emprunts d'Etat et leurs rapports avec la politique internationale', *RGDIP* 14 (1907), 251–87.

——, 'State Loans in Their Relation to International Policy', *AJIL* 1 (1907), 692–726.

Du Cange, Charles Du Fresne, *Glossarium mediæ et infimæ latinitatis*, Conditum a Carolo Du Fresne, domino Du Cange, auctum a monachis ordinis S. Benedicti cum supplementis integris D. P. Carpenterii, Adelungii, aliorums suisque digessit G. A. L. Henschel sequuntur glossarium gallicum, tabulæ, indices auctorum et rerum, dissertationes: Editio nova aucta pluribus verbis aliorum scriptorum a Léopold Favre, Toustain, Le Pelletier, Dantine et al., 7th vol. (new edn., Niort: L. Favre, 1886).

Ducrocq, Louis, *Représailles en temps de paix: Blocus pacifique suivi d'une étude sur les affaires de Chine (1900–1901)*, Thèse pour le doctorat de la Faculté de droit de Paris, soutenue le 20 Mars 1901, à 1 heure (Paris: A. Pedone, 1901).

Dulon, Rudolf, 'The Venezuelan Arbitration Once More. Facts and Law.', *The American Law Review* 38 (1904), 648–61.

Duplessix, E., *La Loi des Nations: Projet d'institution d'une Autorité internationale Législative, Administrative et Judiciaire. Projet de Code de Droit international public*, Ouvrage couronné par le Bureau international de la Paix (Concours 1905–1906 – 1er Prix) (Paris: Libraire de la société du Recueil J.-B. Sirey et du Journal du Palais, 1906).

Eagleton, Clyde, 'The attempt to define war', *IntlConciliation* 15 (1933), 233–87.

Editorial Comment, 'Treaties of Arbitration since the First Hague Conference', *AJIL* 2 (1908), 823–30.

——, 'Mediation in Mexico', *AJIL* 8 (1914), 579–85.

Eiglier, Joseph, *Étude historique sur le droit de marque ou de représailles à Marseille aux XIIIème, XIVème & XVème siècles* (Marseille: Aschero et Sacomant, 1888).

Einspanier, Kathryn L., 'Burlamaqui, the Constitution and the Imperfect War on Terror', *GeoLJ* 96 (2007–2008), 985–1026.

Elagab, Omer Yousif, *The legality of non-forcible counter-measures in international law* (Oxford monographs in international law; Oxford: OUP, 1988).

Elbe, Joachim von, 'The Evolution of the Concept of the Just War in International Law', *AJIL* 33 (1939), 665–88.

Émérigon, Balthazard-Marie, and Boulay-Paty, Pierre-Sébastien, *Traité des assurances et des contrats à la grosse d'Émérigon, conféré et mis en rapport avec le nouveau code de commerce et la jurisprudence; suivi d'un vocabulaire des termes de ma-*

rine et des noms de chaque partie d'un navire, 1st vol. (2nd edn., Rennes: Molliex, 1827).

Erich, Rafael Waldemar, 'Quelques observations sur les mesures de coercition "pacifiques"', *RDI* 4 (1926), 16–9.

Fahl, G., 'Repressalie', in Wolfgang Stammler, Adalbert Erler, Ekkehard Kaufmann et al. (eds.), *Handwörterbuch zur deutschen Rechtsgeschichte*, 4th vol. (Berlin: Erich Schmidt, 1990), col. 911–913.

Falcke, Horst P., *Le blocus pacifique*, trans. Ant. Contat (Leipzig: Rossberg, 1919).

Falcon, Minerva Jean A., 'Reprisals', *PYIL* 10 (1984), 26–37.

Fauchille, Paul, *Du blocus maritime: Étude de droit international et de droit comparé* (Paris: Arthur Rousseau, 1882).

——, *Traité de droit international public*, 2 vols. (8th edn., Paris: Rousseau & Cie, 1921–1926).

Fenwick, Charles G., 'The Arms Embargo against Bolivia and Paraguay', *AJIL* 28 (1934), 534–8.

——, 'Intervention. Individual and Collective', *AJIL* 39 (1945), 645–63.

Ferguson, Jan Helenus, *Manual of International Law: for the Use of Navies, Colonies and Consulates*, 2nd vol. (London: W. B. Whittingham & co., 1884).

Fernandez, Cesareo, *Nociones de derecho internacional maritimo* (Habana: Imprenta del tiempo, 1863).

Field, David Dudley, *Draft. Outlines of an International Code* (New York: Baker, Voorhis & Company, 1872).

Finch, George A., 'The Legality of the Occupation of the Ruhr Valley', *AJIL* 17 (1923), 724–33.

Fiore, Pasquale, *Nouveau droit international public suivant les besoins de la civilisation moderne*, traduit de l'Italien et annotée par Charles Antoine, 2nd vol. (2nd edn., Paris: A. Durand et Pedone-Lauriel, 1885).

——, 'L'organisation juridique de la société internationale', *RDILC* 31 (1899), 105–126 & 209–242.

Flöckher, Adolph von, *De l'intervention en droit international* (Paris: A. Pedone, 1896).

Förster, Robert von, *Schiedssprechung und Repressalie*, Inaugural-Dissertation zur Erlangung der juristischen Doktorwürde der Rechts- und Staatswissenschaftlichen Fakultät der Universität zu Göttingen (Würzburg: Konrad Triltsch, 1936).

François, J.-P.-A., 'Règles générales du droit de la paix', *RdC* 66/IV (1938), 5–294.

Freeman, Alwyn Vernon, *The International Responsibility of States for Denial of Justice* (New York: Kraus, 1938 [Reprod. 1970]).

——, 'Recent Aspects of the Calvo Doctrine and the Challenge to International Law', *AJIL* 40 (1946), 121–47.

Funck-Brentano, Théophile, and Sorel, Albert, *Précis du droit ges gens* (2nd edn., Paris: E. Plon, Nourrit et Cie, 1887).

Garatus Laudensis, Martinus, 'De Represaliis', in Franciscus Zilettus (ed.), *Tractatus illustrium in utraque tum pontificii, tum cæsarei iuris facultate Iurisconsultorum, De Fisco, & eius Priuilegiis. Ex multis in hoc volumen congesti, additis plurimis, etiam nunquam editis, hac nota designatis; & multò, quàm antea, emendatiores redditi; Summariis singulorum Tractatuum locupletißimis illustrati. Indices accessere ita lucupletes, ut omnes materiæ, quæ sparsim leguntur, facillimè distinctæ Lectoribus appareant*, 12th vol. (Venetiis: [s.n.], 1584), fol. 279r- fol. 281r.

Gardiner, Alfred George, *The Life of Sir William Harcourt*, 1st vol. (London/Bombay/Sydney: Constable & Company, 1923).

Gardiner, D. A., 'The History of Belligerent Rights on the High Seas in the Fourteenth Century', *LQR* 48 (1932), 521–46.

Gareis, Karl, *Institutionen des Völkerrechts* (Gießen: Emil Roth, 1888).

Geffcken, Friedrich Heinrich, 'La France en Chine et le droit international', *RDILC* 17 (1885), 145–51.

——, 'Le blocus pacifique. Réponse aux conclusions du rapport de M. Perels', *RDILC* 19 (1887), 377–83.

Gentili, Alberico, *De Iure Belli Libri Tres* (Oxford: Clarendon Press, 1877).

George, Alexander L., *Forceful Persuasion: Coercive Diplomacy as an Alternative to War*, Foreword by Ambassador Samuel W. Lewis (Washington, D.C.: United States Institute of Peace Press, 1991).

Gérard de Rayneval, Joseph-Mathias, *De la liberté des mers*, 1st vol. (Paris: Treuttel et Wurtz/Arthus Bertrand/Delaunay, 1811).

——, *Institutions du droit de la nature et des gens*, 1st vol. (new edn., Paris: Rey et Gravier, 1832).

Gessner, Ludwig, *Le droit des neutres sur mer* (Bibliothèque diplomatique; 2nd edn., Berlin: Charles Heymann, 1876).

Gibson Bowles, Thomas, *Sea law and sea power as they would be affected by recent proposals; with reasons against those proposals* (London: John Murray, 1910).

Giegerich, Thomas, 'Retorsion', in Rüdiger Wolfrum (ed.), *The Max Planck Encyclopedia of Public International Law*, published under the auspices of the Max Planck Institute for comparative public law and international law, 11 vols. (Oxford: OUP, 2012–2013; <http://www.mpepil.com>, accessed 15 December 2017).

Giltaij, Jacob, 'Roman law and the *causa legitima* for reprisal in Bartolus', *Fundamina* 20 (2014), 349–56.

Giraud, Émile, 'La théorie de la légitime défense', *RdC* 49/III (1934), 691–868.

Glafey, Adam Friedrich, *Vernünfft- Und Völcker-Recht: Worinnen die Lehren dieser Wissenschafft auf demonstrative Gründe gesetzet/ und nach selbigen die unter souverainen Völckern/ wie auch denen Gelehrten biß daher vorgefallene Strittigkeiten erörtert werden, Nebst einer Historie des vernünfftigen Rechts/ worinnen nicht nur die Lehren eines jeden Scribenten in Jure Naturæ angezeigt und examinirt werden, sondern auch eine vollständige Bibliotheca Juris Naturæ & Gentium zu befinden ist, welche die biß anhero in dieser disciplin heraus gekommene Bücher, Dissertationes, Deductiones und andere pieçes volantes nach ihren Materien in Alphabetischer Ord-*

nung darlegt, Samt einen vollständigen Real-Register (Franckfurt/Leipzig: Christoph Riegel, 1723).

GLASS, HENRY, *Marine International Law: Compiled from various sources* (Proceedings of the United States Naval Institute, 11, No. 3; Annapolis, Md.: The United States Naval Institute, 1885).

GONSIOROWSKI, MIROSLAS, *Société des Nations et Problème de la Paix*, 2nd vol. (Paris: Rousseau & Cie, 1927).

GOODRICH, LELAND M., and HAMBRO, EDVARD, *Charter of the United Nations: Commentary and Documents*, published under the auspice of the London Institute of World Affairs (The Library of World Affairs, 10; 2nd edn., London: Stevens & sons, 1949).

GÖRTZ, JOHANN EUSTACH von, *Mémoire, ou précis historique sur la neutralité armée et son origine, Suivi de pièces justificatives* (Basle: J. Decker, 1801).

GOTTSCHALK, EGON, 'Die völkerrechtlichen Hauptprobleme des Mandschureikonflikts', *ZVölkR* 17 (1933), 188–259 & 289–341.

GOURDON, ÉDOUARD, *Histoire du Congrès de Paris*, avec une introduction par M. J. Cohen (Paris: Librairie nouvelle, 1857).

GOVER, JOHN M., 'Current notes on international law', *The Law Magazine and Law Review* 22 (4th ser.) (1896–97), 182–94.

GRAHAM-YOOLL, ANDREW, *Imperial Skirmishes: War and Gunboat Diplomacy in Latin America* (Brooklyn, N.Y./Northampton, Mass.: Interlink Books, 2002).

GREWE, WILHELM GEORG, *Epochen der Völkerrechtsgeschichte* (Baden-Baden: Nomos, 1984).

GROB, FRITZ, *The Relativity of War and Peace: A Study in Law, History, and Politics*, Foreword by Roscoe Pound (New Haven: Yale University Press, 1949).

GROS ESPIELL, HÉCTOR, 'La doctrine du Droit international en Amérique Latine avant la première conférence panaméricaine (Washington, 1889)', *JHistIntlL* 3 (2001), 1–17.

GROTIUS, HUGO, *De Jure Belli ac Pacis Libri Tres*, 2 vols. (The Classics of International Law, 3; Oxford: Clarendon Press, 1923–1925).

——, *Le droit de la guerre et de la paix*, Traduction de Jean Barbeyrac, 2 vols. (Bibliothèque de Philosophie politique et juridique: Textes et Documents; Caen [Amsterdam]: Centre de Philosophie politique et juridique de l'Université de Caen [chez Pierre de Coup], 1984 [1724]).

GUANI, ALBERTO, 'Les mesures de coercition entre membres de la Société des Nations envisagées spécialement au point de vue américain', *RGDIP* 31 (1924), 285–90.

GUGGENHEIM, PAUL, *Traité de Droit international public*, avec la collaboration de Denise Bindschedler-Robert, 2nd vol. (Genève: Librairie de l'Université, Georg & Cie, 1954).

GUIZOT, FRANÇOIS, *An Embassy to the Court of St. James's in 1840* (London: Richard Bentley, 1862).

GUTTRY, ANDREA de, *Le rappresaglie non comportanti la coercizione militare nel diritto internazionale* (Pubblicazioni della facoltà di giurisprudenza della università di Pisa, 90; Milano: Dott. A. Giuffrè, 1985).

GUYOT, JOSEPH-NICOLAS, 'Représailles (lettres de)', in Philippe-Antoine Merlin (ed.), *Répertoire universel et raisonné de jurisprudence. Réduit aux objets dont la connaissance peut encore être utile, et augmentée 1° des changemens apportés aux lois anciennes par les lois nouvelles, tant avant que depuis l'année 1814; 2° de dissertations, de plaidoyers et de réquisitoires sur les unes et les autres*, 15th vol. (5th edn., Paris: Garnery, 1828), 48–9.

HAGGENMACHER, PETER, 'L'ancêtre de la protection diplomatique. les représailles de l'ancien droit (XIIe-XVIIIe siècles)', *Relations internationales* 143/3 (2010), 7–12.

HALE, MATTHEW, *Historia Placitorum Coronæ: The History of the Pleas of the Crown*, 1st vol. (new edn., London: T. Payne, H. L. Gardner, W. Otridge, E. and R. Brooke and J. Rider, J. Butterworth, W. Clarke and Son, R. Phenet, J. Cuthell, J. Walker, J. Bagster, and R. Bickerstaff, 1800).

HALL, WILLIAM EDWARD, *A treatise on international law* (4th edn., Oxford: Clarendon Press, 1895).

HANNELL, DAVID, 'Lord Palmerston and the 'Don Pacifico Affair' of 1850. The Ionian Connection', *EHQ* 19 (1989), 495–507.

HAUMANT, ANDRÉ, *Les représailles*, Thèse pour le doctorat en droit présentée et soutenue le 12 Mars 1934, à 14 heures (Paris: Marcel Giard, 1934).

HAUTEFEUILLE, LAURENT-BASILE, *Des droits et des devoirs des nations neutres en temps de guerre maritime*, 3rd vol. (1st edn., Paris: Au comptoir des imprimeurs-unis, 1849).

——, *Des droits et des devoirs des nations neutres en temps de guerre maritime*, 3rd vol. (3rd edn., Paris: Guillaumin et Cie, 1868).

HEBENSTREIT, JOHANNES, *Repressalien im humanitären Völkerrecht* (Völkerrecht und Außenpolitik, 64; Baden-Baden: Nomos, 2004).

HEFFTER, AUGUST WILHELM, *Das Europäische Völkerrecht der Gegenwart* (Berlin: E. H. Schroeder, 1844).

HEILBORN, PAUL, *Das System des Völkerrechts entwickelt aus den völkerrechtlichen Begriffen* (Berlin: Julius Springer, 1896).

HEIMBECK, LEA, *Die Abwicklung von Staatsbankrotten im Völkerrecht: Verrechtlichung und Rechtsvermeidung zwischen 1824 und 1907* (Studien zur Geschichte des Völkerrechts, 28; Baden-Baden: Nomos, 2013).

——, 'Legal Avoidance as Peace Instrument. Domination and Pacification through Asymmetric Loan Transactions', in Thomas Hippler and Miloš Vec (eds.), *Paradoxes of Peace in Nineteenth Century Europe* (Oxford: OUP, 2015), 111–27.

HENDERSON, JOHN BROOKS, *American Diplomatic Questions* (New York/London: The Macmillan Company, 1901).

HENDRICKSON, EMBERT J., 'Root's Watchful Waiting and the Venezuelan Controversy', *The Americas* 23 (1966), 115–29.

HERSHEY, AMOS S., 'The Calvo and Drago Doctrines', *AJIL* 1 (1907), 26–45.

——, *The Essentials of International Public Law* (New York: The Macmillan Company, 1919).

HEYNS, HARALD, *Die Anwendung von militärischen Repressalien unter Völkerbundmitgliedstaaten*, Inaugural-Dissertation zur Erlangung der Doktorwürde der Hohen Rechts- und Staatswissenschaftlichen Fakultät der Christian-Albrechts-Universität zu Kiel (Baruth/Mark-Berlin: J. Särchen, 1938).

HICKS, GEOFFREY, 'Don Pacifico, Democracy, and Danger. The Protectionist Party Critique of British Foreign Policy, 1850–1852', *The International History Review* 26 (2004), 515–40.

HIGGINS, ROSALYN, 'The Legal Limits to the Use of Force by Sovereign States United Nations Practice', *BYIL* 37 (1961), 269–319.

HILL, DAVID JAYNE, 'The Janina-Corfu Affair', *AJIL* 18 (1924), 98–104.

HILLER, ERNST, 'Die Friedensblockade und ihre Stellung in Völkerrecht', Inaugural-Dissertation verfasst und der Hohen Rechts- und Staatswissenschaftlichen Fakultät der Bayer. Julius-Maximilians-Universität Würzburg zur Erlangung der staatswissenschaftlichen Doktorwürde (Würzburg, Hohe Rechts- und Staatswissenschaftiche Fakultät der Bayer. Julius-Maximilians-Universität Würzburg, 1923).

HINDMARSH, ALBERT E., 'Self-Help in Time of Peace', *AJIL* 26 (1932), 315–26.

HO, PAO JIN, 'Reprisals in international law', Master of Arts in Political Science (Urbana, Ill.: University of Illinois, 1922).

——, 'Pacific blockade with special reference to its use as a measure of reprisal', Doctor of Philosophy in Political Science (Urbana, Ill.: University of Illinois, 1925).

HOGAN, ALBERT EDMOND, *Pacific blockade* (Oxford: Clarendon Press, 1908).

HOHL, FRIEDRICH RUDOLF, 'Bartolus a Saxoferrato: Tractatus Represaliarum. Seine Bedeutung für die Entwicklungsgeschichte des Repressalienrechts' (Bonn, Rheinische Friedrich-Wilhelms-Universität Bonn, 1954).

HOIJER, OLOF, *La solution pacifique des litiges internationaux avant et depuis la Société des Nations: Étude de Droit International et d'Histoire Diplomatique* (Paris: Spes, 1925).

——, *Le Pacte de la Société des Nations: Commentaire théorique et pratique*, Préface de M. André Weiss (Paris: Spes, 1926).

HOLLAND, THOMAS ERSKINE, *Studies in international law* (Oxford: Clarendon Press, 1898).

——, 'War *Sub Modo*', *The Law Quarterly Review* 19 (1903), 133–5.

——, *Letters to "The Times" upon War and Neutrality (1881–1920): With some commentary* (3rd edn., London: Longmans, Green, and Co., 1921).

HOOD, MIRIAM, *Gunboat Diplomacy, 1895–1905: Great Power Pressure in Venezuela* (2nd edn., London: George Allen & Unwin, 1983).

HOWARD-ELLIS, C., *The origin, structure & working of the League of Nations* (London: George Allen & Unwin, 1928).

Hübner, Martin, *De la Saisie des Batimens Neutres, ou Du Droit qu'ont les Nations Belligérantes d'arrêter les Navires des Peuples Amis*, 1st vol. (La Haye: [s.n.], 1759).

Hudson, Manley O., 'How the League of Nations Met the Corfu Crisis', *League of Nations* 6 (1923), 176–98.

Hutcheson, Francis, *A Short Introduction to Moral Philosophy: in Three Books; Containing the Elements of Ethicks and the Law of Nature*, translated from the Latin (2nd edn., Glasgow: Robert & Andrew Foulis, 1753).

Huvelin, Paul-Louis, *Essai historique sur le droit des marchés & des foires* (Paris: Arthur Rousseau, 1897).

Hyde, Charles Cheney, *International law chiefly as interpreted and applied by the United States*, 2nd vol. (Boston: Little, Brown, and Company, 1922).

Jackson, A. H., 'An Oracle for Raiders?', *ZPE* 108 (1995), 95–9.

Jaucourt, Louis de, 'Représailles', in Denis Diderot and Jean Le Rond d'Alembert (eds.), *Encyclopédie ou Dictionnaire raisonné des sciences, des arts et des métiers*, 14th vol. (Neufchastel: chez Samuel Faulche & Compagnie, [1751–1765]), 142–3.

Jellinek, Georg, 'China und das Völkerrecht', *DJZ* 5 (1900), 401–4.

Jessup, Philip C., 'The United States and Treaties for the Avoidance of War', *IntlConciliation* 12 (1928–1929), 179–207.

——, 'Force under a Modern Law of Nations', *ForeignAff* 25 (1946), 90–105.

——, *A modern law of nations: An introduction* (New York: The Macmillan Company, 1948).

——, 'Should International Law Recognize an Intermediate Status between Peace and War?', *AJIL* 48 (1954), 98–103.

Johnson, O. Thomas, Jr., and Gimblett, Jonathan, 'From gunboats to BITs. The evolution of modern international investment law', *Yearbook on International Investment Law and Policy* (2010–2011), 649–92.

Joosen, Henry, *Représailles exercées contre des marchands malinois aux foires de Champagne (1300–1305)*, extrait de la Chronique Mensuelle « Mechlinia » (Malines: H. Dierickx-Beke Fils, 1934).

Jouannet, Emmanuelle, 'Emer de Vattel (1714–1767)', in Bardo Fassbender and Anne Peters (eds.), *The Oxford Handbook of the History of International Law* (Oxford: OUP, 2012), 1118–21.

Kalshoven, Frits, *Belligerent Reprisals*, Preface by Jean Pictet (Scientific collection of the Henry Dunant Institute, 1; Leyden: Sijthoff, 1971).

Kamarowsky, Leonid, 'De l'idée d'un tribunal international', *RDILC* 15 (1883), 44–51.

Kamptz, Carl Albert von, *Beiträge zum Staats- und Völkerrecht*, 1st vol. (Berlin: Nicolai, 1815).

——, *Neue Literatur des Völkerrechts seit dem Jahre 1784; als Ergänzung und Fortsetzung des Werks des Gesandten von Ompteda* (Berlin: Duncker und Humblot, 1817).

KAPPUS, GEORG, *Der völkerrechtliche Kriegsbegriff in seiner Abgrenzung gegenüber den militärischen Repressalien* (Abhandlungen aus dem Staats- und Verwaltungsrecht mit Einschluss des Kolonialrechts und des Völkerrechts, 52; Breslau: M. & H. Marcus, 1936).

KAUFMANN, ERICH, 'Règles générales du droit de la paix', *RdC* 54/IV (1935), 313–620.

KEEN, M. H., *The Laws of War in the Late Middle Ages* (Studies in political history; London/Toronto: Routledge & Kegan Paul/University of Toronto Press, 1965).

KELLOR, FRANCES, and HATVANY, ANTONIA, *Security against war*, 2nd vol. (New York: The Macmillan Company, 1924).

KELLY, MICHAEL J., 'Time warp to 1945 – Resurrection of the reprisal and anticipatory self-defense doctrines in international law', *JTransnatLawPol* 13 (2003), 1–39.

KELSEN, HANS, 'The Old and the New League: The Covenant and the Dumbarton Oaks Proposals', *AJIL* 39 (1945), 45–83.

——, *Principles of international law* (New York: Rinehart & company, 1952).

——, *Peace through law* (1st edn. of 1944, Clark, New Jersey: The Lawbook Exchange, 2008).

——, *Collective security under international law* (2nd reprint [originally published: International law studies, 49; Washington: United States GPO, 1957], Clark, New Jersey: The Lawbook Exchange, 2011).

KEYNES, JOHN MAYNARD, *The Economic Consequences of the Peace* (New York: Harcourt, Brace and Howe, 1920).

——, *A Revision of the Treaty: being a Sequel to the Economic Consequences of the Peace* (New York: Harcourt, Brace and Howe, 1922).

KLEEN, RICHARD, *Lois et usages de la neutralité: D'après le droit international conventionnel et coutumier des États civilisés*, 1st vol. (Paris: A. Chevalier-Marescq, 1898).

KLÜBER, JEAN LOUIS, *Droit des gens moderne de l'Europe*, 2nd vol. (Stuttgart: J. G. Cotta, 1819).

KNETSCH, ALFON, 'Repressalien', in Paul Posener (ed.), *Rechtslexikon. Handwörterbuch der Rechts- und Staatswissenschaften*, mit Unterstützung durch zahlreiche Mitarbeiter, 2nd vol. (Berlin: Erich Weber Verlag, 1909), 379.

KOEPPLER, HEINZ, 'Frederick Barbarossa and the Schools of Bologna. Some Remarks on the 'Authentica Habita'', *The English Historical Review* 54 (1939), 577–607.

KOLB, ROBERT, 'The Protection of the Individual in Times of War and Peace', in Bardo Fassbender and Anne Peters (eds.), *The Oxford Handbook of the History of International Law* (Oxford: OUP, 2012), 317–37.

KOSKENNIEMI, MARTTI, *The Gentle Civilizer of Nations: The Rise and Fall of International Law, 1870–1960* (Cambridge, New York: CUP, 2002).

KOTZSCH, LOTHAR, 'Die Blockade gegen Venezuela vom Jahre 1902 als Präzedenzfall für das moderne Kriegsrecht', *ArchVölkR* 5 (1955–1956), 410–25.

——, *The concept of war in contemporary history and international law* (Études d'histoire économique, politique et sociale, 18; Genève: E. Droz, 1956).

Krauss, Axel, 'Bartolus de Saxoferrato (1313/14–1357)', in Gerd Kleinheyer and Jan Schröder (eds.), *Deutsche und Europäische Juristen aus neun Jahrhunderten. Eine biographische Einführung in die Geschichte der Rechtswissenschaft* (6th edn., Tübingen: Mohr Siebeck, 2017), 45–9.

Kreutz, Barbara M., *Before the Normans: Southern Italy in the Ninth and Tenth Centuries* (Philadelphia: University of Pennsylvania Press, 1996).

Kuhn, Arthur K., 'The Lytton Report on the Manchurian Crisis', *AJIL* 27 (1933), 96–100.

Kulsrud, Carl Jacob, *Maritime Neutrality to 1780: A History of the Main Principles Governing Neutrality and Belligerency to 1780* (Boston: Little, Brown, and Company, 1936).

Kunz, Josef L., *Kriegsrecht und Neutralitätsrecht* (Wien: Julius Springer, 1935).

——, 'Sanctions in International Law', *AJIL* 54 (1960), 324–47.

La Mache, Charles, *La guerre de course dans le passé, dans le présent et dans l'avenir* (Paris: A. Pedone, 1901).

Larrain y Zañartu, José Joaquín, *Nociones de derecho internacional marítimo segun los mas recientes progresos de la ciencia: Adaptacion a las leyes i preceptos de Chile, i como testo de la Escuela Naval i libro de consulta para los oficiales de la Marina de Guerra, del testo de A. Lemoine, capitan de fragata i Licenciado en Derecho en Francia* (Santiago de Chile: Imprensa Nacional, 1892).

Lauterpacht, Hersch, '"Resort to War" and the Interpretation of the Covenant during the Manchurian Dispute', *AJIL* 28 (1934), 43–60.

——, *The Function of Law in the International Community* (1st edn. of 1933, Oxford: OUP, 2011).

Laveleye, Émile de, *Des causes actuelles de guerre en Europe et de l'arbitrage* (Bruxelles: C. Muquardt, 1873).

Lawrence, Thomas Joseph, *Essays on Some Disputed Questions in Modern International Law* (2nd edn., Cambridge: Deighton, Bell and Co., 1885).

——, *The principles of international law* (3rd edn., Boston: D. C. Heath & Co., 1900).

——, *The principles of international law* (4th edn., Boston: D. C. Heath & Co., 1910).

——, *Lectures on the League of Nations: delivered in the University of Bristol* (Bristol: J. W. Arrowsmith, 1919).

Le Fur, Louis, *Des Représailles en temps de guerre: Représailles et Réparations* (Comité pour la Défense du Droit International; Paris: Recueil Sirey, 1919).

——, 'Le développement historique du droit international. De l'anarchie internationale à une communauté internationale organisée', *RdC* 41/III (1932), 505–601.

LE LONG, JOHN, *Intervention de la France dans le Rio-de-La-Plata: Motifs et moyens. L'Opposition de l'Angleterre à une intervention armée pourrait-elle aller jusqu'à poser un casus belli?* (Paris: Imprimerie de Madame de Lacombe, 1849).

LÉCRIVAIN, CHARLES-ALBERT, 'Le droit de se faire justice soi-même et les représailles dans les relations internationales de la Grèce', *Mémoires de l'Académie de sciences, inscriptions et belles-lettres de Toulouse* 9 (9th ser.) (1897), 277–90.

LEGNANO, GIOVANNI DA, *Tractatus de Bello, de Represaliis et de Duello*, edited by Thomas Erskine Holland (The Classics of International Law, 8; Oxford: OUP, 1917).

LEISER, BURTON M., 'The Morality of Reprisals', *Ethics* 1975 (1985), 159–63.

LESAFFER, RANDALL, 'The classical law of nations (1500–1800)', in Alexander Orakhelashvili (ed.), *Research Handbook on the Theory and History of International Law* (Cheltenham/Northampton, Mass.: Edward Elgar, 2011), 408–40.

——, 'Peace through law. The Hague Peace Conferences and the rise of the *ius contra bellum*', in Maartje Abbenhuis, Christopher Ernest Barber, and Annalise R. Higgins (eds.), *War, Peace and International Order? The Legacies of the Hague Conferences of 1899 and 1907* (Routledge Studies in Modern History; Abingdon, Oxon/New York: Routledge, 2017), 31–51.

LIANG, YUEN-LI, 'Rechtsprobleme des Mandschureikonflikts', *ZVölkR* 17 (1933), 1–12.

——, 'Some Legal Issues in the Sino-Japanese Controversy before the League Assembly.', *The China Law Review* 6 (1933), 213–24.

LINK, SANDRA, *Ein Realist mit Idealen – Der Völkerrechtler Karl Strupp (1886–1940)* (Studien zur Geschichte des Völkerrechts, 5; Baden-Baden: Nomos, 2003).

LINTOTT, ANDREW, '*Sula*–Reprisal by Seizure in Greek Inter-Community Relations', *The Classical Quarterly* 54 (2004), 340–53.

LISZT, FRANZ VON, *Das Völkerrecht: systematisch dargestellt* (Berlin: O. Haering, 1898).

LITTRÉ, ÉMILE, *Dictionnaire de la langue française, contenant 1° pour la nomenclature: Tous les mots qui se trouvent dans le Dictionnaire de l'Académie française et tous les termes usuels des sciences, des arts, des métiers et de la vie pratique; 2° pour la grammaire: La prononciation de chaque mot figurée et, quand il y a lieu, discutée; l'examen des locutions, des idiotismes, des exceptions et, en certains cas, de l'orthographe actuelle, avec des remarques critiques sur les difficultés et les irrégularités de la langue; 3° pour la signification des mots: Les définitions; les diverses acceptions rangées dans leur ordre logique, avec de nombreux exemples tirés des auteurs classiques et autres; les synonymes principalement considérés dans leurs relations avec les définitions; 4° pour la partie historique: Une collection de phrases appartenant aux anciens écrivains depuis les premiers temps de la langue française jusqu'au seizième siècle, et disposées dans l'ordre chronologique à la suite des mots auxquelles elles se rapportent; 5° pour l'étymologie: La détermination ou du moins la discussion de l'origine de chaque mot établie par la comparaison des mêmes formes dans le français, dans les patois et dans l'espagnol, l'italien et le provençal ou langue d'oc;* 4th vol. (Paris/Londres: Libraire Hachette et Cie, 1874).

LOUTER, JAN de, *Le droit international public positif*, 2nd vol. (Bibliothèque internationale du Droit des Gens; Oxford: OUP, 1920).

LOWELL, ABBOT LAWRENCE, 'The Council of the League of Nations and Corfu', *League of Nations* 6 (1923), 169–75.

MAC FARLANE, CHARLES, *The Cabinet History of England: Being an Abridgment, by the Author, of the Chapters Entitled "Civil and Military History" in "The Pictorial History of England," with a Continuation to the Present Time*, 3rd vol. (London: Charles Knight and Co., 1845).

MACCOBY, SIMON, 'Reprisals as a Measure of Redress Short of War', *CLJ* 2 (1924–1926), 60–73.

MACVEAGH, WAYNE, 'The Value of the Venezuelan Arbitration', *NAR* 177 (1903), 801–11.

MAHAN, ALFRED THAYER, *The influence of sea power upon history, 1660–1783* (12th edn., Boston: Little, Brown and Company, 1890).

MALLARMÉ, ANDRÉ, 'L'arbitrage vénézuélien devant la Cour de La Haye (1903–1904)', *RGDIP* 13 (1906), 423–500.

MANDELSTAM, ANDRÉ NICOLAYÉVITCH, 'La conciliation internationale d'après le Pacte et la jurisprudence du Conseil de la Société des Nations', *RdC* 14/IV (1926), 333–648.

MANNING, WILLIAM OKE, *Commentaries of the law of nations* (London: S. Sweet, 1839).

MARTENS, FRIEDRICH FROMHOLD VON, *Traité de droit international*, traduit du russe par Alfred Léo, 3rd vol. (Paris: Librairie Marescq ainé, 1887).

——, *Par la Justice Vers la Paix: Annexe : Doctrine de Drago ou Note diplomatique du Gouvernement Argentin du 29 Décembre 1902* (Paris: Henri Charles-Lavauzelle, [1904]).

MARTENS, GEORG FRIEDRICH VON, *Précis du droit des gens moderne de l'Europe, fondé sur les traités et l'usage*, Auquel on a joint la liste des principaux traités conclus depuis 1748 jusqu'à présent avec l'indication des ouvrages où ils se trouvent, 2nd vol. (Gottingue: chez Jean Chret. Dieterich, 1789).

——, *Essai concernant les Armateurs, les Prises et sur tout les Reprises. D'après les loix, les traités, et les usages des Puissances maritimes de l'Europe* (Gottingue: Jean Chretien Dieterich, 1795).

——, *Précis du droit des gens moderne de l'Europe fondé sur les traités et l'usage: Pour servir d'introduction à un cours politique et diplomatique* (2nd edn., Gottingue: Librairie de Dieterich, 1801).

MARTENS, KARL VON, *Causes célèbres du droit des gens*, 5 vols. (2nd edn., Leipzig: F. A. Brockhaus, 1858–1861).

MARTITZ, F. VON, 'Über Friedensblockaden', *ZVölkR* 9 (1920), 610–21.

MAS LATRIE, RENÉ DE, *Du droit de marque ou droit de représailles au Moyen-Age: suivi de pièces justificatives* (2nd edn., Paris: Baur, 1875).

MASSÉ, GABRIEL, *Le droit commercial dans ses rapports avec le droit des gens et le droit civil*, 1st vol. (3rd edn., Paris: Guillaumin et Cie, 1874).

MAULDE LA CLAVIÈRE, RENÉ DE, *La diplomatie au temps de Machiavel*, 1st vol. (Paris: Ernest Leroux, 1892).

MAUREL, MARIUS, *De la Déclaration de Guerre: Étude d'Histoire Diplomatique, de Droit Constitutionnel et de Droit Public International*, Préface de A. Mérignhac (Paris: Librairie générale de droit & de jurisprudence, 1907).

MAURICE, JOHN FREDERICK, *Hostilities Without Declaration of War: An Historical Abstract of the Cases in which Hostilities have occurred between civilized Powers prior to Declaration or Warning. From 1700 to 1870* (London: Her Majesty's Stationery Office, 1883).

MCCREDIE, JEFFREY ALLEN, 'The April 14, 1986 Bombing of Libya. Act of Self-Defense or Reprisal?', *CaseWResJIntlL* 19 (1987), 215–42.

MCKINNON, FIONA, 'Reprisals as a Method of Enforcing International Law', *LJIL* 4 (1991), 221–48.

MCNAIR, ARNOLD D., 'The Legality of the Occupation of the Ruhr', *BYIL* 5 (1924), 17–37.

——, 'The Legal Meaning of War, and the Relation of War to Reprisals', *TGS* 11 (1925), 29–51.

——, 'La terminaison et la dissolution des traités', *RdC* 22/II (1928), 463–537.

MÉRIGNHAC, ALEXANDRE, *Traité de droit public international*, Tome premier de la 3ième partie (Paris: Librairie générale de droit & de jurisprudence, 1912).

MEYER, ERWIN F., 'Anent the statute of Westminster I and liability', *Saint Louis LR* 17 (1931), 22–6.

MILLER, DAVID HUNTER, *The drafting of the Covenant*, With an introduction by Nicholas Murray Butler, 2nd vol. (New York/London: G. P. Putnam's sons, 1928).

MITCHELL, ANDREW D., 'Does One Illegality Merit Another? The Law of Belligerent Reprisals in International Law', *MilLRev* 170 (2001), 155–77.

MØLLER, AXEL, 'The Briand-Kellogg Pact', *NordJIntLaw* 3 (1932), 94–107.

MOLLOY, CHARLES, *De Jure Maritimo et Navali: Or, A Treatise of Affairs Maritime and of Commerce. In Three Books.* (7th edn., London: Printed for John Walthoe junior, and J. Wotton, 1722).

MONCHARVILLE, MAURICE, 'Le conflit franco-turc de 1901', *RGDIP* 9 (1902), 677–700.

MONTESQUIEU, CHARLES LOUIS de, *Œuvres complètes de Montesquieu: avec des notes de Dupin, Crevier, Voltaire, Mably, Servan, La Harpe, etc., etc.* (Paris: chez Firmin Didot frères, fils et Cie, 1857).

MOORE, JOHN BASSETT, *History and digest of the international arbitrations to which the United States has been a party, together with appendices containing the treaties relating to such arbitrations, and historical and legal notes on other international arbitrations ancient and modern, and on the domestic commissions of the United States for the adjustment of international claims*, 2nd vol. (Washington: GPO, 1898).

——, *A digest of international law: As embodied in diplomatic discussions, treaties and other international agreements, international awards, the decisions of municipal courts, and the writings of jurists, and especially in documents, published and unpublished, issued by Presidents and Secretaries of State of the United States, the opinions of the Attorney-General, and the decisions of courts, federal and state*, 7th vol. (Washington: GPO, 1906).

Morin, Achille, *Les lois relatives à la guerre selon le droit des gens moderne, le droit public et le droit criminel des pays civilisés*, 2nd vol. (Paris: Imprimerie et librairie générale de jurisprudence Cosse, Marchal et Billard, 1872).

Moser, Johann Jacob, *Versuch des neuesten Europäischen Völker=Rechts in Friedens= und Kriegs=Zeiten: vornehmlich aus denen Staatshandlungen derer Europäischen Mächten, auch anderen Begebenheiten, so sich seit dem Tode Kayser Carls VI. im Jahr 1740. zugetragen haben*, 8th vol. (Frankfurt am Mayn: Varrentrapp Sohn und Wenner, 1779).

Moulin, Henri-Alexis, 'La doctrine de Drago', *RGDIP* 14 (1907), 417–72.

——, *La doctrine de Drago* (Questions de droit des gens et de politique internationale; Paris: A. Pedone, 1908).

Mozo, Manuel J., *Tratado elemental de derecho de gentes y marítimo internacional: con varios apéndices que contienen documentos nacionales y extranjeros referentes al asunto* (Madrid: A. Avrial, 1898).

Müller, Alfred, *Wandlungen im Repressalienrecht*, Inaugural-Dissertation zur Erlangung der Doktorwürde der Hohen Rechts- und Staatswissenschaftlichen Fakultät der Georg-August-Universität zu Göttingen (Göttingen: [A. Stenger], 1933).

Muratori, Ludovico Antonio, *Antiquitates italicæ medii ævi, sive dissertationes: De Moribus, Ritibus, Religione, Regimine, Magistratibus, Legibus, Studiis Literarum, Artibus, Lingua, Militia, Nummis, Principibus, Libertate, Servitute, Fœderibus, alisque faciem & mores Italici Populi referentibus post declinationem Rom.*, 4th vol. (Mediolani: ex Typographia Societatis Palatinæ in Regia Curia, 1741).

Murray, Katherine Maud Elisabeth, *The Constitutional History of the Cinque Ports* (Publications of the University of Manchester: 235. Historical series, 68; Manchester: Manchester University Press, 1935).

Neff, Stephen C., *The rights and duties of neutrals: A general history* (Melland Schill studies in international law; Yonker, N.Y./Manchester: Juris Publishing/Manchester University Press, 2000).

——, 'Peace and prosperity: commercial aspects of peacemaking', in Randall Lesaffer (ed.), *Peace Treaties and International Law in European History. From the Late Middle Ages to World War One* (Cambridge: CUP, 2004), 365–81.

——, *War and the Law of Nations: A General History* (Cambridge: CUP, 2005).

——, *Justice among Nations: A History of International Law* (Cambridge, Mass.: HUP, 2014).

Negrin, Ignacio de, *Tratado elemental de derecho internacional marítimo: Con varios apéndices que contienen la legislacion interior, los tratados de España y otros documentos nacionales y extranjeros referentes al asunto*, Obra de texto en la Escuela Naval Flotante y Academias del Cuerpo Administrativo de la Armada (Madrid: Miguel Ginesta, 1873).

Neumann, Leopold, *Grundriss des heutigen europäischen Völkerrechtes* (2nd edn., Wien: Wilhelm Braumüller, 1877).

NICHOLSON, DAVID, 'Gunboat Diplomacy', in James C. Bradford (ed.), *International Encyclopedia of Military History*, Preface by Professor Jeremy Black (London/New York: Routledge, 2006), 574–5.

NICOGLOU, STÉPHAN PH., *L'Affaire de Corfou et la Société des Nations*, Préface de M. Georges Scelle (Dijon: Libraire générale Félix Rey, F. Mettray et A. Dugrivel, 1925).

NIPPOLD, OTFRIED, 'Die gegenwärtige Stand der Vorarbeiten für die dritte Haager Friedenskonferenz', *ZVölkR* 7 (1913), 286–307.

NOORTMANN, MATH, *Enforcing International Law: From Self-help to Self-contained Regimes* (London/New York: Routledge, 2016).

NYS, ERNEST, *La guerre maritime: Étude de droit international* (Bruxelles/Leipzig: C. Muquardt, Merzbach et Falk, 1881).

——, *Le droit de la guerre et les précurseurs de Grotius* (Bruxelles/Leipzig: C. Muquardt, Merzbach et Falk, 1882).

——, *Les origines du droit international* (Bruxelles: Alfred Castaigne, 1894).

——, *Le droit international: Les principes, les théories, les faits*, 3rd vol. (Bruxelles/Paris: Alfred Castaigne; Albert Fontemoing, 1906).

OBREGÓN, LILIANA, 'The Civilized and the Uncivilized', in Bardo Fassbender and Anne Peters (eds.), *The Oxford Handbook of the History of International Law* (Oxford: OUP, 2012), 917–39.

O'BRIEN, JASONNE GRABHER, 'In Defense of the Mystical Body. Giovanni da Legnano's Theory of Reprisals', *RLT* 1 (2002), 25–55.

O'CONNELL, MARY ELLEN, *The Power and Purpose of International Law: Insights from the Theory and Practice of Enforcement* (Oxford: OUP, 2011).

OGRIS, W., 'Repressalienarrest', in Wolfgang Stammler, Adalbert Erler, Ekkehard Kaufmann et al. (eds.), *Handwörterbuch zur deutschen Rechtsgeschichte*, 4th vol. (Berlin: Erich Schmidt, 1990), col. 913–916.

OLIVI, LUIGI, *Manuale di diritto internazionale pubblico e privato* (Piccola biblioteca scientifica, 8; 2nd edn., Milano: Società editrice libraria, 1911).

OLUSANYA, OLAOLUWA, *Identifying the Aggressor under International Law: A Principles Approach* (Bern: Peter Lang, 2006).

OMPTEDA, DIETRICH HEINRICH LUDWIG von, *Litteratur des gesammten sowohl natürlichen als positiven Völkerrechts*, 2nd vol. (Regensburg: bey Johann Leopold Montags sel. Erben, 1785).

OPPENHEIM, HEINRICH BERNHARD, *System des Völkerrechts* (2nd edn., Stuttgart & Leipzig: A. Kröner, 1866).

OPPENHEIM, LASSA, *International Law: A Treatise*, 2nd vol. (London: Longmans, Green, and Co., 1905).

——, 'The Science of International Law. Its Task and Method', *AJIL* 2 (1908), 313–56.

——, 'Le caractère essentiel de la Société des Nations', *RGDIP* 26 (1919), 234–44.

OPPENHEIM, MICHAEL, *A history of the administration of the royal navy and of merchant shipping in relation to the navy: From MDIX to MDCLX with an introduction treating of the preceding period*, 1st vol. (London and New York: John Lane The Bodley Head, 1896).

ORTOLAN, THÉODORE, *Règles internationales et diplomatie de la mer*, 1st vol. (4th edn., Paris: Henri Plon, 1864).

PADDEU, FEDERICA, 'Countermeasures', in Rüdiger Wolfrum (ed.), *The Max Planck Encyclopedia of Public International Law*, published under the auspices of the Max Planck Institute for comparative public law and international law, 11 vols. (Oxford: OUP, 2012–2013; <http://www.mpepil.com>, accessed 13 December 2017).

——, *Justification and Excuse in International Law: Concept and Theory of General Defences* (Cambridge Studies in International and Comparative Law; Cambridge: CUP, 2018).

PANIAGUA REDONDO, RAMÓN, 'Las represalias en el derecho internacional. Perspectiva histórica', *RevJurCat* 83 (1984), 149–70.

PARKINSON, F., 'Reprisals in international maritime law. A historical paradigm', *Marine Policy* 12 (1988), 276–85.

PARRY, CLIVE, 'British Practice in Some Nineteenth Century Pacific Blockades', *ZaöRV* 8 (1938), 672–88.

PARTSCH, KARL JOSEF, 'Repressalie', in Karl Strupp and Hans-Jürgen Schlochauer (eds.), *Wörterbuch des Völkerrechts*, begründet von Professor Dr. Karl Strupp, 3 vols. (2nd edn., Berlin: Walter De Gruyter & Co., 1960–1962), 3rd vol., 103–6.

PAULSSON, JAN, *Denial of Justice in International Law* (Hersch Lauterpacht memorial lectures, 17; Cambridge: CUP, 2005).

PENFIELD, W. L., 'The Anglo-German Intervention in Venezuela', *NAR* 177 (1903), 86–96.

PENOT, JACQUES, 'L'expansion commerciale française au Mexique et les causes du conflit franco-mexicain de 1838–1839', *Bulletin Hispanique* 75 (1973), 169–201.

PÉPY, ANDRÉ, 'Après les ratifications du Plan Young. Révision et Sanctions', *RDI* 5 (1930), 441–77.

PERELS, FERDINAND, *Manuel de droit maritime international*, traduit de l'allemand et augmenté de quelques documents nouveaux par L. Arendt (Paris: Guillaumin et Cie, 1884).

——, 'Droit de blocus en temps de paix', *Clunet* 14 (1887), 721–9.

——, 'Droit de blocus en temps de paix', *RDILC* 19 (1887), 245–52.

PEREZ GOMAR, GREGORIO, *Curso elemental de Derecho de Gente: Precedido de una Introduccion sobre el derecho natural*, 2nd vol. (Montevideo: Imprenta de El Pueblo, 1866).

PESSÔA, EPITACIO, *Projecto de Codigo de Direito Internacional Publico* (Rio de Janeiro: Imprensa Nacional, 1911).

Petrascu, Nicolas N., *Les Mesures de Contrainte Internationale qui ne sont pas la Guerre entre États Membres de la Société des Nations*, Thèse pour le doctorat de la Faculté de Droit de l'Université de Paris présentée et soutenue le mardi 24 mai 1927, à 2 heures (Paris: Jouve & Cie, 1927).

Phillimore, Robert, *Commentaries Upon International Law*, 3rd vol. (2nd edn., London: Butterworths, 1873).

Phillipson, Coleman, *The international law and custom of Ancient Greece and Rome*, 2nd vol. (London: Macmillan and Co., 1911).

Piédelièvre, Robert, *Précis de droit international public ou droit des gens*, 2nd vol. (Paris: F. Pichon, 1895).

Piggott, Francis Taylor, *The Declaration of Paris, 1856: A Study -documented-* ("Law of the Sea" Series of Historical and Legal Works, 4; London: University of London Press, 1919).

Pillet, Antoine, *Les Lois actuelles de la Guerre* (Paris: Arthur Rousseau, 1898).

Pistoye, Alphonse de, and Duverdy, Charles, *Traité des prises maritimes: dans lequel on a refondu le traité de Valin en l'appropriant à la législation nouvelle*, Ouvrage contenant un grand nombre de décisions inédites de l'ancien Conseil des prises, et les actes émanés en 1854 des gouvernements belligérants et neutres, 1st vol. (Paris: Auguste Durand, 1855).

Planitz, Hans, 'Studien zur Geschichte des deutschen Arrestprozesses. Der Fremdenarrest', *ZRG GA* 40 (1919), 87–198.

Poinsard, Léon, *Études de droit international conventionnel*, Première série (Paris: F. Pichon, 1894).

Politis, Nikolaos Sokrates, 'Les représailles entre Etats membres de la Société des Nations', *RGDIP* 31 (1924), 5–16.

Pollock, Frederick, *The League of Nations* (2nd edn., London: Stevens and sons, 1922).

Polson, Archer, *Principles of the Law of Nations: With Practical Notes and Supplementary Essays on the Law of Blockade, and on Contraband of War.* To Which is Added, *Diplomacy*, by Thomas Hartwell Horne, B. D. (Philadelphia: T. & J. W. Johnson & Co., 1860).

Pothier, Robert-Joseph, and Estrangin, Jean-Julien, *Traité du contrat d'assurance de Pothier: avec un discours préliminaire, des notes et un supplément* (Marseille: Sube et Laporte, 1810).

Pradier-Fodéré, Paul, 'Note sur la question du Luxor', in Institut de Droit International (ed.), *Session d'Oxford – Septembre 1880* (Annuaire IDI, vol. 5; Bruxelles: C. Muquardt, Merzbach et Falk, 1882), 183–200.

——, *Traité de droit international public européen et américain, suivant les progrès de la science et de la pratique contemporaines*, 9 vols. (Paris: A. Durand et Pedone-Lauriel, 1885–1906).

Preston, Anthony, and Major, John, *Send a gunboat! A study of the gunboat and its role in British policy, 1854–1904* (London: Longmans, Green and Co., 1967).

PUFENDORF, SAMUEL von, *Le droit de la nature et des gens*, Traduction de Jean Barbeyrac, 2nd vol. (Bibliothèque de Philosophie politique et juridique: Textes et Documents; Caen [Bâle]: Centre de Philosophie politique et juridique de l'Université de Caen [chez E. & J. R. Thourneisen], 1987 [1732]).

PÜTTER, KARL THEODOR, *Beiträge zur Völkerrechts-Geschichte und Wissenschaft* (Leipzig: Adolph Wienbrack, 1843).

R., 'On the Sulphur Trade of Sicily, and the Commercial Relations between that Country and Great Britain', *JSSL* 2/6 (1840), 446–57.

REDSLOB, ROBERT, *Histoire des grands principes du droit des gens: Depuis l'Antiquité jusqu'à la veille de la Grande Guerre* (Paris: Rousseau et Cie, 1923).

RENAULT, LOUIS, and ROLIN, ÉDOUARD, 'Rapport fait à l'Institut de Droit International au nom de la Commission spéciale constituée en vue de la prochaine conférence de la paix', in Institut de Droit International (ed.), *Session de Christiana – Août 1912* (Annuaire IDI, vol. 25; Paris: A. Pedone, 1912), 23–40.

REYERSON, KATHRYN, 'Commercial law and merchant disputes. Jacques Coeur and the law of Marque', *Medieval Encounters* 9 (2003), 244–55.

RIQUELME, ANTONIO, *Elementos de derecho público internacional: con esplicacion de todas las reglas que, segun los tratados, estipulaciones, leyes vigentes y costumbres, constituyen el derecho internacional español*, 1st vol. (Madrid: D. Santiago Saunaque, 1849).

RISLEY, JOHN SHUCKBURGH, *The Law of War* (London: A. D. Innes & Co., 1897).

RIVIER, ALPHONSE, *Principes du droit des gens*, 2nd vol. (Paris: Arthur Rousseau, 1896).

ROBIN, RAYMOND, *Des Occupations militaires en dehors des Occupations de Guerre (étude d'histoire diplomatique et de droit international)*, avec une Préface de M. Louis Renault (Paris: Libraire de la société du Recueil Sirey, 1913).

RODGERS, W. L., 'Future International Laws of War', *AJIL* 33 (1939), 441–51.

ROELOFSEN, CORNELIS G., 'International Arbitration and Courts', in Bardo Fassbender and Anne Peters (eds.), *The Oxford Handbook of the History of International Law* (Oxford: OUP, 2012), 145–69.

ROLIN-JAEQUEMYNS, GUSTAVE, '[Book Review: *Le droit des neutres sur mer.* By Ludwig Gessner]', *RDILC* 8 (1876), 165–6.

——, 'Chronique du droit international (1885–1886) [Troisième article]', *RDILC* 18 (1886), 591–626.

——, 'L'année 1888 au point de vue de la paix et du droit international', *RDILC* 21 (1889), 167–208.

RONTIRIS, ANTOINE A., 'De l'évolution de l'idée de blocus pacifique', *Clunet* 26 (1899), 225–39.

ROSATE, ALBERICUS de; SAXOFERRATO, BARTOLUS de; NATTA, GIORGIO et al., *Tractatus de statutis, diversorum autorum et JC. in Europa præstantiisimorum,* (Francofurti: ex officina Wolffgangi Richteri, curante Iohanne Theobaldo Schönvvettero & Conrado Meulio ciuibus, 1606).

Rosse, Eugène-Marie-Henri, *Guide international du commandant de bâtiment de guerre: Du droit de la force (D'après Calvo, Fauchille, Ortolan, Hautefeuille, etc.)* (Paris: Librairie militaire de L. Baudoin, 1891).

Roth, Robert, *Die Repressalie: Eine völkerrechtliche Studie*, Inaugural=Dissertation der juristischen Fakultät der Friedrich=Alexanders=Universität zu Erlangen (Nürnberg: Benedikt Hitz, 1918).

Rouard de Card, Edgar, *L'arbitrage international dans le passé, le présent et l'avenir* (Paris: A. Durand et Pedone-Lauriel, 1877).

Rougé, Jean, *La marine dans l'Antiquité* (L'historien, 23; Paris: PUF, 1975).

Ruffert, Matthias, 'Reprisals', in Rüdiger Wolfrum (ed.), *The Max Planck Encyclopedia of Public International Law*, published under the auspices of the Max Planck Institute for comparative public law and international law, 8th vol. (Oxford: OUP, 2012–2013; <http://www.mpepil.com>, accessed 13 December 2017), 927–30.

Rutherforth, Thomas, *Institutes of Natural Law: Being the Substance of a Course of Lectures on Grotius De Jure Belli Et Pacis read in S. Johns College, Cambridge*, 2nd vol. (Cambridge: J. Bentham, 1756).

Saalfeld, Friedrich, *Handbuch des positiven Völkerrechts* (Tübingen: C. F. Osiander, 1833).

Sainte-Croix, Lucien de, *Étude sur l'exception de dol en droit romain/La déclaration de guerre et ses effets immédiats; Étude d'histoire et de législation comparée*, Thèse pour le doctorat; L'acte public sur les matières ci-après sera soutenu le Mercredi 20 Janvier 1892, à 2 heures et demie (Paris: Arthur Rousseau, 1892).

Salpeter, Alan N., and Waller, Jonathan C., 'Armed Reprisals during Intermediacy – A New Framework for Analysis in International Law', *VillLRev* 17 (1971), 270–312.

Sasse, Horst, 'Boedes Lust-Fall', in Karl Strupp and Hans-Jürgen Schlochauer (eds.), *Wörterbuch des Völkerrechts*, begründet von Professor Dr. Karl Strupp, 3 vols. (2nd edn., Berlin: Walter De Gruyter & Co., 1960–1962), 1st vol., 219.

Satow, Ernest Mason, *The Silesian loan and Frederick the Great* (Oxford: Clarendon Press, 1915).

Savigny, Friedrich Carl von, *Geschichte des Römischen Rechts im Mittelalter*, 6th vol. (2nd edn., Heidelberg: J. C. B. Mohr, 1850).

Saxoferrato, Bartolus de, *Omnium Iuris Interpretum Antesignani Consilia, Quaestiones et Tractatus: Nunc recens Quadragintaquatuoraliis Consiliis, tum Criminalibus, tum Ciuilibus, & vno Tractatu de Procuratoribus locupletata; Atque etiam, praeter alias Additiones ad hanc diem editas, Aureis Adnotationibus. Initia Consiliorum, Quæstionum,& Tractatuum ad literarum seriem subsequentia indicabunt*, 10th vol. (Venetiis: apud Iuntas, 1590).

Scelle, Georges, 'Règles générales du droit de la paix', *RdC* 46 (1933), 327–703.

Schachter, Oscar, 'In Defense of International Rules on the Use of Force', *UChiLRev* 53 (1986), 113–46.

Schiattarella, Raffaele, *Il diritto della neutralità nelle guerre marittime* (Sassari: Tipografia Sociale, 1874).

SCHMALZ, THEODOR, *Das europäische Völker-Recht: in acht Büchern* (Berlin: Duncker und Humblot, 1817).

SCHMITT, CARL, '„Inter pacem et bellum nihil medium"', *ZAkDR* (1939), 594–5.

SCHOEN, PAUL, 'Zur Lehre von den völkerrechtlichen nichtkriegerischen Mitteln der Selbsthilfe', *ZVölkR* 20 (1936), 14–64.

SCHOENBORN, WALTHER, *Die Besetzung von Veracruz: (Zur Lehre von den völkerrechtlichen Selbsthilfeakten)*, mit einem Anhang: Urkunden zur Politik des Präsidenten Wilson gegenüber Mexiko (Berlin: W. Kohlhammer, 1914).

SCHRÖDL, MARKUS, *Das Kriegsrecht des Gelehrten Rechts im 15. Jahrhundert: Die Lehren der Kanonistik und der Legistik über De bello, de represaliis et de duello* (Rechtsgeschichtliche Studien, 14; Hamburg: Dr. Kovač, 2006).

SCHÜCKING, WALTHER, 'Rückblick auf den Streit mit Venezuela', *DJZ* 8 (1903), 157–60.

SCHÜCKING, WALTHER, and WEHBERG, HANS, *Die Satzung des Völkerbundes* (2nd edn., Berlin: Franz Vahlen, 1924).

SCHUMANN, ERICH, *Die Repressalie*, Inaugural=Dissertation zur Erlangung der Doktorwürde der Rechts= und Wirtschaftswissenschaftlichen Fakultät der Universität Rostock (Rostock: Carl Hinstorff, 1927).

SCHUMANN, WOLFGANG, *Die Friedensblockade* (Das geltende Seekriegsrecht in Einzeldarstellungen, 9; Frankfurt am Main: Alfred Metzner, 1974).

SCHWARZENBERGER, GEORG, 'Jus Pacis Ac Belli? Prolegomena to a Sociology of International Law', *AJIL* 37 (1943), 460–79.

——, '[Book Review: *Retaliation in International Law*, by Evelyn Speyer Colbert]', *IntAff* 25 (1949), 336–7.

——, *Power Politics: A Study of World Society*, published under the auspices of the London Institute of World Affairs (The Library of World Affairs, 18; 3rd edn., London: Stevens & sons, 1964).

SCOTT, GEORGE WINFIELD, 'International Law and the Drago Doctrine', *NAR* 183 (1906), 602–10.

——, 'Hague Convention Restricting the Use of Force to Recover on Contract Claims', *AJIL* 2 (1908), 78–94.

SCOTT, JAMES BROWN, 'The Work of the Second Hague Peace Conference', *AJIL* 2 (1908), 1–28.

——, *The Hague Peace Conferences of 1899 and 1907: A Series of Lectures delivered before the Johns Hopkins University in the Year 1908*, 2 vols. (Baltimore: The Johns Hopkins Press, 1909).

——, 'The Declaration of London of February 26, 1909', *AJIL* 8 (1914), 274–329.

——, 'Mexico and the United States and Arbitration', *AJIL* 10 (1916), 577–80.

——, *The Spanish Origin of International Law: Francisco de Vitoria and His Law of Nations* (Oxford: Clarendon Press, 1934).

SEEBOHM, FREDERIC, *On International Reform* (London: Longmans, Green, and Co., 1871).

Séfériadès, Stelio, 'La question des représailles armées en temps de paix, en l'état actuel du droit des gens', *RDILC* 63 (1936), 138–64.

Seidl-Hohenveldern, Ignaz, 'Reprisals and the taking of private property', in Redactie van het Nederlands Tijdschrift voor Internationaal Recht (ed.), *De Conflictu Legum. Bundel opstellen aangeboden aan Roeland Duco Kollewijn & Johannes Offerhaus ter gelegenheid van hun zeventigste verjaardag* (Leiden: A. W. Sijthoff, 1962), 470–9.

Sibley, Norman Wise, 'Pacific Blockade.', *The Westminster review* 147 (1897), 679–85.

Simpson, Gerry J., *Great Powers and Outlaw States: Unequal Sovereigns in the International Legal Order* (Cambridge Studies in International and Comparative Law; Cambridge: CUP, 2004).

Skouteris, Thomas, 'The Vocabulary of Progress in Interwar International Law. An Intellectual Portrait of Stelios Seferiades', *EJIL* 16 (2006), 823–56.

Smith, Frederick Edwin, and Sibley, Norman Wise, *International law as interpreted during the Russo-Japanese War* (2nd edn., London: T. Fisher Unwin, William Clowes and sons, 1907).

Snow, Freeman, *Cases and opinions on international law: with notes and a syllabus* (Boston: The Boston Book Company, 1893).

Söderqvist, Nils, *Le blocus maritime: Étude de droit international* (Stockholm: Centraltryckeriet, 1908).

Spiegel, Hans W., 'Origin and Development of Denial of Justice', *AJIL* 32 (1938), 63–81.

Starkey, David J., *British privateering enterprise in the eighteenth century* (Exeter Maritime Studies, 4; Exeter: University of Exeter Press, 1990).

Staudacher, Hermann, *Die Friedensblockade: Ein Beitrag zur Theorie und Praxis der nichtkriegerischen Selbsthilfe* (Staats- und völkerrechtliche Abhandlungen, 7/3; Leipzig: Duncker & Humblot, 1909).

Stelzer, Winfried, 'Zum Scholarenprivileg Friedrich Barbarossas (Authentica „Habita")', *DAEM* 34 (1978), 123–65.

Stone, Julius, *Legal controls of International Conflict: A Treatise on the Dynamics of Disputes- and War-Law* (London: Stevens & sons, 1954).

Stowell, Ellery C., 'Convention Relative to the Opening of Hostilities', *AJIL* 2 (1908), 50–62.

——, 'Military Reprisals and the Sanctions of the Laws of War', *AJIL* 36 (1942), 643–50.

Streit, Georges, 'La question crétoise au point de vue du droit international', *RGDIP* 7 (1900), 301–69.

Strupp, Karl, *Das völkerrechtliche Delikt* (Handbuch des Völkerrechts, 3/3; Stuttgart: W. Kohlhammer, 1920).

——, 'L'incident de Janina entre la Grèce et l'Italie', *RGDIP* 31 (1924), 255–84.

——, 'Ruhreinmarsch, der französisch-belgische', in Karl Strupp (ed.), *Wörterbuch des Völkerrechts und der Diplomatie*, 2nd vol. (Berlin/Leipzig: Walter De Gruyter & Co., 1925), 404–7.

——, 'L'intervention en matière financière', *RdC* 8 (1925), 5–124.

——, *Grundzüge des positiven Völkerrechts* (Der Staatsbürger: Sammlung zur Einführung in das öffentliche Recht, 2/3; 5th edn., Bonn/Köln: Ludwig Röhrscheid, 1932).

——, 'Les règles générales du droit de la paix', *RdC* 47/I (1934), 263–595.

——, 'Problèmes actuels du droit des représailles', in *Mélanges offerts à Ernest Mahaim par ses collègues, ses amis, ses élèves*, Liège, 5 Novembre 1935, 2nd vol. (Paris: Librairie du Recueil Sirey, 1935), 341–56.

Takayanagi, Kenzo, 'On the Legality of the Chinese Boycott', *Pacific Affairs* 5 (1932), 855–62.

Tardieu, André, *La paix*, Préface de Georges Clemenceau (Paris: Payot & Cie, 1921).

Taylor, Amos E., 'Economic Sanctions and International Security', *UPaLRev* 74 (1925), 155–68.

Taylor, Derek, *Don Pacifico: The Acceptable Face of Gunboat Diplomacy* (London/Portland, Oregon: Vallentine Mitchell, 2008).

Taylor, Hannis, *A treatise on international public law* (Chicago: Callaghan & Company, 1901).

Ténékidès, Ciriaque Georges, 'L'évolution de l'idée des mesures coercitives et la Société des Nations', *RDILC* 53 (1926), 398–418.

Testa, Carlos, *Le droit public international maritime: Principes généraux. – Règles pratiques*, Traduction du portugais annotée et augmentée de documents nouveaux, touchant la contrebande de guerre, la neutralisation des mers et des fleuves et la décision de la conférence africaine (1885) en matière de droit maritime suivie d'une table alphabétique et analytique par Adolphe Boutiron (Bibliothèque internationale & diplomatique, 18; Paris: A. Durand et Pedone-Lauriel, 1886).

Teyssaire, Jean, *Le blocus pacifique*, Thèse de Faculté de droit de l'université de Paris pour le doctorat présentée et soutenue le Mardi 8 Novembre 1910, à une heure et demie (Beauvais: Imprimerie centrale administrative, 1910).

Teyssier-Desfarges, 'Revue critique de la jurisprudence du conseil d'État.', *RDFE* 5 (1848), 368–76.

Thomson, Dennis W., 'Prelude to the Sulphur War of 1840. The Neapolitan Perspective', *EHQ* 25 (1995), 163–80.

Tomz, Michael, *Reputation and International Cooperation: Sovereign Debt across Three Centuries* (Princeton, New Jersey/Oxford: PUP, 2007).

Tsagourias, Nicholas, 'Necessity and the Use of Force. A Special Regime', *NYIL* 41 (2010), 11–44.

——, 'Nicolas Politis' Initiatives to Outlaw War and Define Aggression, and the Narrative of Progress in International Law', *EJIL* 23 (2012), 255–66.

TUCKER, ROBERT W., *The Law of War and Neutrality at Sea* (U.S. Naval War College International Law Studies, 50; Washington: GPO, 1957).

——, 'Reprisals and Self-Defence. The Customary Law', *AJIL* 66 (1972), 586–96.

TURNS, DAVID, 'The Stimson Doctrine of Non-Recognition. Its Historical Genesis and Influence on Contemporary International Law', *Chinese JIL* 2 (2003), 105–43.

TWISS, TRAVERS, *The law of nations considered as independent political communities: On the rights and duties of nations in time of war* (2nd edn., Oxford: Clarendon Press; London: Longmans, Green, and Co, 1875).

ULLMANN, EMANUEL von, *Völkerrecht* (Das öffentliche Recht der Gegenwart, 3; 2nd edn., Tübingen: J. C. B. Mohr (Paul Siebeck), 1908).

URRUTIA, FRANCISCO-JOSÉ, 'La codification du droit international en Amérique', *RdC* 22/II (1928), 85–233.

VALIN, RENÉ-JOSUÉ, *Nouveau commentaire sur l'Ordonnance de la marine du mois d'août 1681: Où se trouve la Conférence des anciennes Ordonnances, des Us & Coutumes de la Mer, tant du Royaume que des Pays étrangers, & des nouveaux Réglemens concernans la Navigation & le Commerce maritime. Avec des Explications prises de l'esprit du Texte, de l'Usage, des Décisions des Tribunaux & des meilleurs Auteurs qui ont écrit sur la Jurisprudence nautique. Et des Notes historiques & critiques, tirées de la plupart des divers Recueils de Manuscrits conservés dans les dépôts publics*, dédié à S. A. S. M.gr le Duc de Penthièvre, Amiral de France, 2nd vol. (La Rochelle: chez Jérôme Legier, 1766).

[VARIOUS], 'La doctrine de Monroë. – Une note diplomatique du Gouvernement argentin. – Consultations et avis.', *RDILC* 35 (1903), 597–623.

VATTEL, EMER de, *Le Droit des Gens. Ou Principes de la Loi naturelle, Appliqués à la conduite & aux affaires des Nations & des Souverains*, 1st vol. (Londres: [s.n.], 1758).

——, *The Law of Nations; Or Principles of the Law of Nature, applied to the Conduct and Affairs of Nations and Sovereigns*, edited by Joseph Chitty (6th edn., Philadelphia: T. & J. W. Johnson, 1844).

VAUZANGES, HENRI, *Les Sanctions internationales dans la Société des Nations*, Thèse pour le doctorat de la Faculté de Droit de l'Université de Paris, présentée et soutenue le Vendredi 28 mai 1920 à 3 heures 1/2 (Paris: Jouve & Cie, 1920).

VEC, MILOŠ, 'Intervention/Nichtintervention. Verrechtlichung der Politik und Politisierung des Völkerrechts im 19. Jahrhunderts', in Ulrich Lappenküper and Reiner Marcowitz (eds.), *Macht und Recht. Völkerrecht in den internationalen Beziehungen* (Otto-von-Bismarck-Stiftung Wissenschaftliche Reihe, 13; Paderborn: Ferdinand Schöningh, 2010), 135–60.

VEEDER, VAN VECHTEN, *Legal Masterpieces: Specimens of Argumentation and Exposition by Eminent Lawyers*, 1st vol. (St. Paul, Minn.: Keefe-Davidson Company, 1903).

VENEZIA, JEAN-CLAUDE, 'La notion de représailles en droit international public', *RGDIP* 64 (1960), 465–98.

VERDEBOUT, AGATHA, 'The Contemporary Discourse on the Use of Force in the Nineteenth Century. A Diachronic and Critical Analysis', *JUFIL* 1 (2014), 223–46.

VERDROSS, ALFRED, 'Règles générales du droit international de la paix', *RdC* 30/V (1929), 275–517.

VERZIJL, JAN H. W., *International law in historical perspective*, 12 vols. (Nova et vetera iuris gentium / Publications of the Institute for International Law of the University of Utrecht; Series A. Modern International Law, vols. 4, 6–14, 16, 19; Leiden: A. W. Sijthoff, 1968–1998).

VILLEMAIN, ABEL-FRANÇOIS, *Histoire de Cromwell: D'après les mémoires du temps et les recueils parlementaires.* (Bruxelles: Meline, Cans et comp., 1851).

VISMARA, GIULIO, 'Repressalien(recht)', in Norbert Angermann, Robert-Henri Bautier, Robert Auty et al. (eds.), *Lexikon des Mittelalters*, 10 vols. (München/Zürich/Stuttgart/Weimar: Artemis & Winkler/LexMA-Verlag/J. B. Metzler, 1980–1999), 7th vol., col. 746.

WAGNER, PETER, *Zur Lehre von den Streiterledigungsmitteln des Völkerrechts. Eine historisch-kritische und thetische Untersuchung* (Darmstadt: Chr. Haun, 1900).

WALDOCK, C. H. M., 'The regulation of the use of force by individual States in international law', *RdC* 81 (1952), 451–517.

WALKER, THOMAS ALFRED, *A Manual of Public International Law* (Cambridge: CUP, 1895).

——, *A history of the law of nations*, 1st vol. (Cambridge: CUP, 1899).

WALTERS, FRANCIS PAUL, *A History of the League of Nations* (London: OUP, 1952 [Reprint 1960]).

WARD, ROBERT PLUMER, *An Enquiry Into the Foundation and History of the Law of Nations in Europe, from the Time of the Greeks and Romans, to the Age of Grotius*, 1st vol. (London: J. Butterworth, 1795).

WASHBURN, ALBERT H., 'The Legality of the Pacific Blockade', *Colum. L. Rev.* 21 (1921), 55–69, 227–241, 442–459.

WEBER, LUDWIG, 'Blockade, pacific', in Rudolf Bernhardt (ed.), *Encyclopedia of Public International Law. Use of Force, War and Neutrality, Peace Treaties (A–M)*, 3rd vol., Max Planck Institute for Comparative Public Law and International Law (Amsterdam/New York/Oxford: North-Holland Publishing Company, 1982), 51–3.

WEHBERG, HANS, 'Le problème de la mise de la guerre hors la loi', *RdC* 24/IV (1928), 145–306.

WEIMAR, PETER, 'Bartolus de Saxoferrato (1313/14–1357)', in Michael Stolleis (ed.), *Juristen. Ein biographisches Lexikon; Von der Antike bis zum 20. Jahrhundert* (München: C. H. Beck, 1995), 67–8.

WESTLAKE, JOHN, 'Pacific Blockade', *The Law Quarterly Review* 25 (1909), 13–23.

——, 'Reprisals and War', *The Law Quarterly Review* 25 (1909), 127–37.

——, *International Law*, 2nd vol. (2nd edn., Cambridge: CUP, 1913).

——, *The Collected Papers of John Westlake on Public International Law* (Cambridge: CUP, 1914).

WHARTON, FRANCIS, *A digest of the international law of the United States, taken from documents issued by Presidents and Secretaries of State, and from decisions of federal courts and opinions of Attorneys-General*, 3 vols. (Washington: GPO, 1886).

WHEATON, HENRY, *History of the Law of Nations in Europe and America; From the Earliest Times to the Treaty of Washington, 1842* (New York: Gould, Banks & Co., 1845).

——, *Elements of international law* (3rd edn., Philadelphia: Lea and Blanchard, 1846).

——, *Histoire des progrès du droit des gens en Europe et en Amérique depuis la paix de Westphalie jusqu'à nos jours: Avec une introduction sur les progrès du droit des gens en Europe avant la paix de Westphalie*, 1st vol. (4th edn., Leipzig: F. A. Brockhaus, 1865).

WHITTEN, DOLPHUS, 'The Don Pacifico Affair', *The Historian* 48 (1986), 255–67.

WILDMAN, RICHARD, *Institutes of International Law*, 1st vol. (London: William Benning & Co., 1849).

WILLIAMS, JOHN FISCHER, 'The Covenant of the League of Nations and War', *CLJ* 5 (1933), 1–21.

——, 'Sanctions under the Covenant', *BYIL* 17 (1936), 130–49.

WILLIAMSON, ROSS, 'A Friendly Demonstration of Force. Pacific Blockade, International Law and State Identity, 1827 to 1921', Thesis submitted to the Faculty of Graduate and Postgraduate Affairs in partial fulfillment of the requirements for the degree of Master of Arts in Legal Studies (Ottawa, Ontario: Carleton University, 2013; <http://www.curve.carleton.ca>, accessed 27 December 2017).

WILSON, GEORGE GRAFTON, 'Use of Force and War', *AJIL* 26 (1932), 327–8.

WILSON, GEORGE GRAFTON, and TUCKER, GEORGE FOX, *International law* (New York/Boston/Chicago: Silver, Burdett and Company, 1901).

WINFIELD, PERCY HENRY, 'The History of Intervention in International Law', *BYIL* 3 (1922–23), 130–49.

——, 'The Grounds of Intervention in International Law', *BYIL* 5 (1924), 149–62.

WOLFF, CHRISTIAN, *Jus Gentium Methodo Scientifica Pertractatum*, 2nd vol. (The Classics of International Law, 13; Oxford: Clarendon Press, 1934).

WOOLF, CECIL NATHAN SIDNEY, *Bartolus de Sassoferrato: His position in the history of medieval political thought* (Cambridge: CUP, 1913).

WOOLSEY, L. H., 'The Leticia Dispute between Colombia and Peru', *AJIL* 27 (1933), 317–24.

WOOLSEY, THEODORE DWIGHT, 'The Alabama Question.', *The New Englander* 28 (1869), 575–619.

WOOLSEY, THEODORE SALISBURY, 'The passing of pacific blockade', *YaleRev* 11 (May. 1902, to Feb. 1903), 340–6.

WOUTERS, FÉLIX, *Histoire parlementaire de l'Assemblée nationale, précédée du récit de la révolution de Paris*, sous la surveillance de M. Alexandre Gendebien et de M. Maynz, 4th vol. (Bruxelles: Aux bureaux de l'association des ouvriers typographes, 1848).

WRIGHT, QUINCY, 'Opinion of Commission of Jurists on Janina-Corfu Affair', *AJIL* 18 (1924), 536–44.

——, 'The Neutralization of Corfu', *AJIL* 18 (1924), 104–8.

——, 'The Stimson Note of January 7, 1932', *AJIL* 26 (1932), 342–8.

——, 'When does war exist?', *AJIL* 26 (1932), 362–8.

——, 'The Meaning of the Pact of Paris', *AJIL* 27 (1933), 39–61.

——, 'The Concept of Aggression in International Law', *AJIL* 29 (1935), 373–95.

WURM, CHRISTIAN FRIEDRICH, 'Selbsthilfe (völkerrechtliche)', in Carl von Rotteck and Carl Welcker (eds.), *Das Staats-Lexikon. Encyklopädie der sämmtlichen Staatswissenschaften für alle Stände*, 12th vol. (2nd edn., Altona: Johann Friedrich Hammerich, 1845–1848), 111–32.

——, 'Selbsthülfe der Staaten in Friedenszeiten.', *Deutsche Vierteljahrs-Schrift* 21/4 (1858), 71–94.

YEPES, J.-M., 'L'Affaire de Leticia entre la Colombie et le Pérou. Étude Historique et Juridique', *RDI* 11 (1933), 133–71.

——, 'Les problèmes fondamentaux du droit des gens en Amérique', *RdC* 47/I (1934), 1–143.

YOUNG, CARL WALTER, *Japan's Special Position in Manchuria: Its Assertion, Legal Interpretation and Present Meaning* (Japan's Jurisdiction and International Legal Position in Manchuria, 1; Baltimore: The Johns Hopkins Press, 1931).

ZACHMANN, URS MATTHIAS, *Völkerrechtsdenken und Außenpolitik in Japan, 1919–1960* (Studien zur Geschichte des Völkerrechts, 29; Baden-Baden: Nomos, 2013).

ZIEGLER, KARL-HEINZ, *Völkerrechtsgeschichte: Ein Studienbuch* (Kurzlehrbücher für das Juristische Studium; 2nd edn., München: C. H. Beck, 2007).

ZIMMERN, ALFRED, *The League of Nations and the Rule of Law, 1918–1935* (London: Macmillan and Co., 1936).

ZOLLER, ELISABETH, *Peacetime unilateral remedies: An analysis of countermeasures* (Dobbs Ferry, N.Y.: Transnational Publishers, 1984).

ZORN, ALBERT, *Grundzüge des Völkerrechts* (Webers Illustrierte Katechismen, 79; 2nd edn., Leipzig: J. J. Weber, 1903).

ZOUCHE, RICHARD, *Iuris et Iudicii Fecialis, Sive, Iuris Inter Gentes, et Quaestionum de Eodem Explicatio: Qua Quae ad Pacem & Bellum inter diversos Principes, aut Populos spectant, ex praecipuis Historico-jure-peritis, exhibentur*, 2 vols. (The Classics of International Law, 1; Washington: Carnegie Institution, 1911).